The Politics of Citizenship in Germany

Ethnicity, Utility and Nationalism

Eli Nathans

Oxford • New York

First published in 2004 by
Berg
Editorial offices:
1st Floor, Angel Court, 81 St Clements Street, Oxford OX4 1AW, UK
175 Fifth Avenue, New York, NY 10010, USA

Berg is the imprint of Oxford International Publishers Ltd.

Library of Congress Cataloging-in-Publication Data
A catalog record for this book is available from the Library of Congress.

British Library Cataloguing-in-Publication Data
A catalogue record for this book is available from the British Library.

ISBN 1 85973 776 5 (Cloth)
1 85973 781 1 (Paper)

Typeset by JS Typesetting Ltd, Wellingborough, Northants.
Printed in the United Kingdom by Antony Rowe, Chippenham, Wiltshire.

www.bergpublishers.com

To Caroline

Contents

Contents

Contents

A Note on the Cover

The front cover portrays Germania, a symbol of the German people adorned with the Hohenzollern eagle, guiding ethnic Germans from Russia back to the Motherland. The slogan emblazoned on the branches of the oak tree – another symbol of the German people – enjoins Germans to be unified. The image is taken from *Heimkehr*, a journal published during the First World War by a semi-official Prussian agency whose mission was to promote the immigration of Russian Germans.

Illustrations

Maps

Figures

Tables

Preface

It is a great pleasure to have the opportunity to thank the individuals who have made the completion of this study possible.

This book began as a dissertation at Johns Hopkins University. I thank Vernon Lidtke for his generosity with his time and his wise advice. Those who know his work will recognize the influence of Mack Walker. I wish it were still possible to thank John Higham.

For their detailed comments on the entire manuscript I would like to thank Ben Nathans, Marc Raeff, Anne Raeff and Hartwin Spenkuch. Geoff Cocks, Charles Fairbanks, Robert Forster, Melody Herr, Ann Goldberg, Matt Levinger and Nick Stamos also made valuable suggestions. Ina Paul was exceedingly generous with her expertise and time. At Albion College Russ Clark, Ralph Houghton, Melinda Kraft and Robin Miller all provided most generous and invaluable help with maps and images, as did Juneyeta Gates and Melinda Rains at Ball State University. Ken Ledford gave me the chance to present part of the study at Case Western Reserve University. For this and much else I thank him. I also want to thank Bowdoin College, Albion College, the American Historical Association and the American Society for Legal History for offering venues for presentations and critiques. The anonymous reviewers at Berg Publishers made very helpful suggestions. I also want to thank Kathleen May, Ian Critchley and George Pitcher at Berg.

Financial assistance from various sources made this project possible. The people of the United States provided generous funding for four years through the Jacob Javits Fellowship program; the people of Berlin, through the Berlin Program of the Free University, granted a stipend for one year and office space. A grant from Albion College paid for the images in this book. I thank them all.

Lisa Enders, Shirley Hipley, Charlotte Magnuson, LaVonne March, and in particular the late Sharon Widomski, the staffs of the various history departments where I have studied and taught, provided generous assistance in many matters large and small. The directors of the Berlin Program, Ingeborg Mehser, Dagmar Klenke and Karin Goihl, were also exceedingly generous with their time.

I also received most generous and patient help from the staffs of the Eisenhower Library of Johns Hopkins University, and of the libraries of the Friedrich Meinecke Institute of the Free University, Albion and Bowdoin Colleges, Ball State University, and the University of Michigan. I would especially like to thank Allie Moore and Michelle Gerry of Albion, and to note the marvelous generosity of the University of Michigan in granting borrowing privileges to teachers throughout Michigan. I would like to thank for their assistance archivists from the Geheimes Staatsarchiv in Berlin, the Bundesarchiv in Koblenz and Lichterfelde, the Bayerisches Hauptstaatsarchiv in Munich, the Badisches General-Landesarchiv in Karlsruhe, the Nordrhein-Westfälisches Hauptstaatsarchiv in Düsseldorf, and the Archiwum Panstwowe in Wroclaw (Breslau). Saskia Simons of the Geheimes Staatsarchiv, where I spent most of my time, was of special assistance, as was Margit Ksoll-Marcon in Munich. If I were to name all the archivists and librarians who helped me the list would be long.

In Berlin my family was sustained by friendships with Günter Gebhardt, Ruth and Andreas Hartmann, Ken Ledford, Hartwin Spenkuch, Siegfried Weichlein, Thomas and Sabine Welskopp, and especially Gale and Bill Delaney, Jorg and Sonja Weese and Ina Paul and Uwe Puschner. At Hopkins Robert Mankin, at Bowdoin College Paula and Billy Arsenault, Susan Tananbaum, Dan and Susan Levine, Allen Wells, and Matt Klingle, at Albion College Allen Horstman, Myron and Nancy Levine, Tom Chambers, and Kathe McPhail and Alain Grenier and Caroline and Fong Wang, and at Ball State University Sergei and Irina Zhuk, Jim Connolly, Tony Edmonds, Danny and Marcee Hoyt, Elizabeth Littell-Lamb, and Rene Marion all deserve special thanks for their support.

My greatest debts are to my parents, to my children Hannah and Jenny, and above all to Caroline.

Abbreviations

ALR	*Allgemeines Landrecht für die Preussischen Staaten von 1794*
APW	Archiwum Panstwowe we Wrocławiu, Wrocław (Breslau)
BDF	Federation of German Women's Groups
BGBl	*Bundesgesetzblatt*
BGL	Badisches General-Landesarchiv, Karlsruhe
BHM	Bayerisches Hauptstaatsarchiv, Munich
BA	Bundesarchiv Berlin-Lichterfelde
CDU	Christian Democratic Union
CSU	Christian Social Union
EEC	European Economic Community
EU	European Union
FDP	Free Democratic Party
GPS	*Gesetzsammlung für die Königlichen Preußischen Staaten*
GStA PK	Geheimes Staatsarchiv Preußischer Kulturbesitz, Berlin-Dahlem
IET	Incorporated Eastern Territories
MBiV	Ministerial-Blatt für die gesammte innere Verwaltung in den Königlich Preussischen Staaten
NWH	Nordrhein-Westfälisches Hauptstaatsarchiv, Düsseldorf
RD	Nordrhein-Westfälisches Hauptstaatsarchiv, Düsseldorf, Regierung Düsseldorf
RGBI	*Reichsgesetzblatt*
RS	Reverse Side (back side of a numbered page from an archival source)
SBF	Stenographischer Bericht über die Verhandlungen der deutschen constituirenden Nationalversammlung zu Frankfurt am Main
SBP	Stenographische Berichte über die Verhandlungen des Preussischen Hauses der Abgeordneten
SBR	Stenographische Berichte über die Verhandlungen des Reichstags
SPD	Social Democratic Party of Germany
VDB	Verhandlungen des Deutschen Bundestages

Introduction

It would not have been hard to predict in the mid-nineteenth century that if a German nation-state were founded it would attempt to promote a feeling of ethnic solidarity among its inhabitants. After all, German national feeling did stress the bonds created by a common ethnicity and culture. An astute observer might also have predicted that the new state would more readily grant citizenship to foreigners who were ethnic Germans than to other foreigners. Most nation-states have promoted in various ways the interests and culture of the dominant ethnic group or groups, and this has also frequently been reflected in policies regarding citizenship and naturalization.

Our hypothetical observer would most likely not have predicted, however, the extreme nature of the ethnic preferences some German states adopted. And this does not apply only to the Nazi period. From the 1880s to the 1980s German naturalization policies assumed ethnically exclusive forms that can best be described as anxious and even obsessive. The rigor with which policies of exclusion on ethnic grounds were practiced was, in comparison with the policies of other European states, distinctive. On the other hand, the forms taken by ethnically based naturalization policies in Germany varied considerably over time. They were the focal point of considerable domestic debate and controversy. Over the past fifteen years they have been, to a very significant degree, dismantled. This study examines why ethnically exclusive naturalization policies assumed the forms they did, the controversies they caused, and the reasons for recent changes.

However, ethnicity was frequently not the only factor that determined whether a foreigner might become a German citizen. Decisions about which outsiders would be permitted to live permanently in Germany – or, before 1871, one of the German states – often reflected considerations of interest and utility that were distinct from the pursuit of ethnic homogeneity. The economic utility to the state of different groups of foreigners, or of ethnic Germans living abroad, also played a key role, one that changed over time as the nature of the German economy changed. At certain points state interests in military recruitment were also significant. The treatment of immigrants was also a function of German relations with neighboring states. Harsh treatment of immigrants might have invited retaliation against Germans living abroad or caused other difficulties with the states whose nationals had immigrated to Germany. Until the post-Second World War era German states treated men and women quite differently. This study also explores the ways in which these varied factors affected decisions regarding the inclusion or exclusion of foreigners.

A glance at the ethnic map of Europe and of the German state founded in 1870–1 suggests why ethnicity was, after that date, one central focus of debates regarding which foreigners should be granted citizenship. When nominated to be German Emperor in 1871, the Prussian king promised that the new Reich would give 'the German nation [das deutsche Volk] ... that which it had sought and striven for for centuries', i.e., peace and a common political home.[1] But a fourth of ethnic Germans lived outside the borders of the new state. In 1871 Germany had 41 million inhabitants.[2] There were roughly 9 million Germans in the Austro-Hungarian Empire.[3] Approximately 70 percent of the 2.7 million Swiss spoke German.[4] Some 1.5 million ethnic Germans lived in Russia, many of them descendants of settlers who had journeyed there in the late eighteenth century.[5] More than 2 million Germans had emigrated overseas, most to the United States, and nearly 3 million more followed by the end of the century.[6] Whether, and under what terms, these ethnic Germans would be considered as in some sense belonging to the Reich was a matter of dispute. The state encountered this question when it considered naturalization petitions from ethnic German immigrants. How it determined where to draw this boundary is another central subject of this book.

The central role played by German nationalism in legitimizing the new state created questions regarding the status of the many non-ethnic German groups living within its borders. There were more than 2.5 million ethnic Poles, the largest minority, in 1871, and roughly 300,000 Masurians – Polish-speaking Lutherans who identified more closely with Prussia than with Poland.[7] The conquered territory of Alsace-Lorraine held about 1.5 million inhabitants, most of whom identified politically with France rather than with Germany, even though some were ethnic Germans.[8] There were 512,000 Jews.[9] Smaller ethnic groups included the Danes (200,000), Sorbs (160,000), Lithuanians (120,000), and Czechs (75,000).[10] Almost all of the members of these minority groups were, in 1871, German citizens. Over the next few decades the state attempted in numerous ways to persuade or to compel the members of these minority groups to give up their distinctive practices and identities. But uncertainty about whether this project of cultural homogenization would succeed, the reality of tensions between most of these ethnic minority groups and the German majority, and, especially in the case of Jews, a fear that members of the minority group might be only too successful in integrating into and (as some saw it) infiltrating German society, led the state to view the citizenship applications of foreigners who belonged to several of these groups with hostility. The grounds on which German states and society determined how open or closed the nation was to be to various kinds of ethnic, religious and linguistic differences is also a key theme of this study.

One explanation for the especially tight control German states exercised over the naturalization of foreigners, and the use of these powers to promote the creation of an ethnically homogeneous nation, lies in the demographic facts outlined above. Germany could appeal to the loyalty of ethnic Germans in Russia and Eastern Europe and overseas, and had within its borders several minority ethnic groups that found it difficult to be fully loyal to a German state. There were also other factors. Germany's rapid industrialization from the late nineteenth century made it a magnet for immigration. This led those interested in promoting the ethnic homogeneity of German society to develop rules that would prevent the permanent settlement of foreigners who were not ethnic Germans, while permitting them to work in Germany on a temporary basis. Germany's preeminent military and economic position in continental Europe during the decades following the founding of the nation-state allowed it to give short shrift to the objections of other states concerned about the treatment of their nationals. The experience and loss of two world wars accentuated ethnic nationalism and the ethnic character of German citizenship policies.

Debates regarding citizenship policies were also often debates regarding the desirable form of the state. In the period covered by this study one can identify at least four different kinds of political regime: the authoritarian, bureaucratic government characteristic of the pre-1848 Prussian state; mixed constitutional regimes in which central administrations and rulers generally dominated weak parliaments, which characterized some German states before 1848, Prussia after 1848, and the German national state after 1870; the republican institutions of the period between 1918 and 1933 and after 1949 of the Federal Republic of Germany; and the deeply racist plebiscitary dictatorship of the Nazi period. This study for the most part ignores the German Democratic Republic, a fifth distinct state form. Each regime had a characteristic range of goals and policies regarding citizenship and naturalization. Each was heavily influenced by, and in some cases reacted sharply against, the policies of its predecessors.

Although the purposes which citizenship and naturalization policies served after 1870 reflected to a large degree contemporary conflicts and goals, until the 1990s German citizenship law was based in many respects on a Prussian law adopted in 1842. The 1842 Prussian law gave state administrations almost unlimited discretion over the granting of citizenship to resident foreigners and their progeny. Prussia adopted the 1842 law to help it expel unwanted immigrants and to conscript those who remained, and to reduce conflicts with neighboring states over the status of immigrants. The 1842 law was also a product of a larger conflict between the central administration and local authorities over freedom of movement within Prussia. It gave the state the power to control foreign settlement in part to prevent communities within Prussia from blocking the residence of economically desirable foreigners. The continuity between the citizenship policies of pre-1870 Prussia and the German national state was a general one. Both states assumed that they were entitled to mold society by determining, on a case-by-case basis, which foreigners were entitled to live permanently within their borders.

After the 1880s questions of utility, defined in economic and other ways, continued to play a central role in the making of naturalization decisions. In general, as industrialization progressed and a national and even international economy replaced limited local economies, the poor came to seem more useful. Industry needed labor. The increased willingness to grant citizenship to most ethnic Germans reflected in part the greater economic value of the poor in an industrial society. Germany's international ambitions led it to place a greater emphasis on appealing to the loyalty of Germans who lived outside Germany and even overseas, and citizenship law was one tool employed to this end. On the other hand, Germany's increasingly precarious international position, from the 1890s, led the Kaiserreich, although not its successors, not only to insist that German emigrants who wished to keep their German citizenship fulfill their military obligations to the state but that foreign men who wished to become Germans prove capable of performing military service.

Until the 1950s – and in some respects thereafter as well – German citizenship and naturalization policies were gendered, in the sense that women were subordinated to men. Marriage with a man who was not a German citizen automatically entailed the loss of German citizenship for a German woman. Marriage of a non-German woman with a man who was a German citizen automatically brought German citizenship with it. Why did German women not become more highly valued as citizens as naturalization policies developed a more ethnic focus? After all, the qualities often held to define German culture, language (the mother tongue, 'die Muttersprache'), personal habits of diligence and cleanliness, for some church attendance, were associated at least as much with women as with men, and, it was commonly thought, more likely to be transmitted to the next generation by the mother than by the father. One answer is that the laws governing the citizenship of married women were thought to promote the ethnic homogeneity of the state, since inside Germany the women who married men who were not German citizens were often not ethnic Germans. Another answer is that the German pattern was a pan-European one, one believed to promote a range of state interests. Finally, German (and European) laws were deeply patriarchal, reflecting a much larger pattern, one that had little to do with ethnic nationalism but that was every bit as powerful in its own sphere.

Naturalization policies deeply affected the lives of foreigners living in Germany. The rights and duties linked to citizenship changed over time, but citizenship consistently provided protection from expulsion, superior access to the more privileged forms of work, and, in the nineteenth century, a clearer right to marry. In the course of the nineteenth century an increasing percentage of adult male citizens were granted the right to vote, and after 1918 this right was extended to women. For men, citizenship generally entailed military service. Rejection often led to embitterment and sometimes to emigration. This study also examines the varying reasons why foreigners wished to become German citizens.

The issues examined in the chapters that follow do not belong only to the past. As I researched and wrote this book, German political parties fiercely debated whether the state should grant Germany's 7 million resident aliens, 9 percent of the population, the right to become German citizens.[11] Most of these foreigners belong to groups that are not ethnically German. Many grew up in what before 1990 was West Germany. Very few acquired German citizenship. In 1999 there occurred what can best be described as a revolution in German citizenship policies. A law adopted in that year granted German citizenship at birth to aliens born in Germany to non-German parents, if at least one of the parents had been a legal resident of Germany for eight years and possessed a long-term residence permit. Under its provisions children who acquire German citizenship in this fashion will forfeit it if they do not declare in writing, after reaching maturity but before their twenty-fourth birthday, that they have surrendered all other citizenships. The 1999 law also gives long-term residents a right to naturalization, assuming that they surrender other passports.[12] Beginning in 1993 Germany also adopted a series of measures that restrict the ability of ethnic Germans living in Russia and Eastern Europe to claim German citizenship.[13]

The German state has recently moderated its control over access to citizenship in other ways as well. Citizens of European Union states have the right to live and work where they wish within the Union.[14] Since such rights have, historically, been among the most important conveyed by citizenship, in some respects it is now possible to speak of a common European Union citizenship.[15] But as borders become more open within the Union, many European Union states are taking an increasingly hard line against potential citizens from outside the EU. Both of these phenomena, the breaking down of national barriers and the creation of new barriers at the level of the European Union, parallel the history of German citizenship policies in the nineteenth century.

This study differs from the existing literature on the subject in its emphasis on conflict within German society and on the ways in which citizenship policies have changed to reflect the shifting forms and goals of German states. Recent works on the history of German citizenship have emphasized not conflict but consensus, not change but continuity. One interpretation makes the German yearning for ethnic unity, the Fichtean ideal of the ethnic German nation, the dominant theme. Rogers Brubaker's *Citizenship and Nationhood in France and Germany*, published in 1992, argues that this ethnic conception of the German nation 'determined the tracks along which the politics of citizenship has been driven by the dynamic of interests'.[16] Brubaker sees a more or less continuous – or increasing – focus on ethnic exclusivity as the principal motif of German citizenship law and policy from the late nineteenth century, and argues that this focus reflected in a fairly unproblematic way a broad popular consensus. He contrasts German citizenship policies with those of France, a country whose republican ideology led it, he claims, to be far more open to immigration than Germany.

Another interpretation emphasizes the ways in which German citizenship policies have followed, rather than differed from, larger European patterns. Andreas Fahrmeir, for example, has compared the citizenship and naturalization policies of German states with those of Britain and found significant similarities. Fahrmeir argues that the numerous bilateral agreements governing the deportation of foreigners – into which the German states entered in the early nineteenth century – in practice had the consequence of easing the granting of citizenship to immigrants.[17] Another critique of Brubaker reaches a similar conclusion by an opposite route, i.e., by emphasizing the importance of the Prussian law of 1842. In his recent study of the history of French citizenship policies Patrick Weil argues that the 1842 law merely followed the model of the French Civil Code of 1803. 'In Europe of the mid-nineteenth century, when those in positions of authority in various nations called their civil servants and asked them to "write a citizenship law for me", these jurists did not hesitate to copy the French Civil Code.'[18] The Civil Code granted citizenship automatically only to individuals born to French citizens, although it also gave individuals born in France to aliens a right to naturalization on petition. This emphasis on parentage over place of birth, Weil argues, was the decisive break with the Old Regime focus on long-term residence as the foundation of rights and duties. It was this innovation that Prussia, and other European states, adopted. France broke with its own Napoleonic heritage when it made birth in France a far more significant foundation for citizenship in the late 1880s.

As this line of argument suggests, Weil also calls into question the close connection that Brubaker and others have drawn between forms of national feeling and citizenship law and policy. In the nineteenth century, Weil argues, the formulation of citizenship policy was a matter for administrative elites, who focused on clarity, efficiency and consistency. 'The domination of legal professionals over political considerations, reflecting a perception that citizenship law was a specialty independent of politics, was fundamental in the nineteenth century.'[19] This focus on elite control of citizenship policy has been extended to the post-1945 period by the work of Christian Joppke. Joppke claims that West German and European courts decisively shaped German immigration policies by creating rights that prevented the repatriation of immigrants. 'Filling the vacuum created by the passiveness of the political branches of government, activist courts have expansively interpreted and defended the rights of foreigners.'[20] While judicial elites could not change the terms of citizenship laws, they created the conditions that forced the German Bundestag to make such changes.[21]

A third interpretation of the history of German citizenship policy focuses on 'the historical development of citizenship rules and naturalization policies in Germany in connection with the origins, development, and crisis of the German national state' between 1815 and 1945. Dieter Gosewinkel's history of German citizenship policy emphasizes four aspects of state-building. One was the progressive centralization of state power. Another was the development of strictly legal and uniform rules, rules that replaced legal fragmentation with uniformity, arbitrariness with predictability, and status relationships with a system of individual rights. Third, the modern state sought to police its borders, to 'firmly control access from outside'. Finally, the unification of Germany necessarily resulted in an emphasis on ethnicity in naturalization decisions: 'a state that defines itself as a national state cannot avoid showing national [ethnic] preferences in its naturalization proceedings'. In explaining why German officials refused – in general – to naturalize foreign Poles and Jews from the 1880s, Gosewinkel stresses their fear that the members of these groups lacked 'a readiness to be loyal to the German state'.[22] The same logic determined German policies toward its Alsatian and Danish minorities.

A handful of secondary works have examined aspects of citizenship policies in the course of larger treatments of the Nazi period, and several historical works have appeared recently that focus on the post-1945 period, in part on the basis of administrative records that are becoming accessible to historians. These works, notably Diemut Majer's examination of the Nazi treatment of foreigners, Karl-Heinz Meier-Braun's various books on foreigners in the Federal Republic of Germany, Karen Schönwälder's comparison of the post-war immigration policies of Great Britain and West Germany, Johannes-Deiter Steinert's examination of German migration policies in the 1950s and early 1960s, and Ulrich Herbert's sweeping history of the treatment of foreigners since the Kaiserreich will be discussed in the relevant sections of the text.

This study calls into question the suggestion that the harsh measures taken by German states from the 1880s to the 1980s to prevent the naturalization of individuals from a range of non-German ethnic groups were inherent in the logic of the developing nation-state. Certainly many Germans felt a sense of solidarity with other Germans, and this was bound to have implications for naturalization standards. The Prussian officials who, beginning in the 1880s, prevented the naturalization of foreigners from a range of non-German ethnic groups did in many cases fear disloyalty, as Gosewinkel suggests. However, these fears were out of proportion to the real nature of the threat these groups posed to the state. The rigid treatment of naturalization petitions submitted by foreigners from various non-German ethnic groups was very much the product of domestic political conflicts and, during the Kaiserreich, of the authoritarian nature of the state, of its precarious legitimacy, and of Bismarck's inclination to employ draconian methods. Gosewinkel correctly terms Jews '*the* border group with respect to German citizenship'.[23] They do not readily fit within his overall explanatory scheme, however, for German Jews had no secessionist ambitions or separate political parties, and they were overwhelmingly loyal to

Germany.[24] This study therefore seeks other grounds for the general refusal to grant naturalization petitions from foreign Jews.

Gosewinkel emphasizes the gulf between the citizenship policies of the Kaiserreich and those of the Nazi period. The citizenship law of 1913, which embodied a range of policies characteristic of the Kaiserreich, was, he concludes, 'not a vehicle of the racial state, and can be the foundation of no lines of continuity with the racial policies of the Nazis. It certainly did not lead necessarily to such consequences.' These are, of course, two very different claims, the first quite bold, the second conventional.[25] This study also concludes that the 1913 citizenship law provided only the most modest foundations for accomplishing the Nazi regime's ambitions. However, the anti-Semitic naturalization practices that the 1913 law both sanctioned and strengthened were based on the same fears and prejudices that provided the basis for much of the Nazi government's anti-Semitic program, at least before the inauguration of genocide in 1941.

Finally, this study also considers aspects of the history of German citizenship that have not been paid much attention elsewhere. It examines the ways in which German citizenship was, until very recently, masculine, and the grounds on which German women's groups sought to gain the right to hold citizenship independently of husbands.[26] And it attempts to place the recent, revolutionary changes in German citizenship law in historical perspective, by examining how they reflect larger changes in the nature of the German state and society as well as Germany's position in Europe.

It is possible to discern a large variety of common themes and dissonances in a history as complex as that of a modern nation. German history has in fact produced an unusually large number of generalizations about the nature of long-term historical patterns, often violently contradictory generalizations. The different extant interpretations of German citizenship policy all capture critical aspects of the truth. However, each alone suggests a story that is too linear, too predictable, too simple. Bitter division and conflict, cataclysmic change, and a powerful yearning for unity are the major themes of this study and, arguably, of modern German history.[27] German history is not a teleology, with one internal logic and one predestined outcome.

As Michael Walzer has suggested, 'at stake [in citizenship policies] is the shape of the community that acts in the world, exercises sovereignty . . . Admission and exclusion are at the core of communal independence. They suggest the deepest meanings of self-determination'.[28] And, one might add, in many ways they reveal what the community is.

Notes

1. Letter of Wilhelm I, King of Prussia, to Friedrich I, Grand Duke of Baden, of 14 January 1871. Ernst Huber (ed.), *Dokumente zur Deutschen Verfassungsgeschichte*, vol. 2 (W. Kohlhammer, 1961), p. 284.
2. Results of the census of 1 December 1871. *Vierteljahrshefte zur Statistik des Deutschen Reichs für das Jahr 1873*, vol. 2 (Berlin, 1873), p. 122.
3. Thomas Nipperdey, *Deutsche Geschichte*, vol. 1 (Beck, 1993), p. 10; Peter Urbanitsch, 'Die Deutschen', in *Das Habsburgermonarchie*, vol. 3/1 (Verlag der österreichischen Akademie der Wissenschaften, 1980), pp. 33–7. The figure for Austria-Hungary is a rough estimate, since the census taken in 1880 included German-speaking Jews as Germans, although very few Germans would have considered them part of the historic German nation. In other respects as well the census figures for Austria-Hungary are not entirely reliable.
4. B.R. Mitchell, *European Historical Statistics 1750–1970* (Macmillan, 1975), p. 24; James Luck, *A History of Switzerland* (Society for the Promotion of Science and Scholarship, 1985), p. 534.
5. Detlef Brandes, 'Die Deutschen in Rußland und der Sowjetunion', in K. Bade (ed.), *Deutsche im Ausland – Fremde in Deutschland: Migration in Geschichte und Gegenwart* (Beck, 1992), p. 85; Ingeborg Fleischhauer, *Das Dritte Reich und die Deutschen in der Sowjetunion* (Deutsche Verlags-Anstalt, 1983), pp. 9–13. The first Russian census on nationalities, in 1897, found that 1,790,489 persons reported German as their mother tongue.
6. Peter Marschalk, *Bevölkerungsgeschichte Deutschlands im 19. und 20. Jahrhundert* (Suhrkamp, 1984), pp. 177–8.
7. The exact number can only be approximated, for the national census taken in December 1871 did not systematically record information regarding ethnicity or household language. *Statistik des Deutschen Reichs*, vol. 1, *Die Anordnungen des Bundesrathes für die gemeinsame Statistik der Deutschen Reiches* (Berlin, 1873), pp. 75–6; *Vierteljahrshefte zur Statistik des Deutschen Reichs für das Jahr 1873*, vol. 2, pp. 108–10. While the Prussian censuses of 1861 and 1867 did record the number of individuals in households where a non-German tongue was spoken, the manner in which the surveys were conducted led to the systematic underestimation of the number of non-German speakers. For example, the 1861 census recorded no families in Berlin that spoke a non-German language at home, while

the 1890 census found over 20,000 such individuals. 'Die preussische Bevölkerung nach ihrer Muttersprache und Abstammung', *Zeitschrift des Königlich Preussischen Statistischen Landesamts* 33 (1893), pp. 190, 196. The Prussian census of 1890 inquired more systematically regarding mother tongue. It found 2,765,101 Polish speakers and 103,112 individuals who spoke German and Polish. Ibid., p. 243. These figures exclude individuals identified as Masurian. Few ethnic Poles lived outside Prussia, and this figure therefore gives a rough idea of the number of ethnic Poles living in Germany on this date. For a discussion of the problems with Prussian census results in this period, see Leszek Belzyt, 'Die Zahl der Sorben in der amtlichen Sprachenstatistik vor dem Ersten Weltkrieg', in H. Hahn and P. Kunze (eds), *Nationale Minderheiten und staatliche Minderheitenpolitik in Deutschland im 19. Jahrhundert* (Akademie, 1999), pp. 157–9. The 1858 Prussian census found 466,170 Masurians. 'Versuch einer Statistik der Nationalitäten im preussischen Staate', *Zeitschrift des Königlich Preussischen Statistischen Bureaus* 11 (1871), p. 359. The 1890 Prussian census found 105,755. 'Die preussische Bevölkerung nach ihrer Muttersprache und Abstammung', *Zeitschrift des Königlich Preussischen Statistischen Landesamts* 33 (1893), p. 242. The discrepancy is explained in part by the fact that many Masurians had emigrated to the Ruhr region, where they seem largely to have escaped the notice of those taking the survey, and others had become German-speaking as a result of intensive government efforts at Germanization. Richard Blanke, *Polish-speaking Germans? Language and National Identity among the Masurians since 1871* (Böhlau, 2001).

8. Somewhat more than a tenth of this population emigrated to France following the war. Ernst Huber, *Deutsche Verfassungsgeschichte seit 1789*, vol. 4, *Struktur und Krisen des Kaiserreichs* (Kohlhammer, 1969), pp. 442–3. Huber writes that in 1871 'a large majority of the inhabitants of Alsace and Lorraine would have opposed the annexation of their province by the German Empire...' Ibid., pp. 446–50.

9. The national census of 1871 did inquire regarding confession. *Vierteljahrshefte zur Statistik des Deutschen Reichs für das Jahr 1873*, vol. 2, p. 188D.

10. The statistics regarding Danes and Sorbs are from Hahn and Kunze (eds), *Nationale Minderheiten*, pp. 121, 158. Those regarding Czechs and Lithuanians are based on the Prussian census of 1890.

Introduction

'Die preussische Bevölkerung nach ihrer Muttersprache und Abstammung,' *Zeitschrift des Königlich Preussischen Statistischen Landesamts* 33 (1893), p. 196. All are rough estimates.

11. Ulrich Herbert, *Geschichte der Ausländerpolitik in Deutschland: Saisonarbeiter, Zwangsarbeiter, Gastarbeiter, Flüchtlinge* (Beck, 2001), p. 233.
12. *Gesetz zur Reform des Staatsangehörigkeitsrechts* of 15 July 1999. *Bundesgesetzblatt (BGBl)* I, p. 1618.
13. *Zuwanderung gestalten Integration fördern, Bericht der Unabhängigen Kommission 'Zuwanderung'* (www.bmi.bund.de: 4 July 2001, accessed on 14 July 2003), p. 181; Dietrich Thränhardt, 'Integration und Partizipation von Einwanderergruppen im lokalen Kontext', in K. Bade and J. Oltmer (eds), *Aussiedler: deutsche Einwanderer aus Osteuropa* (Universitätsverlag Rasch, 1999), pp. 229, 233; Paul Harris, 'Russische Juden und Aussiedler: Integrationspolitik und lokale Verantwortung', Ibid., pp. 249, 257–9.
14. See Christian Joppke, *Immigration and the Nation-State: The United States, Germany, and Great Britain* (Oxford University Press, 1999); Christian Joppke, 'The Evolution of Alien Rights in the United States, Germany, and the European Union', in T. Aleinikoff and D. Klusmeyer (eds), *Citizenship Today: Global Perspectives and Practices* (Carnegie Endowment for International Peace, 2001), pp. 48–54.
15. Kay Hailbronner et al., *Staatsangehörigkeitsrecht* (Beck, 2001), pp. 206–44.
16. Rogers Brubaker, *Citizenship and Nationhood in France and Germany* (Harvard University Press, 1992), pp. 1, 6, 17.
17. Andreas Fahrmeir, *Citizens and Aliens: Foreigners and the Law in Britain and the German States 1789–1870* (Berghahn, 2000).
18. Patrick Weil, *Qu'est-ce qu'un Français? Histoire de la Nationalité Française depuis la Révolution* (Bernard Grasset, 2002), p. 196.
19. Ibid., p. 194. Peter Sahlins's recent study, by contrast, gives more weight to the role played by political considerations and actors in the making of French laws and policies in the late eighteenth and early nineteenth centuries. Peter Sahlins, *Unnaturally French: Foreign Citizens in the Old Regime and After* (Cornell University Press, 2004), pp. 215–66, 317–27.
20. Joppke, *Immigration and the Nation-State*, p. 69.
21. For interpretations that place much greater emphasis on economic forces and political decisions, see Herbert, *Geschichte der Ausländerpolitik* and Karen Schönwälder, *Einwanderung und ethnische*

Pluralität: Politische Entscheidungen und öffentliche Debatten in Grossbritannien und der Bundesrepublik von den 1950er bis zu den 1970er Jahren (Klartext, 2001).

22. Dieter Gosewinkel, *Einbürgern und Ausschließen: Die Nationalisierung der Staatsangehörigkeit vom Deutschen Bund bis zur Bundesrepublik Deutschland* (Vandenhoeck & Ruprecht, 2001), pp. 11, 68, 78, 89, 185, 249, 291, 293.

23. Ibid., p. 430.

24. For a recent discussion of this issue see Till van Rahden, *Juden und andere Breslauer: Die Beziehungen zwischen Juden, Protestanten und Katholiken in einer deutschen Großstadt von 1860 bis 1925* (Vandenhoeck & Ruprecht, 2000).

25. Gosewinkel, *Einbürgern und Ausschließen*, 426.

26. On the other hand, there are some subject areas that a more comprehensive work would address that are not covered here, for example German citizenship policies in colonial territories before the First World War. See, on this subject, Lora Wildenthal, 'Race, Gender, and Citizenship in the German Colonial Empire', in F. Cooper and A. Stoler (eds) *Tensions of Empire: Colonial Cultures in a Bourgeois World* (University of California Press, 1997), pp. 263–83; Lora Wildenthal, *German Women for Empire, 1884–1945* (Duke University Press, 2001); Pascal Grosse, *Kolonialismus, Eugenik und bürgerliche Gesellschaft in Deutschland 1850–1918* (Campus Verlag, 2000). Gosewinkel also considers the gendered nature of German citizenship laws and policies.

27. This stress on the central place of political conflict in modern German history is, of course, hardly novel. Max Weber's analysis of the nature of modern society – an analysis that applies especially to Germany of the late nineteenth and early twentieth centuries – breaks with the Rousseauean, Kantian, and Hegelian traditions of political philosophy in part by virtue of its stress on the inevitability of constant conflict over political power. See Max Weber, *Wirtschaft und Gesellschaft: Grundriss der verstehenden Soziologie*, vol. 1 (J.C.B. Mohr, 1956), pp. 20–1 (the concept of conflict), 514–40 (political communities). On the other hand, in abstracting about the nature of modern political and social institutions Weber failed to distinguish sharply between the patterns of conflict prevalent in different modern political regimes. The history of citizenship policies is valuable in part because it illustrates in a very concrete context the numerous changes that have taken place in the intensity of, and forms taken by, political conflict in modern German history,

and the relationship of these changes to domestic and international political structures.

28. Michael Walzer, *Spheres of Justice: A Defense of Pluralism and Equality* (Basic Books, 1984), pp. 61–2.

Part I
The Common Good, State Power, and Local Rights, 1815–1870

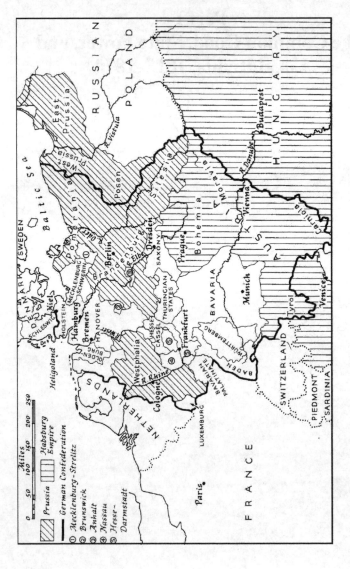

Map 1.1 The German Confederation in 1815. From William Carr, *A History of Germany 1815–1945*, 2nd edn. (Edward Arnold, 1979). Copyright William Carr 1969, 1979. Reprinted by permission of Hodder Arnold. The author acknowledges the assistance of the work of Panikos Panayi in locating several of the maps used in this book.

1

The Narrow-Heartedness of Small States

German states first defined in a systematic way who their citizens or subjects or state members were – the terminology varied – in the first half of the nineteenth century. Their goals included the conscription of eligible males, especially during the Napoleonic Era, avoiding conflicts with other states over deportations of the poor, and promoting the settlement of desirable immigrants. Laws that defined who was a citizen, subject or state member, as well as treaties between states, existed alongside older, generally local, rules and practices regarding the eligibility of outsiders for residence, employment and charitable support. They reflected both the heritage of local practices and conflicts with these practices. To understand state citizenship policies it is therefore necessary first to understand local policies, as they existed in the late eighteenth and early nineteenth centuries. It is necessary also to explore the ways in which social and political change undermined exclusionary local practices at the start of the nineteenth century.

Homelessness in the Old Regime

Above all it was fear of want, both present and expected, that led German villages and home towns in the early modern period jealously to protect their limited economies and communal poverty chests from outsiders. Communities feared competition, for work and for alms. These fears were well-founded. Even in good times most families produced little more than necessary to hold themselves above water. Custom and law required communities to feed and house their permanent residents – those who were 'heimatberechtigt', who belonged to the community – if they became destitute. Certainly they were expected not to slough them off onto some other town or village. And since famine, poverty and early death were part of the fabric of life, most communities assumed responsibility for outsiders only with considerable reluctance. Communities might admit servants and journeymen and laborers on a temporary basis, but most strictly limited grants of permanent resident status.

The economic and social patterns of early modern life led most people to have a long-term connection with a particular place. In Prussia the first thorough census, of 1817, found that 80 percent of the population lived in the countryside, in villages with fewer than 2,000 inhabitants or just 'on the land'.[1] This generally meant a bond with a particular piece of soil, which one's family owned and farmed, or to which it was connected by various rights and obligations other than ownership. In the German states of the south and west, land was usually divided into small or moderate-sized family farms, which had been acquired over generations. Such holdings were given up only with great reluctance, in extreme circumstances. In the east a large part of the population worked on estates owned by the nobility, but here also custom and law emphasized stability, the handing down of peasant positions – whether of serfs or free tenants – from one generation to the next.

In towns the pressure to stay put was perhaps even stronger than in the countryside, for the network of connections on which craftsmen and merchants relied for their livelihoods, the reputations in private and public life that were the currency of communities, were for the most part impossible to transfer from one place to another. As Mack Walker has described in his study of German home towns, the essence of the home town lay in stability and independence from the outside.[2] Everyone had a particular social, economic and political place in a thick web of connections. An outsider who came in without sponsorship, in the form of a spouse or a relative, or because of a particular economic need, might threaten the balance. People stayed put because no other place would take them in, and because if some disaster struck their community might help them through it. In this and other ways 'the experience of want and the need for security were the organizing principles of premodern society'.[3]

Old Regime structures did, however, permit and even demand some mobility.[4] The system of local attachments itself provided for it. Journeymen, servants and farm hands regularly worked away from their homes, either seasonally or for a period of years. In some cases seasonal migrations, to work or sell goods, lasted an entire working life and involved a significant percentage of a local population.[5] But members of these groups did not in most cases become citizens or resident aliens (Schutzverwandte or Beisassen), a lower form of permanent resident status, in their new residences. They usually continued to belong to their own place of origin, to which they could return in the event of

injury or failure or the end of the agreed-upon period of employment
– assuming they were not absent too long. Marriage to someone from
a different place generally led to the acquisition by the woman of the
man's residence status. But this was not automatic. It required, among
other things, the prior approval of the marriage by the man's community
or, for farm laborers in the east, by the local estate owner. There was also
a customary rule that a ten-year residence in a place gave the right to
remain. But it is impossible to know how widely observed this custom
was in practice, and in any event servants, apprentices and journeymen
were generally excluded from the reach of the rule.[6]

Despite the allowance for movement and change, the system of local
attachment regularly broke down. No contemporary figures can be relied
on.[7] One is left with impressions and records of charitable works. The
sense they convey is that the number of unattached individuals was large.
A Berlin journal of the 1780s noted the

> enormous number of people of all backgrounds, men and women, young and
> old, foreign and local, [who] travel around the countryside, from house to
> house, from village to village, from town to town, asking, begging, pleading,
> demanding, insulting, threatening, stealing the necessities of life.[8]

In the town of Erlangen in Franconia, which had at the end of the
eighteenth century 9,000 inhabitants, some 400–500 beggars came to the
town gate each month to receive a card entitling them to free meals for
the day. 'In the smallest, most secluded village near the border with the
Upper Palatinate,' commented an observer in 1802, 'one can often count
thirty to forty beggars each day.'[9] In the winter encounters with beggars
who had frozen or died of hunger were not uncommon. Of course, some
members of these marginal groups might have been able to prove a legal
residence somewhere.

Clearly communities had powerful incentives to rid themselves
of those who were likely to burden the local poor chest and frequent
opportunity to act on these incentives. Because vagrancy was so
widespread, ordinances forbidding begging or ordering the expulsion
of foreign beggars and vagabonds were also common. Prussia ordered
the expulsion of non-Prussian beggars in 1680, 1684, 1696, 1698,
1704, 1710, 1715, 1725, 1735, and 1748.[10] In 1751 Bavaria required
the branding of foreign beggars and, if they repeated the offense, their
execution.[11] The constant repetition of the ordinances regarding foreign
beggars and vagabonds is an indication both of the seriousness of the
problem and – despite the finality of the Bavarian measures – the modest

effectiveness of the tools at the disposal of state administrations to deal with it. The failure of states and other territories to control vagrancy found visible expression in the continued maintenance of town walls, which by the eighteenth century had for the most part lost their military significance. Even if the walls could not keep out armies, at least they were effective against beggars and individual marauders.[12]

While it may seem anomalous, at the same time that many Old Regime towns were busy expelling outsiders, many states assiduously sought to prevent emigration. States could press both more taxes and more conscripts from larger populations. From the late seventeenth or early eighteenth centuries almost all German states imposed a tax on emigration – often on the order of 10 percent or more of assets.[13] Some states prohibited emigration altogether, or required the permission of the central authorities.[14] States' requirements for military service often meant that emigration was prohibited for a fair portion of the population. Eighteenth-century Prussia, for example, required a significant percentage of the adult male population to serve in the army for more than a month each year until they became infirm, a requirement moderated in 1792 to a twenty-year commitment.[15] The institution of hereditary serfdom, common in the eastern part of the Prussian states before 1810, was designed to prevent the emigration of rural labor.[16] Of course, the very existence of a massive legal apparatus aimed at preventing emigration suggests that, in fact, individuals left their homes more frequently than local and state authorities preferred. Old Regime states sought not only to retain existing populations, but in some cases invited outsiders to settle within their borders. Eighteenth-century Russia, Austria and Prussia were among the most active organizers of immigration, to turn wastelands into farmland and to develop new industries.

The contrast between the treatment of the homeless and policies that generally favored population growth reflected in part the differences in the kind of person involved. A poor or elderly person was usually undesirable, a well-off or skilled person might be welcome. In part the differences reflected the conflicting interests of states and local communities. States wished to promote population growth, while communities often were reluctant to permit the permanent residence of any new outsiders.

Building Higher Walls

The early nineteenth century saw an intensification of policies that excluded outsiders.[17] Population growth was one reason. In 1816 there were roughly 23,520,000 people in the lands that after 1870 became the German state. In 1850 there were 33,746,000. An ever larger part of the population had only a marginal basis for existence.[18] Dissolution of the ties that bound individuals, and especially the poor, to a particular place also swelled the number of impoverished vagrants. Following its defeat at the hands of Napoleon in 1806 Prussia ordered an end to hereditary serfdom: 'from Martinmas [11 November] in 1810 there will be only free people'.[19] The process of freeing the peasantry from attachment to the land in fact lasted for decades, in Prussia and in other German states. As it progressed it created a large class of unattached, generally poor, individuals and families. The last mass famine in the German states, at least before the total wars of the twentieth century, took place in the late 1840s and early 1850s. At the height of the famine a fourth to a fifth of the population of Württemberg had to be supported by public charity.[20]

Both local communities and states responded to the multiplying numbers of the poor by closing their doors ever more tightly. In Austria, for example, the state greatly increased the frequency of its mass expulsions (Schübe) of illegal residents from Vienna. In the last decades of the eighteenth century these had taken place twice a year. Beginning in 1817 they occurred twice a month. In 1824 Austrian authorities searched the entire land for undesirable persons. On the evening of the day before the search, officials were required

> to close the doors of churches and cloisters and graveyards, so that no one could flee there, and to adequately man the bridges over the Donau and elsewhere, and especially to shut the gates of towns and enclosed places, and in all other ways to make preparations. On the following day officials, hunters ... and one militarily serviceable man from each house will appear without fail early in the morning ... and examine most thoroughly the local area, including all houses, cellars, lands, stalls, and other suspicious corners, as well as all paths, meadows, and woods...[21]

In this way, throughout Austria, individuals who were living in a place without permission were returned to their legal homes. If foreign, they were expelled. Exactly how vigorously and how often this order was carried out is uncertain, but alone the formulation of such a policy manifested a heightened level of vigilance. From the 1820s to the 1840s police officials in half a dozen German states established journals devoted to describing vagabonds and criminals. The aim was to promote the sharing of information both within and across state boundaries, and in this way to assist in the apprehension, punishment and expulsion of vagabonds and criminals.[22]

By the 1830s and 1840s expulsions from towns and states affected literally hundreds of thousands of Germans. Between 1836 and 1850 Bavaria deported more than 50,000 Bavarian subjects each year from one part of the kingdom to another. This amounted, on an annual basis, to more than 1 percent of the population of the monarchy. In the same period more than 5,000 aliens were expelled annually on similar grounds, between 5 and 10 percent of the alien population.[23] Bavaria was more restrictive than most German states, but the Bavarian statistics at least give a sense of the order of magnitude of the practice. 'Such things [expulsions] used to belong to the daily bread of life everywhere [in Germany], so to speak', Karl Braun, a National Liberal deputy, told the Reichstag of the North German confederation in 1867, during debates on legislation that ended the power of towns to keep out individuals from outside the community.[24] 'Whenever we travel, we find fellow countrymen who have been expelled from their homes through the narrow-heartedness of small state legislation!'[25] As Braun's comment suggests, while the theory of expulsions was to return people to their homes, in practice it often meant removing them from places they had lived for decades to towns or villages to which they had little, if any, real connection.

The increasing frequency of expulsions led states to clarify who their legal residents were. The Prussian treaty with Bavaria of 9 May 1818 served as a model for a series of similar agreements between Prussia and other German states.[26] This treaty, and others like it, attempted to clarify which state was responsible for accepting individuals who were not 'heimatberechtigt', either because they had been born homeless or because by moving they had lost their former citizenship rights.[27] Under its terms only individuals who had a connection with one of the contracting states could be expelled to it. Such a connection included: birth to parents who were state members; birth to homeless parents within the state boundaries; marriage and independent economic activity; and ten years of tolerated residence (except for servants, students, journeymen and the like).[28] The treaty specifically forbade the mass expulsions of vagabonds ('größere, sogenannte Vagantenschube') that Austria and other states continued to practice.[29] Despite the treaties, however, German states frequently found it impossible to agree on where homeless individuals should be permitted to live.[30]

The published documents of the German Confederation, the weak federal institution that after 1815 represented the forty-odd German states, record appeals dating to the 1830s and 1840s from half a dozen individuals expelled or threatened with expulsion from the states where

Figure 1.1 *The Vagabond*, by Ferdinand von Rayski, 1835. The picture illustrates the arrest of the vagabond by two policemen, and suggests little sympathy for him. Rayski was known primarily for his portraits of the nobility, and for his landscapes. From Otto Grautoff, *Ferdinand von Royski* (Grote, 1923).

they lived, but unable to find new residences. Most had committed no crime, but had merely moved away from their original places of birth. After a period they had lost the legal connection to their old home, without acquiring a new legal residence. Several of the individuals practiced itinerant professions.[31] One was a servant.[32] The cases that reached the German Confederation represented only the tip of an iceberg. They illustrate the growing role of German states in excluding outsiders, the conflicts among states these practices caused, and the widespread sense that such expulsions were inhumane, a sign that something was seriously amiss in the German states.

Among the petitions heard by the German Confederation was one from Johann Heinrich Ludwig Hanemann, a former apprentice baker. The Hanemann case enjoyed a certain contemporary notoriety. One reason was that his attempts to find a home lasted some half dozen years. He also seems to have been a colorful character. Finally, his fate had much in common with that of many others. Since Hanemann's troubles shed light on the larger problem, I will describe them in some detail.

Homeless Germans: A Case Study

Hanemann was the kind of subject no German state wanted.[33] As a sixteen-year-old, in 1819, he had moved to the city-state of Hamburg from a village in Hanover to work as an apprentice baker. Apprentices often found work far from their birthplace. The move also reflected other larger patterns. Hamburg was growing, not as quickly as later in the century, but dramatically for the time. In 1817 it had, counting the adjacent suburbs of St. Georg and St. Pauli, roughly 106,000 inhabitants. By 1852 the total was 159,000. Most of this increase came from migration into the city, for Hamburg was relatively open to outsiders.[34] Hanover, on the other hand, was a land where powerful guilds and communal authorities made it hard for many to find an economic foothold outside their own community, and sometimes even inside it.

In 1832 Hanemann took the bold step of applying to become a citizen of Hamburg. He wanted to open his own business, and this required local citizenship. The number of individuals who were citizens of Hamburg was modest, perhaps 20 percent of the adult male population. Citizenship, the Bürgerrecht, was divided into first and second classes, the 'Großbürgerrecht', or first-class citizenship, and the 'Kleinbürgerrecht', or second-class citizenship. Only first-class citizens could practice the most honored and lucrative trades. But even second-class citizenship – one can assume Hanemann sought citizenship of this type – placed the possessor in a privileged position. It cost some forty Marks Current, and applicants had to show ownership of the uniform and weapons of the civil guard, in which male citizens served. For a baker the total expense was roughly equal to a month's wages.[35] Only citizens enjoyed the right independently to operate businesses, to participate in the political life of the city, and to benefit from a range of municipal institutions. Entering the citizenry was therefore a social and economic step of considerable significance for the individual involved.

Hamburg approved Hanemann's citizenship application. But, alas, the citizenship had been obtained by fraud. Hanemann had used the papers and name of his dead and evidently more established brother. In one version of the story he simply wanted to save the costs and trouble of obtaining his own papers. Perhaps he had had a brush with the law, or expressed dangerous political sympathies in the revolutionary years of 1830 and 1831, or in some other way besmirched his reputation. Citizenship required not only payment of a fee, but a showing of good reputation. That he came from outside Hamburg was not enough to prevent the acquisition of citizenship. Many new citizens, and probably an especially large percentage of second-class citizens, were not born in Hamburg.[36] The Hamburg authorities discovered Hanemann's clever maneuver within a few weeks. The city promptly rescinded the grant of citizenship and expelled Hanemann from its territory. Hamburg's openness in granting citizenship rights to newcomers did not extend to the economically marginal and morally dubious.

Hamburg had been Hanemann's home for all his adult life and he was plainly reluctant to leave the area. He attempted to live illegally in the city despite the expulsion order, but Hamburg authorities soon detected, punished and expelled him. Hanemann then moved to Altona, an adjacent city that belonged to the Duchy of Holstein, then ruled by the Danish monarchy, but was also part of the German Confederation. Here he applied for citizenship in his own name. In March 1833 Altona granted his application. Hanemann lived in Altona for the next seven years. In 1839 he again fell afoul of the law. The Altona authorities claimed that he sought out well-to-do young ladies, pretended to be wealthy himself, and made multiple marriage offers, all to the end of finagling money and other valuables from his fiancées. He also declared bankruptcy and apparently attempted to cheat his creditors by failing to provide them with a complete list of personal goods against which his debts might be satisfied. This was, again, how the creditors saw the matter. A more sympathetic account suggests that Hanemann was guilty of no more than quarreling with his fiancée.[37]

Hanemann's legal difficulties led the Altona authorities to rescind his Altona citizenship, on the grounds that when he became an Altona citizen he concealed his previous deception of Hamburg. In October 1840, after Hanemann had served a jail sentence for his other crimes, the Altona police ordered his expulsion. When Hanemann protested, he was informed by the district government, part of the Danish Monarchy, that as a 'highly mischievous, scheming person ('als einen in hohem Grade verschmitzten, ränkevollen Menschen') who was always trying to go behind other people's backs and to earn his living through swindles and frauds', his presence in Altona was undesired.[38]

In the years that followed Hanemann was repeatedly found inside the bounds of both Hamburg and Altona. Each city punished and expelled him, and each denied any responsibility for him. But with such a past no other state in Germany would ever willingly accept him. And so he was expelled from one city to the other, went from one prison to the next, until at last, in the fall of 1844, he sought out the German Confederation in Frankfurt to seek a decision regarding which city or state had an obligation to permit his residence.

The German Confederation had no binding authority in these matters, but it, or rather one of its commissions, attempted to mediate among the states involved. It was clear, after all, that the man had to live somewhere. But the relevant governments refused to back down. Although Hanemann had been born in Hanover and had served in its army, he had been absent from it for some fifteen years. Hanover claimed that in becoming a citizen of a different German state Hanemann had irrevocably lost his citizenship in Hanover. Hamburg took the position that it had never assumed an obligation to him: it had granted citizenship to Hanemann's dead brother, not to Hanemann. That he had lived in Hamburg for over ten years as an apprentice and then journeyman baker did not give him any right to remain there. The commission of the German confederation thought Altona had the greatest responsibility for him, as he had lived there last and had been granted citizenship. But the Danish court vigorously disputed this view. The Danish ambassador to the Diet of the German Confederation took the position that acquisition of local citizenship did not by itself bring with it an irrevocable right to remain in Altona. One had also to live there for fifteen years. The Danish ambassador vigorously disputed the right of the Diet to examine the relevant Danish legislation and draw a different conclusion. Denmark would interpret its own laws, and the German Confederation had to accept Denmark's conclusions on this subject as binding. What eventually happened to Hanemann is not clear from the published records, although it appears that Altona took him back temporarily.

Hanemann's plight illustrates the strict control German states sought to exercise over their borders by the 1830s and 1840s. An issue that had previously been left largely to local communities to resolve had become a matter for states and a source of tension among them. It suggests also the inadequacies of the laws and treaties that governed citizenship and disputes about citizenship. Finally, the Hanemann case and others like it demonstrated how little many German states cared for the plight of individual Germans, or for the idea of a larger German nation. Each state looked out for its own narrow interest, even if it meant the destruction of the lives of those caught by their conflicting laws. As the petitions commission of the German Confederation put it with respect to another instance of someone refused residence by all the states with which he had had a connection, in the late 1830s: 'there cannot be a harder fate than homelessness. What will in the end become of the unfortunate person, who by a chain of accidents for which he is not responsible does not meet the formal conditions for residence imposed by the quite varying state laws, and for this reason faces expulsions everywhere?'[39]

Rethinking Belonging: Smith, Hegel, Fichte

By the 1820s and 1830s many members of the educated elite had come to see the pushing and shoving of an ever growing mass of people across local and state borders as wasteful and cruel. The laments of the representatives of the German Confederation at the misery caused individuals caught between the laws of the different German states were one expression of this critique. Laissez-faire conceptions of the foundations of prosperity, an exalted sense of the mission of the state, and a new humanitarian feeling all played key roles in the new skepticism about the rules that governed residence and citizenship. One also detects the influence of far more traditional concerns for the well-being of the state, especially in Prussia.

The economic critique most directly undermined barriers to movement. Adam Smith's *Wealth of Nations*, published in England in 1776, was the most influential formulation. By the 1790s Smith's book was well known in German administrative and academic circles.[40] Smith attacked restrictions on movement in England as 'an evident violation of natural liberty and justice'.

The very unequal price of labor which we frequently find in England in places at no great distance from one another, is probably owing to the obstruction which the law of settlements gives to a poor man who would carry his industry from one parish to another without a certificate [from his home parish]. A single man, indeed, who is healthy and industrious, may sometimes reside by sufferance without one; but a man with a wife and family who should attempt to do so, would in most parishes be sure of being removed, and if the single man should afterwards marry, he would generally be removed likewise. The scarcity of hands in one parish, therefore, cannot always be relieved by their super-abundance in another...[41]

It was in part the influence of Smith that led Prussia and other German states to abolish serfdom, and to seek to end local exclusionary practices. By the late 1820s a significant part of English society had accepted Smith's critique of the Elizabethan poor-law system, which tied the indigent to their home parish. In the 1830s and 1840s Parliament significantly restricted the rights of parishes to expel outsiders, although thousands of Irish continued to be deported annually from England through the 1850s.[42] The English reforms, and the debates that preceded them, found an echo in the German states, and especially in Prussia.

In the German context Smith's critique of local controls on movement became part of a much larger attack on traditional local powers. The argument, as developed above all in the work of Georg Friedrich Hegel, was that the state was the main instrument for the moral betterment of its inhabitants, that it alone cared for the common good and therefore was capable of freeing individual members of society from their enslavement to private egoism. Smaller associations within the state, such as families, guilds, towns and estates, existed only to serve the needs of their own members. Local controls on movement conflicted with the spirit of Hegel's theory of the state in that they favored one class of subjects – those who belonged to prosperous local communities – over all others, and were aimed at protecting only the local economy and community. The moral grounding of Hegel's thought gave it an intensity even greater than Smith's. It was of little moment to Hegel whether many or most of the inhabitants of the state desired freedom from traditional rules or customs, based on their own selfish interests. 'The objective will is rational, whether individuals recognize this or not, whether they desire it or not.'[43] Narrowness of view was to be expected from most members of society. Communities had to be forced to overcome their narrow interests, and the state was the hand that could and should compel them to do so.

Hegel's philosophy also implied that states had a powerful capacity to integrate foreigners, both those currently in the country and those immigrating from outside. He discussed the question explicitly with respect to adherents of religious sects. 'A state that is strong because its organization is mature may conduct itself all the more liberally... [It] may even tolerate a sect (though, of course, all depends on its numbers) which on religious grounds declines to recognize even its direct duties to the state.' With respect to the Quakers and Anabaptists, who refused to perform military service, the strong state could rely on the 'inner rationality of its institutions' ultimately to integrate them into society. Hegel even advocated full citizenship for Jews, the classic pariah group of the Old Regime.[44] The larger structure of Hegel's argument, the claim that the state should remake all members of society in the most fundamental ways in accordance with universal truths, implied that in principle no individuals need be excluded from full citizenship because of cultural differences between themselves and the majority.

Smith and Hegel found such a welcome reception among the civil servants of German states, and especially in Prussia, in part because they presented in a more systematic – hence also more radical – form conceptions that had been central to the ideology of German state administrations since the late seventeenth century. Cameralism and police science, as they were termed, promoted the oversight of local economies and communities by states for the sake of the common good. Johann Justi, an influential mid-eighteenth-century teacher, writer and administrator, had also attacked local restrictions on admissions to trades. 'Perhaps it will be said that there will be too many masters... But just that is advantageous to the population and economy', he wrote in 1761. Like Hegel, Justi also attacked the way personal interests tended to subvert the common good.[45]

In the same period that Hegel posited that the role of the state in history was morally and spiritually to elevate mankind by overriding local laws and customs, other German writers proposed to improve German society by cultivating local traditions, by enlarging local feeling. Johann Gottlieb Fichte's *Addresses to the German Nation*, delivered in Berlin in the winter of 1807–8, shortly after Napoleon's defeat of Prussia and the dissolution of the Holy Roman Empire, emphasized language as the basis of German national unity. The German nation, he wrote, stretched 'as far as the German tongue was spoken' ('so weit die deutsche Zunge reicht'). Hegel's state dominated and challenged local practices, which Hegel viewed as oriented only to the private interests of the local unit. Only by changing parochial local customs to reflect the needs and moral demands of the larger community could a society that was noble, just and universal come into being. Fichte's German nation, while also in a sense universal, arose organically from local communities. Each community expressed in miniature the constitution of the whole. The national language conveyed to the members of the nation the peculiar national personality and way of thinking (Denkweise) that was the characteristic and essential basis of life.[46]

Fichte's writings contained the seeds of future policies of ethnic exclusion. It is true that he was far from proposing a racial conception of the German nation. His work implied a certain flexibility with respect to the inclusion of non-German groups within German society. Languages can, after all, be learned. Fichte noted that the incorporation of foreigners was a natural and expected part of the history of all nations. All nations, and certainly the German, had become mixed with other ethnic groups, so that 'none of the nations that arose from the Germans can easily make the claim that they had a greater purity of origin [Abstammung] than others'. 'It is not a question of the previous origin of those who carry on the speaking of an original language, but only whether this language has been spoken without interruption, since men are formed much more by their language, than a language by those who speak it.' On the other hand, Fichte also suggested that if a foreign group was large enough or powerful enough to influence the development of the culture and language of the host group, then its influence was likely to be pernicious. Early mixing of German with Slavic peoples had not been harmful because the victors were 'only the Germans'. A nation bound by a common language 'cannot take in another group with a different heritage [Abkunft] and speech and allow itself to mix with it, without itself become confused, and considerably disturbing the smooth progress of its development'.[47] The main target here was the cultural influence of France. In contrast to Hegel, Fichte opposed the integration of Jews, and his treatment of Catholics was also generally intolerant.[48]

Fichte's focus on the linguistically based unity of all Germans implied – although Fichte himself did not dot the i's and cross the t's in this fashion – the possibility of a larger German state, open to all Germans. In the decades that followed the liberation from France his teaching found a wide echo within the educated elite.[49] But the German states of the first half of the nineteenth century existed, and knew they existed, despite such national feeling, in opposition to it. Fichtean conceptions of a common German nationality had little effect on German citizenship policies until well into the second half of the nineteenth century. In the first half of the century German states, and in particular Prussia, focused above all on economic considerations in determining whether outsiders would prove desirable subjects.

Smith and Hegel provided German state administrations, and in particular the Prussian state, with ideological rationales for citizenship policies that were at the same time authoritarian and liberal. These policies were authoritarian in the sense that they flew in the face of traditional rights and customs, and of much popular sentiment, and granted largely uncontrolled powers to central administrations. They were liberal not in the sense that they implied the granting of political rights – they did not – but because they granted subjects, and foreigners whom states made into subjects, social and economic rights, the right to move freely and to find work freely. We turn now to the ways in which Prussia put the teachings of Smith and Hegel into practice.

Notes

1. Johann Gottfried Hoffmann, *Uebersicht der Bodenfläche und Bevolkerung des Preussischen Staats* (Berlin, 1817), p. 49. This percentage of course varied from region to region.
2. Mack Walker, *German Home Towns: Community, State, and General Estate 1648–1871* (Cornell University Press, 1971).
3. Heinz Reif, *Westfälischer Adel 1770–1860: Vom Herrschaftsstand zur regionalen Elite* (Vandenhoeck & Ruprecht, 1979), p. 122.
4. Steven Hochstadt has shown that 'migration was an integral and regular part of a relatively stable social and economic order' in Germany of the seventeenth and eighteenth centuries. Steven Hochstadt, 'Migration in Preindustrial Germany', *Central European History* 16 (1983), p. 213. Hochstadt's most recent work, however, as well as that of James Jackson, make clear that early modern levels of migration were significantly below those experienced from the 1820s to the 1860s in the regions of Germany that were most heavily affected by industrialization. See Hochstadt, *Mobility and Modernity: Migration in Germany, 1820–1989* (University of Michigan Press, 1999), p. 80; James H. Jackson Jr., *Migration and Urbanization in the Ruhr Valley, 1821–1914* (Humanities Press, 1997), p. 72.
5. Klaus Bade, *Europa in Bewegung: Migration vom späten 18. Jahrhundert bis zur Gegenwart* (Beck, 2000), pp. 17–58.
6. The operation of the ten-year rule in Austrian territories is described in Harald Wendelin, 'Schub und Heimatrecht', in W. Heindl and E. Saurer (eds), *Grenze und Staat Paßwesen, Staatsbürgerschaft, Heimatrecht und Fremdengesetzgebung in der österreichischen Monarchie 1750–1867*, (Böhlau Verlag, 2000), pp. 199–213.
7. Ernst Schubert, *Arme Leute: Bettler und Gauner im Franken des 18. Jahrhunderts* (Commissionsverlag Degener & Co., 1983), p. 3.
8. 'Ueber das Betteln auf dem platten Lande und in kleinen Städten', *Berlinische Monatsschrift* 9 (January–June 1787), p. 4, cited in Michael Doege, *Armut in Preußen und Bayern (1770–1840)* (Kommissionsverlag UNI-Druck, 1991), p. 32.
9. *Fränkische Provinzialblätter* 2 (1802), p. 953, cited in Schubert, *Arme Leute*, p. 5.
10. *Corpus Constitutionum Marchicarum, oder Königl. Preußis. und Churfürstl. Brandenburgische in der Chur- und Marck Brandenburg, auch incorporirten Landen publicirte und ergangene Ordnungen,*

Edicta, Mandata, Rescripta, u. von Zeiten Friedrichs I Churfürstens zu Brandenburg, u. bis ietzo (Berlin, 1736), Part Five, Section Five, Chapter 1.

11. 'Armenwesen', in *Meyers Großes Konversations-Lexikon*, 6th edn, vol. 1 (Leipzig: Bibliographisches Institut, 1902), p. 788. I owe the reference to this citation to Hermann Beck, *The Origins of the Authoritarian Welfare State in Prussia: Conservatives, Bureaucracy, and the Social Question, 1815–1870* (University of Michigan Press, 1995), p. 152.

12. Schubert, *Arme Leute*, p. 6. Towns' walls also served a variety of other non-military purposes in the eighteenth century. They protected town markets from competition, and prevented the smuggling of goods into and out of cities to the end of avoiding onerous state taxes. They also kept the soldiers housed in garrisons, which were often located in cities, from deserting. Johannes Ziekursch, *Das Ergebnis der friderizianischen Städteverwaltung und die Städteordnung Steins* (Hermann Castenoble, 1908), pp. 48–9.

13. Hermann Rehm, 'Der Erwerb von Staats- und Gemeinde-Angehörigkeit in geschichtlicher Entwicklung nach römischem und deutschem Staatsrecht', *Annalen des Deutschen Reichs für Gesetzgebung, Verwaltung und Statistik* XXV (1892), p. 169.

14. Hannelore Burger, 'Paßwesen und Staatsbürgerschaft', in Heindl and Saurer, *Grenze und Staat*, p. 132.

15. Heinz Stübig, 'Die Wehrverfassung Preußens in der Reformzeit: Wehrpflicht im Spannungsfeld von Restauration und Revolution 1815–1860', in R. Foerster, (ed.), *Die Wehrpflicht: Entstehung, Erscheinungsformen und politisch-militärische Wirkung* (Oldenbourg, 1994), pp. 40–1; Otto Büsch, *Military System and Social Life in Old Regime Prussia, 1713–1807: The Beginnings of the Social Militarization of Prusso-German Society*, trans. John Gagliardo (Humanities Press, 1997), pp. xxi, 6, 25.

16. Johannes Ziekursch, *Hundert Jahre schlesischer Agrargeschichte: Vom Hubertusburger Frieden bis zum Abschluß der Bauernbefreiung*, 2nd edn (Preuss & Juenger, 1927), pp. 97–101.

17. Leo Lucassen also describes this phenomenon. See his *Zigeuner: Die Geschichte eines polizeilichen Ordnungsbegriffes in Deutschland, 1700–1945* (Böhlau Verlag, 1996), pp. 108–39.

18. The statistics are from P. Marschalck, *Bevölkerungsgeschichte Deutschlands im 19. and 20. Jahrhundert* (Suhrkamp, 1984), p. 145. Alsace-Lorraine is not included in the area for which statistics are given. The increase in the percentage of the population that fell into

the poorest categories is described in Werner Conze, 'Vom "Pöbel" zum "Proletariat". Sozialgeschichtliche Voraussetzungen für den Sozialismus in Deutschland', in W. Conze, *Gesellschaft-Staat-Nation: Gesammelte Aufsätze*, pp. 231–2, and in Doege, *Armut in Preußen und Bayern*, pp. 59–84.

19. *Edikt den erleichterten Besitz und den freien Gebrauch des Grund-Eigenthums, so wie die persönlichen Verhältnisse der Land-Bewohner betreffend* of 9 October 1807, Section 12, *Preussische Gesetz-Sammlung (PGS)*, p. 173.

20. Klaus-Jürgen Matz, *Pauperismus und Bevölkerung: Die gesetzlichen Ehebeschränkungen in den süddeutschen Staaten während des 19. Jahrhunderts* (Klett-Cotta, 1980), p. 57.

21. Wendelin, 'Schub und Heimatrecht', pp. 239–40.

22. Lucassen, *Zigeuner*, pp. 122–62.

23. A. Fahrmeir, *Citizens and Aliens: Foreigners and the Law in Britain and the German States 1789–1870*, Berghahn, 2000, pp. 76, 191.

24. Karl Braun, *Stenographische Berichte über die Verhandlungen des Reichstags des Norddeutschen Bundes*, First Legislative Period, vol. 1 (21 October 1867), p. 564.

25. Ibid. (19 March 1867), p. 254.

26. On the status of the 9 May 1818 treaty between Prussia and Bavaria as a model for the subsequent Prussian treaties with other states, see the analysis of the history of Prussian citizenship policy in von und zur Mühlen, *Vortrag über das Gesetz wegen Entstehung und Auflösung des Preußischen Unterthanen-Verhältnisses*, 26 March 1840, GStA PK I, HA I, Rep. 80 (Drucksachen) Nr. 286, Anlage V, p. 4. Drucksachen were printed collections of proposed laws and memoranda debating the merits of the laws and their histories that were circulated to members of the Staatsrat, the highest advisory council to the Prussian King.

27. Just as it is unclear what percentage of the population of German states lacked a fixed abode, so it is also unclear what percentage was legally homeless. The first Austrian census of the extent to which individuals resided where they were 'heimatberechtigt', in 1869, suggested that virtually every Austrian had a right to reside somewhere in Austria. But then an 1863 law had given the state the right to assign a residence to the homeless, and this suggested that perhaps prior to that date legal homelessness had not been such a negligible phenomenon after all. Heinrich Rauchberg, 'Zur Kritik des Österreichischen Heimatrechtes', *Zeitschrift für Volkswirtschaft, Socialpolitik und Verwaltung* 2 (1893), p. 65. For a discussion of

one group whose members were frequently homeless in the legal sense, see Lucassen, *Zigeuner*.

28. *Ratifikations-Urkunde der zwischen Seiner Majestät dem Könige vom Preußen und Seiner Majestät dem Könige von Baiern am 9ten Mai 1818 abgeschlossenen Uebereinkunft wegen wechselseitiger Uebernahme der Vagabunden und Ausgewiesenen, GPS*, p. 53.

29. Schubert, *Arme Leute*, pp. 219–20.

30. For a more extensive discussion of the effects of the deportation treaties, see my H-Net review of Fahrmeir, *Citizens and Aliens*. The review was published in 2003 at http://www.h-net.org/reviews/showrev.cgi?path=38191059590170.

31. Two of the appeals involved actors, and a third came from a hunter who also had traveled around a great deal. *Protokolle der Deutschen Bundesversammlung* (1831), p. 176 (Johann Friedrich Lemnitzer); Ibid., (1842), pp. 233–6 (Johann Christian Gottlieb Badewitz); Ibid., (1846), p. 91 (Xaver Straßer).

32. Louise Lisette Hasselbaum was a servant living in Frankfurt. When Frankfurt officials demanded in the 1830s that Hasselbaum demonstrate permanent residence status somewhere – eighteen years after she had come to Frankfurt – none of the places where she or her parents had lived would accept her. *Protokolle der Deutschen Bundesversammlung* (1839), p. 522. A survey taken a generation later, in 1858, found that of the 10,101 servants in Frankfurt, only 151 had permanent resident status: the remainder were merely tolerated foreigners. Inge Kaltwasser, *Häusliches Gesinde in der Freien Stadt Frankfurt am Main: Rechtsstellung, soziale Lage und Aspekte des sozialen Wandels 1815–1866* (Waldemer Kramer, 1989), p. 17

33. This account of Hanemann's career is taken from the records of the German Confederation and from Ernst Dronke's *Polizei-Geschichten*, first published in 1846. Dronke had himself been expelled from Berlin and Leipzig in 1845 due to his radical political writings. His subsequent petition to become a Prussian citizen was rejected. He therefore knew first-hand of some of the difficulties Hanemann experienced. See *Protokolle der Deutschen Bundesversammlung* (1845), pp. 391–5, 545, 681–6, 741, 834–7; Ernst Dronke, *Polizei-Geschichten* (Vandenhoeck & Ruprecht, 1968), pp. 141–52, 206–7.

34. Antje Kraus, *Die Unterschichten Hamburgs in der ersten Hälfte des 19. Jahrhunderts: Entstehung, Struktur und Lebensverhältnisse. Eine historisch-statistische Untersuchung* (Gustav Fischer, 1965), p. 34. These statistics, based on surveys conducted for military purposes, probably understated the total population. Ibid., pp. 28–30, 36–8.

35. Ibid., pp. 37–8, 41, 90. While the city authorities kept figures regarding the number of individuals who became citizens, the number of citizens in the city at any moment must be estimated.
36. Ibid., p. 37.
37. Dronke, *Polizei-Geschichten*, p. 146.
38. *Protokolle der Deutschen Bundesversammlung* (1845), p. 393.
39. Ibid. (1838), p. 91 (Johann Conrad Herbig).
40. Smith's influence in Germany, and in particular Prussia, is discussed in Wilhelm Treue, 'Adam Smith in Deutschland: Zum Problem des "Politischen Professors" zwischen 1776 und 1810', in W. Conze (ed.), *Deutschland und Europa, Historische Studien zur Völker- und Staatenordnung des Abendlandes: Festschrift für Hans Rothfels* (Droste-Verlag, 1951), pp. 101–33.
41. Adam Smith, *An Inquiry into the Nature and Causes of the Wealth of Nations* (University of Chicago Press, 1976), p. 157.
42. David Feldman, 'Was the Nineteenth Century a Golden Age for Immigrants? The Changing Articulation of National, Local and Voluntary Controls', in A. Fahrmeir et al. (eds), *Migration Control in the North Atlantic World: The Evolution of State Practices in Europe and the United States from the French Revolution to the Inter-War Period* (New York: Berghahn, 2003), pp. 170–4. Smith was certainly not the only intellectual father of the English poor law reform: Bentham and Malthus also played key roles.
43. Georg Wilhelm Friedrich Hegel, *Grundlinien der Philosophie des Rechts oder Naturrecht und Staatswissenschaft im Grundrisse* (Frommanns, 1952), p. 331 (section 258).
44. Ibid., pp. 353–4 (section 270).
45. Walker, *German Home Towns*, pp. (in order of citation) 167, 165, 156.
46. Johann Gottlieb Fichte, 'Reden an die deutsche Nation', in *Sämmtliche Werke*, pub. by J.H. Fichte, vol. 7 (Berlin, 1846), pp. 392, 481, 470.
47. Ibid., pp. 313–4, 460.
48. In a famous passage in a piece published in 1793, Fichte wrote that 'I see no means of giving Jews the rights of citizens, other than in a single night to remove their heads and replace them with others containing non-Jewish ideas. To protect ourselves from them we have no alternative except to conquer their promised land for them and send them all there.' Johann Gottlieb Fichte, 'Beitrag zur Berichtigung der Urtheile des Publicums über die französische Revolution', in *Sämmtliche Werke*, vol. 6 (Berlin, 1845), p. 150.

49. This brief sketch does not do justice to the many different emphases given to feelings of German national identity in the first part of the nineteenth century. For more detailed and nuanced accounts, see Thomas Nipperdey, *Deutsche Geschichte 1800–1866: Bürgerwelt und starker Staat*, 6th edn. (Beck, 1993), pp. 300–13; Brian Vick, *Defining Germany: The 1848 Frankfurt Parliamentarians and National Identity* (Harvard University Press, 2002), pp. 19–78.

2

'A State that is strong . . . may conduct itself all the more liberally.'

Whereas for local communities control over the admission of outsiders was a matter of fending off hunger, the Prussian central administration, following both Smith and Hegel (the latter of whom quoted for this chapter's title),[1] viewed such restrictions as the product of selfishness. The state aimed to promote the common good in various ways. First, it wanted the poor to find work. If work was not to be had in a particular district, then the poor of that district had to be enabled to move elsewhere. Increased employment would also benefit the state, for economic growth was one foundation of state power. Breaking down communal barriers to movement promoted state interests in a different sense as well: the full integration into the monarchy of the Rhineland and Westphalia, territories acquired (for the most part) in 1815. In 1817 some 3 million of Prussia's 10.5 million inhabitants lived in these two provinces, which were separated from the bulk of Prussia by Hanover.[2] While communal restrictions on settlement existed in various parts of the Prussian monarchy, they were particularly pronounced in the new provinces. Restrictions on settlement maintained the western provinces as distinct and separate enclaves within the Prussian monarchy.

Austria, Baden, Württemberg and Bavaria likewise sought, in the same period, to help the poor find work and to stimulate economic growth. These states had also absorbed significant new territories which their central administrations were intent on integrating. For these varying reasons, 'in one legal form or another [the right to control the admission of new members] was the main issue between the communities and state officials during the first half of the nineteenth century, though the diversity of forms and channels often obscured the unity of the political issue'.[3] But in the south and west of Germany, for the most part, these initiatives failed. The resistance of towns and guilds proved stronger than the authority of central administrations. Policies that promoted the social and economic rights of individuals at the expense of traditional corporate

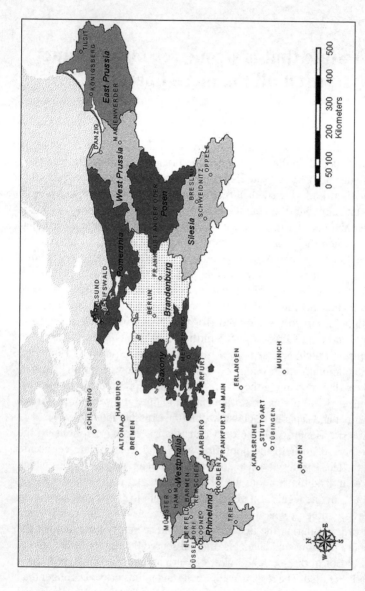

Map 2.1 Prussian Provinces in 1822. Reprinted with the permission of the Institut für Europäische Geschichte at www.ieg-maps.uni-mainz.de, as modified by Dr. Russ Clark, Albion College.

privileges could be put into practice only by central administrations that were insulated to a significant degree from local pressures. In Baden, Württemberg and Bavaria, elected parliaments prevented the adoption of legislation to implement the administrations' plans. When states attempted to carry out such policies through administrative fiat, communal authorities often simply refused to follow instructions or to furnish the information their implementation required.[4]

In Prussia the struggle between local communities and the state had an outcome less favorable for the communities. The reasons were: (1) the dominant position of the central administration and the influence on the administration of the economic principles of Adam Smith and the state-centered morality of Hegel; (2) the historic subordination of Prussian towns to state control and the political weakness of those parts of the state in which town rights were strong; and (3) the political power of East Elbian landowners, who ultimately came to see policies that deprived towns of control over residence as in their economic self-interest. That the debate on local controls over residence lasted nearly a generation, from the late 1810s to the early 1840s, reflected the strength of both sides and the fundamental nature of the issue.

Central Administration and Towns in Prussia

In pre-1848 Prussia there was no parliament that could represent the interests of towns in an authoritative way in disputes with the central administration. The administration viewed itself as the sole legitimate representative of society. There were, it is true, provincial parliaments, created in 1823, that represented society by estates (Stände). The municipal ordinance of 1808 established elected assemblies in towns and cities. But with respect to national legislation the provincial parliaments played only an advisory role, and the towns had no formal role at all.

The structural characteristics of the Prussian central administration lent its self-image as an objective judge of the common good some basis in reality. The state selected its civil servants from among the tiny group of university graduates, who viewed themselves as the intellectual and moral elite of society. The small size of the central administration – it consisted of roughly 1,600 responsible officials in the 1820s and 1830s – promoted its esprit de corps, its sense of being a select group.[5] Perhaps a third of civil servants were themselves sons of civil servants, and most others came from other professional groups or the nobility. Civil servants enjoyed relatively secure tenure once in office. The most senior administrators received incomes that were among the highest in the state.[6] In practice, however, the state's interpretation of the general welfare consistently favored the interests of the East Elbian landowning elite, whose offspring dominated the upper reaches of the ministries and especially the army.

The Prussian state had long stifled communal independence, although the exact degree of control varied from province to province and over time.[7] The experience of Silesia, a province conquered from Austria in the 1740s, and finally conceded to Prussia in 1763, illustrates patterns common in most of pre-Napoleonic Prussia. Approximately 200,000 Silesians lived in towns directly controlled by the state, and another 100,000 in towns governed by estate owners. In both cases the principal goal of the rulers was to extract taxes. Representatives of local inhabitants had at best advisory functions. Many towns housed army garrisons, whose officers were used to ordering local officials about. A Prussian cabinet order of 1752 forbidding officers to strike town officials during disputes gives some sense of the texture of the relationship. Control over the admission of new residents was for the most part in the hands of the state or local estate owners. They made such determinations on the basis of calculations of financial advantage, focusing on whether potential citizens possessed capital or economically valuable skills.[8] This focus on the bottom line sometimes, however, had liberalizing effects. Groups regularly excluded from the home towns of the German south and southwest, such as Jews, were grudgingly accepted in many Prussian communities, in limited numbers, if they possessed economic qualities of benefit to the state.[9]

The legislation of the Prussian Reform Era, 1808–1819, carefully balanced the rights of towns to restrict the settlement of outsiders with individual and state interests in freedom of movement. The municipal ordinance of 1808 provided that 'no one may be denied the right of local citizenship who has settled in the city where he wishes to be a citizen and is of unblemished character'.[10] While the requirement of an unblemished character ('Unbescholtenheit') provided a virtually unpoliceable license for arbitrariness, the statute located the power to rule on applications for local citizenship with magistrates approved by the state, not the elected town council (although the town council's opinion had to be requested in each instance).[11] A similar balance was struck in the matter of the fees charged new local citizens. The Prussian state permitted towns and cities to charge entrance fees, but limited the amount. The fees were not trivial, but they were far less onerous than commonly charged elsewhere in Germany.[12]

Before their acquisition by Prussia in 1815 most of the Rhineland and Westphalia had been subject to much less rigorous central controls than those traditionally imposed on Prussian towns. This tradition of self-governance permitted towns to play a much more active role in the lives of their members. In 1849 for example, 8 percent of the population of the Rhineland received charitable support, compared with less than 2 percent in Posen.[13] The difference in the amount of charitable support that communities in the eastern and western provinces of Prussia offered their residents also reflected demographic and economic differences between them. The western provinces had five or six times the population density of those in the east.[14] The high level of control exercised by Westphalian and Rhenish towns over their members, and also the extent to which individuals were protected by their communities, found expression in relatively low marriage and birth rates (one-half to two-thirds the per capita level found in the rural eastern provinces of Prussia), a far lower level of illegitimate births, and also, a far smaller per capita incidence of suicide.[15]

Rhenish and Westphalian towns viewed control over residence and membership as essential to maintaining local economies, order and a sense of community. All three concerns can be sensed in a comment made in a private letter written in 1830 by Karl Freiherr vom Stein, the great Prussian reformer of the Napoleonic era and a Rhinelander. 'What justifies the state', asked Stein, 'in forcing a community to accept as a member any impoverished wretch, who can provide no assurance of his conduct?'[16] Communities focused especially on the threat to communal funds, often collected over generations. The right permanently to settle in a place meant, as almost all understood it, the right to claim support from the local charity chest.[17] In fact, even Rhenish and Westphalian communities were rather effective in avoiding their obligations in this regard. By modern standards they spent relatively modest sums on charity, even in periods of crisis. In 1835, for example, the city of Cologne spent 90,000 Reichsthaler for its 10,000 poor, hardly enough to feed them for more than a fraction of the year.[18] But in an era in which many lived on the margin of existence and mass famines still occurred, and in which (despite this fact) structural explanations for poverty had not leavened understandings that emphasized individual moral failing, what today might seem small sums loomed large in the popular consciousness. The tangible and economically rational character of the argument may also help explain why the burden of the foreign poor on the local poor chest was usually the focal point of justifications of the right of towns to exclude the penniless.

Restrictions on Residence

That towns in the western part of Prussia systematically excluded outsiders came to the attention of the Interior Ministry in Berlin by way of individual appeals of local decisions. The first case recorded in the Interior Ministry's records involved a retired Prussian soldier, Christian Pohl, whose settlement was prevented by the Westphalian town of Hamm in 1819. Hamm based its decision on an ordinance issued by the district commissioner, the Landrat, in 1817, which required the local authorities to approve the rental of dwellings to persons not from the community. The ordinance permitted towns to prevent the settlement of outsiders who threatened 'the good of the local community'.[19] On 18 September 1820 the Ministry wrote the District Government (the district offices of the central administration were known as 'Regierungen', or Governments), in response to Pohl's appeal, that 'the laws have never given individual communities the right to prevent someone who is in a position to support himself, and who at the time is not impoverished, from establishing his abode where he will'.[20]

In some respects Pohl's appeal presented a special case. The state had a particular interest in seeing that its former soldiers found a place to live. Many had lost all contact with their birthplaces in the course of long years in the military, and it would not do, as a matter of military morale and the state interest in public order, to have them treated as vagabonds. Here the unwillingness of Westphalian towns to accept the settlement of former soldiers collided with long-standing state policies. But Pohl's appeal was followed by others that had nothing to do with the military, and in these as well the Interior Ministry insisted that communities in the Rhineland and Westphalia accept outsiders.[21]

The man who signed the letter to the District Government was Christian Philipp Köhler, the chief deputy of Interior Minister Friedrich von Schuckmann. Köhler wrote many of the letters on the subject of freedom of movement that the Prussian Interior Ministry sent to district governments over the next two decades. Köhler's stature in the government is suggested not only by his position in the Interior Ministry, but by his membership, from 1818, on the Staatsrat, the royal council. The Staatsrat was composed of ministers and other high officials in whom the king had special confidence. In 1818 it had thirty-three members. Köhler remained in his position in the Interior Ministry until 1839, and served in the Staatsrat until 1841. Although little is known about him, his vigorously liberal views are reflected in the many letters, memoranda and laws drafted on the subject of freedom of movement by the Interior Ministry while he was in office.[22]

As in the Pohl decision, the Ministry of the Interior often had to override both local communities and its own regional officials in forcing local authorities to open their doors to outsiders. The provincial governor (the 'Oberpräsident') of Westphalia, Ludwig Freiherr von Vincke, consistently opposed the central administration's efforts to end restrictive communal admissions practices. Vincke, a native of Minden in Westphalia, argued that local authorities had the right to investigate the previous conduct of potential residents and to make sure that they had means to support themselves.[23] Migrants were 'only too often dissolute and suspect', he wrote Schuckmann in 1821. 'In this province, as in the neighboring regions, it is an almost universally followed observance or explicit law, that no one is permitted to settle in a foreign community without having previously received permission.'[24]

A year later the District Government of Münster in Westphalia protested directly to Chancellor Karl August von Hardenberg against the Ministry's directives, most likely with Vincke's encouragement. The Ministry of the Interior had ordered, wrote the District Government, that

every ... criminal, or those who are criminally inclined, has a right ... to establish residence in any city, and no community or higher authority is entitled to expel them ... The Ministry has through this decree not only eliminated the previous general requirement of a good reputation, but also the requirement that there be proof of an honorable means of support ... This principle must be adhered to if the area is not to be made insecure through the activities of criminals and vagabonds.

When criminals grew old, the District Government contended, they would move to cities, where they would take the charity meant for the honorable poor. 'The local sense for charitable deeds will be entirely extinguished, for no one will have the pleasure of seeing their alms given to the truly suffering poor.' And finally, with great bitterness: if their communal rights were no longer to be enforced, and illegally ignored, 'we request that the institutions of the French authorities be applied without delay in Prussia, because at least in the French constitution there were strong rules against suspicious individuals, and the security of individuals and property rights were preserved'.[25] In France the Jean Valjeans ended in the galleys.[26]

In the mid-1820s towns from other parts of Prussia, oppressed by the growing numbers of the poor, began to direct similar appeals to the Interior Ministry. The town council of Schweidnitz, in Silesia, wrote to the Ministry of the Interior in 1826 to protest the refusal of the Magistracy and the provincial government to permit Schweidnitz to charge an entrance fee to newcomers who became resident aliens. The Schweidnitz town council argued that a head of a household need not accept servants he did not want, and the position of the town was similar. The Interior Ministry curtly rejected the argument.[27] Between 1828 and 1831 Königsberg repeatedly pleaded for permission to vet the economic circumstances of newcomers. Stralsund and Frankfurt/Oder also attempted, with limited success, to limit the influx of outsiders.[28]

In some cases the appeals from towns were supported by petitions from the countryside. While towns feared crime and burdens on poor chests, landowners sought to avoid the loss of farm labor. Local exit fees were still often levied in the countryside, on the pretext that they were part of patrimonial jurisdiction, the judicial powers exercised by estate owners.[29] Some landowners viewed restrictions on residence in towns as a means of preventing the exodus of their laborers. In December 1824 the provincial parliament of Pomerania sent Interior Minister Schuckmann a petition asking that towns and cities be allowed to impose strict economic and moral tests for acceptance as a citizen. Although members of all three estates signed the petition, most signers were members of the first estate, reflecting the landowning interest that dominated both the province and the parliament. According to the petition, the result of the freedom of movement created by the edicts of the Reform Era had been overpopulation of the cities and towns and the emptying out of the countryside, 'which has led wages to rise above all normal levels'. Although economic self-interest seems to have been the heart of the matter, the petitioners couched their appeal in moral terms. The migrants wished to move to distant places 'where no one has knowledge of their previous life'. There it would be easier for those who were dissolute to engage in disreputable practices. Particularly the women were attracted by the possibility of avoiding the heavy chores of agricultural labor. And so the migrants believe 'they will be transformed; a common farm worker (Landarbeiter) will supposedly become a town citizen (Bürger)'.[30] Schuckmann rejected the petition out of hand. It was a call, he told the parliament, for the reinstatement of Erbuntertänigkeit, hereditary serfdom.[31]

The reaction against the Interior Ministry's championship of freedom of movement succeeded only at the very center of the monarchy, in Berlin. In July 1822, acting on the instructions of the king, Chancellor Karl August Prince von Hardenberg wrote to the Interior Minister complaining that Berlin was threatening to become the 'principal gathering place for impoverished and work-shy families and individuals'.[32] He asked

Schuckmann to make clear to the police president of Berlin that he was not to permit the residence of all able-bodied adults. The head of the police section of the Interior Ministry, a well-known reactionary, promptly ordered the Berlin police to 'permit settlement in Berlin only with respect to individuals . . . who can demonstrate their previous proper (unbescholten) conduct, and that they have sufficient honorable means of support'.[33] Schuckmann did not challenge this directive with respect to Berlin, but he prevented the application of similar instructions to other cities in Prussia.[34]

Breaking Town Walls

Because it was clear that its orders to communities to permit the settlement of outsiders were encountering massive resistance, at least in the western provinces, the Interior Ministry decided in the early 1820s to propose legislation that would establish the authority of its position. In early 1822 Schuckmann sent Hardenberg a draft law that provided that 'no official might limit an individual's freedom to choose to live where he wished on the grounds that future impoverishment was feared'.[35] Anyone who lived in a community for a year without seeking charitable support would be entitled to remain. The proposed law was first debated in the Staatsrat in 1826. The government sent the proposed legislation to the provincial parliaments for comment in 1831.

The Staatsrat actually sent two laws to the provincial parliaments in 1831. The first of the proposed laws established the obligation of local communities to accept outsiders who were Prussian subjects as permanent residents, except individuals who required charity within a year after their arrival (the residency law).[36] Mere concern about possible or probable future impoverishment did not justify expulsion. The law as eventually adopted gave the central administration, but not communities, the power to prevent the settlement of criminals if they posed a threat to public security in a particular place. The second law made clear the obligation of communities to provide charity to all permanent residents, including adult servants who had resided for more than a year in the community (the law on charitable support). It further provided that an individual's absence from a community for one year in most cases brought an end to his right to charitable support from that community.[37]

The Interior Ministry memoranda that accompanied the legislation sent to the provincial parliaments justified the laws on both economic and moral grounds. The Ministry's memoranda explicitly appealed to the authority of Adam Smith, and in particular, to his critique of the Elizabethan poor laws. The example of England, the Ministry argued, demonstrated the evil of a system in which 'hundreds of hands that might have been usefully employed are tied to places where they remain idle'. The Ministry further argued that

> it corresponds to the general public interest (dem allgemeinen öffentlichen Interesse), that individuals who have committed and been punished for a crime not return to their former place of residence, but, if possible, find a new home. The improvement (Besserung) and rescue of such a man is nowhere so difficult as in the place where he lost his honor and where all who know him will point him out with their fingers. It is much easier where no one, aside from the local authorities, knows anything of him aside from his current behavior. Such a man will also find it hard to find a place to live and a job where everyone knows him, for no one will employ him, and elsewhere he may find both quite easily.

The law demanded of the criminal that 'he improve himself and find an honorable means of support, but whoever has this responsibility, must also have as few encumbrances as possible placed in the way of fulfilling it'.[38]

Against the objections of communities that freedom of movement would require them to accept criminals and other dissolute persons as residents, the Ministry wrapped itself in the cloak of remote neutrality. It argued first that local objections could not be taken at face value.

> It is a great mistake to believe that newcomers, who might support themselves in a certain place, will always be welcomed with open arms. On the contrary, they will be met with Egoism and Prejudice. In every small city the local officials are made up of the local merchants and craftsmen or are dependent on them and reflect their prejudices. But there are almost no trades that do not believe themselves to be too full. No trade will admit that the public is not fully satisfied [with the services it provides]. Every new competitor is one too many, a horror . . .

'In the hands of local officials the common good or interest will almost invariably be sacrificed to momentary individual interests . . .'[39] Secondly, even where communities' fears had some basis, they ignored the larger picture. 'Legislation that follows the most general principle . . . is the best.'[40] Every person had to be taken in somewhere, and the community that was required to accept a criminal might by the same law be freed of having to care for one of its own criminals. The Ministry admitted in passing that its rule was likely to benefit the countryside at the expense of great cities, to which the poor and the criminal gravitated. But this observation had little impact on the argument. 'To the state, from its higher position, all communities are of equal value.'[41]

The provincial parliaments of East and West Prussia and Pomerania approved the laws without objection. The parliaments in Brandenburg, Saxony, and Silesia expressed discomfort with the complete jettisoning of considerations of reputation, especially when the individual had been convicted of a serious crime, but nonetheless also gave their approval. By the mid-1830s, as these votes indicated, the views of the landed interests had shifted. Estate owners had not necessarily become any less hostile to the movement of the rural population to the towns and cities. What was clearly against the interest of landowners was the requirement that they provide charity to persons who had left the countryside. Under existing rules young people who migrated to towns might, upon becoming disabled or too old to work, be sent back to their places of birth for care. The shift in the views of estate owners can be detected both in the votes of the provincial parliaments in the eastern part of the monarchy, and in the fact that the Interior Ministry continued to support the project despite the appointment in 1834 of an Interior Minister, Gustav Adolph Rochus von Rochow, who was a champion of the interests of the Junker class.[42]

Only the Westphalian parliament rejected the legislation outright. The Rhenish parliament, perhaps surprisingly, did not oppose giving all Prussians the right to move freely within the state. But it did object to the law on charitable support. Despite the self-interest at stake, moral arguments dominated. A right to charity 'dissolves the feeling of shame and religiosity on the part of the poor', argued the petition from the Rhineland. A poor man who felt entitled to charity would no longer seek his consolation in Christianity. Charity should be a voluntary matter, argued the Rhineland parliament, for individuals and for communities.[43]

The objections of the Westphalian and Rhineland provincial parliaments found an echo at the highest levels of the Prussian government. It was again the Westphalian provincial governor Vincke who gave the most spirited defense of the rights of towns to exclude foreigners. Vincke argued that the sense of obligation to the entire state had its basis in attachment to local communities. And to preserve communal feeling, he argued, the state needed to permit communities to restrict access to outsiders. If complete freedom of movement were instituted, 'then one will have to do without a sense of loyalty to the community . . . Considerations of educating the individual to belong to the larger state in and through local communities will no longer play a role, and communities will become no more than parts of the state's territory.'[44] Vincke's views were seconded by no less an authority than the crown prince and future king, Friedrich Wilhelm.[45] In 1838, in opposing the Interior Ministry's law establishing freedom of movement, the Crown Prince argued that

> I am convinced that the preservation and promotion of independent life in the communities, which is the basis of the entire constitution of the country, above all depends on not depriving the communities of the right to decide so important a question [as whether to accept newcomers]. One must proceed from the opposite premise, and recognize the power of the communities to decide this question . . .[46]

Despite his opposition as Crown Prince, once ruling as King Friedrich Wilhelm IV he approved both laws. But not all of the protests of the home towns had been in vain. The provincial parliaments of Westphalia and the Rhineland had opposed the language in the residency law that made covenants among homeowners against renting or selling to outsiders unenforceable and illegal, as had the Crown Prince.[47] The residency law as adopted dropped this clause. Evidence from the late 1840s and early 1850s suggests that covenants among homeowners not to rent to particular kinds of outsiders, in particular those without fixed homes somewhere ('Herumtreibende'), were in fact widely used.[48]

The 1831 draft of the residency law indicated that the central administration wished to control the power of communities to prevent the settlement not only of Prussians, but also of non-Prussian foreigners. The draft would have continued the prevailing practice of permitting local communities to grant foreigners permanent residence without the involvement of state authorities.[49] It provided, however, that preventing the residence of a foreigner was a matter for the central administration (a 'landeshoheitliche Frage'). This was new. If a community wished to prevent settlement on the grounds that an individual was not a Prussian subject, then it had to submit the question to the District Government. The District Government was then entitled to rule on whether the individual was a desirable subject. If so, he was to be naturalized and granted the same residency rights as all other Prussians. If not, the community might expel him. In the course of the 1830s, however, the Interior Ministry's views shifted. It came to insist on controlling the naturalization of all newcomers, both those desired by local communities and those rejected by them. Why this change took place is the subject of the next chapter.

Notes

1. G.W.F. Hegel, *Grundlinien der Philosophie des Rechts oder Naturrecht und Staatswissenschaft im Grundrissen*, in *Sämtliche Werke*, vol. 7, Frommanns, 1952, pp. 353–4 (Section 270). 'Der in seiner Organisation ausgebildete und darum starke Staat kann sich hierin desto liberaler verhalten . . .'
2. J. Hoffmann, *Uebersicht der Bodenfläche und Bevölkerung des Preussischen Staats*, Berlin, 1817, p. 8. Hoffmann's report was based on the first thorough census of the Prussian state. A portion of Westphalia had belonged to Prussia before 1807.
3. M. Walker, *German Home Towns: Community, State, and General Estate 1648–1871*, Cornell University Press, 1971, p. 276.
4. See generally Walker, *German Home Towns*, and Edward Shorter, *Social Change and Social Policy in Bavaria, 1800–1860* (Dissertation, Harvard University, 1967).
5. Statistics regarding the number of civil servants in Prussia in the first half of the nineteenth century are given in Reinhart Koselleck, *Preußen zwischen Reform und Revolution: Allgemeines Landrecht, Verwaltung und soziale Bewegung von 1791 bis 1848*, 3rd edn (Klett-Cotta, 1981), pp. 245, 438; John Gillis, *The Prussian Bureaucracy in Crisis, 1840–1860: Origins of an Administrative Elite* (Stanford University Press, 1971), p. 12, n. 25. This figure does not include the personnel of the judiciary or lower-level officials.
6. Gillis, *Prussian Bureaucracy in Crisis*, pp. 22–48, 229. On the high salaries of senior civil servants, see H. Beck, *Origins of the Authoritarian Welfare State in Prussia: Conservatives, Bureaucracy, and the Social Question, 1815–1870*, University of Michigan Press, 1995, p. 139.
7. Francis Ludwig Carsten, *The Origins of Prussia* (Oxford: Clarendon, 1959). Karin Friedrich, 'The development of the Prussian town, 1720–1815', in P. Dwyer (ed.), *The Rise of Prussia 1700–1830* (Longman, 2000), pp. 129–50, provides an overview of Prussian rule of towns that fully confirms its oppressive character and also describes the persistent resistance to state domination in various parts of the monarchy.
8. J. Ziekursch, *Das Ergebnis der friderizianischen Städteverwaltung und die Städteordnung Steins* (Hermann Castenoble, 1908), pp. (in order of citation) 101, 36, 62, 92.
9. Shulamit Volkov, *Die Juden in Deutschland 1780–1918* (Oldenbourg, 1994), p. 4.

The Politics of Citizenship in Germany

10. *Ordnung für sämmtliche Städte der Preussischen Monarchie* of 19 November 1808, *GPS*, p. 326.
11. Ibid., Sections 17 and 24, *GPS*, pp. 326–7. The Städtordnung of 1808 never applied to the Rhineland and Westphalia, as these regions were not a part of Prussia when it was adopted.
12. GStA PK HA I, Rep. 80 Staatsrat (Drucksachen), Nr. 221 (an analysis of practices with respect to Bürgerrechtsgelder, prepared for the Staatsrat in 1837), pp. 6–7.
13. Ilja Mieck, 'Preußen von 1807 bis 1850: Reformen, Restauration und Revolution', in O. Büsch (ed.), *Handbuch der preußischen Geschichte*, vol. 2 (W. de Gruyter, 1992), p. 155.
14. In 1817, Düsseldorf – the most densely populated government district – had 8,109 persons per square Prussian mile, compared to an average for the monarchy of 2,101. Hoffmann, *Uebersicht der Bodenfläche und Bevolkerung des Preussischen Staats*, p. 28. The Prussian mile was equal to 7,532.5 meters, and thus much longer than the British mile (1,609.34 meters). The Prussian square mile was therefore the equivalent of roughly twenty-two English square miles.
15. Johann Gottfried Hoffmann, *Die Bevölkerung des Preussischen Staats nach dem Ergebnisse der zu Ende des Jahres 1837 amtlich aufgenommenen Nachrichten* (Berlin, 1839), pp. 32, 38, 54.
16. Johann Hermann Hüffer, *Lebenserinnerungen, Briefe, und Aktenstücke*, pub. by W. Steffens and E. Hövel (Münster, 1952), p. 242 (letter of November 1, 1830), quoted in Harald Schinkel, 'Armenpflege und Freizügigkeit in der preußischen Gesetzebung vom Jahre 1842', in *Vierteljahrschrift für Sozial- und Wirtschaftsgeschichte* 50 (1964), p. 474.
17. The obligation of local communities to support 'their' poor was of long standing in most Prussian provinces, and was restated, inter alia, in the *Allgemeines Landrecht für die Preussischen Staaten von 1794*, H. Hattenhauer (ed.) (Luchterhand Verlag, 1996) (*ALR*), the national law code promulgated in various parts of Prussia beginning in 1794. *ALR* Part II, Title 19, Section 10 provided, for example, that 'city and village communities must care for the feeding of their impoverished members and residents'. Ibid., p. 669.
18. M. Doege, *Armut in Preußen und Bayern (1770–1840)* (Kommissionsverlag UNI-Druck, 1991), p. 91. Statistics on charitable support by communities available for this period from Württemberg are comparable. K. Matz, *Pauperismus und Bevölkerung* (Klett-Cotta, 1980), pp. 48–9.

19. Order issued by Landrat Wiethaus, dated 19 December 1817. GStA PK, HA I, Rep. 77, Tit. 311, No. 34, Bd. 1, p. 1. See also the discussion of this background in Hans Lippe, *Die preußische Heimatgesetzgebung vom 31. Dezember 1842* (Dissertation, University of Göttingen, 1947). The Landrat was the government official immediately beneath the District Government. He was generally responsible for supervising the enforcement of laws and policies in the region (Kreis) he supervised.

20. Letter of 18 September 1820 from the Prussian Interior Ministry, signed Köhler, to the District Government in Arnsberg. Ibid., p. 2.

21. For other instances of individual appeals to the Interior Ministry in the 1820s from individuals refused permission to settle in towns in the western provinces, see GStA PK, HA I, Rep. 77, Tit. 311, Nr. 34, Bd. 1. Shulamit Magnus's *Jewish Emancipation in a German City: Cologne 1798–1871* (Stanford University Press, 1997) describes the Interior Ministry's intervention in the same period to compel the Rhenish city of Cologne to grant Prussian Jews trade permits. Magnus's statistics show that by 1823 the state had succeeded in breaking Cologne's resistance. The granting of permission to work was tantamount to granting permission to settle in the city.

22. This information regarding Köhler is taken from the *Handbuch über den Königlich-Preussischen Hof und Staat für das Jahr 1818* (Decker), pp. 57, 96–7; 1839 edn at pp. 13, 43; and 1841 edn at p. 47.

23. *Allgemeine Deutsche Biographie*, vol. 39 (Duncker & Humblot, 1895), pp. 736–43.

24. Vincke to the Ministry of the Interior and Police, 17 March 1821, GStA PK, HA I, Rep. 77, Tit. 311, Nr. 34, Bd. 1, p. 12RS.

25. Government of Münster to Hardenberg, 13 July 1822, Ibid., pp. 56–57RS.

26. Jean Valjean was the hero of Victor Hugo's great novel *Les Misérables*. He was condemned to the galleys for stealing a loaf of bread. Hugo wrote *Les Misérables* between 1845 and 1848. Its context was the social and political turmoil common throughout Europe in the post-Napoleonic era.

27. Town council of Schweidnitz to the Interior Ministry, 21 December 1826, GStA PK, HA I, Rep. 77, Tit. 311, Nr. 34, Bd. 2, p. 57.

28. GStA PK, HA I, Rep. 77, Tit. 311, Nr. 34, Bd. 2, pp. 94, 101, 111, 116, 120, 182, 193.

29. J. Ziekursch, *Hundert Jahre schlesischer Agrargeschichte*, 2nd edn (Preuss & Jünger, 1927), pp. 298–9, 368–9.

30. Petition of the Landtag of Pomerania to the King, 15 December 1824, GStA PK, HA I, Tit. 77, Rep. 311, Nr. 34, Bd. 2, pp. 30, 33.

31. Schuckmann to the Oberpräsident of Pomerania and to the Royal Commissarius of the Landtag in Pomerania and Rügen, 27 December 1824, GStA PK, HA I, Rep. 77, Tit. 311, Nr. 34, Bd. 2, pp. 28–9.

32. Hardenberg to Schuckmann, 16 July 1822, GStA PK, HA. I, Rep. 77, Tit. 311, Nr. 34, Bd. 1, p. 50. This conflict is also described in Schinkel, 'Armenpflege und Freizügigkeit'.

33. Order to the Royal Police Presidium in Berlin from the Minister of the Interior and Police, in the absence of his Excellency, signed von Kamptz, GStA PK, HA I, Rep. 80 Staatsrat (Drucksachen), Nr. 286, App. VIII, p. 72. Karl Christoph Albert Heinrich von Kamptz's career is described in an article in the *Allgemeine Deutsche Biographie*, vol. 15, pp. 66–75.

34. Schuckmann to the District Governments, 9 August 1822, GStA PK, HA I, Rep. 77, Tit. 311, Nr. 34, Bd. 1, p. 64.

35. *Allerhöchste Kabinettsordre mit dem Entwurf eines Gesetzes wegen der Armenpflege*, GStA PK, HA I, Rep. 80 Staatsrat (Drucksachen), Nr. 124, p. 11; Letter from Hardenberg to Schuckmann, 16 July 1822, GStA PK HA I, Rep. 77, Tit. 311, Nr. 34, Bd. 1, p. 50RS.

36. *Ursprünglicher Entwurf*, Section 10, *Allerhöchste Kabinettsordre vom 18ten Februar 1838, mit den Gesetz-Entwürfen über die Verpflichtung der Kommunen zur Aufnahme neuanziehender Personen und wegen der Verpflichtung zur Armenpflege*, Appendix A. GStA PK, HA I, Rep. 80, Drucksachen, Nr. 286 c,d, pp. 6–9.

37. *Ursprünglicher Entwurf*, Ibid., Appendix C, pp. 30–4.

38. *Motive zu dem Gesetz-Entwurf 'wegen der Verpflichtung der Kommunen u., neuanziehende Personen aufzunehmen'*, Ibid., Appendix B, pp. 21, 23, 14, 16.

39. Ibid., Appendix B, p. 21.

40. *Motiv zu dem Gesetz wegen der Verpflichtung zur Armenpflege*, Ibid., Appendix D, p. 38.

41. *Motive zu dem Gesetz-Entwurf 'wegen der Verpflichtung der Kommunen u., neuanziehende Personen aufzunehmen'*, Ibid., Appendix B, pp. (in order of citation) 16, 15.

42. Koselleck, *Preußen zwischen Reform und Revolution*, p. 48. A significant percentage of East Elbian landowners remained hostile to the right of peasants to leave their estates. As late as 1868 a majority of the Upper House of the Prussian Parliament voted to permit movement from a community only upon a showing that all existing obligations, including the obligation to support aging

parents, had been fulfilled. *Stenographische Berichte über die Verhandlungen des Preussischen Herrenhauses* (19 December 1868), p. 50. The government prevented the adoption of the law by pointing out that freedom of movement was guaranteed by the constitution. For a discussion of the efforts of the landowners to restrict the free movement of workers during the Kaiserreich, involving fundamentally the same considerations, see George Steinmetz, *Regulating the Social: The Welfare State and Local Politics in Imperial Germany* (Princeton University Press, 1993), pp. 115–18.

43. *Geschichtliche Darstellung der Entstehung der beiden Gesetz-Entwürfe 1. wegen der Verpflichtung der Kommunen u., neuanziehende Personen aufzunehmen, und wegen ihrer Befugniß, dergleichen Aufnahmen zu verweigern, und 2. wegen der Verpflichtung zur Armenpflege*, Appendix G to the *Allerhöchste Kabinettsordre vom 18ten Februar 1838*, GStA PK, HA I, Rep 80 Staatsrat (Drucksachen), Nr. 286 c,d, p. 101.

44. 'Vortrag über das Gesetz wegen der Verpflichtung zur Armenpflege', GStA PK, HA I, Rep. 80, Drucksachen, Nr. 286a, Anl. XV.

45. Friedrich Wilhelm's romantic and conservative conceptions of the Prussian state are described in David Barclay, *Frederick William IV and the Prussian Monarchy, 1840–1861* (Oxford University Press, 1995), pp. 26–37.

46. Separate Opinion of Friedrich Wilhelm of 10 February 1838, *Allerhöchste Kabinettsordre vom 18ten Februar 1838*, GStA PK, HA I, Rep. 80, Drucksachen, Nr. 286 c,d, p. 146.

47. *Geschichtliche Darstellung der Entstehung der beiden Gesetz-Entwürfe 1. wegen der Verpflichtung der Kommunen u., neuanziehende Personen aufzunehmen, und wegen ihrer Befugniß, dergleichen Aufnahmen zu verweigern, und 2. wegen der Verpflichtung zur Armenpflege*, App. G to the *Allerhöchste Kabinettsordre vom 18ten Februar 1838*, GStA PK, HA I, Rep 80 Staatsrat (Drucksachen), Nr. 286 c,d, pp. 84–5.

48. Letter of the Minister of the Interior to the Oberpräsident of East Prussia dated 15 December 1848, GStA PK, HA I, Rep. 77, Tit. 311, Nr. 34, Bd. 6, pp. 216–17.

49. Section 24 of the 1808 Städteordnung, for example, explicitly gave local magistrates the power to make non-Prussians local citizens and, hence, subjects of Prussia. *GPS*, p. 327.

3

'Who belongs to the Brotherhood of the Prussian Nation?'

The Prussian state's assertion of its right to monitor and control the granting of citizenship to foreigners arose initially from its advocacy of freedom of movement for Prussians.[1] The central administration wished to prevent local communities from excluding non-Prussians whose residence the state considered desirable. But with the passage of time other motives became more important than the initial one. Local communities and district governments on the southwestern border of Prussia lobbied the central administration to police immigration more tightly. If local communities were to be denied the right to guard their borders, then the state had to take their place. In fact there was, from the early 1830s, a more cautious attitude toward immigration within the central administration. In part the change of heart in the central administration was a response to the revolutions of 1830 and 1831. The Prussian state feared contamination by revolutionaries and their ideas. The state also hoped to reduce conflicts with other states over deportations. Giving the central administration a direct role in the granting of citizenship would help clarify which foreigners had become Prussians and which remained subject to expulsion. The fact that from 1834 the Foreign Office assumed primary responsibility for drafting the citizenship law indicates the extent to which this last motive had by this date become central to its adoption.

Within the administration the most important conflict over the Prussian citizenship law of 1842, or, as it was called, the law governing the acquisition and loss of Prussian subjecthood (the 'Untertanengesetz'), was generated not by the challenge it posed to the powers of home towns, but by the ways it threatened the privileges of a portion of the landowning nobility. The law made descent from a Prussian father the principal basis for the transmission of status as a Prussian, and also implied that henceforth allegiance to Prussia was to be exclusive. Prussian subjects were to be the subjects of no other state. Nobles who owned land in more than one German state perceived both of these principles as threats to their traditional privileges. The draft law implied that some landowners might forfeit administrative or other powers in Prussia if they did not agree to become exclusively Prussian subjects. Representatives of this part of the nobility were sufficiently well entrenched at the center of the monarchy to force the inclusion of a clause shielding them from the effects of the law. However, their success was to be short-lived.

Changing Immigration Policies

In the 1820s many in the Prussian central administration took the view, one of long standing in Prussia, that immigration benefited the Prussian state. In an 1825 report to Minister Karl von Lottum, the Director of the Berlin Statistical Bureau, Johann Gottfried Hoffmann, opined of the considerable immigration he had documented, of servants and journeymen, that 'this immigration attracts little attention to itself, but it not only increases the number of inhabitants, but also improves their quality, for the newcomers are people who can rely only on their own skills and activity, since they are receiving no special benefits [that is, the assistance Prussia gave settlers of unoccupied lands]'.[2] In its 1831 memoranda in support of the residency law and the law governing the obligation of communities to provide charity, the Ministry of the Interior had supported shortening the period of residence required to make a foreigner a Prussian subject from ten years to one year. It argued that immigration was beneficial to the state. 'This principle [a short residency requirement] is more advantageous and useful than any other. The encouragement of immigration in the Prussian state has in the past gone much further, certainly not to the disadvantage of the state of Prussia. What should it matter to us if foreign countries follow other, to our mind less mature principles?'[3]

From 1815 to the early 1840s Prussia was, in fact, a land with significant immigration. The Prussian statistical office's figures show, in the words of an official summary, that 'in the period from 1816 to 1846 there was an annual average excess of immigrants over emigrants of 30–40,000 per year'.[4] The census showed net immigration of 60,448 between 1824 and 1828; 136,417 between 1829 and 1833; and 337,075 between 1834 and 1838.[5] The heaviest immigration was found in the eastern provinces, although it also took place in the west and south of the monarchy.[6] The immigrants consisted largely of journeymen, servants and students. The total figures for immigration (which are only net figures

– total immigration would have been greater) are quite considerable for a country whose population in 1815 was just over ten million, and in 1848 just over sixteen million.[7]

In the spring of 1830 the District Government of Erfurt, a part of Prussia that protruded like a peninsula into Thuringian territory, complained in one of its periodic reports to Friedrich Wilhelm III of the uncontrolled immigration from the surrounding non-Prussian territory. In a highly unusual displacement of the central ministries, the king then asked the Erfurt District Government to draft a law that would give the Prussian state the power to vet all newcomers. The District Government was happy to oblige. It justified the law it presented to the Ministry of the Interior later in the year as follows:

> not every increase in the population is useful for the state. The maxim previously followed has been that everyone who can show that he is not disreputable, and that he has the physical means to support himself, if he were to find work, must be granted permission to settle in the community he has chosen. No distinctions have been made between foreigners [i.e., non-Prussians] and the native born, and local communities are not granted any special powers of rejection. Under existing conditions this maxim requires modification.

In a highly settled state like Prussia, the District Government argued, inhabitants must have, not merely physical strength and health, but 'spiritual and moral qualities'. In economic hard times foreigners caused unrest and placed demands on the charity chests of local communities. The problem was particularly acute because the social constitution of Prussia was more liberal than those of most of its neighbors. In other states guilds continued to control access to trades, and communities were permitted to reject newcomers. As a result, Prussia had to accept the poor of other states while its own poor were effectively prevented from settling elsewhere.[8]

The complaints from the Erfurt District Government and from the nearby district of Merseburg, and the support they received from the monarch, prompted the central administration to reexamine the premises of its immigration policies. While the Ministry of the Interior objected to considerable portions of the Erfurt government's proposed law, in part perhaps because of the usurpation of its own prerogative to draft legislation, the premise was conceded. An internal Interior Ministry memorandum from July of 1831 concluded that it was necessary that 'immigration not be permitted to continue at the level suggested by long-standing Prussian principles'.[9]

The date suggests that fear of the revolutionary mob also played an important role in the government's change of heart. A wave of revolutions began in July 1830, toppling monarchs or threatening their territories on all sides of Prussia. One of the rebellions occurred in Russian Poland. In 1832, following the suppression of this uprising, Tsar Nicholas I asked Friedrich Wilhelm how it was that a Polish revolutionary was permitted to live undisturbed in Prussian Tilsit. The Prussian King ordered his administration to investigate whether the man was, in fact, a Prussian subject and, again, to clarify the rules governing who was a Prussian.[10] But it required little reinforcement from Nicholas to bring home to Friedrich Wilhelm the danger posed by revolution. A tangible fear of popular rebellion, of a second French revolution, gripped ruling classes throughout Europe. Late in 1830 the Prussian cabinet considered whether the state should temporarily forbid the immigration and emigration of all journeymen, politically the most suspect part of the population. The cabinet recommended against such a general prohibition, but urged that the police be instructed to monitor this group vigilantly.[11] An early draft of the Untertanengesetz, composed by the Prussian Interior Ministry in June 1831, provided that foreigners were to be denied naturalization if they 'were suspected of the intention of causing disorder in this state, or if it is suspected that they may in any way in political matters bring the state into danger'.[12]

While local authorities and the Ministry of the Interior wished to exercise control over who might permanently settle in – or leave – Prussia, the Prussian Foreign Office was concerned primarily with creating a system of rules that established clearly who was and who was not a Prussian subject. The Foreign Office had to determine on a regular basis whether Prussia might expel an individual to another state and whether Prussia had to accept expellees from abroad. Permitting status as a Prussian subject to be acquired merely by a period of residence inevitably led to unclarity, for the state typically was never informed when residence began. The result, as an 1832 Foreign Office memorandum put it, was continuous conflicts and controversies ('Streitigkeiten und Verwicklungen') with other German states.[13] A supporter of the proposed citizenship law, probably from the Foreign Office, commented during debates in the Staatsrat in 1842 that 'the question, whether someone is a Prussian subject, arises in the administration on a daily basis, and leads to the most difficult debates, because there are no authoritative guidelines that determine how the relevant qualities are to be recognized'.[14] The Foreign Office wanted the new law above all because it would require a positive official act to establish status as a subject, and to end it. This would create clarity.

The Foreign Office was much less concerned with restricting immigration than local authorities or even the Interior Ministry. The 1832 Foreign Office memorandum on the subject still took the liberal position that 'entrance and exit from the community of the state [the 'Staatsverband'] should be seen as a right arising from individual freedom, and should be denied to no one'.[15] However, the memorandum continued, the state could require that newcomers be of good character and capable of supporting themselves, and that they have fulfilled their obligations to their previous states. If these qualifications were met, then the Foreign Office thought that immigrants should have a right to become Prussian subjects.

State Citizenship as a Threat to Noble Rights

The citizenship law drafted in 1834 by the Foreign Office, with the advice of the Interior Ministry, had two main principles. First, it provided that mere residence in Prussia would never by itself lead to the acquisition of the status of subject.[16] One could become a Prussian subject only by birth to Prussian parents, adoption, marriage to a Prussian man or by the explicit approval of the central administration, upon petition. Second, although this was implied rather than directly stated, Prussian subjects were to belong only to Prussia, and not to be the subjects of any other state.[17] But it had long been common for nobles owning land in different German states to be subjects of each of the states in which they held property. The Foreign Office's draft Untertanengesetz would have forced the nobility to choose between their loyalties and endangered rights central to their social and economic positions. In Prussia these rights included the right to vote in elections for provincial parliaments and to exercise local police and judicial powers.[18]

It is difficult to say what percentage of the Prussian nobility would have been affected by a prohibition of multiple citizenships. It clearly was not an insignificant number. The phenomenon was most widespread in the territories Prussia had acquired in the eighteenth and early nineteenth centuries.[19] In Silesia as much as 10 percent of the nobility held land abroad.[20] It was especially wealthier members of the nobility, and the nobility that before 1806 had not been subordinate to territorial princes within the Holy Roman Empire, the so-called mediatized nobility, who held land in more than one German state.[21]

The entire nobility, and especially the mediatized nobility, was hypersensitive to state encroachments on their prerogatives. Prince

Chlodwig Hohenlohe, the future Chancellor of the German national state and a member of the mediatized nobility, expressed the general tenor of this feeling in the Bavarian state council in 1869, when he told Prince Ludwig, later King Ludwig III, 'what you are, I am also!'[22] The premise was that the basis of the authority of the landowner was equal to that of the monarch, and, hence, to that of the state. The state had no right to determine that the owner of a noble estate and his offspring could not live within the state, or exercise governmental authority on his estate. It was an argument whose larger theoretical basis had been developed by, among others, Carl Ludwig von Haller, a Swiss political theorist whose 1816 work *Restauration der Staatswissenschaft* (Restoration of the Science of the State) equated royal authority with the patrimonial authority exercised by owners of estates. This work, which influenced both the East Elbian nobility and the future Friedrich Wilhelm IV, implied that the state had no right to alter the traditional package of rights that derived from land ownership.[23]

One purpose of the Untertanengesetz was to clarify the obligation of all males permanently resident in Prussia to serve in the Prussian army. It prohibited the emigration of Prussians serving in the army and of potential draftees seeking to avoid military service.[24] In defending the draft Untertanengesetz in administrative debates, the Foreign Office treated the duty to perform military service in Prussia as one, if not the crucial, defining element of the relationship of the subject to the state. In determining who was a Prussian, proponents of the law argued in the Staatsrat, one must ask: 'Who is bound to the King and to the State with his entire person? Who belongs to the brotherhood (Genoßenschaft) of the Prussian nation (Volk)?' The answer: 'only those whose bodies and property (Blut und Gut) belong to the state, and who are obliged to perform military service . . .'[25] That foreigners residing in Prussia were often able to avoid military service, although they enjoyed all the local benefits of citizenship, was one of the reasons the bureaucracy wished to define more precisely who was a Prussian.[26]

The implications of the Untertanengesetz for military service placed that part of the nobility with property in several German states in a particularly difficult position. In the Staatsrat those who sought to preserve noble rights were required to defend the position that nobles alone, with a few despised minority groups, were under no obligation to serve in the Prussian army.

The determination that foreign owners of noble estates in Prussia should be freed of the military service requirement does not destroy the basis of their status as subjects. There are numerous classes of persons who are incontestably Prussian subjects who are freed of this requirement. This applies to members of families of noble houses directly subordinate to the former Holy Roman Empire, to members of collateral lines of ruling princely houses, to Jews in Posen and to Mennonites.[27]

Once the nobility had to appeal to the status of Posen Jews and Mennonites to preserve its special privileges the game was up. What the claim made in the Staatsrat shows most decisively is the tacit acceptance by at least a portion of the nobility of the state's intellectual framework as the basis for claims of rights. But the attempt to defend the nobility's privileges on the basis of principles applicable to the entire population could only end in failure.

The Untertanengesetz was never considered by the provincial parliaments. In part this was because it was developed later than the companion pieces of legislation and in part because it did not seem as significant. Nonetheless, the nobility was able, through its representatives on the Staatsrat and in the ministries, to influence the drafting of the law. Under the threat of losing its law altogether, the Foreign Office conceded that an estate owner who was deemed a subject of another state could enjoy the prerogatives of landownership in Prussia, including patrimonial jurisdiction and the right to vote in elections for provincial parliaments. Section 11 of the adopted law provided that 'nothing in the present law will change any of the rights and duties that relate to the quality as a subject that arise from the ownership of real property, namely from the ownership of a noble estate and from the oath of loyalty to the Monarch'. This exemption contained no hint of the principle on which it was based, however, or how broadly the exclusion offered was to be drawn. The Staatsrat also amended the law to give an influential role to local communities in the making of naturalization decisions. The Staatsrat required the central administration to consult the community where a foreigner wished to settle as to whether the law's standards for naturalization had been met.

Although the Untertanengesetz made significant concessions to the traditional rights of the nobility and indicated that communities would retain some control over the admission of foreigners, the interpretation of the law lay in the hands of the central administration. And as the process of drafting the law showed, the central administration interpreted all traditional rights through the prism of the interests of the state and the common good. In part as a result, by the time of the founding of the German Empire in 1871 the clauses that protected local rights had lost almost all of their significance.

The claim that the Prussian state might determine who was a subject implied that it would be entitled to expel individuals whom it chose not to accept, no matter how long they had dwelt in Prussia. This message was directed primarily at the foreign states surrounding Prussia, the states which had to accept most of the expellees.[28] The new law did not nullify the deportation treaties Prussia had signed with other German states, but it was meant in the long run to modify the way they worked. The civil servants who drafted the law explicitly noted their intention that it serve as a model for all German states.[29] In fact, Prussia withdrew from the deportation treaties in 1850 and 1851, and at the same time entered into a new multilateral deportation agreement with the other German states that was based on the theory of the Untertanengesetz.[30]

Foreign Models?

To what extent was the Untertanengesetz the product, not of interests and institutions indigenous to Prussia, but of foreign influences? A recent book on the history of French citizenship by Patrick Weil suggests that Prussian officials essentially copied the Untertanengesetz from the French Civil Code of 1803, that Prussia's political goals and traditions were of relatively little significance in the formulation of the law.[31] This issue is worth exploring.

It is certainly true, as Weil suggests, that the Prussian officials who drafted and debated the terms of the Untertanengesetz were familiar with the French Civil Code, and were aware that in important respects the changes they proposed followed the direction suggested by the French legislation. It was the Civil Code that first broke with the Old Regime practice of permitting the automatic acquisition of citizenship on the basis of long-term residence in a place. As an 1830 Interior Ministry memorandum put it, 'one can almost claim that . . . the concept of naturalization was hardly employed in Germany in 1804. At that time the neighboring republican countries had only just begun to . . . [employ] this concept when they determined the political rights of the inhabitants (or, as they were then called, citizens).'[32] Foreign Office memoranda defended the draft law in part on the grounds that it ensured that foreigners who became Prussian subjects wished this result, since naturalization could take place only on petition. This respect for the desires of the individual certainly had some relationship to republican ideologies that emphasized individual autonomy and rights, even though in pre-1848 Prussia no political rights followed from citizenship. Prussian civil servants rejected the British policy of granting citizenship based on birth in Britain, and also, of compelling emigrants and their children to remain British. As an 1832 Foreign Office memorandum put it, 'there is nothing in the nature of being a subject that permits a state to hold someone against his will'.[33] In this regard Prussia also followed the French Civil Code.

Nonetheless, while the French model doubtless had some influence, the evidence to support the claim that it played a decisive role in the formulation of the Untertanengesetz is modest. It was opponents of the Untertanengesetz within the administration who repeatedly claimed that the draft law was permeated with French ideas: these claims were intended to discredit it.[34] Those who drafted the law explicitly denied, in internal memoranda, that foreign law codes had played a significant role as models.[35] Perhaps they did not wish openly to acknowledge their indebtedness to France. Their own explanations suggest, however, that it was not so much the Civil Code as the world the French Revolution and Napoleon's armies had created that helped bring the Untertanengesetz into being. The Prussian civil servants who drafted the Untertanengesetz were very much aware of the fact that it reflected conditions created by the abolition of serfdom, the expansion of freedom to move and to practice trades, and the development of a national conscript army.[36]

The Gender of Citizenship

While the Untertanengesetz permitted the central administration to supervise local decision-making regarding naturalization, one institution remained sacrosanct, or arguably became more so: the family. The Untertanengesetz provided that marriage between a Prussian man and a non-Prussian woman automatically meant that the woman became a Prussian subject. If a Prussian woman married a non-Prussian man she ceased to be a Prussian. All children of a Prussian couple were Prussian, as were children adopted or legitimated by a Prussian man. In this way the state lent its sanction to decisions of a largely private character, or, rather, assigned them public significance. And it did so in a way that made the civic status of females, as that of male children below military age, entirely a function of their position within the family.

Legal subordination of wives to husbands was hardly a novelty. The Prussian General Law Code, the Allgemeines Landrecht, assigned to the husband ultimate authority on all questions involving the marriage. He controlled the wife's property, determined if she might practice a trade, and decided how the children were to be raised.[37] Yet Old Regime rules subordinating the wife to the husband did not necessarily imply that wives had to hold their husbands' citizenship. For example, if a master's widow married a journeyman it was generally the journeyman who acquired the woman's local citizenship.[38] In early discussions of the Untertanengesetz some consideration was given to providing for certain exceptions to the general rule that the citizenship of the wife would follow that of her husband.[39] But the Interior Ministry insisted that wives share the citizenship of their husbands on the grounds that a contrary rule would endanger 'the holiness of the marriage bond'.[40]

The primacy of the citizenship status of the husband in the Untertanengesetz also reflected a range of administrative objectives and priorities. It may also have been influenced by the example of the French Civil Code.[41] As noted earlier, enforcing military service requirements was a central purpose of the Untertanengesetz. The state had no reason to seek to control the nationality of women to prevent avoidance of conscription. There is also some reason to believe that Prussian officials wished to prevent the breaking up of families in the event of the need for poor relief, something that might well have happened had the spouses had different citizenships. This kind of thing happened with some frequency in South German states, where marriage usually required the approval of the local community. An 1839 Prussian Interior Ministry memorandum described the operation of these rules and the problems they created for Prussia:

> by virtue of laws existing in the majority of German states . . . the permissibility and validity of entering into marriages by the male subjects of the states is made dependent on the prior concurrence of communal authorities. It has frequently happened that individuals who have lived for a shorter or longer period in the royal states [Prussia] have married Prussian women without having obtained this permission. Such occurrences have had the unfortunate consequence . . . that the marriages are declared invalid by local authorities of the husband. The wives and children of such foreigners have then been denied permission to settle in the home of the husband and father, and have therefore burdened the poor chests of Prussian communities.[42]

'Barbarism and Arbitrariness', was the marginal comment of one Prussian Interior Ministry official, perhaps Köhler, on such rules.[43] By granting non-Prussian women automatic Prussian citizenship upon marriage to a Prussian, the Untertanengesetz guaranteed them the right to live inside Prussia with their families. Wives of Prussians could not be expelled by the state or by a local community.

The liberalizing tendency of the Prussian law was applauded at the Frankfurt Parliament of 1848. Johann Peter Werner, a lawyer who represented Koblenz in the Prussian Rhineland, urged that the laws governing the citizenship of wives enacted in Prussia be applied to all Germans. 'It is in accordance with the principles of German Freedom, that every woman who marries a German man, even if it takes place abroad, now has a direct relationship to [i.e., citizenship in] Germany.'[44] Wives of Germans, he argued, had the right not to be treated as foreigners.

Exclusion and Inclusion

The dual functions of the Untertanengesetz, exclusion and inclusion, are shown by administrative actions in the half dozen years that followed its adoption. A brief comparison of Prussian policies with those in Baden highlights what was distinctive in the Prussian approach.

While the constitution of Baden provided that anyone who resided for ten years in the state – with the exception of servants and other dependent individuals – would be considered a permanent resident, in practice the tolerance of local communities was required. Individuals who wished to marry, or to operate a business independently, generally had to petition for some variety of local citizenship, and the policy of the state was to defer to the wishes of local communities with respect to such petitions. As the Ministry of the Interior of Baden put it in a memorandum in 1836: 'citizenship is not granted [to an individual] against the will of a community' unless the person's residence in the state was especially desirable from the point of view of the general interest.[45]

The files of the Interior Ministry in Karlsruhe contain a rich collection of appeals dating from the 1830s and 1840s from foreigners seeking to reverse citizenship denials by local communities. In almost all of the cases Grand Duke Leopold of Baden, to whom they were directed, supported the decisions of the local communities. Most of the cases turned on communities' fears of competition by foreign tradesmen. A Frenchman, Peter Chevard, who had worked as a journeyman tailor in the city of Baden from the early 1830s, sought in the middle of the decade to open his own shop. The local guild requested his expulsion. To avoid this fate, and to obtain the legal right to become a master, Chevard petitioned to become a citizen of Baden and of the community. The town council sided with the guild, and Chevard, after losing an appeal to the provincial government, in vain petitioned Leopold for a reversal.[46] Even if a town sided with the petitioner a guild's opposition might prove sufficient to prevent naturalization. Katherine Wolf, a resident of Nieder Emmendingen, petitioned Leopold in 1838 for the naturalization of the carpenter Ludwig Nast, from Württemberg, with whom she had already had two children. The town council had approved, and promised Nast local citizenship. But the local carpenters, fearing competition, protested to the District Government, which sided with them. The Ministry and the Grand Duke affirmed the decision of the District Government. Since there were already too many carpenters in Nieder Emmendingen, and 'since the local master carpenters have filed an objection, this is decisive'.[47] Perhaps the height of communal egoism was reached in an 1838 case involving a Württemberg man, Friedrich Kleinfelder, and the town of Brazingen. Kleinfelder wished to marry the widow of a vintner, and brought to the proposed marriage the sizable sum of 3,941 Gulden. But the widow was young and well to do, and the Mayor of Brazingen managed to persuade the town council to reject the petition for citizenship 'because he intended to win the widow of the vintner Mäßener for his own son'. Kleinfelder's prospective father-in-law penned an appeal of the decision to the king. This case came close to the line, but even here the Ministry of the Interior sided with the town. The principle was that a foreigner could be granted citizenship against the will of the community only if his residency in Baden was especially desirable as a matter of the general interest. And that was not the case here. Whether the vintner's widow ever married the mayor's son falls outside the ambit of the records.[48]

Even in Baden a community might go too far, especially as a procedural matter, and cause the Ministry and the Grand Duke to reverse a decision rejecting an application. Where a town had indicated to an applicant that he would be granted local citizenship, and he, in reliance on this assurance, had incurred considerable expense, the Ministry showed itself inclined to force the town to live up to its initial assurance.[49] A town's cockiness could lead to trouble. Durlach denied citizenship to a baker from Württemberg, and in defending its decision simply stated that 'a foreigner has no right to become a citizen, even when he has filled the legal conditions'. The Ministry of the Interior decided against the town, and when, in an appeal to Leopold, the town supplied further reasons, it was too late. Durlach had another baker.[50] Another case involved a town that apparently discovered that a considerable profit could be made from selling local citizenships to foreigners who had no intention of settling in the town. Once made citizens of Baden, the foreigners found it much easier to move to the larger towns that had been their true destinations all along, but which had denied their petitions for residence. The Ministry of the Interior intervened to stop the sales.[51]

While the Prussian Untertanengesetz had granted local communities the right to object to applicants for the status of a Prussian subject, it had limited the grounds on which these objections could be proffered. These were: did the applicant have his own dwelling?; could he support himself and his family?; and, had he conducted himself reputably? These grounds left the community considerable discretion, but they excluded many of the reasons for rejection found acceptable in Baden. Second, while the Untertanengesetz did not specify which institution in the community was empowered to object to newcomers, the Prussian Ministry of the Interior soon made it clear that only the magistracy, and not the elected assembly or guilds, was responsible. In fact, the Ministry, with the support of the king, positively forbade magistracies from consulting with local elected assemblies, in all but exceptional cases, when making recommendations regarding naturalization petitions.[52] The central administration considered illegitimate the interests of the type to which elected assemblies were likely to give voice. This was the point of an April 1844 memorandum from the Königsberg District Government to the Interior Ministry in Berlin, a memorandum prompted by the protests of an elected council at its exclusion from the decision-making process. The objections of the elected representatives to the proposed naturalization of two merchants from Denmark and Norway, the District Government wrote, were due 'to the private interest of individual merchants, who fear from the naturalization . . . a disadvantage for their own businesses'.[53] Such considerations were to be ignored.

In interpreting the law the Prussian Interior Ministry focused primarily on whether potential citizens would prove economically productive members of society. This focus on the economic well-being of the state is reflected in the statistics collected regarding naturalizations. Beginning in June 1845 the Prussian Statistical Bureau asked each District Government to report how many individuals had emigrated from and immigrated into the district in the previous year, based on the number of exit certificates issued and naturalization petitions granted.[54] Individuals were asked to state the value of the assets they had with them when they departed or arrived. Statistical reports published in the 1850s carefully compared the amount of assets lost to, or gained by, the state by virtue of migration. The tables divided both emigrants and immigrants into those over and those under fourteen years of age, the point being, apparently, to determine how many of the immigrants might earn their own keep and contribute to the economy of the state, and how many were as yet unable to do so. For the same reason, apparently, the tables indicated the gender of emigrants and immigrants.[55] The state viewed men as the more valuable economic commodity.[56] In collecting data the state displayed no interest in the ethnicity, confession, or other individual characteristics of those naturalized.

There was, however, one distinct subgroup of foreigners that the Untertanengesetz singled out for particularly restrictive treatment: Jews. Even the most enlightened Christian advocates of Jewish emancipation in Prussia, such as late eighteenth-century civil servant and philosopher Christian Wilhelm Dohm, generally opposed increasing the number of foreign Jews permitted to settle in the state.[57] The Untertanengesetz provided that all Jewish applicants for naturalization had to be approved by the Interior Minister instead of by the District Governments, as was the norm. In practice foreign Jews were naturalized only when they were particularly well off, which generally meant that they were required to possess capital in the amount of at least 5,000 Reichsthalers or to demonstrate knowledge of a useful trade.[58] In addition, Jewish petitioners were required to pay a fee amounting to 1 to 2 percent of their net assets.[59] A special set of rules applied with respect to that portion of the Prussian Jewish community that, while permanently resident in the monarchy, had not been granted full citizenship. Before 1848 the Jews of Posen, one-third of the Jews in Prussia, had had to meet a range of tests demonstrating their acculturation as Germans before being naturalized as full citizens, as well as economic tests similar to those applied to foreign Jews.[60] In those parts of Prussia acquired in 1815 from Saxony, Hessen and Nassau the central administration permitted far more restrictive rules on Jewish settlement to remain in effect.[61]

While Prussian rules regarding the naturalization of Jews were hardly liberal, they compared favorably with the practices of most of the south German states. Bavaria, for example, entirely prohibited the naturalization of foreign Jews.[62] Baden permitted the naturalization of Jews, but prevented Jews from settling in communities where Jews did not already live. Since 90 percent of the communities in Baden had no Jews, this meant that in practice Jews found it difficult to migrate to or move within the country.[63] Quite apart from these formal rules, the freedom given local communities to act on their prejudices in most German states meant that the settlement of foreign Jews was quite restricted.

From a modern perspective the Untertanengesetz does not appear liberal. It discriminated against the poor, against women, and against Jews. It required all emigrants to forfeit their citizenship immediately upon leaving Prussia. It privileged the landed nobility. And it gave unlimited discretion to state authorities over naturalization decisions. But in the context of the age, compared with the laws of other German states and with Prussia's own past practices, it was relatively tolerant and open. The discretion over naturalization it gave the state was intended to be used, and in fact was used, to combat the arbitrariness (Willkühr) of communal practices. The privileges granted the nobility were given grudgingly and interpreted narrowly. The Untertanengesetz, and the companion laws on residence and charitable support, were the products of a self-confident, liberalizing administration.

Notes

1. Quoted in English as this chapter's title, 'Wem gehört zum Genossenschaft des Preussischen Volkes?' From the 1842 Staatsrat debates on the proposed Prussian citizenship law, session of 2 February 1842. GStA PK, HA I, Rep. 80 I, gen, Nr. 4a, Bd. 26, Debates of the Staatsrat, p. 62. It is not clear who spoke the words in question, as the identity of speakers was generally not noted in the minutes of Staatsrat debates.

2. GStA PK, HA I, Rep. 89, Nr. 16786, p. 13. And similarly in Johann Gottfried Hoffmann, 'Über die Besorgnisse, welche die Zunahme der Bevölkerung erregt', in Johann Gottfried Hoffmann, *Sammlung kleiner Schriften staatswirtschaftlichen Inhalts* (Berlin, 1843), pp. 30–77 (this article was first published in 1835). The colonists' benefits to which Hoffmann referred were grants of land or loans from the state.

3. 'Motive zu dem Gesetz-Entwurf wegen der Verpflichtung zu Armenpflege', in *Allerhöchste Kabinetsordre vom 18ten Februar 1838, mit den Gesetz-Entwürfen über die Verpflichtung der Kommunen zur Aufnahme neuanziehender Personen und wegen der Verpflichtung zur Armenpflege*, Exhibit D. GStA PK, HA I, Rep. 80, Drucksachen, Nr. 286a, pp. 41–2.

4. 'Statistische Uebersicht der in dem Zeitraum von 1sten October 1844 bis zum 30sten September 1848 zur amtlichen Kenntniß der Regierung gekommenen Zahl der Ein- und Ausgewanderten im Preußischen Staate', *Mittheilungen des statistischen Bureaus in Berlin*, published by F.W.S. Dieterici, vol. 2 (1849), p. 130.

5. Mack Walker, *Germany and the Emigration 1816–1885* (Harvard University Press, 1964), p. 56.
6. Marschalck, *Bevölkerungsgeschichte Deutschlands im 19. und 20. Jahrhundert* (Suhrkamp, 1984), p. 180.
7. Horst Matzerath, *Urbanisierung in Preußen, 1815–1914* (Kohlhammer, 1985), pp. 75–80.
8. Memorandum of 22 October 1830, from the Government in Erfurt, Abtheilung des Innern, to the Ministry of the Interior. GStA PK, HA I, Rep. 77, Tit. 227, Nr. 4, Bd. 1, pp. 21RS–24RS.
9. Memorandum of the Interior Ministry to the Ministry of Foreign Affairs, 15 July 1831. GStA PK, HA I, Rep. 77, Tit. 227, Nr. 4, Bd. 1, p. 62RS.
10. Memorandum dated July 1833 of the Ministry of the Interior and Foreign Office regarding a proposed law on citizenship. GStA PK, HA I, Rep. 77, Tit. 227, Nr. 4, Bd. 1, p. 230. The role of Russian intervention was emphasized in the history of the *Untertanengesetz* composed by the Prussian Staatsministerium in 1838. *Allerhöchste Kabinetsordre vom 18ten Februar 1838*, GStA PK, HA I, Rep. 80, Drucksachen, Nr. 286a, p. 4.
11. Report from the Prussian Cabinet to Friedrich Wilhelm III dated 31 December 1830, GStA PK, HA I, Rep. 89, Nr. 15692, pp. 12–14.
12. Memorandum of 15 July 1831 of the Minister of the Interior and Police, von Brenn, to be sent to the Ministry of Foreign Affairs, Exhibit C. GStA PK, HA I, Rep. 77, Tit. 227, Nr. 4, Bd. 1, p. 58RS.
13. Letter of 13 February 1832 from the Prussian Ministry of Foreign Affairs (signed Eichhorn) to the Minister of the Interior and Police von Brenn, GStA PK, HA I, Rep. 77, Tit. 227, Nr. 4, Bd. 1, p. 1.
14. Staatsrat session of 2 February 1842. GStA PK, HA I, Rep. 80, I gen Nr. 4a (Staatsrat protocols), Bd. 26, p. 62.
15. Letter of 13 February 1832 from the Prussian Ministry of Foreign Affairs (signed Eichhorn) to the Minister of the Interior and Police von Brenn, GStA PK, HA I, Rep. 77, Tit. 227, Nr. 4, Bd. 1, pp. 5RS, 9–9RS.
16. *Gesetz über die Erwerbung und den Verlust der Eigenschaft als Preußischer Unterthan, so wie über den Eintritt in fremde Staatsdienste*, Section thirteen.
17. See the commentary of von Eichmann, GStA PK, HA I, Rep. 80, Drucksachen, Nr. 286a, p. 8.
18. GStA PK, HA I, Rep. 80 Staatsrat (Drucksachen), Nr. 286, Anlage V, pp. 20–2.

19. Heinz Gollwitzer, *Die Standesherren: Die politische und gesellschaftliche Stellung der Mediatisierten 1815–1918* (Friedrich Vorwerk Verlag, 1957), pp. 47–51, 251–8.
20. J. Ziekursch, *Hundert Jahre schlesischer Agrargeschichte*, 2nd edn (Preuss & Jünger, 1927) p. 46. Ziekursch's statistics refer to the late eighteenth and early nineteenth centuries and must be treated cautiously when applied to the 1830s and 1840s.
21. The rights of nobles who before 1806 had been independent of territorial princes had been guaranteed by Article fourteen of the Bundesakte of 1815. *Bundes-Akte* of 8 June 1815, E. Huber, *Dokumente zur Deutschen Verfassungsgeschichte* (Kohlhammer, 1961), vol. 1, pp. 78–9.
22. 'Was Sie sind, bin ich auch!' Quoted in Gollwitzer, *Die Standesherren*, p. 68.
23. Haller's influence on the East Elbian estate owners is discussed in Robert Berdahl, *The Politics of the Prussian Nobility: The Development of a Conservative Ideology 1770–1848* (Princeton University Press, 1988), pp. 232–46 and T. Nipperdey, *Deutsche Geschichte 1800–1866*, 6th edn (Beck, 1993) pp. 317–18. His influence on the Crown Prince is noted in D. Barclay, *Frederick William IV and the Prussian Monarchy, 1840–1861*, (Oxford University Press, 1995), p. 36.
24. Articles 17–19, *GPS* (1843), p. 17.
25. Debates of the Staatsrat, 2 February 1842, GStA PK, HA I, Rep. 80 I, gen, Nr. 4a, Bd. 26, pp. 62–62RS.
26. The partially successful attempts of the Prussian state to make conscription a general duty imposed on all male subjects during and after the Napoleonic Era are described in H. Stübig, 'Die Wehrverfassung Preußens in der Reformzeit' in R. Foerster (ed.), *Die Wehrpflicht* (Oldenbourg, 1994), pp. 49–53.
27. Debates of the Staatsrat, 2 February 1842, GStA PK, HA I, Rep. 80 I, gen, Nr. 4a, Bd. 26, p. 70RS.
28. GStA PK, HA I, Rep. 80 I, gen, Nr. 4a, Bd. 26, p. 64.
29. Letter of 13 February 1832 from the Ministry of Foreign Affairs to the Minister of Interior and Police, GStA PK, HA I, Rep. 77, Tit. 227, Nr. 4, Bd. 1, p. 5.
30. D. Gosewinkel, *Einbürgern und Ausschließen* (Vandenhoeck & Ruprecht, 2001), pp. 150–7.
31. P. Weil, *Qu'est-ce qu'un Français?* (Bernard Grasset, 2002), pp. 188, 196. Professor Weil's argument stimulates reflection on an important issue. Unfortunately, I, or rather the German colleague

who undertook to assist me, since Weil's book appeared after the completion of my primary research in Germany, could not locate a number of the key passages in the original sources that Weil cites, or found that his paraphrases were not entirely accurate. Some of the difficulties may arise from Weil's apparent reliance on Hans Lippe's 1947 dissertation, *Die preußische Heimatgesetzgebung vom 31. Dezember 1842* (Göttingen). Compare Weil's claims on page 191 of his book with the statements in the Lippe dissertation on pp. 160–1. It was Professor Weil who graciously pointed out the Lippe manuscript to me as one likely source of his evidence.

32. Interior Ministry memorandum of 9 March 1830 regarding the citizenship status of a Dutch citizen, Verhoff. GStA PK, HA I, Rep. 77, Tit. 227, Nr. 4, Bd. 1, pp. 181, 181RS.

33. Letter of 13 February 1832 from the Prussian Ministry of Foreign Affairs (signed Eichhorn) to the Minister of the Interior and Police von Brenn, GStA PK, HA I, Rep. 77, Tit. 227, Nr. 4, Bd. 1, p. 9.

34. Memorandum of Interior Minister von Rochow of 24 July 1834. GStA PK, HA I, Tit. 227, Nr. 4, Bd. 2, p. 29; Chart summarizing the views regarding the Untertanengesetz of Ministers von Brenn, von Kamptz, Mühler and von Rochow, undated but most likely from 1835. GStA PK, HA I, Tit. 227, Nr. 4, Bd. 2, p. 48; *Vortrag über das Gesetz wegen Enstehung und Auflösung des preussischen Unterthanenverhältnisses* of 26 March 1840, GStA PK, HA I, Rep. 80 (Drucksachen), Nr. 286, Anlage V, p. 16.

35. Memorandum of the Ministry of the Interior and Police and the Foreign Office of 19 July 1833, pp. 236–236RS. I would like to express my gratitude to Ina Paul for her generous assistance in transcribing the relevant portion of this document.

36. The Joint Memorandum of the Interior and Foreign Ministries of July 1833 contains an extended discussion of the social and legal changes that had taken place in Prussia since the late eighteenth century and how these changes had created a need for clear rules governing citizenship. GStA PK, HA I, Rep. 77, Tit. 227, Nr. 4, Bd. 1, pp. 231–6.

37. *ALR*, Part II, Title 1, Section 4, Paragraphs 184, 195; Section 5, Paragraph 205, at p. 357; *ALR*, Part II, Title 2, Section 1, Paragraph 74; Section 2, Paragraphs 66–9, at pp. 390–1; Marianne Weber, *Ehefrau und Mutter in der Rechtsentwicklung: Eine Einführung* (J.C.B. Mohr, 1907), pp. 274–6; E. Schubert, *Arme Leute* (Degener, 1983), p. 107.

38. In Alsace it was the custom, before the Revolution, to consider as French a foreign man who married an Alsatian woman. Weil, *Qu'est-ce qu'un Français?*, p. 42.

39. Letter of 13 February 1832 from the Prussian Ministry of Foreign Affairs (signed Eichhorn) to the Minister of the Interior and Police von Brenn, GStA PK, HA I, Rep. 77, Tit. 227, Nr. 4, Bd. 1, p. 12. A similar position was taken in the joint memorandum of the Prussian Interior Ministry and Foreign Ministry of July 1833, GStA PK, HA I, Rep. 77, Nr. 4, Bd. 1, pp. 247, 247RS.

40. Letter from Interior Minister von Brenn to the Prussian Foreign Minister, von Ancillon, of 14 September 1833. GStA PK, HA I, Rep. 77, Tit. 227, Nr. 4, Bd. 1, p. 274; Memorandum of the Prussian Interior and Justice Ministries to the Foreign Ministry of 21 February 1834, GStA PK, HA I, Rep. 77, Tit. 227, Nr. 4, Bd. 2, pp. 9, 9RS. The 1834 memorandum also stated that 'it would be . . . unnatural as well as politically inadvisable . . . to divide the citizenship of a married couple . . .'

41. Weil, *Qu'est-ce qu'un Français?*, pp. 42, 213. But with respect to the treatment of women, German states – even those most subject to the influence of the French example – did not blindly follow it. See Isabel Hull, *Sexuality, State, and Civil Society in Germany, 1700–1815* (Cornell University Press, 1996), pp. 371–406.

42. Circular of 4 May 1839 from the Ministry of Interior and Police to all the Prussian District Governments (except in the Rhineland) and to the Police Presidium in Berlin. GStA PK, HA I, Rep. 77 (Interior Ministry), Tit. 227, Nr. 4, Bd. 3, p. 29. For an examination of nineteenth-century south-German rules governing marriage, and their relationship to support for the poor, see K. Matz, *Pauperismus und Bevölkerung* (Ernst Klett, 1973).

43. Memorandum of 22 October 1830 from the Erfurt District Government to the Prussian Ministry of the Interior, GStA PK, HA I, Rep. 77, Tit. 227, Nr. 4, Bd. 1, p. 28RS. The description of the laws of other German states is in the letter, the characterization of their practices as 'Barbarei und Willkühr' is a marginal notation.

44. Werner of Koblenz, in *Stenographischer Bericht über die Verhandlungen der deutschen constituirenden Nationalversammlung zu Frankfurt am Main*, F. Wigard (ed.), 9 vols (1848–1849) (*SBF*), vol. 1, p. 761.

45. Baden Ministry of the Interior to the Mittelrheinkreis, 2 May 1836, Badisches General-Landesarchiv, Karlsruhe (BGL), Abteilung 236,

Nr. 10656; Memorandum of the Ministry of the Interior to Leopold of 28 November 1838. BGL Abt. 233, Nr. 32588.

46. Baden Ministry of the Interior to Leopold, 8 January 1838, recommending denial of the petition. BGL, Abt. 233, Nr. 32558.

47. Baden Ministry of the Interior to Leopold, 22 February 1839; final order in the appeal dated 6 April 1839. Ibid.

48. Baden Ministry of the Interior to Leopold, 28 November 1838, decision of 13 December 1838. Ibid.

49. Baden Ministry of the Interior Ministry to Leopold, 9 May 1840, Ibid. The final decision in this case is not made clear, although the memorandum indicates the way the Ministry is leaning.

50. Baden Ministry of the Interior to Leopold, 20 December 1839. Ibid.

51. Baden Ministry of the Interior to Leopold, 18 April 1844. Ibid.

52. As one example among many, see the memorandum to the Erfurt Government from the Ministry of the Interior, 30 June 1844. GStA PK, HA I, Rep. 77, Tit. 227, Nr. 4, Bd. 4, p. 259.

53. District Government of Königsberg to the Ministry of the Interior, 26 April 1844. GStA PK, HA I, Rep. 77, Tit. 227, Nr. 4, Bd. 4, p. 218. This does not mean that the Interior Ministry always ignored local wishes. See letter from the Ministry of the Interior to the District Government in Erfurt dated 28 August 1845, GStA PK, HA I, Rep. 77, Tit. 227, Nr. 4, Bd. 5, pp. 60–2.

54. The Royal Statistical Bureau Decree of 16 June 1845 is described in the Circular of 31 March 1862 of the Prussian Minister of the Interior, *Ministerial-Blatt für die gesammte innere Verwaltung in den Königlich Preußischen Staaten* (1862) (*MBiV*), p. 181.

55. See, for example, the conclusion in T. Bödiker, 'Die Auswanderung und die Einwanderung des preussischen Staates', *Zeitschrift des Königlich Preussischen Statistischen Bureaus* 13 (1873), p. 12, that the 'gender and age structure of the immigration is extremely favorable. The male sex is almost twice as strongly represented as the female, the number of adults (over fourteen years old) is greater than the number of children by a factor of four.'

56. The statisticians attempted to quantify this. Ibid., p. 16.

57. J. Katz, *Out of the Ghetto: The Social Background of Jewish Emancipation, 1770–1870* (Harvard University Press, 1973), p. 58.

58. Joint Memorandum of the Prussian Interior Ministry and Foreign Ministry of July 1833, GStA PK, HA I, Rep. 77, Nr. 4, Bd. 1, p. 249. The memorandum here summarized the provisions of decrees issued in 1817 and 1822. In the 1840s, or perhaps after the revolution of

1848, the amount of this wealth required of Jews was increased. See the memorandum from Interior Minister Westphalen to Friedrich Wilhelm IV dated 21 July 1857. GStA PK, HA I, Rep. 89, Nr. 15704, p. 114RS.

59. Memorandum to the King from the Minister of the Interior and the Minister of Finance dated 6 May 1848. GStA PK, HA I, Rep. 89, Nr. 15694, pp. 115–16, 120–3.

60. *Vorläufige Verordnung wegen des Judenwesens im Großherzogtum Posen* of 1 June 1833, *GPS*, p. 66. 'Patriotic behavior [that] rendered a special service to the state' provided another, distinct grounds for naturalization. Approximately 7,500 Posen Jews were naturalized before this law was suspended in 1848. Stanisław Navrocki, 'Die Polen unter preußischer Herrschaft 1815–1848', in H. Boom and M. Wojciechowski (eds), *Deutsche und Polen in der Revolution 1848–1849: Dokumente aus deutschen und polnischen Archiven*, (Harald Boldt Verlag, 1991), p. 5.

61. *Gutachten der Abtheilungen des Königlichen Staatsraths für die Innern und Justiz-Angelegenheiten betreffend die Regulierung des Judenwesens* of 20 October 1839. GStA PK, Rep. 80 (Drucksachen), Nr. 266.

62. Stefan Schwarz, *Die Juden in Bayern im Wandel der Zeiten* (Günter Olzog, 1963), pp. 183–6.

63. Reinhard Rürup, 'Die Emanzipation der Juden in Baden', in A. Schäfer (ed.), *Oberrheinische Studien*, vol. 2 (Druckerei Esser, 1973), p. 13.

–4–

Paths Not Taken

Both the revolutionaries of 1848, who attempted to create a national state and failed, and Bismarck, who succeeded, thought it possible to include large numbers of foreigners who were not ethnic Germans in the German state, to make them full German citizens. They hoped for eventual assimilation. Bismarck's approach hardened over time. By the 1880s the relative openness of the 1860s had been replaced by far more combative tactics. Many liberals also became skeptical of the possibilities of a multi-ethnic state. But the initial openness – as a relative matter – was nonetheless significant. There is a tendency to see the liberalism of 1848 and the 1860s as a passing enthusiasm, sentimental and unrealistic, so superficial as to be almost a mirage, or, in the case of Bismarck, whom no one can accuse of sentimentality, as a matter of adaptation to transient political needs. There is some truth in this perception. But the citizenship policies of the 1848 revolutionaries and of the 1860s also serve to suggest real alternatives, alternatives that a German state founded in a different way, that had a more federal structure and included Austria, would have been more likely to pursue.

A large part of the explanation for the initial openness to including individuals who were not ethnic Germans in the new state lies in the territorial ambitions both of the revolutionaries and of Bismarck. The leaders of the revolution sought to create a Germany that would incorporate the entirety of the German Confederation, as well as adjacent lands in which significant numbers of Germans lived. This implied a willingness to accept as citizens numerous individuals who were not ethnic Germans. Bismarck's plans were less ambitious. But in taking Schleswig from Denmark and Alsace-Lorraine from France he also accepted the need to extend German citizenship to a significant number of individuals who were not ethnic Germans. Moreover, the fate of the inhabitants of these territories was not decided only by Prussia, but was the subject of treaties with the defeated powers. These treaties required Prussia to give the inhabitants the chance of becoming Prussian or – in the case of Alsace-Lorraine – German citizens.

Both the revolutionaries and Bismarck, the latter at least until the early 1870s, were confident of the assimilatory powers of the German nation and state. The confidence of the revolutionaries rested to a large degree on the belief that fair treatment and the attractiveness (and, for many, superiority) of German culture would lead foreigners to assimilate. Bismarck emphasized more the efficacy of official policies promoting and compelling assimilation.[1] For the liberals equal treatment of individuals who were not ethnic Germans was also a matter of political principle, and they hoped that a state founded on a constitutional basis would prove attractive to a range of nationalities. The optimism of both Bismarck and the 1848 revolutionaries was probably influenced by the limited appeal of competing nationalisms in the pre-1848 era, especially in the East. In 1848 the spread of nationalistic sentiments among the peasantry of Eastern Europe was only just beginning. This made the project of integrating non-German foreigners into a German state seem less daunting.[2] In the case of the Alsatians there was the hope that they might come to view their German ethnic roots as more important than their political loyalty to France.

The industrialization of the German states also promoted an expansive and assimilatory citizenship policy. From the 1840s, in the Ruhr Valley and in Saxony, but not only there, 'railroads and machine shops, coal mines and iron foundries . . . seemed to spring out of the ground'.[3] The growth of cities accelerated. Industrialization created a demand for labor that, at least where it was most intense, could not be met as long as customary communal standards of reputation and solvency were maintained. In the new cities the notion of a limited and regulated economy became increasingly unworkable. And in the countryside landowners felt an ever greater need for labor, as peasants left to find work in cities and overseas, and new and often labor-intensive commercial crops were introduced. Industrialization contributed to a revaluation of the economic value of the poor that promoted a more liberal citizenship policy.

While industrialization occurred more or less continuously during this period, the political changes were fitful, a matter of explosive stops and starts and reversals of direction. Fundamentally different political conceptions opposed each other. Were the German states to remain independent, or become part of a national state? Would Austria belong to a new nation-state or not? Would German states have constitutions and parliaments, or be run primarily by monarchs and administrations? The back and forth on these issues led also to a back and forth on citizenship policies.

A National and Liberal Citizenship

The end of the French monarchy on 24 February 1848 sparked popular uprisings throughout the German Confederation. The German states quickly yielded to popular pressure and permitted the election of a national parliament on the basis of nearly universal manhood suffrage. One can compare the events of the spring of 1848 to those of the autumn of 1989, when communist rule collapsed throughout Eastern Europe. In both cases a seemingly stable authoritarian system based on military force buckled in the face of popular unrest and the reluctance – in large part based on fear – of key leaders to give their armies the orders to shoot to kill on a massive scale. In 1848, in contrast to 1989, the old elites recovered their nerve and attempted with some success to restore the status quo ante.

The leaders of the 1848 revolution in Germany pressed for a national citizenship. Unity and Justice and Freedom (Einigkeit und Recht und Freiheit): each of the great goals of the 1848 revolution implied changes in the laws that governed citizenship. How could Germans feel a sense of unity, asked delegates to the Frankfurt Parliament, the revolutionary assembly, if they were not allowed to live and work where they wished within Germany? Louis Tellkampf, a professor of political science from Breslau who had spent eight years teaching in the United States, told the assembly that 'the unity of Germany can only become a reality when there is complete freedom of movement . . . Only in this way will the nation become melded together, only in this way will a truly brotherly feeling arise . . .'[4] 'Without the general right [to move freely] the German will still feel himself a foreigner on German soil, because the police can arbitrarily expel him from where he chooses to settle', argued Gustav Gulden, a lawyer from the Palatinate.[5] What would freedom mean, if Germans were not free to settle where they chose? Admittedly these terms were ambiguous. Freedom might also refer to the freedom of local authorities to establish their own rules governing membership in communities and admission to trades, and right might refer also to the traditional rights of towns and guilds. But most of the Frankfurt delegates believed that the cruel expulsions of Germans from one town to another and one state to another should cease.

Freedom to live and work where one pleased was the answer most delegates to the Frankfurt Parliament gave to pauperism, the pressing social problem of the 1830s and 1840s. 'There is none among us under whose feet the ground is not burning, as he sees the masses of starving peasants, the confused and aroused workers, the despairing tradesmen, who are looking over our shoulders . . .', Friedrich Vischer, a Tübingen professor of art and German literature, told the Assembly at the start of its deliberations.[6] The poor demanded to be allowed to work, and this demand could be met only if they were permitted to move to where jobs could be found. 'Nothing', the Economics Committee reported, 'promotes the evil whose healing is the most important task of the present, Pauperism, than a narrow-hearted limitation of freedom of movement.'[7] 'There is no question, but that this matter [freedom of movement] is the most important of all, for it concerns not only the rich and the well-to-do, but will also give the poorest of our fellow citizens a Fatherland . . .' commented Adolph Lette, a senior Prussian civil servant and a member of the center right.[8]

Agitation to break down barriers to movement in part reflected the new economic conditions, the establishment of factories and the building of railroads, which required the use of non-local labor. Bruno Hildebrand, an economist at the University of Marburg and the spokesman for the Economics Committee, argued that 'every worker who simply relies on the strength of his arms to earn his bread, for example railroad and factory workers, must have the right to settle anywhere in Germany'.[9] But it was not just a matter of helping the poor, although they received the most consideration. 'The new industry', stated Tellkampf, 'demands a greater balance of capital and work force. And this is only possible if we permit workers to go where capital can be efficiently employed.'[10]

The demands of the majority in the Frankfurt Parliament for a lowering of barriers to movement were opposed by a not inconsiderable minority that wished to preserve and strengthen the rights of communities to control their borders. Tradesmen 'above all want to be freed from freedom of movement', argued August Reichensperger, a Prussian judge and delegate from the Rhineland, which knew of the effects of such legislation first hand.[11] Friedrich Hermann, an economics professor and civil servant from Bavaria, urged the assembly to respect local rights: 'Let us not diminish the autonomy of the individual states where it is not necessary for the unity and political freedom of Germany.'[12] Even supporters of freedom of movement purported to respect the 'independent position and honor' ('selbständige Haltung und Ehrenhaftigkeit') of local communities.[13]

While a majority of the delegates demanded greater freedom of movement, the question of whether this should be stated as a goal or accomplished forthwith was something about which the assembly was uncertain. Two committees considered that question for the assembly. The Constitutional Committee proposed to grant each individual the same freedom to move as possessed by the citizens of each state, and to leave the creation of a uniform law governing settlement to future legislation. The problem with this idea was that most German states permitted communities to restrict entrance by those not from the community. The Constitutional Committee's draft would have permitted these restrictions to remain in effect. Just as important, the Constitutional Committee's proposal would have opened all of Prussia to the poor of other states, while leaving the other states in practice closed to Prussians. Given the fact that Prussia had in 1842 made mere settlement the basis for entitlement to poor relief, the Constitutional Committee's plan might well have had the effect of making Prussian communes responsible for supporting the poor who migrated from other German states.

The Economics Committee supported granting all German citizens the right to settle where they pleased, without regard for local laws. This was a more radical approach. While the Assembly eventually voted to accept the Economics Committee's proposal, it was only by a vote of 244 to 242 that it authorized the committee to draft the law that would state the conditions under which residence and the practice of a trade would be permitted. Actually implementing the principle, the Assembly realized, was a recipe for trouble. This vote showed, as one might expect, that supporters of more rapid action tended to come from the states where freedom of movement already prevailed, Prussia and Saxony, and those favoring slower action came from the south and west, where local communal rights were still entrenched.[14] In fact the Economics Committee never got around to drafting the measures.

The primary difference in substance between the debates on freedom of movement at Frankfurt in 1848 and those within the Prussian ministries in the 1820s and 1830s was the failure of the Frankfurt Parliament to tackle head-on the issue of poor relief. Even the Economics Committee draft, while it granted individuals the right to move where they pleased, did not entitle them to poor relief in the new location.[15] The delegates thought that in this way communities might be persuaded that freedom of movement posed less of a threat. But this left unclear exactly from where poor relief would come. There was some vague talk of states assuming responsibility. The 1842 legislation creating freedom of movement inside Prussia had attracted the support of the landed interests largely because it had freed them from the burden of supporting former residents who had left for towns and cities. But the landed interests were not well represented at Frankfurt – it was not their revolution.

The unity the revolution sought was one that made as many ethnic Germans as practicable part of a larger political unit. Creating the new state on an ethnic basis suggested that non-Germans might become second-class citizens. The Frankfurt Parliament sought to allay the fears thus aroused among non-Germans by promising to respect the distinct languages and cultures of subgroups within the new state. All individuals born and raised within the German state would be treated as full citizens, the Parliament promised. Johann Peter Werner, an attorney from Koblenz in the Prussian Rhineland, who was associated in the Frankfurt Parliament with the center left, asked the assembly 'if every slave, every serf, who puts his foot on German soil is to be free, why then not the child who is born on German territory and has grown up among Germans . . . Why should not this child also have an expectancy of obtaining German citizenship?'[16] Wilhelm Jordan, a writer from East Prussia and one of the most charismatic figures of the assembly, took the same position: 'I think we can calmly say that everyone is a German who lives on German soil.'[17] The radical nature of the assembly's willingness to expand the boundaries of who might be considered German is suggested by its treatment of Jews. Not only did the constitution prohibit discrimination based on confession, but the assembly elected Gabriel Riesser, a practicing Jew, vice president. Its president from December 1848 was Eduard Simson, who had converted from Judaism to Protestantism as a young man.[18]

The Frankfurt Assembly's guarantees of cultural tolerance and civic openness also had limits. The provision guaranteeing ethnic minorities the right to preserve their own culture and language was meant to operate only in areas where the non-German group was in the majority. It was unclear whether members of minorities outside these areas, or at national institutions like parliaments and universities, would enjoy any special cultural rights. Some deputies, like Wilhelm Jordan, accepted the idea of granting civic rights to ethnic minorities, but only in the expectation that the minorities would, sooner or later, merge culturally with the German majority.[19] It is also true that many of the leaders of the German national movement viewed various foreign nationalities and states as hostile, or potentially hostile, and often as culturally inferior.[20] The development of German national feeling for much of the nineteenth century owed a great deal to enmity toward France, and the 1848 revolution was accompanied by a German war with Denmark, and armed ethnic clashes in Posen and Bohemia. In half a dozen German or partly German cities and towns the revolution brought pogroms rather than civic equality for Jews. The Frankfurt Parliament itself urged the German states to make war on Denmark to protect the German minority in Schleswig. Non-German national groups in border regions of the future German state often resisted efforts to persuade them to participate in the Frankfurt Parliament. The Czech historian Frantisek Palacky's 11 April 1848 letter rejecting such an invitation is one of the seminal documents of Czech national history. Palacky argued that Bohemia's future lay in a largely Slavic Austria. At the Slavic Congress in Prague, in June 1848, deputies adopted a manifesto that attacked the 'lust for domination' of the Romance and Germanic nations.[21] The revolution planted seeds both of ethnic and religious tolerance and of chauvinism.

Reaction, Sexual Morality, and Prussian Citizenship

The suppression of the revolution in the autumn of 1848 and the spring of 1849 led to an official reaction against the ideals the revolution had expressed, ideals that had also, to some degree, animated state policies before the revolution. Liberalism became associated with the revolution, treason to the state. For a decade after 1848 Prussia viewed all foreigners, and especially the young men who formed a disproportionate percentage of immigrants, as potential carriers of revolutionary ideas. The Prussian central administration not only reestablished some degree of local control over the residence of non-Prussians, but forced the hand of communities inclined to be more open than the state now considered appropriate. The confidence and optimism about the future that had characterized much of the central administration before 1848, and its certainty that it would play the key role in shaping this future, had been irretrievably shaken. Foreigners were among the main victims.

The ideals inscribed on the banner of the Reaction were order, morality and Christianity. In the face of the humiliation of the state at the hands of the revolution, the Hegelian ideals of creating a more just and free society that had animated at least a good portion of the Prussian civil service in the period before 1848 gave way to fear for the survival of the state and the social order on which it was based. Civil servants now focused less on easing social misery and promoting economic growth – admittedly these had been priorities only for a part of the civil service even before 1848 – and more on strengthening the existing order. Administrative rules were modified in 1849 (and codified as law in 1851 and 1852) to permit the firing of high-level officials who displeased their superiors. The state administration itself was suspected of complicity in the revolution.[22]

Among the first orders of business was punishing, or ridding society of, the revolutionaries. Bernhard Becker, a contemporary, wrote in a history of the reaction that 'expulsions were the order of the day . . . There arose a class of homeless people who were pushed from one state to another'.[23] Prussia banned from its territory journeymen who had worked in the politically suspect states of Switzerland and Bremen. The Prussian Trades Ordinance of February 1849 prohibited the naturalization of foreign journeymen absent significant justification. It also required the approval of the local community and the relevant local guild and handicrafts board.[24] The pre-1848 guarantees of freedom of movement for Prussians were undermined by government policies designed to rid cities of domestic troublemakers. The infamous police commissioner of Berlin, Karl Ludwig von Hinckeldey, expelled a considerable number of Prussians from the city, despite the freedoms contained in the 1842 laws.[25] Even deputies to the Prussian national parliament, created as a concession to the revolution, were not free of the danger of expulsion from Berlin in the 1850s.[26]

The Reaction viewed the revolution not merely as a political failure, but as a sign of society's moral degeneration. In the first part of the nineteenth century all political and economic problems and interests tended to be expressed in moral terms. The Prussian state therefore undertook to punish not just political deviance, but immorality. Prussia launched a vigorous attack on cohabitation outside of marriage. Since, for the reasons discussed below, foreigners were often offenders, and since the state had a ready instrument of punishment, expulsion, they were perhaps the chief victims of this campaign.

As Dirk Blasius writes, 'the cohabitation of the nineteenth century had nothing to do with alternative lifestyles. It was rather the expression of a life without alternatives, the inability of the lower classes to organize their lives in the socially privileged legal form of marriage'.[27] Roughly 7.5 percent of all births in Prussia took place out of wedlock in the period from 1830 to 1869.[28] When one considers the number of occasions on which marriage occurred after conception of a child, and also the fact that the percentage of first children born or conceived out of wedlock must have been much higher than the percentage of all illegitimate births, one obtains an impression of the extent to which living together or having sexual relations before marriage was a common practice for many Prussians (as for many Europeans).[29]

Foreigners in Prussia lived in 'concubinage', as the authorities often referred to it, with special frequency. First, as a group foreigners were almost certainly poorer than the average for Prussian society as a whole. Second, they were frequently young and single, and subject to little oversight and control by their families. Third, Prussian laws made it difficult for foreign men to marry in Prussia. Laws of 28 April 1841 and 13 March 1854 required foreign men to obtain permission for marriage from their home authorities. As a result, male immigrants often could enter into marriage only after a long delay, either to obtain the necessary local permission or to seek Prussian citizenship. Furthermore, foreigners often had good reason to postpone seeking naturalization until the last possible moment. By attracting the attention of the authorities they ran the risk of being expelled. There was also the prospect of conscription. It appears that intimate relationships between foreign men and Prussian women outside of formal wedlock were common and often existed for long periods.[30]

The tightening of rules governing cohabitation actually began before 1848, and was a consequence of Friedrich Wilhelm IV's assumption of power in 1840. While for most of the first half of the nineteenth century Prussian officials had assumed a tolerant attitude toward cohabitation, in general taking no action against the parties unless one of those involved was married to someone else, in July 1841 this policy was changed to permit the police to intervene to separate the couple when the cohabitation was a cause of 'public offense', i.e., became notorious.[31] But it was only after 1848 that the state administration began to pursue this new direction with vigor. In a decree issued on 5 November 1852 the Minister of the Interior, Ferdinand von Westphalen, ordered police to 'deprive all those foreigners who are living in "concubinage" of permission to live in the community, and then immediately to provide for their expulsion from the place where they have provided such an evil example . . .'[32] Having had children out of wedlock, or cohabiting, became grounds for denial of a citizenship petition.

The central administration undoubtedly hoped that its moral strictures would be enforced by local authorities. The 1849 Trades Ordinance required local guilds and town authorities to approve the employment and naturalization of foreign craftsmen. This gave these groups a free hand to determine whether the settlement of such individuals was desirable. Guilds had traditionally enforced rigid moral standards on masters and journeymen.[33] But the central administration soon discovered that its own moralism far exceeded that of the average Prussian. A series of appeals to Friedrich Wilhelm IV from disappointed petitioners for naturalization provides several examples of such differences between the central administration and local authorities.

In approximately 1850 the Danish shoemaker journeyman Skjellet sought naturalization in Greifswald. Although the shoemakers' guild supported the petition, the District Government rejected it, on the grounds that the exceptional circumstances for naturalization required by the 1849 Trades Ordinance were not present. In 1852 Skjellet renewed his petition. By this time he had become engaged to the widow of an innkeeper and had left off shoemaking to help his fiancée operate the inn. The strictures of the Trades Ordinance were therefore no longer applicable. Again the guild spoke in favor of the naturalization petition. Unfortunately, however, Skjellet's relationship with the innkeeper's widow had already led to the birth of a child, and on this ground the District Government again denied the petition. When Skjellet appealed directly to Friedrich Wilhelm to permit his naturalization, the king rejected the plea on the advice of Westphalen. If Skjellet's naturalization were approved, Westphalen wrote Friedrich Wilhelm, it would only encourage others to enter into similar immoral relationships.[34]

The hardships the Ministry's moralism worked on thousands of immigrants is suggested by an 1859 petition to the King from Heinrich Schmidt, a weaver living in Barmen in the Rhineland, seeking a reversal of an order for his expulsion. Schmidt was at the time nearly forty years old. He explained that he had come to Barmen over twenty years earlier, and had several times before sought Prussian citizenship. While he was waiting for a response to his first petition, which was apparently filed after 1849, his first child was born,

> and because I did not want them [his partner and child] to fall into the hands of the Poor Administration, I took them to me. In this way our cohabitation came into being, and we have since had five children. I do not seek to avoid my deep guilt. God knows how this guilt has oppressed and anguished my soul all these years.

He could not obtain permission to marry from his home town, in Hesse, 'because I was absent too long and had too large a family, and also could not produce the amount of money required for the acceptance there of my wife and children'.[35] Because he had had children out of wedlock his naturalization petitions were repeatedly denied, although supported by numerous neighbors.

Much of the Prussian central administration had doubts about the practicality and wisdom of the rigid orders emanating from Berlin. In an April 1851 letter to the Landräte of his province, the Provincial Governor of Posen wrote that:

> While it is in the interest of an orderly police and poor-support administration to prevent marriages where only one of the spouses is a Prussian citizen, and

when means to support the family are precarious, it is nonetheless undeniable that it is also morally dubious to prevent those involved from entering into a religiously sanctioned and legal sexual relationship. They are usually young persons, and have been granted permission to remain in Prussia for not a short period. The very fact of their migration to Prussia has made it almost completely impossible for them to obtain the necessary papers (from their homes) . . . The acceptance of these individuals as Prussian citizens seems the best way to legalize what often cannot be prevented, or only with great hardship. Marriage is often the only means of reclaiming these individuals from the attractions of an unsteady life, and also is beneficial from the point of view of the police, as it makes the person less and less of a threat to public security.[36]

While this letter was written before the harsh ministerial directive of November 1852, it reflected an almost unavoidable response to the position of foreigners in Prussia. Especially in the eastern provinces, where much of the Catholic Church was Polish, and priests were often sympathetic to the desire of foreign Poles to marry, it happened not infrequently that a priest would perform a marriage despite the legal prohibition.[37]

Morality and Industry in Düsseldorf

The shifts in the political and economic tides that determined citizenship policies in the period between 1848 and 1870 are displayed graphically by the example of the Düsseldorf district of Prussia. This district contained the Ruhr Valley, whose numerous coal mines and iron works attracted labor from abroad, and at least a portion of the foreign work-force eventually became Prussian. Of the 108,260 naturalization petitions granted in Prussia between 1844 and 1871, 8,238 were from the Düsseldorf district. Only in Berlin, Merseburg, and Schleswig were the numbers higher.[38]

Before the Reaction took hold we observe essentially the pattern found in the administrative correspondence of the 1820s and 1830s. Communities did their best to keep out foreigners who might burden their poor chests, while the Düsseldorf District Government sought to prevent them from imposing onerous and illegal conditions for settlement. A series of exchanges regarding a naturalization case in Remscheid illustrates the dynamic. The town council of Remscheid voted in November 1847 to approve the naturalization of a weaver, Andreas Fischer, on the condition that he either marry the daughter of Peter Wilhelm Günter, apparently a well-off local resident, or that Günter guarantee Fischer's ability to support himself for the next ten years.[39] The Düsseldorf government disapproved of these conditions on two grounds: 1) the council had no business becoming involved in such questions; and 2) there was no legal basis for imposing a requirement for a ten-year guarantee, or the entrance into a marriage, as a condition for local support for a naturalization. The Mayor of Remscheid did not back down an inch in his response of January 1848.

> People who want to be accepted as Prussian subjects frequently offer such guarantees of their own volition, and it does not seem at all incorrect to take advantage of such offers, for the community has unfortunately had the most bitter experiences in this regard and the communal assembly has under these circumstances no desire to accept a single additional foreigner.[40]

The District Government also did not budge. While it may have won the battle – Fischer was naturalized without conditions – it was clear that the larger conflict had not ended. In the usual case the District Government learned of the imposition of conditions by communities only if the petitioner for naturalization thought the terms too onerous and was willing to risk permanently alienating the community by appealing to a higher authority.

The District Government's efforts to force communities to abide by the letter of the Untertanengesetz and to accept as permanent residents foreigners who seemed capable of supporting themselves was undercut in mid-1851 by a sharp shift in the policy of the central administration. In July the Prussian Ministry of the Interior chastised the District Government for naturalizing a butcher living in the city of Düsseldorf against the wishes of the local authorities. The District Government had compared the number of butchers in Düsseldorf with the numbers found in other cities, and concluded that Düsseldorf was not suffering from a surfeit. The Interior Ministry objected. 'The Ministry does not find it justified, when the administration of the community, the community council, and the Trades Council unanimously declare that no significant local interests would be served by permitting residence, for the District Government nonetheless to find that such grounds are to be assumed . . .'[41] The Ministry further ordered the District Government rigorously to enforce the clause of the February 1849 Trades Ordinance that permitted the naturalization of foreign journeymen only for 'significant reasons'.[42] With this directive the Ministry essentially ordered the Government to reject most of the naturalization petitions that came before it.

One year later, in November 1852, Interior Minister Westphalen ordered the expulsion of foreigners living out of wedlock with Prussian or foreign women. By this time the District Government understood the new direction. It ordered local police officials to expel the offenders and to 'make sure that naturalization petitions from craftsmen and workers are judged more strictly by the communal authorities than was previously the case'.[43] The police chief of Barmen and Elberfeld, Hermann Hirsch, reported that in response to the Interior Ministry order he had separated 120 unmarried couples with 300 children and shipped the husbands and fathers, all foreigners, out of the country. Another 400 other individuals who were illegally in the city were either expelled or forced to obtain papers. In the latter case he granted permission to reside only for three to six months. Hirsch reported: 'I . . . performed this rigorously and with severity.'[44]

The expulsion of the foreigners in Barmen and Elberfeld marked a shift in the positions of the local community and the state. Hirsch was appointed directly by the Interior Ministry: after 1848 the local government in Barmen and Elberfeld was not trusted to run its own police department. The Mayor of Barmen protested the expulsions to the District Government. Almost all the journeymen in Barmen were foreigners, he wrote, and roughly half of the masters. Many lived in illicit relationships because it was impossible to obtain approval for marriage from their home communities. He noted that many of the partners and children of expelled workers would become impoverished and that the city would be forced to pay for their support. Given the clarity of the orders from Berlin, neither argument had much effect. If the expulsions created problems for the city, responded the police chief, this was just a result of previous negligence, whose fruits must be borne. Delay would simply make the problem worse.[45]

In the late 1850s city officials in the Düsseldorf district, now joined by local business leaders, renewed their efforts to persuade the state to relax its naturalization policies. In response to local pressure the District Government suggested to Berlin that perhaps a more liberal naturalization policy was in order, but was rebuffed.[46] The Mayor of Remscheid then informed the District Government that 'existing industrial conditions are such that the help of foreign workers is absolutely necessary'. As a result a large number of workers came from abroad, and in particular from the Grand Dukedom and Electorate of Hessen. The work required a long-term commitment, and the skills they learned were useless back in Hessen. Factories could not afford to lose these skilled workers. In January 1859 the city council of Barmen sent a petition to the District Government that made a similar argument, and enclosed a protest from thirty-eight local businessmen.[47] In a second letter the Mayor of Remscheid also attacked directly the official argument for denying naturalization petitions where the individuals in question had lived in 'concubinage'. It was in the nature of the industry that foreign workers would live in the city for long periods, and it was impossible to prevent them from forming families. They wished to live honorable lives, and were prevented from doing so by government policy.[48] The District Government in Düsseldorf stuck by the policy mandated in Berlin, but it also was clearly unhappy with the orders it was required to enforce. In January 1860 it granted the naturalization petition from Heinrich Schmidt, the Hessian native who had been threatened with expulsion for cohabitation.

By the late 1850s the dam had begun to give way. On 7 October 1858 Prince Regent Wilhelm replaced Friedrich Wilhelm as monarch. Wilhelm dismissed Interior Minister Westphalen the following day, and a few weeks later replaced Minister-President Manteuffel.[49] The change in the opinions of the reigning monarch corresponded to a larger change in mood. The government also relaxed its manipulations of elections. While conservative deputies held 236 seats in the Prussian parliament elected in 1855, and liberals only 57, in 1858 these figures were reversed. The liberals won 210 seats and the conservatives 57.[50] In February 1860 the Ministry of Trade asked District Governments throughout Prussia to indicate whether they believed the provision of the February 1849 Trades Ordinance that prevented the naturalization of foreign journeymen should be changed. This was a strong indication that Berlin was rethinking its position.[51] On 22 June 1861 the offending article of the February 1849 law was repealed, permitting the naturalization of foreign journeymen without special circumstances.[52]

In addition, the Interior Ministry's policies regarding foreigners living in illicit relationships seems to have fallen into abeyance in the early 1860s.[53] Perhaps just as significant were legal changes that eliminated the barriers to the marriage of foreigners in Prussia. Most German states eliminated the requirement that their citizens obtain local approval for marriage. Prussia did away with the requirement that the permission of the home community be obtained prior to marriage for the citizens of numerous foreign states. Such rules were adopted with respect to the subjects of Great Britain (1856), France (1858), Belgium (1869), most of Austria-Hungary (1869), and Russia (1871).[54]

The importance of economic motives in the development of liberal naturalization policies in the 1860s is reflected, as in the 1840s, in the data sought by the central administration regarding who was becoming naturalized. The Prussian statistical office revised its forms in 1862 to eliminate questions regarding net worth and put in their place inquiries regarding the trades practiced by both immigrants and emigrants.[55] The dropping of questions relating to net worth was attributed primarily to the unreliability of the data obtained on this point. Perhaps the reduced significance of a person's wealth also played a role. This was increasingly a society in which wealth could be created, not merely inherited. As with earlier data-collection efforts, the state saw no need to inquire regarding ethnicity, religion or other non-economic characteristics. In 1871 the Bundesrat required all states in the new German federation to employ a form similar to Prussia's in gathering information regarding individuals who were naturalized.[56]

Compulsion and Free Will

Government fiat determined most of the changes in citizenship status that accompanied the unification of Germany. Subjects of the German territories annexed by Prussia following the war with Austria in 1866, Hanover, Kurhessen, Nassau and Frankfurt, were simply made into Prussians. In 1870 the North German Federation, composed of the German states north of the river Main, created a common North German citizenship held by all subjects of the member states of the Federation. Each individual retained his citizenship in one of the member states, and became a citizen of the North German Federation by virtue of the state citizenship. The same method was employed with respect to the citizens of Baden, Württemberg and Bavaria when the German national state came into being.

In areas that were ethnically mixed and, probably even more important, had been taken from a foreign state that continued to exist, inhabitants were given a choice between retaining their previous citizenship or assuming a German citizenship. The 1864 treaty that ended the war with Denmark gave the residents of Schleswig the right to remain Danish or to become Prussians. Those who chose to remain Danish citizens were permitted to remain residents of Schleswig. In the decades that followed, Prussian policy wavered between allowing the Danish citizens in Schleswig to more or less live in peace and coercive measures designed to force them to assume the burdens of Prussian citizenship and become loyal Prussians, or to emigrate. In 1883, for example, the Prussian Interior Minister ordered the draft-age sons of the roughly 25,000 Danish citizens living in Schleswig to report for military service or to face expulsion. By a quirk in Danish law children born before 1898 to those who had opted for Danish citizenship became stateless, and subjection to Prussian conscription was one of the numerous burdens associated with their status. In 1907 Prussia agreed to grant all the stateless Danes in Schleswig Prussian citizenship, thus giving up its powers of expulsion in exchange for the clear recognition of its right to draft the young men in the group.[57]

The 1871 treaty that ended the war with France permitted the 1.5 million inhabitants of Alsace-Lorraine to choose between German and French citizenship. Those who chose to remain French were required to move to France. Those who stayed – the vast majority – became German citizens.[58] For decades there were conflicts about whether individuals who had opted for France and actually emigrated might be permitted to return to Alsace-Lorraine and become German citizens, as well as over the status of emigrants to France who had never formally renounced German citizenship. Frequently, as in Schleswig, the focus of tension was the status of young men of military age. In the mid-1870s the Prussian policy of forcing aliens to choose between expulsion and Prussian citizenship was extended to the thousands of Dutch citizens living in Prussia. The purpose was to prevent the avoidance of service in the Prussian army. Most, apparently, chose to become Prussians.

The other side of Prussian citizenship policy in the era of unification was a comparatively liberal naturalization policy. One has to stress the word comparative. The easing of the Reaction did not mean that the state immediately ceased to be suspicious of politically active individuals. But many of the restrictions that had previously prevented the naturalization of particular subgroups were eliminated or ameliorated. The results can be read in part in the naturalization statistics. Between 1850 and 1857 the number of naturalization petitions granted each year in Prussia never exceeded 3,300. In the period from 1860 to 1866, the year before Prussia incorporated the new territories won in the war with Austria, the annual number never fell below 4,000 (see Table 4.1, depicting the number of individuals naturalized in Prussia from 1845 to 1887).

In the 1850s and early 1860s the treatment of Polish applicants for citizenship underwent repeated change, in response to waxing and waning fears of Polish disloyalty and the persistent pressure of East Prussian landowners to permit the residence of Polish farm workers.[59] In 1853, most likely as a reaction to the revolutionary sympathies of many Prussian Poles during the 1848 revolution, and the Polish nationalist rebellion in Posen, the Interior Ministry required central approval of all Polish applications for citizenship. In 1857 this decree was restricted

Table 4.1 Individuals Naturalized in Prussia, 1845–1887

Year	Number of individuals naturalized in Prussia	Year	Number of individuals naturalized in Prussia	Year	Number of individuals naturalized in Prussia
1845	3,534	1860	4,179	1875	7,883
1846	3,074	1861	4,253	1876	2,060
1847	3,092	1862	4,728	1877	1,832
1848	2,783	1863	4,444	1878	1,697
1849	2,221	1864	4,626	1879	2,616
1850	2,481	1865	5,309	1880	3,079
1851	2,733	1866	4,023	1881	3,468
1852	2,859	1867	5,715	1882	2,728
1853	2,752	1868	6,188	1883	2,173
1854	3,254	1869	6,862	1884	2,220
1855	2,644	1870	10,022	1885	2,544
1856	3,027	1871	3,086	1886	unpublished
1857	3,296	1872	1,505	1887	3,281
1858	3,469	1873	1,543	1888	unrecorded
1859	3,606	1874	4,413	1889	unrecorded

Source: T. Bödiker, 'Die Auswanderung und die Einwanderung des preussischen Staates', The large number of naturalizations granted between 1867 and 1871 reflects the incorporation of Schleswig into Prussia: two-thirds of the 1870 naturalizations took place in Schleswig, and presumably involved Danes opting for Prussian citizenship. The spike that occurred in 1874 and 1875 was the result of a Prussian campaign to force foreigners living in the Rhineland, many of them Dutch, to accept Prussian citizenship. Prussia gave these foreigners a choice between naturalization and expulsion. The decline in the number of persons naturalized each year after 1870 reflects the fact that immigrants from other German states ceased, after unification, to be foreigners.

to Poles belonging to the upper middle class and the nobility, whom the central administration viewed as the most likely troublemakers.[60] In 1863, during the Polish rebellion in Russian Poland, the Ministry again centralized control of all naturalizations of Poles. (Table 4.2 depicts the naturalizations of Poles in Prussia from 1849 to 1880.)

Despite the Interior Ministry's efforts to control the immigration of Poles, at the local level both landowners and Landräte often did little to stop movement across the border. In part this was a matter of the means at their disposal. The District Government of Oppeln wrote to the Provincial Governor of Silesia in 1851 that 'only by a great increase in the size of the police administration . . . would it be possible to determine who is a Polish immigrant, when he immigrated and where he lives. To my knowledge such a capacity of the police administration is nowhere to be found in the countryside'. Another reason was that the

Table 4.2 Naturalizations of Poles in Prussia, 1849–1880

Year	Naturalizations granted to immigrants from the Polish provinces of Russia who were Christian (excluding data from the Marienwerder district government)	Year	Naturalizations granted to immigrants from the Polish provinces of Russia who were Christian (excluding data from the Marienwerder district government)
1849	89	1865	300
1850	67	1866	360
1851	180	1867	338
1852	174	1868	367
1853	104	1869	289
1854	122	1870	196
1855	180	1871	135
1856	126	1872	98
1857	358	1873	100
1858	189	1874	74
1859	364	1875	126
1860	358	1876	125
1861	188	1877	86
1862	331	1878	107
1863	121	1879	103
1864	192	1880	52

Source: GStA PK, HA I, Rep. 77, Tit. 1176, Nr. 2a, Adh. I. The figures given include the family members of individuals who were naturalized. The statistics were compiled in 1881 on Bismarck's orders. The survey attempted to determine the number of Jews and Poles naturalized each year in Prussia. Since district governments did not record information regarding ethnicity before the mid-1880s, it was necessary to attempt an estimate on the basis of the confession and place of origin of each immigrant. The resulting figures therefore provide only a very crude estimate of the number of Poles naturalized, since they include immigrants who were Christian but not Polish, and exclude immigrants from Austria. Moreover, the chart does not include figures from the Marienwerder District Government, which apparently did not systematically keep track of the religion of the individuals it naturalized. Since approximately one fourth of the naturalizations granted in Prussia in this period were in the Marienwerder district, this means that the table significantly understates the true figures.

Polish immigrants were welcomed by landowners. The Oppeln District Government noted that 'the Polish immigrant is a powerful man, used to obedience. When he is tolerated this attitude remains as long as he fears that he can be expelled'.[61]

An unscientific sampling of naturalization petitions from Polish farm workers in the second half of the 1860s and early 1870s indicates that naturalization was commonly granted when the individual's employers supported the application. Almost always the only references provided for

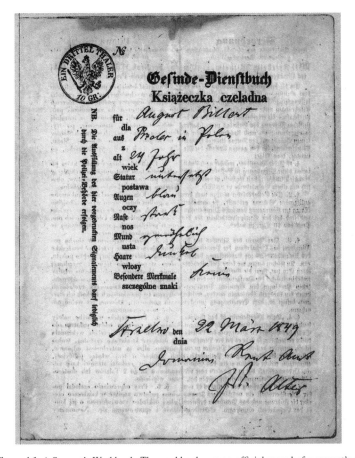

Figure 4.1 A Servant's Workbook. The workbook was an official record of a servant's or laborer's employment history. The laws of various German states required both native and foreign servants and laborers to keep such workbooks. In some cases these requirements remained in effect until the end of the First World War. Employers' evaluations in this passport-like document often formed the basis for official decisions about whether to grant naturalization petitions. This example was found in the archival records of naturalization petitions in the District Government of Bromberg, in the Prussian province of Posen, and was begun in 1849. The workbook pictured here is written in both German and Polish. The cover page, illustrated here, provides a description of the individual whose record it contains. Photographs were not yet employed. After stating the individual's name and place of birth, it gives the age, stature (here not as a numerical measurement, but as a description – in this case, short and stocky or muscular), color of the eyes, shape of the nose and mouth, color of the hair, and any other noticeable features. This workbook belonged to August Billert. The picture is taken from GStA PK, HA XVI (Posen), Rep. 30, Abt. 1, Nr. 1048, Bd. X. Reprinted with the permission of the Geheimes Staatsarchiv Preussischer Kulturbesitz.

Tag Dzień des wstąpienia Dienst. w eintritts. służbę.	Name Nazwisko der Dienstherrschaft. państwa.	Der Inhaber ist Właściciel został angenommen przyjęty		Tag Dzień des wyjścia Dienst. ze anstritts. służby.
		auf na welche jaki Zeit? czas?	in w jakim welcher Ei stosunku genschaft? służbowym?	
Den 1ten Tag *[illegible]* 1848.	*Mühlenbesitzer Frie drich Vilinger zu Bronislaw*	*1ten Januar 1849.*	*[illegible]*	*Den 1ten Januar 1849*
1/1. 49	*Müller Patzer in Góra*	*1/2.*	*[illegible]*	*D. 26 December 1849*
Den 26 December 1849	*Müller Meyer in Góra*	*2 J*	*als Knecht*	*D. 20/12 51.—*

Figure 4.1 continued. The employer and/or the police were required to provide the following information (reading from left to right): the day employment began; the name of the employer, the agreed upon period of employment; the capacity in which the individual was employed (here as Knecht, or servant or laborer); the last day of employment; the police office that granted the individual a visa and where the police records were located; remarks

of police officials; and the employer's evaluation of the conduct of the employee and an explanation of the reasons for the end of the employment relationship. The evaluation of Billert in the far right column, at the top, states: "He hopes to find a better position, his conduct was from every point of view good."

farm workers were the evaluations in the Gesinde-Buch, the passport-like document that contained the written evaluation of the individual's work by his employer. Asked for information about Johann Jankowski, who applied to be naturalized in 1870, a communal official in Marienwerder replied that 'he has worked here for the past ten years as a stableboy and nothing derogatory is known about his conduct'. Such a judgment was enough to justify naturalization in this and numerous similar cases. This is not to suggest that employers always readily supported naturalization. As the District Government of Oppeln noted, there was always a danger that Poles would cease to be subservient when expulsion no longer could be threatened. Naturalization was a carrot to be held in front of workers for as long as possible. But if someone had worked in Prussia for a long time, was a steady and desirable employee and wished to marry, many employers apparently were willing to support naturalization petitions. The records of several Landräte in the Danzig district record that Polish immigrants often sought naturalization in order to obtain permission to marry. So, in a typical formulation in a letter from 4 July 1870, one man wrote (or rather, since he was illiterate, someone wrote on his behalf): 'in 1868 I left my Fatherland Poland and came here. I have worked ever since, do not desire to return home, and wish to marry and become a Prussian subject'.[62]

The modestly liberal spirit of the 1860s and 1870s was reflected in, among other ways, the lessening of discrimination against Jews. The requirement in the Untertanengesetz that the Interior Minister approve all naturalizations of Jews was suspended by the administration in December 1848, as a consequence of a law of 6 April 1848 that made the enjoyment of civic rights independent of an individual's religious faith. It was reinstated in the 1850s, and apparently enforced with more animus than had been general before 1848.[63] For example, the District Government of Trier rejected the naturalization petition of Gottlieb Rosenburger in 1854, despite the approval of the elected council of the local community and the long residence of Rosenburger in the community, on the grounds that 'the settlement of Jews in villages is never desirable, because the well known business methods of Jews lead only too frequently to the impoverishment of those living in the countryside'.[64] In December 1860 the Interior Ministry again changed direction, ending the Minister's personal involvement in the naturalization of Jews.[65] When the Untertanengesetz was applied to the entire North German Confederation in 1870, and in 1871 to all the states of the new Reich, the provision requiring that the Interior Minister personally approve the naturalization of Jews was dropped.[66]

Despite the change made in 1860 the naturalization statistics suggest that fears of the type expressed by the Trier District Government continued to restrict significantly the number of Jews accepted as new citizens. The number of Jews naturalized each year in the eastern part of the monarchy jumped from virtually nil in the 1850s to as many as sixty in the 1860s.[67] This was liberalization, but of a very modest sort. Only after 1871 did Jewish naturalizations reach significant levels. (Table 4.3 depicts the naturalization of Jews from Russian Poland from 1849 to 1880.) While statistics regarding the number of individuals who applied for naturalization were generally not kept, a study of naturalization practices in Breslau has found that between 1865 and 1875, of the 62 Jews who petitioned for naturalization 56 were supported by the Magistracy and approved by the District Government.[68]

For Poles the liberal era came to an end shortly after the founding of the national state. Bismarck viewed Prussian Poles as a potential fifth column. In 1873 he ordered District Governments to deny all naturalization petitions from Poles, Austrian as well as Russian, 'in which there was

Table 4.3 Naturalizations of Jews in Prussia, 1849 to 1880

Year	*Naturalizations granted to immigrants from the Polish provinces of Russia who were Jewish (excluding data from the Marienwerder district government)*	*Year*	*Naturalizations granted to immigrants from the Polish provinces of Russia who were Jewish (excluding data from the Marienwerder district government)*
1849	12	1865	15
1850	0	1866	31
1851	0	1867	19
1852	0	1868	29
1853	0	1869	5
1854	1	1870	13
1855	2	1871	61
1856	1	1872	234
1857	2	1873	295
1858	3	1874	153
1859	0	1875	110
1860	13	1876	34
1861	11	1877	51
1862	60	1878	61
1863	23	1879	80
1864	31	1880	26

Source: GStA PK, HA I, Rep. 77, Tit. 1176, Nr. 2a, Adh. I. The limitations noted with respect to Table 4.2 apply here as well.

not complete confidence that they kept away from politics'.[69] A similar request was made of other federal states in the new Reich. Bismarck's anti-Catholic campaign of the 1870s, the Kulturkampf, was directed with special vigor at the Poles. The number of naturalizations of Poles was significantly lower in the 1870s than in the previous decade.[70]

Even after the 1850s, rules governing local residence rights remained an important instrument of social control with respect to both aliens and German citizens. Carl Zuckmayer's famous play *The Captain of Köpenick*, first produced in 1931, satirized Wilhelmine society's awe of an officer's uniform, and also castigated harsh police controls on residence. Based on a true story that took place in 1906, Zuckmayer described the attempt of a man who had been expelled from Berlin because of his criminal record to steal a residence permit from the local police station by masquerading as an army officer, and the magical way in which the sight of the uniform produced obedience.[71]

Bavaria employed residence rules with special severity. In the 1860s officials might still expel a servant girl from a city at the request of the family that had employed her and had developed an aversion to her, or expel a woman who had become an embarrassment to a civil servant whose child she had born.[72] After 1870 such arbitrary use of state powers of expulsion appears to have diminished, but it remained the norm well into the twentieth century that Bavarians convicted of crimes such as begging, theft or prostitution were forced to live for a year or two in the communities in which they were born after serving their (sometimes much shorter) jail sentences. It is unclear whether the chief purpose was to relieve the communities where the crimes had been committed of the burden of the presence of criminals, to enforce on local communities their obligation to police the conduct of their current and former residents, or to further punish criminals by shaming them. Bavaria regularly expelled from its territory non-Bavarians who had committed crimes in Bavaria, including individuals from other German states, after they had served their prison sentences.[73]

German national feeling in the pre-1848 era, and through the 1860s, was in fact far more accepting of ethnic difference than it was to become. It is true that many of the revolutionaries of 1848 were not free from chauvinistic attitudes regarding the relative merits of German culture, as Günter Wollstein and others have shown. And perhaps these attitudes would have hardened when confronted with the realities of ethnic tensions in Central Europe even had the 1848 revolution been successful. What is clear is that the exclusionary policies inaugurated by Bismarck in the 1880s represented a dramatic change from those practiced by Prussia in the 1860s and early 1870s, and, a fortiori, from the plans of the leaders of the 1848 revolution. The next chapter explores the reasons for this transformation.

Notes

1. Some of the delegates to the 1848 Parliament were not averse to the use of compulsion as an instrument of Germanization. Günter Wollstein, *Das "Großdeutschland" der Paulskirche: Nationale Ziele in der Bürgerlichen Revolution von 1848/49* (Droste, 1977), p. 172.

2. As Oswald Hauser argues. See his 'Polen und Dänen im Deutschen Reich', in T. Schieder and E. Deuerlein (eds), *Reichsgründung 1870/71: Tatsachen Kontroversen Interpretationen* (Seewald, 1970), p. 300.

3. Max Wirth, *Geschichte der Handelskrisen* (Frankfurt am Main, 1858), p. 348, quoted in Theodore Hamerow, *The Social Foundations of German Unification, 1858–1871* (Princeton University Press, 1969), p. 5.

4. Tellkampf from Breslau, *SBF*, vol. 1, p. 763 (6 July 1848). The description of Tellkampf's career, and of the careers of other deputies discussed below, is based on Heinrich Best and Wilhelm Weege, *Biographisches Handbuch der Abgeordneten der Frankfurter Nationalversammlung 1848/49* (Drost, 1996).

5. Gulden from Zweibrücken: *SBF*, vol. 1, p. 768 (6 July 1848).

6. Vischer from Tübingen: Ibid., vol. 1, p. 45 (19 May 1848).

7. Rationale of the Economics Committee for its Proposal Regarding Freedom of Movement. Ibid., vol. 1, p. 690 (3 July 1848).

8. Lette from Berlin: Ibid., vol. 1, p. 777 (6 July 1848).

9. Hildebrand from Marburg (for the Economics Committee): Ibid., vol. 1, p. 756 (6 July 1848).

10. Tellkampf from Breslau: Ibid., vol. 1, p. 763 (6 July 1848).

11. Reichensperger from Trier: Ibid., vol. 2, p. 870 (13 July 1848).

12. Hermann from Munich: Ibid., vol. 1, p. 757 (6 July 1848). Hermann spoke for the minority of the Economics Committee.

13. This language is taken from the Constitutional Committee's rationale for its plan to create freedom of movement. Ibid., vol. 1, p. 684 (3 July 1848).

14. Ibid., vol. 2, pp. 1077–82 (20 July 1848).

15. Bernhard Eisenstück from Chemnitz, a leading member of the Economics Committee, claimed that the Economics Committee had no intention of requiring communities to open their poor chests to outsiders. Ibid., vol. 1, p. 760 (6 July 1848).
16. Werner from Koblenz: Ibid., vol. 1, p. 761 (6 July 1848).
17. W. Jordan from Berlin: Ibid., vol. 1, p. 737 (4 July 1848). And even more explicitly Tellkampf from Breslau, who proposed that a German citizen be defined as 'every man who was born and grew up within the territory of the German Federal State, or who has satisfied the requirements of a forthcoming law governing naturalization'. Ibid., vol. 1, p. 740 (4 July 1848). The biographical information on Jordan is from Frank Eyck, *The Frankfurt Parliament* (St Martin's Press, 1968), pp. 182–4, 276–9, 284, 296.
18. The decision of the Frankfurt Parliament to grant full economic, civic, and political rights to Jews was bitterly resisted by a small minority of delegates, and a significant proportion of those who supported the emancipation of Jews probably were far from willing to consider any Jews as fully German. B. Vick, *Defining Germany: The 1848 Frankfurt Parliamentarians and National Identity* (Harvard University Press, 2002), pp. 83–109. Many Catholic delegates accepted the emancipation of Jews as an unfortunate sacrifice, one required to protect their own confession from discrimination. Ibid., pp. 106–7.
19. Ibid., pp. 110–38.
20. Günter Wollstein's *Das 'Großdeutschland' der Paulskirche* illustrates, in the context of disputes over territory with Danes, Poles, Czechs, and other ethnic groups, the often chauvinistic views of many 1848 revolutionaries.
21. Stanley Pech, *The Czech Revolution of 1848* (University of North Caroline Press, 1969), pp. 80–2, 133.
22. Gillis, *The Prussian Bureaucracy in Crisis* (Stanford University Press, 1971), pp. 139–40.
23. Bernhard Becker, *Die Reaktion in Deutschland gegen die Revolution von 1848 beleuchtet in sozialer, nationaler und staatlicher Beziehung*, 3rd edn (W. Bracke Jr., 1873), p. 466.
24. *Verordnung betreffend die Errichtung von Gewerberäthen und verschiedene Abänderungen der allgemeinen Gewerbeordnung* of 9 February 1849, Section 67. *GPS*, p. 108. This restriction was limited to journeymen coming from states that did not provide reciprocity to Prussian journeymen, and seems to have been designed in part to force freedom of movement à la Prusse on all German states.

Initially, however, few German states made the sought-after change, and the law simply became a vehicle for excluding outsiders deemed as a class to be politically dangerous.

25. Comments of Deputy Hans Victor von Unruh, *Stenographische Berichte über die Verhandlungen des Reichstags des Norddeutschen Bundes*, First Legislative Period, 1867, vol. 1 (21 October 1867), p. 558. von Unruh, the son of a Prussian Major General, was for a brief period in 1848 President of the Prussian National Assembly.

26. Remarks of Eduard Lasker, Ibid., p. 559.

27. Dirk Blasius, *Ehescheidung in Deutschland, 1794–1945* (Vandenhoeck & Ruprecht, 1987), p. 82.

28. T. Nipperdey, *Deutsche Geschichte 1800–1866*, 6th edn (Beck, 1993), p. 110.

29. In a study of a sample of Bremen families from the early nineteenth-century Peter Marschalck has shown that roughly 40 percent of first-born children were conceived before the marriage took place, while some 8 percent were born out of wedlock. Peter Marschalck, 'Demographische Aspekte der Familienbildung in Bremen in der ersten Hälfte des 19. Jahrhunderts', in Jürgen Schlumbohm (ed.), *Familie und Familienlosigkeit: Fallstudien aus Niedersachsen und Bremen vom 15. bis 20. Jahrhundert* (Hahnsche Buchhandlung, 1993), p. 210. The prevalence of wilde Ehen in poorer parts of society is discussed in Karin Gröwer, '"Wilde Ehen" in den hansestädtischen Unterschichten 1814–1871', *Archiv für Sozialgeschichte* 38 (1998), pp. 1–22; and Lynn Abrams, 'Concubinage, Cohabitation and the Law: Class and Gender Relations in Nineteenth Century Germany', *Gender & History* 5 (1993), pp. 81–100.

30. In naturalization petitions there are occasionally veiled or open references to the desire to avoid the shame of an out-of-wedlock birth. See, for example, the letter of 11 July 1860 from the Police Directory of Barmen and Elberfeld to the District Government in Düsseldorf, in Nordrhein-Westfälisches Hauptstaatsarchiv Düsseldorf (NWH), Regierung Düsseldorf (RD), Nr. 11979, urging rapid action on a naturalization petition due to 'unexpected intervening conditions'; Letter of 18 September 1865 from Hermann Lowenstamm to the District Government in Marienwerder, asking for rapid approval of his naturalization petition to avoid shaming his fiancée, GStA PK HA XIV, A205, Nr. 2.

31. Blasius, *Ehescheidung in Deutschland*, pp. 88; Letter of 13 March 1862 from the Landrat of Strasburg to the District Government in Marienwerder asking for rapid naturalization of several individuals

who wished to marry or, if this were not possible, permission to permit the marriages.

32. *Cirkular-Verfügung . . . wegen des Verfahrens gegen Ausländer, die in diesseitigen Staaten in Konkubinat leben* of 5 November 1852, *MBiV* 12 (1852), p. 293.
33. M. Walker, *German Home Towns* (Cornell University Press, 1971), pp. 73–7.
34. Westphalen to Friedrich Wilhelm IV, 14 December 1853, GStA PK, HA I, Rep. 89, Nr. 15704, pp. 28–30.
35. Petition of 29 August 1859, from Heinrich Schmidt to the Ministry of the Interior, NWH, RD, Nr. 582.
36. Letter of 16 April 1851 from the Oberpräsident of Posen to the Landräte of the province, in GStA PK, HA XVI, Rep. 30, Abt. I, Nr. 1048, Bd. 10, pp. 80–3.
37. See GStA PK, HA I, Rep. 76IV, Sekt. 1, Abt. XVI, Generalia Nr. 10, Bd. 1. This file contains correspondence regarding numerous instances in which priests and ministers performed marriages for foreigners without the permission required by the law.
38. Bödiker, 'Die Auswanderung und die Einwanderung des preussischen Staates', p. 13. Schleswig is not really comparable, as most of those naturalized were Danes who became Prussians after the conquest of 1864.
39. Report from the Lenneper Kreisblatt of 11 November 1847; letter from Bürgermeister Schall of Remscheid to the District Government of 26 January 1848, both in NWH, RD, Nr. 9157.
40. Letter of Mayor Schall to the District Government, 26 January 1848. Ibid.
41. Letter of 10 July 1851 from the Ministry of the Interior to the Government in Düsseldorf. After much hemming and hawing the Interior Ministry acknowledged, in 1854, that the Gemeinderat was usually not supposed to be consulted. Letter of 17 April 1854 from the Ministry of the Interior to the Government of Düsseldorf. Ibid.
42. *Erlaß an die Königl. Regierung zu N.N., die Zulassung von Ausländern zum Betriebe stehender Gewerbe und die Naturalisations-Anträge ausländischer Gewerbsgehülfen betreffend* of 16 November 1851, *Ministerial-Blatt für die gesammte innere Verwaltung in den Königlich Preussischen Staaten (MBiV)* 12 (1851), pp. 309–10; NWH, RD, Nr. 9157.
43. Letter of 17 February 1853 from the District Government of Düsseldorf to the Mayor of Barmen. Ibid.
44. Letter from the Police Directorship of Elberfeld and Barmen, 26 February 1853, to the District Government in Düsseldorf. Ibid.

45. Letter of 4 December 1852 from the Mayor of Barmen to the District Government in Düsseldorf; Response dated 17 February 1853 from the District Government in Düsseldorf to the Mayor of Barmen; Letter of 26 February 1853 from the Prussian Police Directory of Elberfeld and Barmen to the District Government in Düsseldorf. NWH, RD, Nr. 11979.
46. Letter of 9 December 1857 from the District Government of Düsseldorf to the Ministry of the Interior. Ibid.
47. Letter of 13 January 1858 from the Mayor of Remscheid to the District Government in Düsseldorf; Letter of 25 January 1859 from the City Council of Barmen to the District Government in Düsseldorf. Ibid.
48. Letter of 1 March 1859 from the Mayor of Remscheid to Landrat von Bernuth; Letter of 21 March 1859 from the Mayor of Remscheid to Landrat von Bernuth. Ibid.
49. D. Barclay, *Frederick William IV and the Prussian Monarchy, 1840–1861* (Oxford University Press, 1995), p. 280.
50. Hamerow, *The Social Foundations of German Unification*, p. 374.
51. Letter of 15 March 1860 from the Ministry of the Interior to the Oberpräsident of the Rhine Province. NWH, RD, Nr. 558.
52. *Gesetz, betreffend die Abänderung einiger Bestimmungen der Allgemeinen Gewerbe-Ordnung vom 17. Januar 1845* of 22 June 1861, Article three. *GPS*, pp. 441–5.
53. List of proposed naturalizations submitted by the Magistrate of Lautenberg to the Landrat in Strassburg, 16 February 1865. GStA PK, HA XIV, Rep. 205, Nr. 2.
54. *Erlaß an die Oberpräsidenten zu Schleswig, Hannover und Cassel vom 12. April 1889, betreffend die Eheschließung von Ausländern*, *MBiV* 50 (1889), pp. 118–19. See also pp. 85–6.
55. *Cirkular-Verfügung an sämmtliche Königliche Regierungen und an das Polizei-Präsidium hierselbst, betreffend die Einsendung der Nachweisungen der in Preußen vorgekommenen Ein- und Auswanderungen* of 31 March 1862, *MBiV* 23 (1862), pp. 181–3.
56. Bödiker, 'Die Auswanderung und die Einwanderung des preussischen Staates', p. 1.
57. D. Gosewinkel, *Einbürgern und Ausschließen* (Vandenhoeck & Ruprecht, 2001), pp. 200–11.
58. This agreement did not apply to individuals who were not French citizens. Fritz Stern, *Gold and Iron: Bismarck, Bleichröder, and the Building of the German Empire* (Alfred A. Knopf, 1977), p. 147.
59. For a general description of Prussian policies toward ethnic Poles in this period, see William Hagen, *Germans, Poles, and Jews: The*

Nationality Conflict in the Prussian East, 1772–1914 (Chicago: University of Chigaco Press, 1980), pp. 120–8; W. J. Rose, 'Prussian Poland, 1850–1914', in W.F. Reddaway et al. (eds), *The Cambridge History of Poland From Augustus II to Pilsudski (1697–1935)*, (Cambridge University Press, 1941), pp. 409–31.

60. Decrees of 20 January 1853 and 9 October 1857. NWH, RD, Nr. 9157.

61. Letter from the District Government of Oppeln to the Oberpräsident of Silesia of 9 March 1851. APW, Police Presidium of Breslau, Nr. 341, pp. 49RS, 52–5.

62. Letter from Sokolowski of 4 July 1870. GStA PK, HA XIV (Danzig), Rep. 205, Nr. 16. The petition is signed with an 'X'.

63. *Verordnung über einige Grundlagen der künftigen Preußischen Verfassung* of 6 April 1848, *GPS*, p. 87.

64. Letter of the District Government of Trier to the Ministry of the Interior dated 19 January 1856. GStA PK, HA I Rep. 77, Tit. 227, Nr. 4, Bd. 7, pp. 62RS–3. Letter of the Interior Ministry to the District Government of Trier of 7 February 1856. Ibid., p. 64.

65. Circular from the Minister of the Interior to all District Governments and the Police Präsidium of Berlin, December 1860. GStA PK, HA I, Tit. 227, Nr. 4, Bd. 7, pp. 188–9.

66. In 1869 the North German confederation freed Jews from all the special legal restrictions to which they had previously been subjected. *Gesetz betreffend die Gleichberechtigung der Konfessionen in bürgerlicher und staatsbürgerlicher Beziehung* of 3 July 1869. *RGBl* I, p. 292.

67. These figures are incomplete, as the District Government of Marienwerder was unable to determine the number of Jews and Poles it had naturalized when this data was requested in 1881.

68. Till van Rahden, 'Die Grenze vor Ort – Einbürgerung und Ausweisung ausländischer Juden in Breslau 1860–1918', in *Tel Aviver Jahrbuch für deutsche Geschichte* 27 (1998), pp. 54–5. Petitions were generally forwarded to District Governments with recommendations by Landräte, which were in turn based on opinions expressed by estate owners and town officials. The Landräte often did not retain records regarding individuals whose petitions they refused to support, and the same was also true at the local level.

69. Letter of 17 March 1873 from Bismarck to the District Governments, in GStA PK, HA I, Rep. 77, Tit. 1176, Nr. 2a, Bd. 4, p. 57RS.

70. There is some reason to wonder, however, about whether the table significantly understates the number of Poles naturalized in the 1870s. Compare the figures in the charts with those published

in 'Der Erwerb und Verlust der Reichs- und Staatsangehörigkeit im preussischen Staat während des Jahres 1874', *Zeitschrift des Königlich Preussischen Statistischen Bureaus* 15 (1875), p. 295; 'Der Erwerb und Verlust der Reichs- und Staatsangehörigkeit im preussischen Staat während des Jahres 1875', *Zeitschrift des Königlich Preussischen Statistischen Bureaus* 16 (1876), p. 83. These also are not conclusive.

71. The historical background of the play is described in Hartmut Scheible, *Erläuterungen und Dokumente: Carl Zuckmayer, Der Hauptmann von Köpenick* (Philipp Reclam, 1977) and Benjamin Carter Hett, 'The "Captain of Köpenik" and the Transformation of German Criminal Justice, 1891–1914', *Central European History* 36 (March 2003): 1–43.

72. In 1868 Ursula Mayer appealed to Ludwig II to reverse her one-year expulsion from Rosenheim, which she stated was the result of her employer's wife's jealousy of her. 'Because a jealous woman has testified against me, and the local officials and court officials did not see other grounds for the conflict between the Mühlberg couple . . . the servant must be made to sacrifice her reputation, and cloud her already dark future.' Petition of Ursula Mayer to Ludwig II dated 20 February 1868. BHM, Interior Ministry, Nr. 46204. Another petition from the same file of appeals to the king, also dating from 1868, is from a single woman expelled from Munich because she had given birth to the child of a (married) civil servant, and her presence had become unpleasant for him. Petition of Theresa Furcht to Ludwig II of 24 February 1868. Ibid.

73. Stadtarchiv Munich, RA 48062–48111 are a small sample of the hundreds of files in the Munich city archives that describe these expulsions. One example will serve to show the severity with which the Bavarian government carried out these measures. In 1881 the Munich District Government ordered Katherina Achter to leave Munich for two years, to live in her birthplace, following her conviction for theft. Achter had been sentenced to jail for four months. Achter's husband, a 64-year-old cabbie, protested vigorously. 'Have the police perhaps overlooked that I am a tax-paying citizen and may demand from the state that it permit my wife to be at my side . . .' The appeal was rejected. Appeal of 22 June 1881, Stadtsarchiv Munich, RA 48096.

Part II
Citizenship Policy as a Political Weapon, 1871–1918

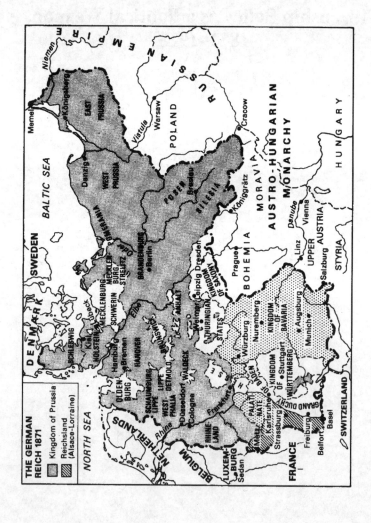

Map 5.1 The German Reich in 1871. From Gordon Craig, *Germany: 1866–1945* (1980), vi. Reprinted by permission of Oxford University Press.

−5−

Bismarck Punishes his Opponents

Lady Emily Russell, the wife of the British ambassador to Germany, wrote to Queen Victoria in 1880 that Bismarck '[has] his own way in *everything*; and the great Chancellor revels in the absolute power he has acquired and does as he pleases'. He had, she reported, turned the government into 'a Ministry of Clerks ... who do as they are told'.[1] From 1871 until his ouster by Wilhelm II in 1890 Bismarck was both Chancellor of the German state and Minister-President of Prussia, in both capacities responsible only to the monarch. The domestic and foreign policies of the German state in this period bear the stamp of Bismarck's calculations of the national interest, of his defense of the authoritarian political institutions he had helped create, and of his own combative personality. He was used to overriding opposition through tactics that combined surprise and violence, intimidation and seduction. Certainly Bismarck operated within the constraints placed on him by domestic interests and beliefs and foreign power. But these constraints left him considerable independence.[2]

It was Bismarck, in his capacity as Prussian Minister-President, who in March 1885 ordered the expulsion of foreign Jews and Poles living in the eastern provinces of Prussia and, by implication, an end to further Jewish and Polish immigration. Between 1885 and 1888 Prussia pushed some 20,000 foreign Poles, as well as a further 10,000 foreign Jews, across its eastern borders.[3] The expulsions of the Jews originated in Bismarck's fear of future Jewish immigration. The pogroms that followed the assassination of Tsar Alexander II in March 1881 had led tens of thousands of Jews to flee Russia. Bismarck feared that this exodus would continue, for there were in 1881 some five million Jews in the Russian Empire.[4] The deportation of foreign Jews was a signal that Jewish refugees from Russia were not welcome in Germany. It also reflected the increasingly anti-Semitic climate of German society.

The expulsion of foreign Poles, most of whom were farm laborers, was based more on long-term fears regarding the growth of the Polish population of Prussia and the apparent failure of Prussian efforts to

Germanize this group. Although most of the state administration, as well as the landowners of the eastern provinces of Prussia, considered Polish farm workers vital to the economy, for Bismarck the political interests of the state in limiting the number of ethnic Poles in Prussia took priority over private economic interests, even those of the landowning elite to which he himself belonged. There was also a foreign-policy aspect, as frequently encountered in Bismarck's policies. Bismarck feared that the very liberal policy followed by Austria-Hungary in the largely Polish province of Galicia, a policy that permitted the Polish majority in the province a significant degree of cultural and political autonomy, would lead Prussian Poles to seek similar conditions, and that this autonomy would necessarily end in a loss of state control over the largely Polish parts of Prussia.[5] Prussian policy had to be especially rigorous to suppress these hopes. Bismarck also feared that France might find Polish nationalist agitation useful in creating an anti-German coalition, and that Russia might be persuaded to join this coalition.[6] He hoped that anti-Polish measures would create a bond with Russia, for Russia ruled its Polish subjects with an iron hand.

The chronology of the expulsion orders suggests that another reason for them, and their immediate cause, was the defeat of the parties on which Bismarck relied in the Reichstag in the national elections held in 1881 and 1884. Bismarck's focus on the urgency of expelling foreigners rose dramatically in the aftermath of each election. Bismarck apparently believed he could improve the fortunes of the government parties by limiting the growth in the number of Jewish and Polish voters – for Poles and Jews generally voted for political parties that were in the opposition – and by arousing public sentiment against these minority groups. It is also possible that he simply sought a target for his frustration. Bismarck's nature was combative, and he had no compunctions about attacking those of his enemies – as he saw them – who seemed most vulnerable. It is hardly a novel observation that Bismarck often interpreted national interests in a way that was compatible with a desire to manipulate the electoral system to his own advantage. The expulsions of foreign Poles and Jews must be seen as having a character similar to that of Bismarck's anti-Catholic measures, the Kulturkampf, and the laws that repressed the organizations and activities of the Socialist Party.

To what extent did the expulsions also reflect social and cultural forces or currents not specific to Germany? Can they be understood as a product of the racism and nationalism (and anti-Semitism) that were infecting many Western societies, or of more amorphous forces of 'modernization'? Racism explained and justified admirably the empires that Europeans had created around the world, and it was therefore pervasive in European societies. Citizenship policy in the modest German empire begun in 1884 in Africa and the South Pacific reflected this pan-European racism. Between 1905 and 1912 German colonial governors introduced bans on official recognition of marriages between Germans and the indigenous peoples, to prevent the development of a 'mixed-race' group of German citizens.[7] While the peoples of Eastern Europe had not been colonized, the industrial revolution had created a sizable gap in prosperity between Eastern and Western Europe. This gap led some West Europeans to consider themselves racially superior to Slavs and other East European ethnic groups. One can also ask whether the impulse to control immigration more tightly had any relationship to efforts by Germany and other states to regulate and reform their societies in new ways. In the late nineteenth and early twentieth centuries various Western states, foremost among them Germany, enacted laws that protected workers, and created welfare, public hygiene, health care and pension programs.

These questions are prompted in part by the reflection that restrictions on immigration were imposed or considered by various Western countries in the period between the 1880s and the First World War. But in none of the other major Western nations did programs of exclusion from citizenship along ethnic lines reach the proportions that they assumed in Germany, at least until the First World War. The exclusionary measures that most closely resembled those adopted by Bismarck were found in the United States, which in 1882 effectively closed its borders to Chinese immigration. And one can compare Bismarck's employment of ethnically exclusive citizenship policies to prevent some members of disfavored ethnic groups from having access to the ballot with the way in which white Americans used legal chicanery and extra-legal violence to prevent African Americans from exercising their formal right to vote. But it was only during the First World War, and in its immediate aftermath, that the United States imposed tight restrictions on immigration from Europe. In the United Kingdom, efforts to limit immigration – and in particular Russian-Jewish immigration – began in the 1880s, although it was only in 1905 that Parliament first adopted very modest controls. As in the United States, the era of the First World War was a turning point in British policy. From 1889 France compelled the children of immigrants to become full citizens – that is, it responded to immigration by compelling legal integration in French society. Throughout this period, and through the 1920s, France remained open to immigration.[8] In Austria-Hungary, Emperor Franz Joseph and the government of Prime Minister Taafe

(1879–1893) opposed, with mixed success, anti-Semitic agitation aimed at hindering the migration of Jews from the Austrian province of Galicia to Vienna.[9] This very rough comparison suggests that the forces that led to the development of exclusionary policies were certainly not limited to Germany, but also that, for the reasons explored below, neither can they be seen simply as a necessary corollary of the development of the nation-state or of the racism prevalent in European societies.

The expulsion of foreign Poles and Jews, and the tightening of access to citizenship by members of these groups, was part of a much larger change in Bismarck's political course. At the end of the 1870s Bismarck made the Conservatives rather than the National Liberals the principal government party. He started to back away from his anti-Catholic campaign, creating the possibility of a working relationship with the Catholic Center Party. He outlawed many socialist organizations. Bismarck did not bring the new orientation of the state into being on his own. The economic depression that started in 1873 had changed the national mood. Economic liberalism fell out of favor. The late 1870s and early 1880s saw a palpable increase in anti-Semitism in many parts of society, in part as a consequence of the economic depression, in part as a result of jealousy and fear of German Jews' comparative economic and social success. This is the backdrop and larger stage on which the development of naturalization policies were played out.

Fears of Poles and Jews

Bismarck's belief that many Prussian Poles were disloyal to Germany was not entirely without foundation, although his own policies significantly sharpened Polish alienation from the state. After 1849 many Prussian Poles were represented in the Prussian Parliament and, later, in the Reichstag, by the Polish Party, the Kolo Polski. The leader of the Party in the Prussian Landtag, Kazimierz Kantak, asserted in 1877 – admittedly after the experience of the Kulturkampf had radicalized Polish national feeling – that 'all Poles hope for and expect national independence . . . We believe in, we hope for and we pray for the restoration of Poland, for Poland is our faith, our hope, and our love'.[10] Russian Poles had undertaken armed rebellions in 1830 and 1863. An 1846 plot involving rebellion in all three parts of occupied Poland had been nipped in the bud. In 1848 Prussian Poles had created a Polish militia and appeared on the path to secession, an initiative that was repressed by force.[11] The examples of Italian and German unification undoubtedly gave hope to nationalist Poles. On the other hand, there was after 1871 no imminent danger of a rebellion.[12] Expressions of hope for a Polish state can be compared with Socialists' hope for a revolution. Had the power of the Prussian or German states been seriously shaken, Polish nationalist sentiment would likely have led to rebellion, but otherwise it was compatible with law-abiding conduct.

Bismarck's attack on the Catholic Church, which began in 1871, radicalized most Prussian Poles. The Archbishop (from 1874 Cardinal) of Gnesen-Posen, Miecislaus Johann Ledóchowski, was imprisoned for two years after he promoted resistance to a law requiring religious instruction in school to take place in German rather than Polish and then refused to resign from his position.[13] Hundreds of priests were imprisoned or expelled. And these are just examples of the measures Bismarck employed, and give a sense of why the Kulturkampf so deeply alienated Prussian Poles from the state.

The failure of Prussian efforts to force its Polish minority to surrender its distinct cultural identity was exacerbated, from Bismarck's point of view, by the unfavorable demographic trends in the eastern provinces that began in the 1870s. In a May 1885 speech in the Prussian Lower House Interior Minister Robert von Puttkamer presented evidence that in Posen the Polish population had grown by 10 percent from 1870 to 1880, while the German population had increased only by 1.9 percent. 'The Polish element, supported by migration from the East, will in the next decades likely . . . push back the German element in the border provinces of the monarchy', Puttkamer told the chamber.[14] Bismarck clearly feared that these trends would lead to pressure to grant the largely Polish districts greater autonomy or even independence. 'The Poles can say . . . "Our Flag is advancing",' Bismarck told the Prussian Lower House in 1886.[15]

In almost all respects the demographic, economic, cultural and political profile of German Jews stood in sharp contrast to that of the German Poles. The Jewish population was growing more slowly than that of Germany as a whole, although the increasing concentration of Jews in the major cities, and especially in Berlin, in many ways made them more visible to those running the German state. German Jews played leading roles in the commercial sector of the economy and were, on average, wealthier than other Germans. They attended universities in disproportionate numbers, and the same applied to the numbers of Jews in professions like law, medicine and journalism. Unlike most Poles, German Jews avidly sought cultural integration into German life. But the high level of Jewish integration prompted more hostility than Polish efforts to remain separate.

Fritz Stern has amply demonstrated in his account of the relationship between Bismarck and his Jewish banker, Gerson Bleichröder, that Bismarck shared much of the contempt with which Junkers as a class viewed Jews. He despised the leading liberal Jewish Reichstag members, Ludwig Bamberger and Eduard Lasker, and expressed this dislike through anti-Jewish slurs.[16] On the other hand, Bismarck treated almost all those around him with contempt. He was willing at times, before the late 1870s, to champion Jewish rights. It was with his approval that the Reichstag of the North German Confederation eliminated all discrimination based on confession, in 1869.[17] The measures Bismarck took in the 1880s to stop further Jewish immigration reflected a hardening of his own anti-Jewish views and, more importantly, political calculations about how to appeal to voters.

Popular novels clarify both the attitudes to which Bismarck appealed and perhaps also his own views regarding Jews and Poles. Gustav Freytag's *Debit and Credit* (*Soll und Haben*), first published in 1855, is a leading example. The book was one of the most widely read novels in Germany in the second half of the nineteenth century. By 1871 it had gone through 15 editions, by 1890 36 and by 1922 114.[18] The novel attempted to reconcile two groups that had for the most part opposed each other during the 1848 revolution (which Freytag was careful not to mention), the middle class and the landed nobility. The instrument of reconciliation was what Freytag described as a common devotion to honest industriousness, a sphere far from politics. 'This novel', a prefatory quotation stated, 'should find the German nation where its virtues are, namely, at its work.'[19]

The main foil to German honesty and humility and industriousness was the Jew. The hero, Anton Wohlfart, and the anti-hero, the Jew Veitel Itzig, are both young men training to be merchants in Silesia. But here the similarity ends. Whereas Wohlfart is noble, honest, courageous and modest, Itzig is a scoundrel, the devil in human form. Wohlfart's Christian employer primarily buys and ships goods, while the merchant for whom Itzig works focuses on money lending, generally to those in trouble and at high interest rates. With one exception all the major Jewish figures in the novel share Itzig's characteristics: his cowardice, his dirtiness, his dishonesty, his dangerous cleverness and constant scheming, his sycophancy to superiors, in short, his grotesqueness, in appearance and character. For most Jews, Freytag suggested, education and manners and friendliness were mere veneer. Freytag's Jews are not merely contemptible, but dangerous. Itzig 'had the virtue of never tiring . . . he would run after every penny, was as happy as a king at every conquered thaler, and shook off every curse – of which he heard many – like a poodle shakes off blows'. Jews' indefatigable energy was placed in the service of their overweening ambition. The very honesty and naiveté of many of the German characters makes them vulnerable to Jewish business methods. For Jews business is a form of swindle and theft.[20]

While Freytag's venom is reserved primarily for Jews, Polish defects provide a second basis on which the German nation 'is helped to find itself in its virtues'. A revolution in Poland breaks out. 'The people on the other side of the border, aroused by old memories and by the landowners, had risen up, and bands marauded along the border, led by fanatical priests, holding travelers and goods, plundering and burning . . .' Freytag puts his views in the mouth of Schrötter, the head of Wohlfart's merchant house. 'There is no race that is less well equipped to make progress, to acquire humanity and education through its capital, than the Slavic . . . As if nobles and serfs can be a state!' But if the Poles are to be pitied, Freytag suggests little grounds for hatred. The problem is that they lack a middle class, and tend to disorder, not that they are essentially evil.[21] They are unfortunate, not dangerous.

The anti-Semitic prejudices that Freytag's novel articulated hardened and took new political forms in the 1880s. Beginning in 1880 German anti-Semites circulated a petition urging that Jewish immigration and Jews' access to positions of power be restricted. The petition, which was presented to Bismarck in April 1882, garnered 225,000 signatures, most from northern and eastern Prussia.[22] Fear of Jewish success and power was the leitmotif.

> In all districts of Germany the conviction has prevailed that the growth of the Jewish element contains most serious dangers for our nation. Everywhere that Christian and Jew enter into social relations we see the Jew as the master, and the indigenous Christian population in the position of servants. The Jew plays only a very modest part in the hard labor of the great mass of our nation . . . but the fruit of the work is earned above all by the Jew . . . Not only do the proudest palaces of our great cities belong to Jewish owners, whose fathers or grandfathers crossed our Fatherland's borders as peddlers, but even the ownership of land . . . is falling more and more into Jewish hands.[23]

The petition expressed in a compressed form common stereotypes and fears, some new, others quite ancient. It echoed the main themes of an article published in 1879 by the prominent nationalist historian Heinrich von Treitschke, the editor of the respected journal *Preußische*

Jahrbücher. Treitschke had warned that Jewish immigrants from Eastern Europe would come to play a dominant role in the German economy, as had, he implied, earlier Jewish immigrants.[24]

The anti-Semitic aspects of naturalization policies mimicked on the national level the 'no-Jews' clauses introduced in the governing charters of many German social and political groups in the 1890s. Examples include the Agrarian League (the Bund der Landwirte, founded in 1893 with a charter excluding Jews), the National Union of Commercial Employees (the Deutschnationaler Handlungsgehilfenverband, founded with a charter excluding Jews in 1893), and the student Burschenschaften, or fraternities (which adopted a rule excluding Jews in 1896).[25] On the other hand, the ever more strenuous efforts of the Prussian administration to keep foreign Jews from becoming German citizens, as well as the exclusionary rules of a range of groups inside Germany, also reflected the fact that many of the older barriers to Jewish integration into German society, formal and informal, had disappeared or diminished in importance.[26] Perhaps the single most significant indication of the social acceptance by Jews on the part of at least some Christian Germans comes from the statistics regarding intermarriage. Between 1910 and 1913, 12 percent of German Jews married Christians, roughly double the percentage of a generation earlier.[27] The Prussian state was not simply following the dominant anti-Semitic mood of the country.

Excluding Foreign Poles and Jews

Bismarck first proposed restricting Jewish immigration into Prussia in May 1881. The immediate cause was not the anti-Semites' petition but the increase in Jewish emigration from Russia. On 13 March 1881 Russian populists assassinated Tsar Alexander II. Jews played an important role in the populist movement, although they were not strongly represented in its terrorist wing. The assassination sparked a wave of anti-Jewish pogroms, which the Russian government did little to stop and which in turn led to increased Jewish emigration. Bismarck reported to the Prussian cabinet on 22 May 1881 that he had met with Interior Minister Puttkamer to make sure that the state would do its utmost to prevent the immigration of such 'unwanted elements'. Bismarck pushed Puttkamer during the cabinet meeting to expel all foreigners who 'lived from usury', code words for Jews. The conviction that Jews, and in particular East European Jews, were economic parasites was widely held in the Prussian state administration.[28] Puttkamer argued against mass expulsions, for the moment, and Bismarck, for the moment, was content to accept lesser measures.[29]

The practical consequences of the change in state policy were several. First, in May 1881 Puttkamer issued an edict to the provincial governors in the eastern part of Prussia ordering them to permit the naturalization of Russian subjects only under exceptional circumstances, and then only if this was 'compatible with our state interests or at least in no way disadvantageous'. The order's discussion of which groups were to be permitted to reside in Prussia clarified exactly what the basis of this judgment was to be. 'In particular the residence of such persons who earn their living as farm laborers is in general not to be hindered.' These were commonly Poles. But those who 'make their living by exploiting the neediness or inexperience of Prussian subjects . . . are to be prevented with ruthlessness from further residence in Prussia'.[30] Those who received this missive understood who was meant by this last clause. Second, Puttkamer ordered, on Bismarck's instructions, that statistics be gathered regarding the number of immigrants from Russia who had settled in the eastern territories since 1848, a date chosen because, as Bismarck noted, this was the date the Prussian Interior Minister had first given up personal control over the naturalization of Jews.[31] Once it became clear that not all the District Governments had obtained information regarding the confession of individuals naturalized, the Prussian cabinet ordered a revision of the forms to generate this information, again on Bismarck's orders. Bismarck in fact insisted that this information be collected not only by Prussia, but by all the German states. The Bundesrat ordered the collection of this information in December 1882.[32] Third, in October 1881 Bismarck's close associate Christoph von Tiedemann assumed the office of District Government President in Bromberg, in the province of Posen, next to the Russian border. Tiedemann's appointment was made on the basis of an express request from Bismarck.[33] Tiedemann used this position both to carry out the expulsions of foreign Jews with a greater sharpness than previously practiced and to report directly to Bismarck on the situation in the east.

The Reichstag election held on 27 October 1881 was a disaster for Bismarck. The government parties, the National Liberals, Conservatives and Free Conservatives, won 125 seats in the Reichstag, less than a third of the total, whereas in the previous Reichstag they had held 215, a majority. Bismarck identified Jewish voters with the opposition Progressive Party.[34] 'The Jews have always been advocates of the Progressives', he told Puttkamer before the 1884 elections.[35] In fact, most of the Jews sitting in the Reichstag in the 1880s were Progressives, and most Jewish voters did support this party (and its successors) after 1880.[36] Bismarck wanted to intimidate and punish the Progressive Party and its supporters, and, if possible, to prevent the party's constituency from growing. On 11 February 1882 Bismarck wrote to Puttkamer that 'since Jews [who are to be forced out of Russia] *will not be taken back again*, it may be advisable to have the provincial authorities direct their attention in particular to border movements, so that an unusual immigration of a Jewish proletariat is prevented'.[37] In the following months Bismarck repeatedly forwarded to Puttkamer reports from the German ambassador in Russia describing anti-Jewish pogroms and the government's failure to protect the victims.[38]

The pause in 1883 and 1884 in Bismarck's pressure on Puttkamer came to an end after the Reichstag elections of 28 October 1884. Despite the government's strenuous efforts, the results were hardly better than three years earlier. The governing coalition increased its strength by 31 seats, but still remained distinctly in the minority. Three weeks later Bismarck complained sharply to Puttkamer about an incident in Danzig in which forty-two Russian Jews had voted in a race won by the Progressive leader Heinrich Rickert, an opponent of Bismarck and a leader, although not Jewish, of the Association for Defense against Anti-Semitism (Verein zur Abwehr des Antisemitismus).[39] Bismarck ordered the expulsion of those who had voted illegally. In unusually sharp language he also criticized the previous policies of the Interior Minister. This was a distinct reprimand, in German, a 'Rüge'.

> There are at the moment still many Russian subjects in Prussia who appear to have the intention of acquiring German citizenship as a result either of tacit toleration or naturalization. It therefore seems that the deportation measures against Russian subjects, who illegally and, in our opinion, in an undesired way remain in Prussia, have not reached the extent that his Honor [Bismarck] expected following oral discussions with your Excellency on this subject.[40]

Bismarck pressed Puttkamer again on 22 February 1885. But this time he focused less on Russian Jews than on Russian Poles. He sent Puttkamer a long letter from the Minister for Religious Affairs, Gustav von Goßler, describing in detail the growth of the Polish population in the eastern provinces, and the problems created for Germanization efforts in general and German schools in particular. 'I have the hope that Your Excellency, after you have examined the enclosed letter, will share my oft repeated impression that concern for the public good and for the inner peace and security of the state make decisive measures against these evils necessary.'[41] That Bismarck's focus had shifted to Polish immigrants, although Jews remained a target, reflected both the momentarily reduced danger of a vast immigration of Russian Jews and the domestic political threat posed by Poles. There were certainly far more Poles in Prussia than Jews. The 1890 census counted 2,765,440 Prussian Poles, some 9 percent of the population of Prussia.[42] The same census found 372,059 Prussian Jews. While there were no electoral districts in the state whose residents were mostly Jews, there were a number of such Polish districts, and several more that appeared likely to become Polish. Since 1871 roughly fifteen Polish Party delegates had been elected to the Reichstag each term.[43] However, the political dangers posed by Poles and Jews seem to have somehow become connected in Bismarck's mind. After the 1884 elections Bismarck gave instructions that the press friendly to the government should, in its articles on the election, 'emphasize that [during the election] the Jews worked closely with the Poles'.[44]

In the face of Puttkamer's continued reluctance to act with the harshness he desired, even after the election of October 1884, Bismarck made his orders crystal clear and assumed personal responsibility.[45] In a letter of 11 March 1885, which he signed with Goßler, Bismarck proposed making the policy of expulsions one to be decided upon by the cabinet as a whole, and not just by the Interior Minister. And then he again pushed for harsher measures. It was not enough to expel individuals who were politically active.

> We cannot agree that the needs for labor of border regions are more important than the dangers to the state and the political order which a Polonisation of a large part of the Prussian people entails . . . We ask your Excellency whether you should not instruct the Oberpräsidenten that they should in principle and generally prohibit Russian-Polish subjects from residing on our territory, and not only those who are seen as burdensome . . .[46]

This time Puttkamer followed Bismarck's instructions to the letter.[47] The expulsions began within weeks, at the end of April. Even after the expulsions began, however, Puttkamer sought to ameliorate Bismarck's orders. In the meeting of the Prussian Staatsministerium of 24 September 1885 Puttkamer asked whether 'the expulsions were to be carried out against those Galician Jews who, if judged by their language, belong to the German rather than to the Polish nationality'. Bismarck curtly rejected Puttkamer's distinction: 'For us Galicians of either category are Poles'.[48]

Although Bismarck argued to Puttkamer that the expulsions reflected popular sentiment, in fact they had at best modest support outside the office of the Chancellor, at least insofar as they concerned Poles.[49] There had been, it is true, articles in the press following the 1884 elections that warned of the Polish danger, and some of these at least were not planted by the government.[50] But most agricultural interests in the east viewed Polish farm workers as essential to the local economy, and were inclined to complain that there were too few of them.[51] When the expulsions began in earnest, in April 1885, both industrialists and landowners in the eastern provinces of Prussia protested vigorously.[52] Bismarck forced through the expulsions against the will of much of the economic elite of the four eastern provinces.

The most significant critique of the expulsions came from the Reichstag, which voted on 16 January 1886 that 'in their extent and manner [the Prussian actions] . . . do not appear justified and are not compatible with the interests of the citizens of the Reich'.[53] The Center, Progressive, Polish and Socialist parties were the main supporters of the motion. Ludwig von Jazdzewski, the representative of the Polish Party, opened the debate by attacking the expulsions as inhumane and contrary to international law and Prussian treaty obligations. He denied Puttkamer's claims that the growth in the Polish population was to a significant extent the product of immigration, and also that Germany's Polish citizens posed a threat to the state. The Social Democrat delegate Wilhelm Liebknecht termed the expulsions 'an act of barbarism committed in the name of [German] culture'. German patriotism, he told the Reichstag, did not require opposing the Polish desire for a national state. Julius Möller, from the Progressive Party, criticized the expulsions as entirely unnecessary and counterproductive: 'the German nationality has no need for this kind of assistance'. The Center Party leader Ludwig Windthorst also attacked the claim that those who opposed the expulsions were somehow unpatriotic.[54]

In defending the expulsions after the Reichstag censure, Bismarck made little attempt to conceal that one of his main goals was to limit the demographic (and electoral) growth of groups he considered disloyal to the state. In an extraordinarily bitter and threatening speech, Bismarck told the Prussian Lower House on 28 January 1886 that it was the policy of the government to increase the number of those loyal to the Prussian state. This might be accomplished both by

> increasing the German population and reducing the Polish . . . To achieve the last purpose we have no other legal means than the expulsion of those Poles who do not belong to the country and who have no right to be tolerated here. We were convinced that we had enough of our own Poles, and that we had to

reduce the number of Polish agitators by the number of the foreigners who are found here.[55]

Bismarck made much of the possibility that Poles might be used as a fifth column by France in the case of a European war, or that a Polish rebellion might provide an excuse for international intervention. The speech touched only momentarily on the anti-Semitic aspect of the expulsions. Bismarck suggested in very veiled terms that those who opposed his policies belonged to a 'nihilistic fraction' and also deserved expulsion. Bismarck made clear that in his view what made the Polish Party dangerous was that it was one of several opposition parties: it was the parliamentary system, with its possibility of an anti-government majority, that Bismarck feared.[56] Bismarck closed his speech with a discussion of the possibility of sharply reducing the power of the Reichstag, a coup d'état against the constitution.

Bismarck tacitly acknowledged that public debate of the treatment of immigrants might not be in his interests through his efforts to suppress publication of information regarding the naturalization policies of the different German states. The first parliamentary debate regarding the expulsions took place in the Prussian Lower House on 6 May 1885. Three weeks later, on 26 May, Bismarck wrote to Puttkamer asking whether he would agree to ask the Reich statistical office to cease publication of statistics regarding naturalizations, ostensibly to save time and money.[57] On 29 January 1886, two weeks after the Reichstag had condemned the expulsions and the day after Bismarck had defended them in the Prussian Lower House, Bismarck again wrote Puttkamer on this subject, this time with more urgency. 'I allow myself here to confirm', Bismarck stated, 'that this matter will be acted on.'[58] The central statistical commission of the German states considered the Prussian request on 26 February 1886, but refused, by a vote of 9–8, to follow Bismarck's instructions – they had been presented as a technical improvement by Becker, the director of the Reich statistical office.[59] The Bundesrat prevented the publication of the data through the expedient of ordering the different German states to cease collecting the information.[60]

After the Expulsions

The expulsions of 1885 and 1886 established the principle that further Polish and Jewish – 'Russian Jewish' soon became 'Jewish' – immigration was dangerous and to be prevented. They lent this policy the prestige of Bismarck. The very difficulty of carrying out the expulsions led to the development of methods designed to prevent the need to resort to such measures in the future. Firm policies against the naturalization of Poles and Jews, which would serve to deter potential immigration, were among the principal weapons created.

Despite Bismarck's claims that the expulsions were in the long run important to amicable relations with Russia and Austria-Hungary, the measures in fact led to tension. Austria accepted the expellees, but its government was clearly not happy about the sudden impoverishment of a large number of its subjects, a common consequence of the uprooting. Austria needed German diplomatic support, however, and was in no position to make an issue of the matter. Russia took a harder line. In September 1885 Russian border guards began to refuse to accept the formerly Prussian spouses of Russian citizens, and shortly thereafter its own subjects as well.[61] This eventually forced Puttkamer to order a halt to the expulsions. The Russian press called for a suitable response against Germans who lived in Russian Poland. The result was a March 1887 Russian decree ordering the expulsion of foreigners who worked as factory or estate administrators in Russian Poland and prohibiting foreigners from purchasing real estate in Russia's western territories.[62] It is not clear how many Germans actually were expelled pursuant to this law, but the worsening of German-Russian relations that it reflected was clear.

While the Prussian state attempted to prevent all new immigration of Poles and Jews for the remainder of Bismarck's term of office, his forced resignation immediately led to a slackening of the controls he had created. A week after Bismarck's departure on 20 March 1890 the East Prussian Agrarian Association petitioned the new Reich Chancellor and Prussian Minister-President Leo von Caprivi 'to permit Russian workers to be temporarily employed in Prussia for a period adequate for the needs of agriculture'.[63] The situation had become so desperate in the late 1880s that landowning circles near Danzig had given serious consideration to importing laborers from China.[64] Local authorities knowingly permitted the violation of the central government's prohibitions on the employment of Russian Poles. In September 1890 the Interior Ministry consulted with the provincial governors of the four Eastern provinces regarding the advisability of relaxing the border controls. All concurred (with some hesitation on the part of Schlieckmann in East Prussia) that the controls should be relaxed. On 26 November 1890, following a discussion in the Prussian cabinet, the Minister of the Interior instructed the provincial governors of the four eastern provinces to permit Russian migrant laborers (later this was extended to Austrians) to work in Prussia from 1 April to 15 November.

Bismarck's departure also led to serious consideration by the government of relaxing government controls over access to citizenship. In 1892 the Governor of Alsace-Lorraine, the future Chancellor Chlodwig zu Hohenlohe-Schillingsfürst, proposed to Chancellor Caprivi that the citizenship law of 1870 be amended to provide that children born in Alsace-Lorraine – or, alternatively, anywhere in the territory of the German state – to foreigners be considered German citizens. Hohenlohe's proposal was a response to problems faced by the German administration in Alsace and Lorraine, where young men who had not become German citizens often left German territory when they reached military age and then came back when their age made military service unlikely or impossible. The proposal was almost certainly inspired by French legislation adopted in 1889.[65] While Caprivi apparently took the idea seriously, it was killed by the opposition of Count Botho zu Eulenburg, from 1892 to 1894 both Prussian Minister-President and Interior Minister. On 29 March 1894, after surveying the views of the Prussian administration, Eulenburg wrote to Caprivi that the proposal would deprive the administration of a useful tool for dealing with undesirable immigrants. Eulenburg argued that a change in the law would primarily benefit 'the Polish-Russian, Galician, and particularly Jewish proletariat, which crowds over the border . . .'[66]

Although Prussian policies of Germanizing the eastern provinces led to a significant sharpening of tensions between the state and Prussian Poles after the mid-1890s, the demand for foreign workers was so great that the Prussian government chose to continue its policy of permitting Russian Poles to work in Prussia on a seasonal basis. In April 1894 the government extended the policy indefinitely, while at the same time warning that foreign migrants had to be closely watched. In 1898 the Interior Ministry permitted Polish farm workers to remain in Prussia from 1 March to 1 December. In 1900 this was extended to the period between 1 February and 20 December. The numbers involved grew explosively. In 1894 25,403 seasonal workers came to Prussia; in 1905 there were 454,348; in 1914 900,780.[67] After 1905 the solicitation and control of the migrants was no longer primarily a matter for each provincial government. Prussia established a central bureau to issue permits for residence within its borders, to prevent competition among the different provinces for workers and to ensure that the Poles worked on farms and not in industry and that they returned to Russia. The Prussian migrant labor system expanded rapidly both because of the emigration of Germans from the eastern provinces and the increasing use of labor-intensive crops. Drawn by the high wages of Prussian industry, roughly 5 percent of the population of the four eastern provinces and Pomerania, 473,000 persons, emigrated between 1895 and 1900.[68] At the same time, landowners in the east were steadily increasing the amount of land devoted to the sugar beet, a commercial crop that required several times as much manpower per acre for the fertilization of fields and clearing of weeds as rye and wheat.[69]

Even apart from migrant farm laborers, the number of foreigners living in Prussia and the new German state grew rapidly during the Kaiserreich. Industry's demand for labor could not be satisfied by Germans. After 1905 more than 100,000 Dutch and roughly the same number of Italians worked in Prussia, some as migrants, some on a long-term basis.[70] Industry also managed to employ tens of thousands of foreign Poles, both in the non-Prussian states of the Empire and also, despite the rules against this, in Prussia.[71] In 1890 the census calculated that there were 164,805 foreigners – that is, non-German citizens – living in Prussia and 433,254 in the entire Reich.[72] By 1910 the census found that there were 688,839 foreigners in Prussia, and 1,259,873 in the Reich as a whole, out of a total population of 35,426,335 and 64,568,000, respectively.[73]

Historical Judgments

Bismarck's explanation of the reasons for the expulsions of foreign Poles and Jews influenced not only the policies of his successors, but also the historical treatment of this episode in Germany.[74]

The standard German work on the expulsions, written by Helmut Neubach and published in 1967, concludes that they were in principle justified but should have affected fewer people, especially fewer Poles, and been carried out in a more humane manner. The foreign-policy damage done to Germany was greater than the gains the expulsions achieved, even though the bad press in large part reflected untrue horror stories. Neubach characterizes a National Liberal Prussian Landtag deputy who opposed the Reichstag condemnation of Bismarck's measures as displaying a 'very objective' approach (he made a 'sehr sachlichen Rede') and describes Heinrich von Treitschke as a 'great historical scholar of the Reichstag' in the same sentence in which he notes Treitschke's attack on the Reichstag's vote of censure. Neubach claimed that his book revealed the previously concealed anti-Semitic origins of the expulsions.[75] This claim was entirely justified. Unfortunately, Neubach also concludes that the anti-Semites were correct: the book reproduces more or less verbatim the stereotypes found in *Debit and Credit*. According to Neubach, Prussian Interior Minister Robert von Puttkamer's assessment that Jewish immigrants were 'a true plague on the countryside' ('eine wahre Landplage') was no more than a statement of the truth ('so ist wohl auch Puttkamer . . . Recht zu geben'), overlooking in the process that even with respect to foreign Jews Puttkamer sought to ameliorate Bismarck's orders. Neubach also accepts as true the Berlin Police President's reports of the 'moral depravity' ('die moralischen Tiefstand') of Jewish immigrants.[76] If one takes this view of the matter, then the expulsion of members of such a useless group seems only natural, requiring little further explanation.

Oswald Hauser's studies of Bismarck's policies in the eastern provinces also remain influential. In an essay published in 1971 Hauser accepts Bismarck's claim that Polish nationalism was 'a danger to the state' ('staatsbedrohend'). He argues that Bismarck pursued Germanization only to the extent he believed necessary to counter the Polish threat. It was when the 'leniency' ('Milde') of his measures 'was not honored by [Polish] nationalists bent on secession' that Bismarck was forced to adopt 'hard and nationally intolerant measures'. 'The government undoubtedly proceeded, as a subjective matter, from the point of view of defending itself against a danger . . . for the aggressive actions of Polish nationalism had for a long time required energetic action.' The expulsions 'definitely (durchaus) arose from the effort to protect the state from the danger of Überfremdung (roughly: alienation by the growth of a foreign population) through dangerous elements'. Hauser accepts Bismarck's claims that Polish immigration had reached a 'dangerous level' and that 'the inner peace and the security of the state' required decisive measures.[77]

One early dissenting opinion to the general willingness to accept – for the most part – Bismarck's perspective on the expulsions was voiced by Martin Broszat, in his *Zweihundert Jahre deutsche Polenpolitik*. Published in 1963, this study is still widely considered a standard work on Polish-German relations. Broszat, in contrast to Hauser, found that liberal Prussian policies between 1840 and 1870 led to a moderate degree of integration of Poles into German society, and that the radicalization of Polish national sentiment was primarily a consequence, not a cause, of Bismarck's harsh anti-Polish measures. Bismarck's policies, Broszat concludes, were too aggressive and left too little room for compromise.[78] Hans-Ulrich Wehler reached similar conclusions in an essay first published in 1968.[79]

Dieter Gosewinkel's recent study of German citizenship policies accepts Hauser's claim that the rising tide of Polish national feeling required defensive measures by the German state. 'The growing tendency of the Polish minority towards political secession exerted pressure on the formally uniform legal institution of citizenship.' There was a 'genuine Polish-national consciousness and desire to be separate that was not only a reaction to Prussian-German discrimination'. But, following both Broszat and Thomas Nipperdey, Gosewinkel rejects Hauser's suggestion that the Poles posed an immediate danger to the inner peace and security of the Prussian state. He stresses more than Hauser the role played by Bismarck's harsh measures in radicalizing Polish national feeling. Still, Gosewinkel argues that by the early 1890s, as shown by internal debates regarding the possible amendment of the citizenship law along French lines, the senior levels of the Prussian civil service had come to believe that both Polish and Jewish immigrants lacked 'the capacity to be loyal to the German state'. Gosewinkel further appears to argue that this judgment was accurate. The belief that it would prove difficult to assimilate Poles and Jews was a conclusion 'contemporaries drew from political experience'. 'In this situation the introduction of a territorial element into German citizenship law could have been seen as a surrender of the state's control over the naturalization and expulsion of individuals considered as potentially dangerous foreigners, and it was overwhelmingly so seen.'[80]

Certainly Bismarck believed that he was acting in the interests of the German state and nation. His view that Polish nationalism posed a potential threat to Prussian and German interests was undoubtedly correct. But the evidence suggests that Bismarck's expulsions also served as a weapon – one of many – to stabilize his system of rule, to secure his own power in the face of a hostile electorate. And while the claim that many or most Poles desired eventual secession is undoubtedly true, at least in the period after the Kulturkampf, there are no grounds that support the suggestion that most Jewish immigrants were not capable of becoming loyal to the German state.

Even those historians most inclined to give credence to Bismarck's own depiction of the reasons for his actions have generally concluded that in the end the expulsions damaged German interests. The question of whether the expulsions damaged Bismarck's own political interests has been largely ignored. The expulsions were one of numerous measures Bismarck deployed after 1884 with the aim – in part – of politically polarizing society in a way that would aid government parties. The success of the government parties in the 1887 elections suggests that these measures were, in the short term, successful.

The expulsions and the ethnically exclusive naturalization policies they inaugurated were not a necessary consequence of German national self-interest or feeling, any more than were the Kulturkampf and the anti-Socialist laws. While Bismarck ended the Kulturkampf and his successors repealed the anti-Socialist laws (while continuing to view the socialists as enemies of the state), the rigid rules against the naturalization of foreign Poles and Jews that the expulsions inaugurated remained in effect. One reason for the difference is that the measures taken against foreign Poles and Jews harmed relatively helpless minorities. This applies especially to the foreigners who were expelled and whose applications for citizenship were rejected, but also to some degree to German Poles and Jews. They could be kept secret, or at least publicly denied. In addition, the government-sponsored system of Polish migrant labor turned out to have important economic advantages for Prussian landowners. By keeping foreign Polish workers in a position of permanent legal subordination, and preventing them from working in industry, the Prussian migrant labor system depressed farm wages and promoted subservience. Restrictions on the naturalization of Jews doubtless corresponded to widespread anti-Jewish prejudices. That these prejudices could be reproduced more or less verbatim in the leading post-1945 German study of the expulsions is only one indication of their pervasiveness.

Notes

1. Letter of 27 December 1880. G. Buckle (ed.), *The Letters of Queen Victoria*, Second Series, 3 vols (John Murray, 1928), vol. 3, pp. 169–70.
2. The question of how much power came to be exercised by political parties or extra-parliamentary organizations of various kinds during the Kaiserreich has been the subject of intensive study over the past thirty years. In general the research has emphasized the degree of independence that characterized these groups and the real power they came over time to acquire. But Bismarck's domination of the political system while he was in office, and the continuing authoritarian character of the state even after his forced resignation, are clear. The title for the second volume of Thomas Nipperdey's classic history of the Kaiserreich, *Machtstaat vor der Demokratie* (Beck, 1993), captures this reality.

3. Helmut Neubach, *Die Ausweisungen von Polen und Juden aus Preussen 1885/1886* (Harrassowitz, 1967), pp. 128–9.
4. The 1897 Russian census found 5,189,636 Jews. *Encyclopedia of Judaism*, vol. 14 (Jerusalem: Keter, 1971), p. 450 (entry for Russia).
5. Martin Broszat, *Zweihundert Jahre deutsche Polenpolitik* (Ehrenwirth, 1963), pp. 98–101.
6. George F. Kennan, *The Decline of Bismarck's European Order: Franco-Russian Relations, 1875–1890* (Princeton University Press, 1979), pp. 27–82.
7. The ban on official recognition of 'mixed-race' marriages was introduced in 1905 in Southwest Africa, in 1906 in East Africa, and in 1912 in Samoa. Grosse, *Kolonialismus, Eugenik und bürgerliche Gesellschaft in Deutschland 1850–1918*, pp. 160–8; Lora Wildenthal, *Colonizers and Citizens: Bourgeouis Women and the Women Question in the German Colonial Movement, 1886–1914* (Phd Dissertation, University of Michigan, 1994), pp. 233–377.
8. John Higham, *Send These to Me: Immigrants in Urban America* (Johns Hopkins University Press, 1993); David Feldman, 'Was the Nineteenth Century a Golden Age for Immigrants? The Changing Articulation of National, Local and Voluntary Controls', in A. Fahrmeir, et al. (eds), *Migration Control in the North Atlantic World: The Evolution of State Practices in Europe and the United States from the French Revolution to the Inter-War Period* (Berghahn, 2003), pp. 167–77; David Feldman, *Englishmen and Jews: Social Relations and Political Culture 1840–1914* (Yale University Press, 1994), pp. 268–90; Gérard Noiriel, *The French Melting Pot: Immigration, Citizenship, and National Identity*, trans. G. de Laforcade (University of Minnesota Press, 1996), pp. 54–61; Klaus Bade, *Europa in Bewegung* (Beck, 2000), pp. 209–22. At approximately the same time, however, France undertook to distinguish more sharply between the rights of citizens and those of aliens. Restrictions were placed on the employment of aliens by the state.
9. Simon Dubnov, *History of the Jews*, vol. 5, *From the Congress of Vienna to the Emergence of Hitler*, trans. M. Spiegel (Thomas Yoseloff, 1973), pp. 476–505.
10. Blanke, *Prussian Poland in the German Empire (1871–1900)* (Columbia University Press, 1981), p. 29.
11. Broszat, *Zweihundert Jahre deutsche Polenpolitik*, pp. 78–85.
12. Blanke, *Prussian Poland*, p. 12. Martin Broszat comes to a similar conclusion in *Zweihundert Jahre deutsche Polenpolitik*.
13. Blanke, *Prussian Poland*, pp. 25–6.

14. *SBP* (6 May 1885), p. 1757D. The percentage of the population of these districts that was German had been growing through the 1860s, but emigration of Germans to higher-paying jobs in the west of Prussia, or overseas, reversed this trend. In 1860 the German population of Posen amounted to 41 percent of the population. In 1890, 34 percent of the province was German. And these were the official statistics: one can assume that the reality was worse, from the point of view of the Prussian government.

15. Blanke, *Prussian Poland*, pp. 41–2; *SBP* (28 January 1886), p. 170C.

16. F. Stern, *Gold and Iron* (Alfred A. Knopf, 1977), pp. 146, 198. Bismarck's hatreds extended past the grave. When the American Congress sent the Reichstag a note of sympathy on Lasker's death, Bismarck refused to accept it. Jacob Toury, *Die politischen Orientierungen der Juden in Deutschland: Von Jena bis Weimar* (Mohr, 1966), p. 195.

17. Stern, *Gold and Iron*, pp. 356, 370.

18. Broszat also notes the book's popularity, and the prevalence of the stereotypes it contained. Broszat, *Zweihundert Jahre deutsche Polenpolitik*, p. 90. See also George Mosse, 'The Image of the Jew in German Popular Literature: Felix Dahn and Gustav Freytag', in G. Mosse, *Germans and Jews: The Right, The Left, and the Search for a 'Third Force' in Pre-Nazi Germany* (Wayne State University Press, 1987), p. 70; T. van Rahden, *Juden und andere Breslauer* (Vandenhoeck & Ruprecht, 2000), p. 275.

19. 'Dieser Roman soll das deutsche Volk da suchen, wo es in seiner Tüchtigkeit zu finden ist, nämlich bei seiner Arbeit.'

20. Gustav Freytag, *Soll und Haben* (Verlag Dietmar Klotz, 1992), pp. (in order of citation) 17, 90–92, 79, 85–7. Itzig literally makes a pact with the devil to learn how to cheat people legally.

21. Ibid., pp. 244, 251, 264–6.

22. Peter Pulzer, *The Rise of Political Anti-Semitism in Germany and Austria*, rev. edn (Harvard University Press, 1988), p. 91.

23. Ernst Reventlow, *Judas Kampf und Niederlage in Deutschland: 150 Jahre Judenfrage* (Andermann, 1937), pp. 342–3.

24. 'Unsere Ansichten', *Preussische Jahrbücher* 44 (1879), pp. 572–3.

25. Pulzer, *Rise of Political Anti-Semitism*, pp. 186, 214, 248.

26. The Prussian state's vigorous efforts to prevent the naturalization of foreign Jews fits the larger pattern described by Peter Pulzer. 'As antisemitism lost broad political appeal [after the 1890s], though gaining in intellectual acceptance, its advocates became more desperate and more conspiratorial.' Peter Pulzer, 'The Return of Old Hatreds', in M. Meyer (ed.), *German-Jewish History in*

Modern Times, vol. 3, *Integration in Dispute 1871–1918* (Columbia University Press, 1997), p. 250. It is clear that anti-Jewish feeling of various grades of intensity was widespread in the middle-class and other social and economic circles throughout the Kaiserreich. Marion Kaplan, *The Making of the Jewish Middle Class: Women, Family, and Identity in Imperial Germany* (Oxford University Press, 1991), pp. 129–130; Dietz Bering, *The Stigma of Names: Anti-Semitism in German Daily Life, 1812–1933*, trans. N. Plaice (University of Michigan Press, 1992); Helmut Walser Smith, *The Butcher's Tale: Murder and Anti-Semitism in a German Town* (Norton, 2002). Till van Rahden argues in his *Juden und andere Breslauer* that Breslau Christians were most accepting of Jews in 1900, not in the 1860s, and that by the later date Jews were not generally excluded from non-Jewish German middle-class society. The argument is not entirely persuasive, with respect to both Germany (or Prussia) as a whole and Breslau in particular. Richard Levy and John Kulczycki describe some of the reasons for the unusual degree of integration of Jews into German society in the eastern provinces in 'Germans, Poles and Jews', *East European Quarterly* 17 (September 1984), pp. 365, 372.

27. Kaplan, *Making of the Jewish Middle Class*, pp. 81, 258; Monika Richarz, 'Demographic Developments', in M. Meyer (ed.), *German-Jewish History in Modern Times*, vol. 3, p. 14. Kaplan and Richarz give somewhat different figures for the percentage of Jews who married non-Jews in Prussia during the Kaiserreich, but the general order of magnitude of the statistics is similar.

28. Neubach, *Die Ausweisungen*, pp. 12, 16, 20, 55.

29. Meeting of the Prussian Staatsministerium, 22 May 1881, GStA PK, HA I, Rep. 90a, Abt. B, Tit. III/2b, Nr. 6, Bd. 93, p. 107.

30. Order of 28 May 1881 from the Prussian Minister of the Interior, Puttkamer, to the Oberpräsident in Posen, Günther, with copies to the provincial presidents of East Prussia, West Prussia, and Silesia. GStA PK, HA I, Rep. 77, Tit. 1176, Nr. 2a, Bd. 4, pp. 89, 90–90RS.

31. Letter of 11 May 1881 from the Foreign Office to Interior Minister Puttkamer, GStA PK, HA I, Rep. 77, Tit. 1176, Nr. 2a, adh. I, pp. 1–2.

32. Letter from Bismarck to Puttkamer of 11 September 1881; Memorandum of the Prussian Staatsministerium of 18 April 1882; Letter from Bismarck to Puttkamer of 29 June 1882; Letter of Beckes, Director of the Kaiserliches Statistisches Amt, to Boetticher, Director of the Reich Office of the Interior of 16 August 1882.

Bundesarchiv Berlin-Lichterfelde (BA), R 1501, Nr. 108249, pp. 12, 15, 38, 44, 208.

33. Neubach, *Die Ausweisungen*, p. 14.

34. From 1861 to 1884 the Party was named the Progressive Party (Fortschrittspartei). In March of 1884 it joined with the Liberal Union (Liberale Vereinigung) to form the German Liberal Party (Deutsche-Freisinnige Partei). Other mergers and name changes followed. At the expense of some precision all these parties will be referred to in the text as the Progressive Party.

35. Hans-Ulrich Wehler, *Das deutsche Kaiserreich: 1871–1918*, (Vandenhoeck & Ruprecht, 1973), p. 113.

36. Peter Pulzer, *Jews and the German State: The Political History of a Minority, 1848–1933* (Blackwell, 1992), pp. 102, 190–1; Toury, *Die politischen Orientierungen*, pp. 177–92, 275; van Rahden, *Juden und andere Breslauer*, p. 248 ('an essential part of urban left-wing liberalism – the main force behind it – was Jewish').

37. Letter of 11 February 1882 from Bismarck to Puttkamer, GStA PK HA I, Rep. 77, Tit. 1176, Nr. 2a, adh. I, pp. 193–193RS. Emphasis in original.

38. Prussian Foreign Office to Puttkamer, 2 March 1882; Prussian Foreign Office to Puttkamer, 2 May 1882, Ibid., pp. 195–214.

39. This incident is discussed in Neubach, *Die Ausweisungen*, p. 16. Rickert's activities are described in Pulzer, *Jews and the German State*, pp. 123–4, 330–1.

40. Letter of 17 November 1884 from the Prussian Foreign Office to Puttkamer. GStA PK, HA I, Rep. 77, Tit. 1176, Nr. 2a, Bd. 4, pp. 302–302RS.

41. Letter of 22 February 1885 from Bismarck to Puttkamer, GStA PK, HA I, Rep. 77, Tit. 1176, Nr. 2a, Bd. 5, pp. 23RS–24.

42. A. Fircks, 'Die preussische Bevölkerung nach ihrer Muttersprache und Abstammung', *Zeitschrift des Königlich Preussischen Statistischen Bureaus* 33 (1893), p. 243.

43. Results of Reichstag Elections, 1871–1912, in E. Huber, *Dokumente zur Deutschen Verfassungsgeschichte*, vol. 2 (Kohlhammer, 1961), pp. 536–9. While the small number of Jews suggests that their political influence was less than that of Polish voters, Prussian election laws and Jews' above-average wealth tended to give them a weight greater than their numbers. In Prussia the electorate was divided into three parts based on the amount of taxes each individual paid: the wealthiest individuals who together paid a third of a district's taxes were in the first group, the individuals who together

paid the next third in the second, etc. As a result, in a handful of urban districts Prussian Jews possessed far greater political power in local and state elections than their numbers alone would have suggested. In Breslau, for example, although Jews composed only 5 percent of the local population in 1888, they amounted to a fourth of the first (wealthiest) class of the electorate, and nearly a fifth of the second class. van Rahden, *Juden und andere Breslauer*, p. 248. In Reichstag elections, by contrast, all votes had equal weight. Gerrymandering of districts at both state and national levels favored rural voters: this to some degree enhanced the electoral power of ethnic Poles.

44. Wehler, *Das Deutsche Kaiserreich, 1871–1918*, p. 112. How much Bismarck actually believed this claim is unclear.
45. Letter of 26 February 1885 from Puttkamer to Bismarck, GStA PK HA I, Rep. 77, Tit. 1176, Nr. 2a, Bd. 5, p. 35RS.
46. Letter of 11 March 1885 from Bismarck and Goßler to Puttkamer, GStA PK HA I, Rep. 77, Tit. 1176, Nr. 2a, Bd. 5, pp. 88–9.
47. Letter of 26 March 1885 from Puttkamer to Bismarck and Goßler, Ibid., pp. 92RS–93.
48. GStA PK, HA I, Abt. B, Tit. III/2b, Nr. 6, Bd. 97, pp. 175–175RS. I would like to thank Hartwin Spenkuch for bring this exchange to my attention.
49. As noted also in Richard Blanke, 'Bismarck and the Prussian Polish Policies of 1886', *Journal of Modern History* 45 (1973), p. 216. The conservative press welcomed the expulsions of Jews and in some measure that of the Poles as well. See T. van Rahden, 'Die Grenze vor Ort – Einbürgerung und Ausweisung ausländischer Juden in Breslau 1860–1918', in *Tel Aviver Jahrbuch für deutsche Geschichte* 27 (1998), pp. 56–7.
50. Bismarck took pains to convince Puttkamer that the expulsion measures were popular. In March 1885 he sent Puttkamer a newspaper clipping that supported his views, and claimed that 'public opinion spontaneously expressed' the same fears. Letter from Bismarck to Puttkamer dated 14 March 1885, GStA PK, HA I, Rep. 77, Tit. 1176, Nr. 2a, Bd. 5, p. 100. But it is clear that Bismarck's evidence was thin. Neubach, *Die Ausweisungen*, pp. 23–6.
51. Letter of 3 May 1882 from the Oberpräsident of West Prussia to Puttkamer, Minister of the Interior, GStA PK HA I, Rep. 77, Tit. 1176, Nr. 2a, Bd. 4, pp. 98–105. The Oberpräsident of East Prussia had written in a very similar vein to the then Interior Minister Friedrich von Eulenburg in 1874. Letter of 30 April 1874 from

Oberpräsident Horn to Interior Minister von Eulenburg, Ibid., pp. 64–5.

52. Neubach, *Die Ausweisungen*, pp. 233–4.

53. *SBR, Anlagen zu den Verhandlungen des Reichstags* (II Session, 1885/6), Anlage 85, p. 506.

54. *SBR* (16 January 1886), pp. 526–36, 537D, 538, 541C, 551.

55. *SBP* (28 January 1886), p. 173A.

56. Ibid., p. 171C.

57. Letter of Bismarck to Puttkamer, of 26 May 1885 (the letter was actually signed by Boetticher, State Secretary of the Reich Office of the Interior). BA, R1501, Nr. 108249, p. 216.

58. Letter from Bismarck (signed by a subordinate) to Puttkamer of 29 January 1886, Ibid., p. 221.

59. Minutes of the meeting of the Statistical Central Commission of 26 February 1886, BA, R1501, Nr. 108249, p. 257.

60. Notation regarding the decision of the Bundesrat of 9 December 1887, BA R1501, Nr. 108250, p. 4.

61. Neubach, *Die Ausweisungen*, pp. 76–81.

62. Ibid., p. 182.

63. Johannes Nichtweiss, *Die ausländischen Saisonarbeiter in der Landwirtschaft der östlichen und mittleren Gebiete des Deutschen Reichs* (Rütten & Loening, 1959), p. 35.

64. Ibid., pp. 38–9. This project never got off the ground.

65. Letter from Hohenlohe to Caprivi of 16 July 1892, BA, R 1501, Nr. 108005, p. 70.

66. Letter from Prussian Prime Minister and Interior Minister Eulenburg to Reich Chancellor Caprivi of 29 March 1894, Ibid., pp. 91RS–92.

67. Nichtweiss, *Die ausländischen Saisonarbeiter*, pp. 43–9; Klaus Bade, 'Arbeiterstatistik zur Ausländerkontrolle: die "Nachweisungen" der preußischen Landräte über den "Zugang, Abgang und Bestand der ausländischen Arbeiter im preußischen Staat" 1906–1914', *Archiv für Sozialgeschichte* 24 (1984), pp. 256, 272.

68. Klaus Bade, '"Preußengänger" und "Abwehrpolitik": Ausländerbeschäftigung, Ausländerpolitik und Ausländerkontrolle auf dem Arbeitsmarkt in Preußen vor dem Ersten Weltkrieg', *Archiv für Sozialgeschichte* 24 (1984), p. 96.

69. Nichtweiss, *Die ausländischen Saisonarbeiter*, p. 31.

70. 'Zusammenstellung einiger Hauptzahlen der Ergebnisse über die Beschäftigung ausländischer Arbeiter in Preußen in den Jahren 1905/11', *Zeitschrift des Königlich Preussischen Statistischen Landesamts* 53 (1913), p. 26.

71. U. Herbert, *Geschichte der Ausländerpolitik in Deutschland* (Beck, 2001), pp. 45–6; Karl Marten Barfuß, *'Gastarbeiter' in Nordwestdeutschland 1884–1918* (Selbstverlag des Staatsarchivs der freien Hansestadt Bremen, 1986).

72. 'Reichsausländer im preußischen Staate', *Zeitschrift des Königlich Preussischen Statistischen Bureaus* 41 (1901), p. 60.

73. 'Die Reichsausländer im Staate, in den Provinzen und Regierungsbezirken am 1. Dezember 1910', *Zeitschrift des Königlich Preussischen Statistischen Landesamts* 52 (1912), pp. 42–3; 'Die Ausländer im Deutschen Reich nach den Volkszählungen von 1900, 1905, 1910', *Statistisches Jahrbuch für das Deutsche Reich* 33 (1912), p. 7. Because the censuses that collected these figures took place on 1 December, most of the migrant laborers working in the eastern part of Prussia had already left for home, and therefore were not included in the totals.

74. For a more complete discussion of the historical literature regarding Prussian efforts to Germanize Prussian Poles that also considers the very significant Polish scholarship on the subject, see Witold Molik, 'Die preußische Polenpolitik im 19. und zu Beginn des 20. Jahrhunderts: Überlegungen zu Forschungstand und -perspektiven', in H. Hahn and P. Kunze (eds), *Nationale Minderheiten und staatliche Minderheitenpolitik in Deutschland im 19. Jahrhundert* (Akademie, 1999), pp. 29–39. Unfortunately, I cannot read Polish.

75. Neubach, *Die Ausweisungen*, pp. (in order of citation) 221, 100, 103, ix.

76. Ibid., pp. 12, 20. That Neubach often repeated the 'language and judgment of the documents' with which he worked was commented on at the time of publication by Hans-Ulrich Wehler. See Wehler's review of Neubach's book in *Jahrbücher für Geschichte Osteuropas* 17 (September 1969), p. 462. Wehler also noted that this meant that Neubach gave credence to prevailing anti-Semitic prejudices.

77. Oswald Hauser, 'Polen und Dänen im Deutschen Reich', in T. Schieder and E. Deuerlein (eds), *Reichsgründung 1870/71: Tatsachen, Kontroversen, Interpretationen* (Seewald, 1970), pp. (in the order of citation) 298, 299, 300, 298, 303, 304.

78. Broszat, *Zweihundert Jahre deutsche Polenpolitik*, pp. (in order of citation) 101–4, 92–3. One indication of the extent to which Broszat's perspective on Bismarck's anti-Polish measures broke with the historical consensus of the time, at least in Germany, was the harshly critical review his book received in *Historische Zeitschrift* 198 (1964), pp. 397–406 (review by Horst Jablonowski).

79. Hans-Ulrich Wehler, 'Von den "Reichsfeinden" zur "Reichs-kristallnacht": Polenpolitik im Deutschen Kaiserreich 1871–1918', in Hans-Ulrich Wehler, *Krisenherde des Kaiserreichs 1871–1918* (Göttingen: Vandenhoeck & Ruprecht, 1970), p. 184.

80. Gosewinkel, *Einbürgern und Ausschließen* (Vandenhoeck & Ruprecht, 2001), pp. (in order of citation) 212, 218, 291, 293. The reference to Nipperdey is to *Deutsche Geschichte 1866–1918*, vol. 2 (Beck, 1993), pp. 278–9.

6

Enemies and Friends: A Hierarchy

To prevent the naturalization of foreigners it considered undesirable, Prussia instituted in the 1890s and early 1900s an increasingly centralized and elaborate structure for ruling on naturalization petitions. The Interior Ministry required District Governments to report detailed information regarding each naturalization, to permit oversight; issued numerous decrees guiding decision-making at the district level; took direct control of the granting of naturalization petitions submitted by individuals from groups considered undesirable; and pressured the other German states to conform to Prussian policies.

The Prussian Interior Ministry resumed collecting data on individual naturalizations in 1892, two years after Bismarck's departure from office, although this information was now kept entirely secret. Each District Government reported to the Interior Ministry in Berlin the name, religion and ethnicity of every individual naturalized. To promote the conscription of new citizens, information needed by the army was also provided. It was on the basis of this flow of information to Berlin that the Prussian Interior Ministry attempted to control tightly which groups would be favored and which disfavored in the naturalization process. The way this control was exerted can be seen in Prussian Interior Minister (and Minister-President) Eulenburg's response to the first annual reports from District Governments regarding naturalizations. Eulenburg noted all instances in which Jews had been naturalized – in 1892 there were 24 – and wrote to the responsible District Governments demanding explanations. In some instances Eulenburg ordered the District Governments to send the relevant files to Berlin. In 1893 two-thirds of the District Governments received letters from the Minister demanding that they justify particular naturalization decisions. By 1904 the Interior Ministry required District Governments to submit to the Interior Minister all proposed naturalizations of Jews, Poles, Czechs, priests and politically active individuals.[1]

Although certain categories of naturalization petitions had to be forwarded to Berlin for approval, the principal responsibility for determining who should be naturalized remained with the District Governments. With respect to individuals from disfavored groups, petitions were forwarded to Berlin only if the District Government proposed naturalization. The District Governments therefore had to be aware of what the general policies of the Prussian Interior Ministry were. To this end Prussian Interior Ministers issued numerous orders guiding the District Governments in their decisions.

In 1904 the Interior Ministry compiled the guidelines it had issued to District Governments, together with a discussion of numerous individual decisions, in a narrative summary of its policies. The resulting treatise, some 150 handwritten pages, contained an elaborate categorization of desirable and (mostly) undesirable potential citizens. Its rules were designed to sift out individuals with the undesirable qualities particularly associated with a range of groups. With respect to the most strongly stigmatized groups, and in particular Jews, the primary message of the treatise seemed to be that local officials had to ignore all the evidence relating to individual worthiness to become a citizen, that the assumption of unworthiness or potential disloyalty based on ethnicity (or perhaps 'race') outweighed all contrary evidence, even if the contrary evidence was overwhelming. While it is not clear exactly how much authority the treatise had, the fact that it was closely held – the treatise itself, and all the letters that refer to it, are marked secret – suggest that the Ministry considered it an official statement of its views.

The 1870 revision of the citizenship law required District Governments to consult the 'higher administrative officials' of the community where a petitioner lived with respect to his reputation and economic status. It is striking that the 1904 Treatise makes no reference to this consultation. The District Governments were instructed to consult the 'appropriate records' in making their determinations, and one can assume that in almost all cases this meant the records of communal authorities.[2] But it is clear that the only level of the state whose views were important in this structure was the central administration. The comments of local authorities were to be considered as evidence, and to be given weight just as evidence from any other source might be. It seems that localities were often inclined to be more permissive than the central administration, at least with respect to naturalization petitions from economically useful individuals who had long resided in the community.[3]

The Prussian Interior Ministry also sought in various ways to influence the naturalization policies of the other German states. In 1891 the Bundesrat ordered all German governments that received naturalization petitions from individuals who had previously resided in a different

German state to consult that state as to whether a previous petition had been denied. In this way Prussia sought to prevent individuals who had been denied naturalization in Prussia from becoming naturalized elsewhere in Germany. To promote conformity with Prussian policies the Prussian Foreign Office sent copies of the 1904 treatise to the Interior Ministries of various German states.

From the 1880s Prussia and other German states maintained the policy of secrecy regarding naturalization decisions that Bismarck inaugurated. The grounds for this secrecy were rarely discussed, at least in a way that found written memorialization. The only explicit explanation I have found is contained in a memorandum probably drafted by the Reich Office of the Interior early in 1911. The context was negotiations regarding what became the citizenship law of 1913. Bavaria had proposed that the Bundesrat, the council of representatives of the federal states of Germany, establish general guidelines for naturalization. The Reich Office of the Interior criticized the Bavarian proposal in part on the grounds that the Reichstag would almost certainly insist on reviewing the guidelines, which in this way would be made public.

> Public disclosure of the guidelines would have most undesirable consequences for our internal and our external policies. At home the most vigorous attacks would be directed at all guidelines that have anything to do with confession or the political views of the petitioner. As a matter of foreign policy it would seriously endanger our relations with our ally Austria-Hungary if nationalities like the Czechs and the Poles, which form large parts of this Monarchy, are publicly declared unacceptable.[4]

It may be that Prussian officials were aware that other aspects of their policies were also likely to prove unpopular, for example the tight-fisted treatment of returning German emigrants. Prussian officials were perhaps also concerned that disclosure of their policies would expose them to the charge of arbitrariness, even illegality. The law provided no clear basis for the disparate treatment of different ethnic groups, or for discrimination against individuals with political views anathema to the state. In 1911 the Interior Minister warned District Governments not to reveal that certain categories of applicants required his approval. 'It is neither desired, nor does it correspond to the interests of the state, that . . . internal administrative measures applied to individual cases be revealed to the outside.'[5]

The result of this centralization of control was that the number of Prussian naturalizations granted annually was comparatively low, at least

Table 6.1 Persons Naturalized in Prussia, 1904–1920

Year	Persons Naturalized	Year	Persons Naturalized	Year	Persons Naturalized
1904	7,798	1910	8,665	1916	8,403
1905	7,312	1911	9,389	1917	4,824
1906	7,974	1912	6,748	1918	3,366
1907	13,813	1913	7,727	1919	8,837
1908	9,074	1914	5,695	1920	13,627
1909	10,244	1915	8,437		

Source: 'Erwerb der Reichs- und Staatsangehörigkeit in Preussen, insbesondere im Jahr 1920', *Zeitschrift des Preussischen Statistischen Landesamts* 62 (1922), pp. 37–8. The unusually large number of naturalizations in 1907 reflected the naturalization of a large number of stateless Danes in Schleswig-Holstein in that year. The fact that this table gives significantly higher figures for 1919 and 1920 than found in Table 8.1 (see p. 207) is due to the fact that the figures here include all the persons naturalized, not merely the number of naturalization petitions granted. Since naturalization petitions extended to entire families, it is not surprising that the figures given here for 1919 and 1920 are roughly three times as large as those found in Table 8.1.

in relation to the number of foreigners living in the state. (Naturalization figures for the Reich as a whole do not exist.) In 1892 and 1893 the state granted only some 1500 naturalization petitions, roughly the same number as in the late 1870s, although in the meantime the number of foreigners in Prussia had more than tripled.[6] As Table 6.1 shows, between 1905 and 1914 some 9,000 naturalizations were granted each year, on average.[7] Since there were by 1905 over half a million foreigners in Prussia – not including Polish migrant laborers – this figure is still modest.

General Principles

The principles that governed Prussian naturalization decisions after 1890 are best described in the treatise compiled in 1904. Its provisions remained in force until the monarchy collapsed in 1918.

The treatise first admonished District Governments to make sure that applicants had a 'good reputation' and were 'politically above suspicion'. If these qualities could not be reliably confirmed, then applicants were to be asked to wait two to three years, to permit the state better to judge their conduct.[8] The principal object of this suspicion of political activity was the Social Democratic Party and its constituency.[9] Cases in the Prussian Interior Ministry's files make clear that the government consistently denied petitions submitted by individuals active in organizations affiliated with the Social Democrats.[10] While examples given in the treatise make clear that members of the working class were in fact naturalized, this happened only if the individual seemed politically unobjectionable and capable of supporting himself and his family.

The antipathy to political activity was not limited to Social Democrats. The Interior Ministry considered sympathy for the Polish national cause equally reprehensible, and one suspects that the Progressive Party also fell under a similar ban. In the 1913 Reichstag debate regarding an amended citizenship law a Center Party deputy from Alsace-Lorraine, Franz Haegy, attributed the rejection of a naturalization petition from a Swiss man to the fact that he was an 'enthusiastic advocate of the positions of the Catholic Church and the Center Party'.[11] There is no indication, however, that the mere fact that an applicant for citizenship was Catholic was an obstacle to naturalization.

Another basis for concern with respect to the naturalization of members of the working class was the possibility of burdening local and state social programs. The Ministry of the Interior admonished district governments that 'special care must be taken with respect to the naturalization of persons with modest incomes, who belong to the working class or are tradesmen. Such persons, due to their uncertain situations, cannot be seen as a desirable addition to the domestic population'.[12] Starting in 1898 the Prussian government sought information regarding the annual income of each petitioner for naturalization.[13] The Social Democrats accused Prussia of denying naturalization petitions of foreign workers because their status as foreigners made it easier for employers to exploit them economically, and in this way to hold down the wages of all workers. 'You want foreign workers to come to Germany,' Social Democratic Deputy Karl Liebknecht told the Reichstag in the 1912 debate regarding the amended citizenship law, 'but they should be in Germany as slaves, to be exploited . . . Whoever has some idea of what it means to be a foreigner in Prussia or various other German states, knows that such persons are entirely in the hands of the police.'[14]

While military considerations had always played a significant role in shaping Prussian citizenship and naturalization laws, the 1904 treatise went considerably further in this respect than the law itself, or Prussian practice before 1890. Whereas the law sought to prevent avoidance of military service through emigration, the treatise made the capacity to serve in the army, at least for men, a precondition for becoming a subject. 'The naturalization of persons, who either themselves or whose sons can still be called for active military service, but whose advanced age or other personal qualities lead to the assumption that they would not actually be enrolled, is in general to be rejected, unless a particular state interest in their naturalization exists.' The treatise noted, however, that this rule did not apply to certain classes of applicants, such as pastors, nor was it always strictly applied. It seems, as will be discussed in more detail below, that the rule was applied primarily with respect to individuals belonging to suspect groups. The same can be said for the statement that individuals who came to Prussia to avoid military service in their native countries were in general not to be naturalized. The treatise noted that this last rule did not apply in the western parts of Prussia. It was an instrument of administrative control in the east, and hence, primarily directed at Poles and Jews from Russia and Austria.[15] Polish and Jewish men who migrated to Prussia from Russia often did so to avoid conscription.

The treatise stated that 'emigration with the intention of avoiding domestic military service especially took place to America. A mild treatment of such emigrants on their return would stimulate imitation'.[16] An 1868 agreement with the United States, the Bancroft Treaty, prevented states of the North German confederation from conscripting returning German-Americans who had not performed their German military service, if they had lived in the United States for at least five years and had been naturalized; this followed over two decades of bitter disputes on this subject.[17] But the need to placate the United States government was less pressing after the completion of the wars of unification. Although the Bancroft Treaty was not repudiated, a Prussian edict of 1885 provided that all returning German-Americans who had avoided military service by leaving Germany were to be granted only a limited right to stay in Prussia – to be measured in weeks or months. They were to be expelled immediately if 'by forwardness, by calling attention to their exceptional position, or in any other way they make themselves unwelcome (unbequem) or burdensome'.[18]

These comments support Alfred Vagts's claim, in his monumental study of German-American relations, that 'those in charge of the Wilhelmine state had no special warm feelings, such as ethnic fellowship, for German-Americans'.[19] If anything, wrote an American consul in Germany in 1896 in a confidential report to the State Department, there was

> more ill-will toward their emigrant brethren than towards Americans of a different descent. It is said with some appearance of truth that Germans who have emigrated as children, or the children of German emigrants, only return

to the Fatherland to be met by evidences of a rooted dislike as would not be observed by visitors from France or Great Britain.[20]

In fact, not only German-Americans, but all returning Germans who had somehow avoided military duty were treated with rigor by the Prussian government, as the files of the District Governments that shared borders with Holland and Belgium attest.[21]

The lengths to which Prussia would go to punish German-Americans who had failed to fulfill their military obligations, even if this was done in a legal manner, is suggested by the experience of Wilhelm Nikolaus Müller. Müller emigrated to the United States as a fourteen-year-old, in 1891. At this time he sought and received a release from Prussian citizenship, in order to prevent his later prosecution for failure to perform his military service. Müller served in the Spanish-American War as a cook in the American forces, during which time a mishap resulted in the amputation of one leg at the knee. In 1900 he returned to Germany, and petitioned for naturalization. This petition was denied, since he was no longer capable of serving in the army, and the District Government President ordered him to leave Prussia. When Müller appealed the decision to the Kaiser, Prussian Interior Minister Hans von Hammerstein urged the denial of the petition, on the grounds that a significant number of young men in the city of Stade, where Müller lived, sought to avoid military service by temporary emigration, and Müller's presence might encourage this tendency. 'This practice of [temporary] migration takes place in particular to North America, and it is therefore generally prescribed, that [former Germans who are] citizens of the United States and who have not performed their German military service . . . are to be granted permission to remain in the country only on a temporary basis.'[22] The Kaiser apparently found the recommendation too harsh, and ordered that Müller be at least granted permission to remain in the country.

The 1870 citizenship law provided that former Germans who lost their citizenship by virtue of a ten-year absence abroad were entitled as a matter of right to become citizens of the German state in which they settled if they returned to Germany.[23] This clause was unpopular within the administration, as it deprived it of the discretion to deny returning Germans citizenship. Fortunately, from the point of view of the administration, this part of the 1870 law was, as the German vice consul in New York put it in 1910, 'almost unknown, and it is taken as a firm fact, that the failure to perform one's military duty is a complete barrier to a return to the home'.[24] The popular interpretation was not, however, without a basis. While former Germans might be entitled to regain their citizenship upon returning to Germany, if they had failed to fulfill their military service obligations they might, upon becoming citizens, be subjected to imprisonment and fines. If they were young enough they might well be conscripted.

With respect to foreigners born in Germany the treatise suggested that naturalization was generally desirable, so long as they could be drafted and were not on particular ethnic, political or economic grounds undesirable. 'It can in general not be seen as desirable, that such foreigners should enjoy the advantages of residing in Prussia without fulfilling the duties imposed on its subjects by the state.'[25] Part of the problem was a practical one. It often was difficult to expel men born in Prussia to the state in which they were nominally citizens. If the person could not be gotten rid of, or controlled by the threat of expulsion, state interests were in general better served by forcing him to become a Prussian, so long as he at least theoretically accepted the possibility of having to serve in the army.

The apotheosis of the hardy soldier as the model citizen had certain corollaries. A few rough edges might be expected in such a package, and the Ministry made clear that this was acceptable. Crimes involving physical injury were not to be considered insuperable barriers to naturalization as long as the offenses had only been subject to a fine. Crimes associated with financial dishonesty, however, were a different story. The treatise made clear that these in principle were not to be tolerated.[26]

Jews, Poles, Czechs and Danes

The 1904 treatise singled out Jews, Poles, Czechs and Danes for especially discriminatory treatment, in descending order of severity. The same scale of stigmatization was also apparent in the gathering of statistics. In the Prussian Statistical Bureau's analysis of naturalization statistics, which were prepared for the use of the Ministry of the Interior from 1904, members of the first three groups were tallied separately. In numerous statistical compilations Interior Ministry officials underlined or circled statistics having to do with Jews, a sign of their obsession with this group. Although the treatise treated Jews as a confession, the extent of the barriers it imposed on the naturalization of members of this group implied that the discrimination had an ethnic or even 'racial' basis.

The Interior Ministry's treatise decreed that the naturalization of Jews born outside of Prussia 'in principle does not take place'. The reasons were 'in part political, in part national, in part of an economic nature'.

'Exceptions have only occurred rarely and after a thorough examination, in which considerations of a personal nature are in general not given decisive weight.'[27] The political reasons have been discussed above. Jews voted predominantly for the Progressive Party, which was, at least in the 1890s, in the opposition. The fact that from 1906 until 1909 both progressive parties belonged to the governing coalition at the national level does not appear to have had much effect on Prussian naturalization policies. When Hugo Agular, an Austrian Jew, sought naturalization in 1913, the Breslau District Government rejected the application with the remark that 'his political conduct and party membership have given rise to questions, since one can assume that he – like most of those belonging to the Jewish religion – belongs to the Progressive Party'.[28] While the treatise does not explain what it meant by 'national grounds', the reasoning appears to have been that Jews could in general not be assimilated into the German nation, even if they successfully mimicked its outward cultural forms. In contrast to the instructions regarding most other ethnic groups, the acquisition of the cultural accoutrements of Germanness – for example, the ability to speak and write German – was not mentioned as a positive factor in considering naturalization petitions from Jews.

While the treatise in general displayed a bias against the working class, in the case of Jews middle-class or lower-middle-class occupations were singled out for punitive treatment. The treatise prohibited the naturalization of Jews born outside of Germany who worked in commerce ('dem Handel oder Gewerbestande angehörigen Personen').[29] Since most Jews in Germany, native and almost certainly also foreign, earned their living in some aspect of commerce, the effect of the rule was to preclude most foreign Jews from eligibility for citizenship. While it is possible that the strictures against the naturalization of Jews active in commerce may have reflected in part the anti-capitalist backlash that characterized certain parts of Wilhelmine society, the limitation of this concern to Jews shows that it was not commerce in general to which the drafters of the treatise objected, but what were perceived as Jewish business methods.[30] Freytag's *Debit and Credit (Soll und Haben)*, for example, is full of praise for what it considers the German bourgeoisie, but only contempt for the Jewish variant. Behind the fear of Jewish business methods lay the fear of Jewish success and power. The treatise mentioned several instances in which Jewish factory owners and other professionally successful individuals were denied citizenship.[31] The fundamental problem was not that these individuals had succeeded by fraudulent methods, but that they had succeeded – and that they were Jewish.

While the rules restricting the naturalization of Jews born outside of Germany were developed in particular for the eastern provinces, in fact, as the treatise noted, 'on the basis of these instructions approval for the naturalization of Jews born abroad has frequently been denied in all parts of the Monarchy'.[32] The treatise then gave instances. Even former German Jews who sought to regain their citizenship were subject, unless the law required that their requests be granted, to the rule that the Minister of the Interior had to personally approve their petitions. Whether the rules governing foreign Jews generally were to be applied to them was to be 'determined in each individual case'.[33]

In 1911 the screws were turned one rotation tighter. In instructions to the District Governments the Interior Minister ordered that 'the petitions of originally Jewish foreigners who have converted to Christianity' also were to be forwarded to him for final decision.[34] This treatment of conversion was rationalized on the grounds that conversion to Christianity displayed a character flaw. In 1912 the Interior Ministry reported to the Reichstag Commission considering revisions to the citizenship law that

the Prussian Minister of the Interior considers it undignified when an individual changes his professed faith for the sake of material advantage. The government can even cite cases where the Minister of the Interior rejected an application for naturalization precisely because the applicant had expressed his intention to give up the Jewish confession for the sake of naturalization or because the applicant had already converted in order to acquire citizenship.[35]

In internal documents the Interior Ministry provided a rationale that reflected a bias against all Jews, not merely a concern regarding individuals whose actions displayed a flawed character. A marginal comment on the Interior Ministry's file copy of the February 1911 instructions regarding Jews who had converted stated that 'the basis for the refusal to naturalize foreign Jews is not their religious beliefs, but the characteristics they owe to their origins (Abstammung) and race. These characteristics are generally not eliminated by baptism, which is generally sought for business reasons'.[36] On these grounds the Police President of Berlin rejected the naturalization petition of Albrecht Gruenbaum in 1913, despite his conversion to Protestantism and thirty-year residence in Germany.[37]

Foreign Jewish males who had been born in Prussia were permitted to become citizens only if they were physically capable of serving with the regular army ('Dienst mit der Waffe'), and were actually enrolled with a unit. Service in the reserves in general did not suffice. If foreign Jewish men were found medically unqualified to serve in the army, then the administration could – at least if some other state was willing to accept the person – order expulsion.[38] In this requirement that Jews actually serve in the active army, commented the Provincial Governor of East Prussia to the Interior Minister in 1904, 'there is a valuable means to counter the inclination of Jewish foreigners to avoid military service, to exercise an educational influence on their views and actions and to reduce considerably the number of Jewish foreigners naturalized'.[39] The rules governing Jews' military service are only comprehensible in light of prevailing views that (a) Jews generally did all they could to avoid military service (which, given their treatment while in the army, had a certain logic), and (b) that they were as a group physically incapable of serving.[40] It was assumed that few Jews would be able to meet the army's physical requirements. Apparently the administration concluded, after some experience with this rule, that too many Jewish foreigners were being found capable of active service in the military. In a 1910 letter the Minister of the Interior informed the President of the District Government in Cologne that 'in examining naturalization petitions of foreign Jews who . . . have grown up in Prussia, one must first consider . . . whether the petitioner, in the event of the rejection of the naturalization petition is likely sooner or later to emigrate. If this is the case, then the petition must be rejected.' If the petitioner was likely to remain in Prussia, and it appeared impossible to force his emigration, then and only then was he to be required to serve in the army and naturalized.[41]

Poles were subject to a somewhat lower level of discrimination, although the grounds were different and in some cases diametrically opposite to the reasons for the exclusion of Jews. The treatise provided that 'the naturalization of foreign Poles [not born in Germany] in principle is not to take place for national and political reasons'. But exceptions were possible. 'If doubts with regard to politics are not present, the applicant has adequately mastered written and spoken German, and if either the personal circumstances of the applicant permit an exception or if there is a special [state] interest in the naturalization of the applicant', then naturalization might be permitted.[42] The treatise described nine examples of exceptional naturalizations of foreign Poles. Among those so favored had been a boilerman in a state institution in Cologne (the state had an interest in the naturalization), a man who married a Prussian woman and agreed to support her German children by a previous marriage (they might otherwise have required charitable support), a man who married a Prussian woman and agreed to support her elderly parents and, perhaps most remarkable, a man who had an illegitimate child with a Prussian woman – naturalization would permit the marriage to take place. The treatise stressed that these were all exceptions and that naturalizations of Poles were best avoided altogether.[43] Nonetheless, they indicated a degree of flexibility absent with respect to Jews.

The difference in the way the administration viewed naturalization petitions from Poles and Jews reflected in part the view that at least some Poles could in fact become Germans. First, there were a considerable number of individuals of mixed ancestry, and the administration was willing to view all such persons of mixed background as assimilable.[44] The treatise mentioned, for example, the case of an illiterate farm worker who 'was brought up with Polish habits and customs' but who was apparently of German ancestry, and whose mother tongue was German. The man was naturalized.[45] Secondly, individuals who had no German roots might choose to become German. The treatise mentioned a Czech – a group treated in most respects like Poles – who, although of entirely Czech ancestry, 'only used German at home and was giving his children a purely German education'.[46] He, too, was naturalized. Jews were not considered assimilable, no matter how well they had mastered German or other aspects of German culture.

The difference in the treatment of cultural leaders from each group is also telling. The treatise in general prohibited the naturalization of non-German priests.[47] The state feared that Polish priests, in particular, would serve to perpetuate and propagate Polish national identity. By contrast, at least according to the treatise, Jewish religious functionaries were among the most welcome group of foreign Jews. Individuals who earned their livings as officials in a Jewish community were not engaged in commerce, and this was explicitly noted as the basis for the decision to permit naturalization in several cases.[48] Perhaps the administration sought in this way to encourage a separate and traditional Jewish identity.[49] Complaints from the Jewish community in the years before the First World War suggest, however, that the administration in fact granted naturalizations even to Jewish religious officials quite selectively.[50]

While commercial activities were absolutely forbidden to foreign Jews who wished to become Prussian citizens (at least with respect to those born abroad – the prohibition did not apply with the same severity to foreign Jews born in Prussia), the rules directed at Poles in many respects favored the middle class. In particular, the requirement that Poles seeking naturalization know spoken and written German clearly was biased in favor of individuals who had had the chance to receive an education. Unlike foreign Jews born in Prussia, foreign Poles generally did not have to show physical capacity to perform military service, or be accepted by a regular army unit. Should Poles born in Prussia before 1885 refuse, upon mustering, to apply for citizenship, or if they did not provide the necessary medical certificate or certificate regarding ability to speak and read German, then they were to be expelled, if possible. On the other hand, the treatise urged that alien Poles born in Prussia after 1885 in general be sent back to their country of origin to perform their military service.[51]

In practice it often proved difficult to enforce the treatise's requirements with respect to foreign Jews and Poles born in Germany. Jews and Poles who had themselves immigrated could generally be expelled, and especially in Prussia the police made frequent use of this power. It was more difficult to expel individuals born in Germany, at least those whose parents came from Russia. But even if the state could not legally expel an individual, it had numerous means of making life miserable. It could threaten expulsion even if the administration realized that it would prove difficult to carry out the threat. In this way the state could deprive the individual in question of all sense of confidence about his future.[52]

Despite the special harshness of the rules that governed the naturalization of Jews, the state generally naturalized more Jews each year than Poles. In 1905 there were 63 naturalizations of Jews and 87 of Poles;[53] in 1906 110 and 56;[54] in 1907 91 and 37;[55] in 1908 65 and 4;[56] in 1909 80 and 31.[57] Why this was so is a matter for conjecture. One reason is that Jews applied to be naturalized in far greater number than Poles: the files of the central administration leave no doubt on this point. Since Jews more frequently lived in cities, and owned businesses, they may well have been more visible to the authorities and felt a greater need to gain German citizenship to protect themselves from the danger of expulsion. A significant percentage of the Jewish applicants for citizenship were well-off. They were often able to generate considerable support from local officials for their petitions.[58]

The strictures imposed on Poles were followed with reduced severity with respect to Czechs and Danes. In both cases the administration was concerned primarily with individuals who resided in the provinces immediately adjacent to the borders with Bohemia and Moravia, and Denmark, respectively. The state administration generally assumed that in areas of Prussia where Czechs and Danes were a barely noticeable minority no threat was presented. Here the state could assume that the minority would assimilate and, even if it did not, would not be in a position to influence elections or provide a basis for challenges to German borders. Thus, the treatise ordered that Czechs residing in Silesia, but not elsewhere in Prussia, were to be treated like Poles.[59] In 1912 the District

Government of Breslau rejected the naturalization of a Czech man, Josef Heinsch, even though he was married to a German woman, spoke only German, had no relationships with other Czechs, was not politically active and had hung a picture of the Kaiser in his house.[60]

With respect to Danes, but not Czechs, the government relaxed the requirement for political reliability. Naturalization petitions were not to be rejected merely because the individual displayed a strong Danish consciousness.

> One can usually assume that [ethnic Danes who applied for Prussian citizenship] incline towards the Danish party or are open to Danish national influences. Nonetheless naturalization is generally to be approved if the person is capable of military service. This reflects the view that in most cases a very clearly developed political viewpoint will not yet have emerged, and that on the one hand army service is admirably suited to remove young people from the influence of their Danish environment, and, on the other hand, it is not appropriate [to permit them to escape military service].[61]

One can detect here the influence of calculation based on both ethnicity and politics. The Prussian administration viewed the Danes as among the most assimilable minority groups. They presented a much smaller political threat. The Danish party, after all, usually had only one seat in the Reichstag. The Poles, by contrast, won between thirteen and twenty seats in Reichstag elections between 1870 and 1913.[62] There was also the fact that the 1864 treaty that ended the war with Denmark required Prussia to permit the continued residence in Schleswig of Danish citizens: expulsion was not as ready an option.

Among the hardships created by the treatise's strictures was that they often resulted in the splitting up of families. A Polish family that had for generations moved between Russian Poland and Prussia experienced this fate in the first decade of the twentieth century. One son, Johann Kluza, was found to be incapable of serving in the army, and ordered deported to Russia. A younger brother, however, was drafted and naturalized. On the other hand, it commonly happened that the expulsion order was not effective. Johann, who had been raised in Prussia, illegally returned shortly after being deported, and the authorities were unable to find him.[63]

Following the Prussian Example

Prussia pressured the other German states to follow its example, and it was for the most part successful in this endeavor. Bavaria, Saxony, Baden,

Mecklenburg-Schwerin and Anhalt all received copies of the treatise in 1905, with 'a request to preserve the strictest secrecy'.[64] The responses of Bavaria and Saxony to the Prussian treatise are extant. Saxony was closest to the Prussian model. In 1906 the Saxon Foreign Office sent the Prussian Interior Ministry a description of its rules governing naturalization that, while much shorter than the Prussian treatise, in most respects adhered to the Prussian model. The guiding principle was that 'a significant increase of state members in Saxony through ways other than the natural increase of the population is undesired, as is any reduction in the capacity [of the state] to rid itself of foreign elements by expulsion whenever they make themselves in any respect burdensome or their conduct raises doubts'.[65] While the Saxon guidelines contained no discussions of the treatment of Poles or Czechs or religious officials, they reproduced verbatim the essential provisions of the Prussian rules regarding Jews and the role of military service.

A 1907 memorandum from the Bavarian Royal House and Ministry of Foreign Affairs to the Bavarian Embassy in Berlin, which apparently was meant to be passed on to the Prussian government, indicated that in Bavaria local communities played a far more important role in naturalization decisions than in Prussia. Bavaria interpreted the 1870 citizenship law as mandating that naturalization required the approval of the community in which the foreigner dwelled. But in practice the results were similar to the Prussian policies, Bavaria reported. 'The handling of naturalization petitions in Bavaria is dominated by the effort to keep out elements that, either thanks to their uncertain economic position, or on political or national grounds, are seen as an undesirable addition to the population.'[66] The requirement for approval by a local community usually guaranteed this result, for communities were 'extremely cautious' in granting residence rights to foreigners. Even without general rules to guide them, local communities considered nationality, origin, religion, reputation and political preferences, stated the memorandum. Jews in particular were rarely accepted. The Bavarian files contain directives from the Interior Ministry from the late 1880s warning against the naturalization of Russian Jews, at least those who had lived in Prussia, and ordering that German-Americans who had not fulfilled their military obligations be permitted to remain in Bavaria only for a brief period.[67] The only significant difference with Prussia related to military service. In Bavaria, reported the memorandum, the capacity of potential citizens to serve in the army was not as important as in Prussia.

The Interior Ministry of Baden reported to the Baden Foreign Office in 1907 that it would essentially follow the guidelines in the Prussian treatise.[68] The Prussian embassy in Stuttgart reported in 1907 that Prime Minister von Weizsäcker had informed it that Württemberg had since 1885 generally denied naturalization petitions from Russian Poles and Austrian Galicians.[69] Oldenbourg and Lippe indicated in 1907 that they followed, or intended to follow, Prussia's lead.[70]

The Unwanted

How many of Germany's long-term resident aliens attempted to become German citizens? It is impossible to determine the answer, since German states did not generally keep track of the number of petitions for naturalization they received. Many foreigners who wished to stay may have decided that it was simply better not to risk the dangers that came with official attention.[71] Stringent naturalization requirements clearly also played a key role.

As before 1870, the desire to marry a Prussian woman remained the reason for which many foreigners living in Prussia sought naturalization. This applied in particular to Russians. In 1871 Prussia granted resident aliens who were Russian the right to marry in Prussia without Russian approval. Prussia rescinded this right in 1889. The reason for the change in the law, presumably, was to make it more difficult for Russian immigrants to settle in Prussia, and also easier for Prussia to expel Russian men and their families. In 1885 and 1886 Russia had often refused to accept the formerly Prussian wives of expelled Russians. Many of these Russian men had, presumably, married without the permission of their Russian communities.[72]

To marry, Russians living in Prussia could apply either for naturalization or for exemption from the requirement for Russian approval of a marriage. Prussia granted the latter far more readily, since it involved less of a firm commitment to the person. But before permitting a marriage to take place in Prussia without the approval of Russian authorities, Prussian officials examined whether they wanted the applicant to remain in Prussia even for a moderate period. If they did not, then they denied the request. When the cigar-maker Lipa Leibow applied for a dispensation from the requirement for approval by the Russian government in 1894 so that he could marry a Prussian woman, the President of the District Government in Danzig rejected the petition. The state had no interest in permitting the residence of Leibow, he concluded, and the petition was made the occasion of Leibow's expulsion.[73]

Even foreign men from countries with respect to which Prussia no longer required home approval for marriage sometimes found it essential to become Prussian subjects before they married. This applied in particular to citizens of Catholic countries, like Austria, which applied conservative Catholic teachings in their marriage laws. Prussia permitted a foreign man to marry in Prussia only if the marriage was valid under his country's laws. Austrian and Italian laws prohibited marriages between Catholics and Protestants, as well as the marriage of those who had divorced. Naturalization was the only recourse. The naturalization petition that Anton Truka submitted in 1905 illustrates a common situation. Truka, an Austrian Catholic, petitioned for naturalization in order to marry Minna Piltz, a Prussian Protestant. Piltz pleaded with the government to grant the request. 'I was divorced from my previous husband Piltz because of his brutality, but am Protestant, and so cannot marry [a Catholic] according to Austro-Hungarian laws.'[74] Prussia rejected the petition: the man was a Social Democrat. In 1906 the Prussian Interior Ministry rejected a petition from Joseph Groos, an Austrian Jewish watchmaker who wanted to marry Laura Kluth, a Prussian Christian. Austria also forbade marriages between Jews and Christians. The intervention of Laura's father, 'who together with his daughter enjoys the best reputation', and also Groos's own previous good conduct, led the local Landrat and District Government to support the petition. But the Interior Ministry in Berlin overruled the District Government.[75]

An impending marriage was often the occasion for a petition for naturalization even when no legal impediments existed. The possibility of expulsion hung over the head of every foreigner, especially those who were Jewish or Polish. This, and the fact that women who married foreigners lost their Prussian citizenship, meant that women and their families would sometimes only permit a marriage to take place if the groom became a Prussian. In 1907 the District Government of Marienwerder rejected a naturalization petition from Julius Groß, an Austrian Jew, submitted in these circumstances. Groß's lawyer wrote to the Interior Ministry, in an appeal of this decision, that 'the parents of the bride have made their acceptance of the marriage dependent upon his naturalization'.[76] The District Government justified the decision as a means of keeping Jews from settling in Prussia: 'through the need periodically to renew their residence permits foreign Jews will always remain conscious of the fact that in Prussia they are only tolerated guests'.[77] The Interior Ministry agreed.

If a marriage took place despite the failure of the man to obtain Prussian naturalization, the sacrifice made by the woman might trouble the relationship for years to come. This seems to have been the case especially with respect to Jews, the most stigmatized and endangered group. Fischel Freundlich's appeal to the Kaiser to grant his naturalization petition in 1906 stressed this aspect of his situation. 'My nationality has previously been the only matter', he wrote, 'which now and then cast a shadow on my family life, in that my wife, the most tender spouse and mother, never was able to get over the fact that by marrying me she lost her home, her citizenship.'[78] Freundlich pleaded for a grant of naturalization on the occasion of the Emperor's twenty-fifth marriage anniversary. The Interior Minister denied the request.

Foreign families living for long periods in Germany often found, especially if they had middle-class aspirations, that the failure to possess German citizenship led to serious disabilities for their children. After numerous rejections Ludwig Arpadi, a Jewish restaurant owner who had emigrated to Prussia from Hungary around 1890, appealed to Kaiser Wilhelm in 1909 to grant him Prussian citizenship. Arpadi explained that he 'often had had difficulties when he attempted to smooth the way for the future of my children, because I am not a Prussian subject'. Both his son and his daughter had attended a Gymnasium, and his daughter wished to become a schoolteacher, a profession that required citizenship. The Interior Ministry rejected the petition.[79]

Certainly many petitioners hoped through naturalization to improve their own positions, and not merely that of wives or children. Wilhelm Castellaz, an Austrian, informed the District Government of Arnsberg that he wanted to become a Prussian citizen in order to be able to qualify for a position with the railroad administration, a state company that employed only German citizens. This frankness did not help him. The District Government justified its rejection of the petition in part on the grounds that it was designed 'only to achieve personal advantage'.[80]

Some foreigners may have sought naturalization to protect themselves from personal or business enemies, who might inform the authorities of their status. In the aftermath of the expulsions of foreign Poles and Jews in the mid-1880s an anonymous letter from the Breslau district called the authorities' attention to Casimir Kukuta, a Russian Polish miner. The letter denounced Kukuta as a danger to Prussia: 'his expulsion from this state is long overdue'.[81] The authorities were reluctant to act on an anonymous denunciation, and after interviewing Kukuta permitted him to stay.

Some petitioners for naturalization may have based their desire for Prussian citizenship on the wish to exercise the right to vote. This usually was not, of course, mentioned in petitions to the government, but was sometimes surmised by officials. When Rudolf Czech, an

Austrian locksmith, sought naturalization in Altona in 1906, the District Government feared such motives.

> The Social Democratic press has undertaken a lively agitation in the vicinity of Hamburg to encourage non-Prussian workers to apply for Prussian citizenship, so as to gain political rights, in particular the right to vote. This circumstance forces me to show special caution with respect to naturalization petitions from persons who, due to their social position, are especially vulnerable to the influence of Social Democracy.[82]

While the District Government had no special reason to suspect Czech, aside from the fact that he was a worker, its more general anxieties led to the denial of his petition. Active involvement in social democratic unions, subscription to the Socialist daily *Vorwärts* or participation in May-first festivities all provided a concrete and individual basis for such fears and led almost invariably to the rejection of petitions.[83]

Prussia never officially informed rejected petitioners for naturalization of the grounds for their rejection, although these often were surmised. This fact, and the general strictness of the naturalization policies, produced frustration and humiliating attempts to adapt to the vaguely grasped demands of the state administration. Workers cut off their involvement with the Social Democrats, usually in vain.[84] An editor of a newspaper for butchers claimed that his journal was strongly monarchical ('Königstreu') and had opposed Social Democratic agitation among butchers. His only fault, he wrote, 'was to be born a Jew and, furthermore, in Galicia'.[85] The thousands of pathetic letters to the 'most illustrious, most almighty Kaiser, all merciful King and Lord' may have followed ritual formulas, but they also reflected a real self-abasement and despair.

Desirable Citizens

While the records preserved in the files of the Prussian Interior Ministry focus primarily on excluding undesirable individuals, it is possible from other evidence to piece together the characteristics that the Ministry found especially appealing in potential future citizens. Independent wealth and a habitus seen as aristocratic were certainly of considerable assistance, as were connections with officials in high places. An Italian lawyer naturalized in 1908, Luigi Guio Bertolini, had all these characteristics. The Police President of Berlin reported to the Interior Ministry that Bertolini was able to support himself from his private fortune and his legal practice. He could speak German, and had contacts with 'respected circles of the intellectual elite [Intelligenz] and society'. '[His] deportment is that of an educated man.' While Bertolini had written articles for Italian journals, none had had anything to do with politics, and Bertolini himself had no political attachments. On the other hand, Bertolini was clearly politically well connected in a sense the Prussian government approved, for the decision that his naturalization was approved was forwarded to the Italian ambassador.[86]

The largest group of especially favored foreigners, at least in the period immediately preceding the First World War, were members of the ethnic German agricultural communities in Russia, amounting in 1900 to roughly three-quarters of the 1.8 million Russian Germans.[87] As noted above, the need for migrant farm workers from Poland and other East European countries grew to major proportions in the years before the First World War. The annual migration of nearly a million Polish farm workers into the eastern provinces of Prussia increased Germany's dependence on the good-will of outside governments at a time when Russia, in particular, was becoming more and more firmly part of a hostile coalition. And it was impossible to prevent at least some of the immigrants from settling permanently in Prussia, despite all the government's efforts to prevent this. For these and other reasons, from early in the twentieth century the German and Prussian governments showed increasing interest in encouraging immigration from the ethnic German communities in Russia.

In 1908 the Prussian government created a bureau whose mission was to assist Russian Germans to migrate to Prussia. Between 1908 and 1914 the agency brought some 30,000 Russian Germans to Prussia.[88] The Russian Germans, as a publication of this agency described them, were 'used to keeping their meager possession clean, understood patriarchal relationships, and were religious'. Some were, admittedly, 'not used to intensive work', and not completely honest.[89] Many were illiterate. But the Russian Germans might take the place of Polish migrant laborers and were as a whole immune from the influence of the Social Democrats. As the Landrat of Hohensalza reported to the District Government President of Bromberg in the fall of 1912, the German returnees (Rückwanderer, as they were usually referred to in official memoranda) 'voted in a completely German way'.[90] On the other hand, the Russian Germans often showed little understanding of the ethnic struggle in which they were supposed to serve. They frequently brought non-German servants with them from Russia, whose presence then usually had to be tolerated.[91]

In theory ethnic German farm workers from Russia were supposed to be naturalized either immediately, or, unless economically or politically suspect, after the passage of several months or a year from the time they entered Prussia.[92] In practice matters did not always work this smoothly. In October 1918 Reichstag Deputy Franz Behrens complained to the Prussian Interior Minister about the treatment of Russian German families living on an estate in West Prussia. They had immigrated before the start of the war, and had repeatedly petitioned for naturalization. These petitions had been denied at the request of the estate owner, Count Waczmirs, on the grounds that 'once the returnees are naturalized, they will have the opportunity to find work elsewhere'.[93] Restricting the movement of the returned Russian Germans, at least until they were naturalized, was apparently a general practice.[94]

Notes

1. Document entitled 'Verleihung und Wiederverleihung der preußischen Staatsangehörigkeit auf Grund der Sek. 8 und 21 des Reichsgesetze vom 1. Juni 1870' (henceforth cited as the 'Prussian Administrative Treatise on Naturalization'), GStA PK, HA I, Rep. 77, Tit. 227, Nr. 53, Beiheft 2, pp. 33–4, 35–6, 45, 59, 67.

2. Ibid., pp. 19–22.

3. See Till van Rahden, 'Die Grenze vor Ort – Einbürgerung und Ausweisung ausländischer Juden in Breslau, 1860–1918' *Tel Aviver Jahrbuch für deutsche Geschichte* 27 (1998), pp. 47–69.

4. 'Bemerkungen zu den Ausführungen der Königlich Bayerischen Regierung über die Aufnahme von Ausländern', undated, in BA, R 1501, Nr. 108013, pp. 129RS–130. The memorandum was a response to a Bavarian memorandum dated 5 December 1910. Ibid., pp. 125–7. It was forwarded to the Bavarian government.

5. Instructions of the Minister of the Interior to the District Government Presidents dated 30 June 1911. GStA PK, HA I, Rep. 77, Tit. 227, Nr. 4, Bd. 22, p. 87.

6. GStA PK, HA I, Rep. 77, Tit. 227, Nr. 4, Beihefte 1–2. These figures apparently did not include relatives that were naturalized with heads of families.

7. See the confidential analysis of naturalizations prepared by the Prussian Statistical Bureau for the Prussian Interior Ministry, 29 June 1908, GStA PK, HA I, Rep. 77, Tit. 227, Nr. 4, Bd. 21, p. 18RS.

8. Prussian Administration Treatise on Naturalization, GStA PK, HA I, Rep. 77, Tit. 227, Nr. 53, Beiheft 2, pp. 19–20.

9. During Bismarck's tenure in office the government had gone so far as to propose a law permitting the state to deprive active Social Democrats of citizenship, to permit their expulsion from the Reich. The clause was not adopted. GStA PK, HA I, Rep. 90, Nr. 2253, pp. 48–52.

10. See for example GStA PK, HA I, Nr. 42G, p. 61; GstA PK, HA I, Nr. 42T, 3, pp. 60–73, 110.

11. *SBR* (28 May 1913), p. 5290A.

12. Prussian Administrative Treatise on Naturalization, GStA PK, HA I, Rep. 77, Tit. 227, Nr. 53, Beiheft 2, pp. 21–2. And similarly with respect to the naturalization of Dutch workers. Ibid., p. 94.

13. Compilation of forms containing information regarding naturalizations filed by the District Governments with the Interior Ministry, 1898. GStA PK, HA I, Rep. 77, Tit. 227, Nr. 4, Beiheft 6.

14. *SBR* (23 February 1912), p. 254C. As noted above at page 94, such goals certainly occurred to the administration.

15. Prussian Administrative Treatise on Naturalization, GStA PK, HA I, Rep. 77, Tit. 227, Nr. 53, Beiheft 2, pp. 22–5.

16. Ibid., pp. 138–9.

17. D. Gosewinkel, *Einbürgern und Ausschließen* (Vandenhoeck & Ruprecht, 2001), pp. 158–62, 260. A report of the United States Congress from 1860 describes in great detail, with numerous examples, the forced enlistment of German-Americans in the Prussian army in the 1850s. See Document No. 38, United States Congress, 36th Congress, First Session.

18. Prussian Administrative Treatise on Naturalization, GStA PK, HA I, Rep. 77, Tit. 227, Nr. 53, Beiheft 2, p. 140.

19. Alfred Vagts, *Deutschland und die Vereinigten Staaten in der Weltpolitik*, vol. 1 (Macmillan, 1935), p. 600.

20. Ibid., p. 579.

21. See for example the disputes described in GStA PK, HA I, Rep. 77, Tit. 1176, Nr. 68, Beiakte 3.

22. Memorandum from Minister of the Interior von Hammerstein to Wilhelm II dated 11 January 1903. GStA PK, Rep. 89, Nr. 15713, p. 291.

23. *Gesetz über die Erwerbung und den Verlust der Bundes- und Staatsangehörigkeit* of 1 June 1870, Section 21, paragraph 5. *RGBl* I, p. 355.

24. Memorandum from Vice Consul Hossenfelder to Chancellor Bethmann Hollweg of 1 April 1910, BA, R1501, Nr. 108012, p. 331.
25. Prussian Administrative Treatise on Naturalization, GStA PK, HA I, Rep. 77, Tit. 227, Nr. 53, Beiheft 2, p. 26.
26. Ibid., p. 20. On the glorification of violence in elite circles, see Kevin McAlee, *The Cult of Honor in Fin-de-Siècle Germany* (Princeton University Press, 1994).
27. Prussian Administrative Treatise on Naturalization, GStA PK, HA I, Rep. 77, Tit. 227, Nr. 53, Beiheft 2, pp. 69, 73.
28. GStA PK, HA I, Rep. 77, PK 227, Nr. 42A, Bd. 1, p. 129.
29. Prussian Administrative Treatise on Naturalization, GStA PK, HA I, Rep. 77, Tit. 227, Nr. 53, Beiheft 2, pp. 69, 76.
30. The conservative attack on the spirit of capitalism in this period, and the association of capitalism with Jews, is discussed in Kenneth Barkin, *The Controversy Over German Industrialization* (University of Chicago Press, 1970), pp. 131–85.
31. Prussian Administrative Treatise on Naturalization, GStA PK, HA I, Rep. 77, Tit. 227, Nr. 53, Beiheft 2, pp. 70–1.
32. Ibid., pp. 69–70.
33. Ibid., p. 130. How such petitions were likely handled is suggested by the difficulties in regaining German citizenship experienced by a formerly Prussian Jewish woman who had lost her citizenship upon marriage with a non-German Jew. The President of the District Government in Oppeln objected to the renaturalization request, which was made in 1910 to the Hamburg District Government. He pointed out that one result might be that her sons would in turn have to be naturalized. Letter of the District President in Oppeln to the Prussian Interior Minister of 4 June 1910, GStA PK, HA I, Rep. 77, Tit. 227, Nr. 4, Bd. 21, p. 216.
34. Decree of the Prussian Interior Minister of 7 February 1911. GStA PK, HA I, Rep. 77, Tit. 227, Nr. 4, Bd. 22, p. 42.
35. Citation from the *Geschäftsbericht des Verbandes der deutschen Juden* 8 (1913), printed in Wertheimer, 'Jewish Lobbyists and the German Citizenship Law of 1914: A Documentary Account', *Studies in Contemporary Jewry* 1 (1984), p. 153.
36. GStA PK, HA I, Rep. 77, Tit. 227, Nr. 4, Bd. 22, p. 40. I owe the reference to this citation to Dieter Gosewinkel, '"Unerwünschte Elemente" – Einwanderung und Einbürgerung der Juden in Deutschland 1848–1933', *Tel Aviver Jahrbuch für deutsche Geschichte* 27 (1998), p. 95.

37. Letter of the Police President of Berlin to the Oberpräsident of Potsdam of 13 April 1913. GStA PK, HA I, Rep. 77, Tit. 227, Nr. 42G, Bd. 1, p. 152.
38. Prussian Administrative Treatise on Naturalization, GStA PK, HA I, Rep. 77, Tit. 227, Nr. 53, Beiheft 2, p. 56.
39. Letter of 19 December 1904 from the Oberpräsident of East Prussia to the Minister of the Interior, GStA PK, HA I, Rep. 77, Tit. 227, Nr. 4, Bd. 19, p. 122.
40. As to the treatment of Jews while in the Prussian army, see D. Bering, *The Stigma of Names: Antisemitism in German Daily Life, 1812–1933*, trans. N. Plaice (University of Michigan Press, 1992), pp. 243–54. With respect to common prejudices regarding Jews' military capacities, see Sander Gilman, *The Jew's Body* (Routledge, 1991), especially pp. 38–59.
41. Letter from the Prussian Minister of the Interior to the President of the District Government in Cologne, 7 March 1910. GStA PK, HA I, Rep. 77, Tit. 227, Nr. 4, Bd. 21, p. 139.
42. Prussian Administrative Treatise on Naturalization, GStA PK, HA I, Rep. 77, Tit. 227, Nr. 53, Beiheft 2, p. 47.
43. Ibid., pp. 48–52.
44. For example, a chart published by the Prussian Statistical Office in 1893 regarding the ethnic origins of the population of Prussia claimed that 45,000 to 75,000 of the Poles in Prussia were 'of purely German ethnicity, although they have lost the ability to speak German'. *Zeitschrift des Königlich Preussischen Statistischen Landesamts* 33 (1893), p. 196.
45. Prussian Administrative Treatise on Naturalization, GStA PK, HA I, Rep. 77, Tit. 227, Nr. 53, Beiheft 2, p. 51.
46. Ibid., p. 63. This unclarity regarding the group to which an individual belonged worked in the other direction as well. In a 6 December 1906 memorandum the Landrat of Schubin reported to the District Government President regarding a man who 'was taken until recently to be a German, but through a perfidious sale of German land to a Pole has lost stature among Germans'. GStA PK, HA XVI (Posen), Rep. 30 (Bromberg District Government), Abt. I, Nr. 1849.
47. Prussian Administrative Treatise on Naturalization, GStA PK, HA I, Rep. 77, Tit. 227, Nr. 53, Beiheft 2, p. 36.
48. Ibid., pp. 73–5.
49. The administration also pursued the goal of inhibiting Jewish assimilation by preventing Jews from changing their first or last names to ones that sounded more 'Christian'. All name changes in

Prussia required official approval. Bering, *The Stigma of Names*, pp. 87–118.

50. Wertheimer, 'Jewish Lobbyists and the German Citizenship Law of 1914', pp. 149–52.

51. Prussian Administrative Treatise on Naturalization, GStA PK, HA I, Rep. 77, Tit. 227, Nr. 53, Beiheft 2, p. 56.

52. As reported by the Bavarian Ministry of the Interior in a memorandum to the Bavarian Royal House and Ministry of Foreign Affairs of 8 February 1914. BHM, Interior Ministry, Nr. 71641. The Interior Ministry reported that it was quite difficult to expel individuals to Russia, but that the threat of expulsion usually sufficed to persuade those threatened to move to some other state. This technique was certainly not limited to Bavaria.

53. Report of the Prussian Statistical Office to the Prussian Interior Minister of 25 August 1906, GStA PK, HA I, Rep. 77, Tit. 227, Nr. 4, Bd. 20, p. 59.

54. Report of the Prussian Statistical Office to the Prussian Interior Minister of 1 July 1907, Ibid., p. 189.

55. Report of the Prussian Statistical Office to the Prussian Interior Minister of 29 June 1908, GStA PK, HA I, Rep. 77, Tit. 227, Nr. 4, Bd. 21, p. 18.

56. Report of the Prussian Statistical Office to the Prussian Interior Minister of 9 July 1909, Ibid., pp. 85, 85RS.

57. Report of the Prussian Statistical Office to the Prussian Interior Minister of 25 August 1910, Ibid., pp. 274RS, 275.

58. For example, an Austrian Jew from Breslau, whose net worth the Interior Ministry estimated to be 800,000 Marks, and who had given generously to local charities and promised to establish a foundation to support needy persons previously employed by his firm, had little difficulty being naturalized (David Grünbaum). Letter of the Interior Ministry of 4 October 1910. GStA PK, HA I, Rep. 77, Tit. 227, Nr. 42G, Bd. 1, p. 96. The same applied to a doctor in Berlin whose net worth was estimated at 400,000 Marks. The fact that he had converted to Christianity was not held against him (Eugen Oppenheimer). GStA PK, HA I, Rep. 77, Tit. 226b, Nr. 65, Bd. 1, p. 95.

59. Prussian Administrative Treatise on Naturalization, GStA PK, HA I, Rep. 77, Tit. 227, Nr. 53, Beiheft 2, pp. 59–63.

60. APW, Neurode Nr. 88 (Einwanderungen 1911–1925). The modesty of Heinsch's salary apparently played a role as well his ethnicity.

61. Prussian Administrative Treatise on Naturalization, GStA PK, HA I, Rep. 77, Tit. 227, Nr. 53, Beiheft 2, p. 121.

62. E. Huber, *Dokumente zur Deutschen Verfassungsgeschichte* (Kohlhammer, 1961), vol. 2, pp. 536–9.

63. Letters of the Landrat of Hohensalza to the District Government President in Bromberg dated 4 February 1907, 10 March 1908, and 18 May 1911. GStA PK, HA XVI (Bromberg), Rep. 30, Abt. I, Nr. 1120.

64. Letter of the Prussian Foreign Office to the Prussian Interior Ministry dated 31 December 1905. GStA PK, HA I, Rep. 77, Tit. 227, Nr. 4, Bd. 20, p. 1.

65. The Saxon memorandum is appended to a letter from the Prussian Foreign Office to the Prussian Interior Ministry of 3 August 1906, GStA PK, HA I, Tit. 77, Rep. 227, Bd. 4, Nr. 20, p. 53.

66. Memorandum of 23 March 1907, in BHM, Berlin Embassy, Nr. 1133.

67. Letter from the Ministry of the Interior to the District Government of Oberfranken of 1 September 1893. BHM, Bavarian Ministry of Foreign Affairs, Nr. 92681; Circular from the Bavarian Ministry of the Interior to the District Governments of 3 August 1886. BHM, Berlin Embassy, Nr. 1133.

68. Letter from the Baden Ministry of the Interior to the Ministry for the Royal House and Foreign Affairs of 13 February 1907. BGL, Abteilung 233, Nr. 11143.

69. Letter to the Prussian Interior Ministry from the Prussian Embassy in Stuttgart dated 26 February 1907, GStA HA I, Rep. 77, Tit. 227, Nr. 4, Bd. 20, p. 144.

70. Letter of the Staatsministerium of Oldenbourg to the Prussian Ambassador of 16 February 1907; Letter of the Staatsministerium of Lippe to the Prussian Ambassador of 19 February 1907, Ibid., pp. 148–50.

71. Till van Rahden describes several instances in which Breslau authorities sought to expel foreign immigrants who had attracted scrutiny by seeking naturalization. Van Rahden, 'Die Grenze vor Ort' pp. 60–1. An article from 1908 in the *Allgemeine Zeitung des Judentums* gives a sense of how widespread was the appreciation of the dangers of seeking naturalization. 'There are foreign Jews who have lived and worked here for three or four decades; they have children and grandchildren. When, in the interests of their wives, their German-born children, and their grandchildren, they seek naturalization, they are informed by those who know – even

by well-meaning officials – [to remain silent]. They are better off not reminding people that they are foreigners.' Quoted in Jack Wertheimer, *Unwelcome Strangers: East European Jews in Imperial Germany* (Oxford University Press, 1987), p. 60.

72. Since the Russian population in Prussia was disproportionately male – as was the foreign population generally – marriages between foreigners and Prussians usually involved a foreign man and a Prussian woman.

73. Letter from the President of the Danzig District Government to the Prussian Minister of the Interior, GStA PK, HA I, Tit. 227, Nr. 8, Bd. 21, p. 98.

74. Letter of 16 January 1905 from Minna Piltz to Kaiser Wilhelm II, GStA PK, HA I, Rep. 77, Tit. 227, Nr. 42T, p. 5. Prussia likewise rejected Ferdinand Stary's petition for naturalization in 1909. He also was unable to marry under Austrian laws because he was divorced. The denial was based on the fact that he was a Czech. GStA PK, HA I, Rep. 77, Tit. 227, Nr. 42 St, Bd. 1, pp. 57–9.

75. Letter of the Prussian Interior Ministry of 15 November 1906, GStA PK, HA I, Rep. 77, Tit. 227, Nr. 42G, Bd. 1, pp. 38–9. A petition by a Catholic Austrian man to marry a Jewish Prussian woman met a similar fate. Prussian Interior Ministry letter of 29 June 1908, GStA PK, HA I, Rep. 77, Tit. 227, Nr. 42C, Bd. 1, p. 30. Oliver Trevisiol has found a similar pattern in naturalization petitions of Italians in Baden. Since Italy prohibited divorce, becoming the citizen of a state with more liberal rules was often the only means of gaining the right to remarry. The authorities in Baden generally took a liberal position with respect to the granting of such naturalization petitions. Oliver Trevisiol, *Scheidung vom Vaterland: Die Einbürgerung von italienischen Migranten im Deutschen Kaiserreich am Beispiel von Konstanz* (www.magi-e.historicum.net/reihe/magi-e_band_03.pdf, 01.04.2003: accessed on 4 August 2003), pp. 56–71.

76. Letter from Groß's lawyer to the Prussian Minister of the Interior of 28 June 1907, GStA PK, HA I, Rep. 77, Tit. 227, Nr. 42G, Bd. 1, p. 52.

77. Letter from the District Government of Marienwerder to the Prussian Interior Minister of 3 August 1907, Ibid., p. 50RS.

78. Letter of Fischel Freundlich to Kaiser Wilhelm II of 22 February 1906, GStA PK, HA I, Rep. 77, Tit. 227, Nr. 42F, Bd. 1, pp. 26–26RS.

79. Letter from the Prussian Interior Ministry of 11 August 1909, GStA PK, HA I, Rep. 77, Tit. 227, Nr. 42A, Bd. 1, p. 84. For a similar

appeal see the letter of Alois Adler to the Prussian Interior Ministry of 11 October 1909. Ibid., pp. 86–8.

80. Letter of the District Government of Arnsberg to the Prussian Minister of the Interior of 13 March 1913. GStA PK, HA I, Rep. 77, Tit. 227, Nr. 42C, Bd. 1, p. 68.

81. APW, Breslau, Nr. 359, pp. 6–11. For another instance of the attempted use of expulsion to further a personal grudge, in this case of a man against his former wife, see *SBR* (27 February 1893), p. 1302; and similarly *SBR* (15 December 1898), p. 92.

82. Letter of the President of the District Government of Schleswig to the Prussian Interior Minister of 11 April 1906. GStA PK, HA I, Rep. 77, Tit. 227, Nr. 42C, Bd. 1, pp. 5–9.

83. This was, for example, the grounds on which the Breslau District Government rejected repeated naturalization petitions from Richard Palm, formerly an American citizen, shortly before the First World War. When he first submitted an application, the District Government noted, he was a member of the Social Democratic Union of German Carpenters. Letter from the Breslau District Government to the Prussian Interior Ministry of 20 November 1913, GStA PK, HA I, Rep. 77, Tit. 226b, Nr. 65, Bd. 1.

84. Letter from the Breslau District Government to the Prussian Interior Ministry of 20 November 1913, GStA PK, HA I, Rep. 77, Tit. 226b, Nr. 65, Bd. 1.

85. Letter of John Goldstaub to Chancellor Bethmann-Hollweg of 7 February 1906. GStA PK, HA I, Rep. 77, Tit. 227, Nr. 42G, Bd. 1, p. 33.

86. Report from the Police President of Berlin to the Prussian Interior Ministry of 25 September 1908. GStA PK, HA I, Rep. 90, Nr. 2253, pp. 287–8, 336.

87. I. Fleischhauer, *Das Dritte Reich und die Deutschen in der Sowjetunion* (Deutsche Verlags-Anstalt, 1983), p. 12.

88. Alfred Borchardt, 'Deutschrussische Rückwanderung', *Preußische Jahrbücher* 162 (1915), p. 139. Borchardt was head of the agency for Russian German returnees established by Prussia. During roughly the same period the Pan-German League transported an additional 20,000 Russian Germans to Baltic countries, where their mission was to strengthen the existing German population. Fleischhauer, *Das Dritte Reich und die Deutschen in der Sowjetunion*, pp. 21–3.

89. Booklet entitled *Deutsche Rückwanderer aus Rußland, Ein Leitfaden für ländliche Arbeitgeber* (Berlin: Selbstverlag der Rückwandrerstelle, 1908), pp. 10–11. GStA PK, HA I, Rep. 77, Tit. 226b, Nr. 63, Bd. 1.

90. Report from the Landrat of Hohensalza to the Bromberg District Government President of 16 October 1912. GStA PK, HA XVI (Bromberg), Nr. 1048, Bd. 64.
91. Ibid.; Report of the Bromberg District Government President to the Oberpräsident of Posen of 30 January 1904, in GStA PK, HA XVI, Rep. 30, Abt. I, Bd. 1060. The absence of a highly developed sense of German national feeling among the Russian Germans also proved frustrating for the Pan-German League. Fleischhauer, *Das Dritte Reich und die Deutschen in der Sowjetunion*, pp. 20–3.
92. In a circular of 13 July 1910 to the District Governments the Prussian Interior Minister ruled that the immediate naturalization of ethnic Germans from Russia was appropriate when they had secured steady employment, and that otherwise naturalization should be delayed a year. GStA PK, HA I, Rep. 77, Tit. 227, Nr. 4, Bd. 21, pp. 252–3. Letter from the President of the District Government in Posen to the Prussian Interior Minister of 14 June 1910. Ibid., pp. 214–15.
93. Letter from Reichstag Deputy Behrens to the Prussian Minister of the Interior dated 21 October 1918. GStA PK, HA I, Rep. 77, Tit. 226b, Nr. 63. Bd. 1, p. 221.
94. Letter of the Fürsorgeverein für deutsche Rückwanderer of 26 April 1918 to the Prussian Minister of the Interior. GStA PK, HA I, Rep. 77, Tit. 226b, Nr. 63a, Bd. 3, p. 156.

7

Civis Germanus Sum

'Our German state has become a world state', Wilhelm II proclaimed in January 1896. 'Thousands of fellow Germans live around the earth. German goods, German learning, German industriousness have traveled across the ocean. As a result we have the responsibility of binding the larger German empire firmly to the homeland.'[1] Weltpolitik, as the Wilhelmine program of extending German trade and power around the globe came to be known, led to a reorientation of official attitudes regarding German emigrants. More than five million Germans emigrated overseas in the course of the nineteenth century, most to the United States.[2] Disinterest, a sense in the various German state administrations that the emigrants were renegades or troublemakers, was displaced by the hope – at least among the chief advocates of Weltpolitik – that Germans living abroad would prove valuable allies.

The revisions to the citizenship law adopted in 1913 reflected the goals of Weltpolitik, and also, the German government's need at least to appear to consider the views of political parties and the public in formulating policy. The 1870 citizenship law deprived emigrants of citizenship either upon their departure from Germany or, at the latest, ten years after they left. This rule had long been unpopular, and the 1913 amendments abolished it. In this way the 1913 citizenship law promoted the Kaiser's goal of 'binding the larger German empire firmly to the homeland', for it suggested that Germans who emigrated could remain German citizens indefinitely. The revision, promised the State Secretary of the Reich Interior Office in the Reichstag in 1912, would help bring into being a 'polity of all Germans', a 'Civis Germanus Sum'.[3]

As with many aspects of Weltpolitik, there was much in the new citizenship law that was bluster. The most vocal advocates of strengthening ties with Germans overseas were right-wing organizations outside the Prussian and Reich central administrations. They found some allies in official positions, most importantly the Kaiser and the State Secretary of the Reich Naval Office, Alfred von Tirpitz, the architect of the naval build-up. But most of the Prussian and Reich ministries viewed the proposed changes in the citizenship law as a product of unrealistic calculations regarding the behavior of Germans abroad and a threat to the strength of the army at home. As a result, while the final version of the law promised continued citizenship to all future German emigrants, it made maintenance of citizenship depend on the fulfillment, for men, of military service obligations. This requirement had the effect of annulling most of the intended consequences of the law.[4]

Appealing to Germandom Abroad

Both the Prussian Untertanengesetz of 1842 and the national citizenship law of 1870 deprived individuals of their citizenship upon emigration or, if the emigrant failed to obtain an emigration certificate, after an absence of ten years. These provisions had, in many respects, a liberal pedigree. Old-regime laws and customs had severely restricted emigration. During the Napoleonic era a series of treaties among German states had abolished exit taxes and fees. Section 18 of the Bundesakte, the agreement that created the German Bund, or Confederation, applied the terms of these treaties to all the German states. This clause stated that all subjects of German states had the right to migrate to any German state that was prepared to accept them, without payment of a fee, provided only that military service obligations had been fulfilled.[5]

General acceptance of the right to emigrate freely, at least to other German states and after the performance of military service, was in part a product of early nineteenth-century efforts to promote patriotic feeling. Patriotism, wrote Carl von Rotteck in the famous liberal *Staats-Lexikon* published in the 1830s, 'is the true virtue of the citizen. Its absence can be replaced by nothing else; not through obedience . . . nor through the threats of state power'.[6] But how could patriotic feeling be expected of people kept by force within the boundaries of a state? When leading Prussian generals were asked, in 1817 and 1818, whether they supported permitting the right to emigrate freely in peacetime, the question of the implications for communal spirit provided one of the bases for their responses. General August Graf Neidhardt von Gneisenau, one of the heroes of the war of liberation from Napoleon, stated that

> the undersigned supports granting the greatest possible freedom to emigrate in times of peace, only with the proviso, that those who have not fulfilled their military service not be permitted to receive inheritances from within the monarchy, and that those who emigrate in order to avoid military service in time of war be permanently deprived . . . of all the rights of Prussian citizens

(Staatsbürger) . . . If one permits (families) the right of emigration in time of peace, and they remain within the country, then they conclude in this way a free contract, whereby they recognize their duty [to the state]. This is not the case when emigration is forbidden or made difficult, for in this case they will feel as if they have been kept in a prison against their inclination and will.[7]

Gneisenau assumed that when a Prussian subject emigrated, he terminated his contract with the state, and therefore ended his status as a citizen or subject.

Both in 1869, when the Prussian Lower House had considered a reenactment of the Untertanengesetz, and in 1870, when the Reichstag of the North German Confederation extended the law to the entire confederation, the National Liberals had challenged the rule depriving emigrants of citizenship immediately or ten years after emigration. Initially the Prussian Lower House voted to abolish this clause.[8] Bismarck refused to acquiesce. The National Liberal proposal, he wrote to Interior Minister Friedrich von Eulenburg in 1869,

> would have the effect that all those Prussians who for a long period remain abroad, without acquiring a new citizenship, would receive a guarantee that they would be able to retain their citizenship without having to make any special declaration. This would apply irrespective of the length of the absence, even for generations. In this way there would soon probably arise a very numerous class of foreign Prussians, who, while removed from all personal control and oversight [by Prussia], would enjoy a privileged position in a double sense. This would arise first with respect to the state where they live, to which they in fact, although not legally, belong, and second with respect to their former Fatherland, whose protection they will still be able to claim, without fulfilling the duties that arise from the relationship of a subject . . .[9]

The principal duty to which Bismarck referred was, of course, military service. Bismarck's view prevailed in the North German Reichstag, to which he sent the proposed law to avoid the need to compromise with the Prussian Parliament. In keeping with Bismarck's rationale, the 1870 law provided two exceptions to the rule governing the expiration of citizenship. First, emigrants might obtain permission from a German consulate to retain their citizenship. German consulates granted this permission, to men, only if they could demonstrate that they had satisfied their military service obligations.[10] Second, if emigrants returned to Germany after having lost their citizenship by virtue of the ten-year rule, they were entitled to again become citizens.[11] As citizens, however, they again became subject to the draft.

The 1870 law had very different practical consequences for German emigrants living in different countries. Roughly 90 percent of the 2.7 million Germans who emigrated between 1871 and 1907 journeyed to the United States, and almost all of these became United States citizens.[12] The vast majority never wished to live again in Germany, nor did they require the assistance of German consulates. On the other hand, many Germans who migrated to Russia or to Latin America did not become citizens of the countries in which they lived, because of the oppressiveness or lawlessness of the foreign regime. For these Germans retention of German citizenship was useful as a source of diplomatic protection. In Russia foreigners without papers from their homelands were subject to expulsion, and for this reason, among others, a large number of the German citizens living in Russia placed their names on the lists kept by the German consulates.[13]

Beginning in 1894 nationalistic groups like the Pan-German League, the Colonial Society, and the National Liberal Party pushed successive national governments to introduce legislation that would permit German emigrants and their children to remain German citizens until they became citizens of a different state.[14] As the State Secretary of the Reich Office of the Interior, Count Arthur von Posadowsky-Wehner, put it in a 1906 memorandum to Chancellor Bernhard von Bülow, 'the agitation for a change in the citizenship law . . . came from outside [the administration], from the Pan-German League and from the German Colonial Society, and at the same time from foreign Germans who had been aroused by the Pan-German League'.[15] Composed for the most part of members of the middle class, with the active membership numbering at the most in the thousands, the Colonial Society and especially the Pan-Germans nonetheless managed to exert an extraordinary influence on the government. The Pan-German League's first general meeting, in 1894, called for a revision of the law to prevent the loss of citizenship through mere residence abroad and to further restrict naturalizations inside Germany. The President of the League, Ernst Hasse, a National Liberal Reichstag deputy, introduced a resolution that would have accomplished this result in the 1895 Reichstag. Hasse wanted the state not only to permit Germans to retain their citizenship indefinitely while abroad, but to grant all ethnic Germans (deutsche Volksgenossen) the right to be naturalized in Germany.[16] Hasse also sought to restrict the naturalizations of Poles and Jews.

While Hasse's motion was defeated, the proposal that emigrants no longer be deprived of citizenship after a ten-year absence found wide support. From 1895 to 1898 the newspaper of the Colonial Society, the *Deutsche Kolonialzeitung*, repeatedly published articles calling for a revision of the ten-year rule. In 1896 a Reichstag Commission appointed to consider the Pan-German League's petitions proposed that the government introduce legislation prolonging or ending the ten-year period. The proposal even won the support of August Bebel, a leader of the Social Democratic Party Reichstag faction. In 1896 the Reichstag adopted a motion urging the government to introduce a revised citizenship law.[17]

In July 1898, on the basis of a decision of the Colonial Society's executive committee, the president of the society wrote to Chancellor Chlodwig zu Hohenlohe-Schillingsfürst urging a revision of the law.

In the opinion of the Society the dignity of a great and strong state requires that it release its subjects from the bond of citizenship only when they themselves request this. This is not only because the subjects are of value to the state, but primarily because citizenship in the Reich is a means of binding together all foreign Germans that, in its consequences for Germany's position as a world power, should not be underestimated.[18]

The Colonial Society's petition apparently prompted Wilhelm II to state his support for the proposed revision. A Foreign Office memorandum from August 1898 noted that Wilhelm had ordered the ministries to begin drafting a new law, an order with which the ministries complied.

The revival of agitation to eliminate the ten-year rule was in part a consequence of larger structural and political changes in Germany. As a result of the economic boom of the 1890s the value of trade with foreign countries jumped dramatically, almost doubling between 1890 and 1906.[19] German emigrants were potential consumers of Germany's industrial products. Industrialization also slowed the rate of emigration, for it created jobs at home for those who might have left. Whereas considerably more than 100,000 Germans emigrated each year between 1880 and 1893, on average, between 1894 and 1914 the annual figure never exceeded 50,000, and in many years was less than half this number.[20] The fear that more lenient treatment by the German state of Germans abroad might fuel the emigration therefore subsided. Finally, due to the growing significance of international markets, and a widespread sense that conflicts with other leading powers over access to markets were unavoidable and would determine Germany's economic future, Wilhelm II and much of German society – excepting primarily the working class – determined to expand German influence around the world. Weltpolitik found expression in part in the rapid expansion of the navy, but also in a range of other efforts to spread German power and to prepare for military conflict with other states. In these imperialist plans German emigrants played a key role.

Inside the administration it was Alfred von Tirpitz, from 1897 the State Secretary of the Naval Office, a confidant of the Kaiser and the architect of Germany's naval buildup, who stated most forcefully the imperialist rationale for amending the citizenship law.[21] For Tirpitz Germany's future 'lay on the sea', and it was around this plan, or dream, that all else turned.[22] Tirpitz argued that the whole question of whether emigrants should be permitted to retain their citizenship could be summed up as follows: 'Should or should not the German state, which had determined to conduct Weltpolitik, employ the most important tool at its disposal to preserve Germandom, namely Germans living abroad?'[23] For Tirpitz German emigrants were an 'instrument of state power' ('Machtmittel des Staates').[24] 'It would in my opinion not be responsible to take from the Fatherland such a mass of intelligence, energy, and capital and to drive it into the arms of our competitors.'[25] The mirror image of the central administration's fears of the disloyalty of domestic ethnic Poles, Czechs, Danes, etc. was the hope that German emigrants might be persuaded to remain loyal to Germany.

Part of Tirpitz's thinking was economic. 'Everything that has the effect of promoting [German] prestige abroad and increasing the sale of German products must be accomplished.'[26] German emigrants would purchase German goods and introduce them to their neighbors, and would promote German investment abroad. 'Since matters have developed that the German nation . . . must turn abroad to find buyers for its goods, raw material for its factories, and investments for its capital, we must rely more than ever on our countrymen abroad, for whom the preservation of the Reich is an imperative of their own self-interest.'[27]

But the most important considerations were political or military in nature. Where large parts of the population of a foreign country consisted of German emigrants, then the foreign government could be pressured to 'accommodate German wishes and . . . German interests'.[28] 'Without the help of [foreign Germans] the supply of his Majesty's ships with news and materiel would in crises become impossible.'[29] Emigrants were also potential soldiers and sailors. 'It is a significant matter whether the 10,000 Germans [who serve in the British merchant marine] in the event of a war with England feel themselves repulsed by us and as our opponents, or whether they at least give up their employment on English ships . . .'[30] Germans serving on foreign warships in the service of an enemy power would during wartime be guilty of treason if they retained their citizenship, and this would make them more likely to resign their positions, Tirpitz argued.

Although Tirpitz made military considerations his central focus, he argued in internal memoranda against the position of most of the administration that the maintenance of citizenship be made to turn on fulfillment of military obligations. In Tirpitz's view 'the [emigrant] German is proud of his nationality and wishes to preserve, with his Fatherland, his own being and convictions'.[31] If he often had failed to meet his military obligations, this was in large part due to antipathy to the bureaucratic methods of the German state. Tirpitz expressed confidence that in a time of crisis German emigrants would rally to Germany. He also pointed out the class bias of the military service requirements supported by most of the administration. The Foreign Office intended to exempt individuals who owned businesses or had fixed positions from having to return to Germany to perform their annual army service. 'The relief granted [with respect to military service] offers little benefit to many of those subject to military obligations, i.e., sailors and workers, who do not have fixed positions', wrote Tirpitz. And as a result 'many good Germans would fail to perform their military service'.[32]

Tirpitz claimed to be entirely indifferent to the fears of the Foreign Office that too successful an effort to retain German emigrants as citizens would lead to repeated military interventions to protect these citizens, and to possible conflicts with foreign states. Probably the most significant danger was of conflict with the United States, which had made clear that it looked unfavorably on the gunboat diplomacy of European powers in Central and Latin America.[33] Tirpitz did not appear to consider the antagonism his policy might create in the United States a serious problem. 'In an increase in such appeals for help I see no disadvantages. One cannot overlook the fact . . . that every successful completed action in support of an appeal for help strengthens the prestige of the Reich and the self-assurance of foreign Germans . . .'[34] Foreign concerns that the preservation of the citizenship of emigrants was intended in some cases as a step towards colonization also mattered little: 'colonies are almost always acquired in this way'.[35] Similarly, Tirpitz had few fears about the possibility that German emigrants might hold dual citizenship. In countries where local citizenship was necessary to own land or practice a trade, one could assume that the emigrants 'remain in their hearts German', and should therefore be permitted to retain their German passports.[36] As had the Pan-German League, Tirpitz proposed that all German emigrants, and their children and grandchildren, be granted the right to retain their citizenship, unless a foreign citizenship was acquired by choice and without a pressing economic rationale.

The Prussian Interior and War Ministries, and the Reich Foreign Office, as well as almost all the other ministries consulted with respect to the proposed law, steadfastly insisted that the law make fulfillment of military service obligations a condition for retaining German citizenship. The rationale was not that foreign Germans were likely to agree to perform reserve duty in great numbers, or that those who fulfilled the conditions imposed on them in peacetime would prove of much use in the event of a war. It was rather 'pour encourager les autres'. As Posadowsky, the State Secretary of the Reich Interior Office, put it in a 1906 memorandum to Bülow, the administration feared that the number of Germans resident in Germany who 'would attempt to avoid military service would considerably increase, especially in times where there was the danger of war . . .'[37] In a memorandum dated July 1910 Posadowsky, by then no longer State Secretary but a member of the Prussian Upper House, warned that in the future it might be necessary 'to raise the defensive capability of the country to a much greater extent than is now the case'. At the same time, he believed that larger social forces were leading to a growing disinclination to serve. 'The responsibility [for this tendency] lies with the long period of peace, increasing well-being and the resulting softness [Verweichlichung] of the lower classes, the social democratic propaganda, and a certain decadent disinclination to subject oneself to the pressures of discipline.'[38] Under these circumstances a relaxation of the rules that suggested to Germans that they might escape their military obligations by crossing the border into Belgium or Holland or Switzerland was to be avoided. The Foreign Office also took issue with Tirpitz's expansionist plans, and implied that his desire to increase the number of emigrants who remained citizens might be based on the desire to justify the building of a larger fleet.[39]

The Foreign Office took a skeptical view of claims that German emigrants fervently wished to share the burdens of German citizenship, a conclusion that reflected its extensive contacts with emigrants. The comments of the German consul in New York, Hossenfelder, were representative of those of most embassies and consulates, as reflected in a 1910 survey conducted by the Foreign Office. Hossenfelder wrote that 'whoever believes that Germans living abroad . . . will promptly report to the colors in the event of a crisis would, if this proposition were ever tested, experience great disappointment'. In the Balkan crisis of 1908 the consulate had alerted officers of the reserves that they might be called up. 'The General Consulate was thereupon flooded with written and oral requests, in which petitioners (from all classes and circles) sought "freedom from military service."' 'Even the most respected firms had no difficulties of conscience in supplying false affidavits to help their employees avoid their military obligations.' 'And if the petitions of these individuals, who with a beer in hand or in [German] clubs always stressed their Germanness, were rejected . . . then one always heard the same cynical question: did one really think they were so stupid as to risk their lives in a war that had nothing to do with them?' It would require 'very strong pressure' to force Germans living abroad to perform their military duty, and the German state had only limited means to exert this pressure.[40]

Hossenfelder also criticized one of the key premises of the whole enterprise of revising the citizenship law, that the retention of German citizenship would promote a common German identity. German emigrants felt a special attachment to Germany, he argued, but it had little or nothing to do with their citizenship. 'The feeling that most deeply moves the German living abroad is not his political connection with the Reich or a German state, nor with a particular ethnic group or nation, but the love of the soil on which he was born, where his childhood memories are.'[41] The overwhelming majority of German emigrants in the United States had freely become American citizens, yet many were active in German societies and clubs, and helped promote trade with Germany.[42] Hossenfelder advised insisting on the military-service obligation as a condition for retention of citizenship, not because German-Americans were likely to serve, but because it would function as a deterrent to emigration to escape the draft.

Despite the lukewarm attitude of most in the state administration, the agitation for the abolition of the ten-year rule became by the first decade of the twentieth century too great for the national government to ignore. Virtually all the parties in the Reichstag supported the change, as did scores of newspapers.[43] On at least two occasions, in 1901 and 1908, the Bülow government promised the Reichstag to introduce the amended law.[44] Each time it failed to do so. The main reason for this failure was disagreement within the Reich and Prussian administration regarding the requirement that German emigrants perform their military obligations. Tirpitz, Bethmann Hollweg (from 1907 State Secretary of the Interior) and, it seems, Bülow, all inclined not to include this requirement in the law. The sense that such a requirement would prove highly unpopular seems to have played an important role in forming the positions of both Bülow and Bethmann Hollweg.[45] But the Foreign Office and the Prussian Interior and War Ministries insisted on military service. The key point was, as the Prussian Interior Ministry put it, that a considerable number of individuals subject to military service emigrate abroad, primarily to countries in Europe, not from urgent economic reasons, but with the unmistakable intention to escape their service obligations. To keep open to individuals who have grossly violated their duties to the Fatherland the possibility of enjoying the full protection of the Reich and of returning unhindered after they have reached an age that prevents their conscription would not correspond to a sense of justice and the demand for equal completion of their civic duty by all subjects.[46]

Bülow was not prepared to take on virtually the entire administration, and in the end decided not to submit the bill.

It was during Bethmann Hollweg's chancellorship that the revised citizenship law was finally introduced and adopted. But Bethmann, like Bülow, in the end accepted the position of almost all the administration, apart from Tirpitz, that satisfaction of the military service requirement be a condition for the maintenance of citizenship.[47] Because it imposed the requirement for military service on (male) emigrants who wished to remain German citizens, the law of 1913 in fact had only modest consequences for most German emigrants. The law aided men who emigrated or worked as merchants abroad after they had fulfilled their military service requirements at home, emigrants who had before 1913 lost their German citizenship immediately upon emigration (they now could claim citizenship automatically upon returning to Germany), and single adult women, who were not subject to military service and whose citizenship status was not tied to that of their fathers or of a husband. German emigrants who lost their citizenship after 1913 no longer had a right to revive their citizenship upon returning to Germany. The law made no special concessions to ethnic Germans who had never been citizens of the nation state. As before, the treatment of such questions was left entirely in the hands of the administration. What was new was the grandiose claim of principle, the suggestion that all Germans – at least outside of Austria-Hungary – in some sense belonged to the Reich, and might look to it for protection.

The guidelines prepared by the Foreign Office for use of its embassies and consular officials in applying the new citizenship law fully justified Tirpitz's fears of class bias. The guidelines gave consular officials the power to excuse Germans living overseas from having to report for military service in Germany, but only if fixed employment or property would be thereby endangered. Individuals who had lost their German citizenship would be permitted to reacquire it, but only if they were 'of use to Germandom abroad'.

This group includes in particular members of commercial circles. Our economic relationships with the outside world, our exports and our shipping is based to a very significant degree on our merchants who dwell abroad. Not a few German families overseas have been active in this sense for generations . . .[48]

German missionaries were also to be especially favored, as well as all those who were active in promoting German churches, schools, and communal life. The guidelines required embassies and consulates to report on the national feeling of the applicant for citizenship, his position within the German community, and his conduct generally.

Although the terms of the law made it unlikely that large numbers of emigrants would maintain their German citizenship, the fact that the law explicitly made it possible for Germans to hold dual citizenships, and had been advertised as a vehicle for appealing to the loyalties of German emigrants, aroused fears in Russia that Germany would employ the Germans in that country as a fifth column.[49] Ethnic Germans in fact held a range of high offices in the Tsarist state. The German Ambassador in St. Petersburg, Count von Pourtales, reported to Bethmann Hollweg in March 1912 that various Russian officials, including Foreign Minister Sazonov, were concerned about the dual loyalties such a legal provision promoted. Pourtales quoted anonymously an official who attacked the law quite aggressively, claiming that it demonstrated the 'moral uncleanliness of our good neighbor'.[50]

Limiting Naturalizations

The 1913 citizenship law also created an instrument for national, and, in practice, Prussian, control of the naturalization policies of the different German states. The Prussian Interior and War Ministries and the Reich Foreign Office had originally advocated giving the Chancellor a veto over all naturalization decisions. Bavarian objections led to the placement of this veto power in the Bundesrat, the federal council comprised of representatives of the different federal states. Despite the change, Prussian objectives were accomplished. While Prussia controlled only 17 of the 58 votes in the Bundesrat, this bloc was sufficient to permit it to enforce its will in most matters.[51]

By 1912 it was an open secret that Prussia strictly limited the naturalization of Jews and Poles. During Reichstag debates Social Democratic Reichstag Deputy Eduard Bernstein described instances in which Jewish applicants for naturalization had been directly informed by lower-level officials of the policy, and advised not to waste their time submitting petitions.[52] Jewish organizations began in 1908 to keep track of how many Jewish applicants were accepted and rejected, and in this way to introduce statistical evidence of the policy.[53] The anti-Polish tenor of Prussian naturalization policies was also a matter of public record, although only the Polish Party focused on this aspect in the Reichstag debates.[54]

Despite the overwhelming evidence to the contrary, Prussia steadfastly denied in public that it discriminated on the basis of confession. 'Confession does not play a decisive role in the judgment of naturalization requests', a Reich Interior Office official, Lewald, assured the Reichstag in 1913, on behalf of the Prussian Interior Minister.[55] While it was clear from the public record that this assurance was false, even with the slippery term 'decisive' (massgebend), the Center, National Liberal, and Progressive parties claimed to interpret the words as admitting previous error and promising future change.[56] Exactly how much they desired Prussian policies to change is, however, unclear. The Conservatives and the Anti-Semites, of course, simply applauded the exclusion of Poles and Jews.

The Center Party's criticisms of Prussian policies were so oblique as to amount almost to an endorsement. 'In the press much has been written suggesting that confession has until now had a great influence on naturalizations in Germany, especially in Prussia', Center Party Deputy Emil Belzer commented to the Reichstag.[57] Without making clear his views on the truth of the charges, Belzer stated that he believed Prussia had promised to change its policies. Belzer assured the Reichstag that his party held itself 'distant from all anti-Semitism', although he was then quick to note that 'we do not wish a mass naturalization of Galician peddlers'. Nor, for that matter, did the Center Party desire the naturalization of 'thousands of impoverished farmworkers'. 'We are obliged to take care that our communities are protected from the naturalization of morally or economically doubtful elements.' His party believed that in certain states naturalizations were made too lightly, and therefore 'it is natural that other states be given the right to have a say in the matter'.[58]

Anton Beck, a National Liberal deputy, was almost as cautious as Belzer in his criticism of Prussian policies. He acknowledged that there had been instances 'that at least have created the impression that the application of the law was not entirely uninfluenced by anti-Semitic inclinations and tendencies'.[59] He noted that Jewish organizations had urged the Reichstag to include a provision in the law prohibiting discrimination on the basis of confession, but rejected this possibility because 'we did not want to shake the principle that no right [to naturalization] exists'. And therefore, continued Beck, his party had accepted the assurances of the Prussian government that 'confession as such would not be a decisive consideration for the administration in decisions regarding naturalizations'. In response to heckling from the Social Democrats, Beck claimed to believe that 'we are in the position to check the carrying out of this assurance [on the part of Prussia] . . .' At the same time Beck affirmed that 'under certain circumstances political considerations could influence the decision [regarding a naturalization petition]. The state must certainly consider what political elements it wishes to accept . . .'[60]

The Progressive representative who spoke during the debate, Andreas Blunck, rejected Prussian claims that it did not discriminate on the basis of religion as 'completely groundless and contradicted by the facts'. 'We have ascertained the existence of a broad policy whose principal purpose is to prevent the naturalization in Prussia of individuals from a certain confession.' At the same time Blunck claimed to believe that Prussia had promised to change its policies in the future. 'We therefore lay great weight on the fact that [the granting of power to the Bundesrat] represents a complete break with current Prussian naturalization policies . . .'[61]

Only the Social Democratic Party consistently opposed Prussian efforts to centralize control over naturalizations in Berlin. The Social Democrats went so far as to advocate that foreigners 'be granted a right to citizenship when they have lived for a certain period in Germany'.[62] Social Democratic deputy Otto Landsberg openly attacked Prussia's duplicity. Prussia had assured the Reichstag commission considering the proposed law that 'confessional considerations are not given weight in the examination of petitions for naturalization'.[63] But this assurance had been accompanied by the words 'exactly as little as previously', which, Landsberg pointed out, meant that the assurance was meaningless. Landsberg read into the minutes a 1901 letter from the Prussian Interior Minister prohibiting the naturalization of foreign Jews born and raised in Prussia, unless active service in the army was guaranteed. As a result of granting the veto to the Bundesrat, Landsberg told the Reichstag, 'Prussia will be in a position to enforce its [current] naturalization principles'.[64]

Women without a Fatherland?[65]

That German women lost their citizenship upon marriage with a man who was not a German citizen, a norm established in the Untertanengesetz and restated in the 1870 citizenship law, first became a matter of public controversy shortly before the First World War, thanks to the development of an organized, largely middle-class, women's movement. While women's groups capable of agitation on local issues had existed in Germany since the 1860s, it was only at the very end of the nineteenth century that the preconditions for effective national lobbying had begun to exist, although German women did not gain the right to vote until after the First World War. The national woman's magazine *Die Frau* began publication in 1893. The umbrella organization for middle-class women's groups, the Federation of German Women's Groups (Bund Deutscher Frauenvereine, or BDF) was formed in 1894. It was only after 1908 that these organizations and individual women were permitted to engage in political activities in all the German states.[66] The BDF played the leading role in the effort to persuade the government and the Reichstag to permit women to retain their citizenship upon marriage with a foreigner. The Social Democratic Party, once stimulated by the agitation of women, also advocated a change, as did German Jewish organizations.[67]

In petitions to the Reichstag in 1912 and 1913 the BDF argued that existing laws harmed women's interests. German women who married foreigners faced expulsion if their husbands became impoverished or were convicted of a crime. BDF petitions emphasized the ways in which the operation of the law might harm women's ability to fulfill their traditional domestic roles. For example, women who married foreigners in a second marriage and who were expelled might be separated from their children from the first marriage, for these children would remain German. There was the element of unchivalrous intrusion into a woman's private sphere: 'for a woman devoted to her Fatherland,' wrote the BDF, 'it can possibly be as much of an imposition [to be forced] to change her citizenship as her religious faith'.[68] In an article published in *Die Frau* Helene Lange, the editor, wrote that 'what is most important for us is that the old dominance of the man (die alte Ehevogtei des Mannes) still rules . . . The State is the Fatherland of the man, and the woman belongs to it only indirectly.'[69] While a woman might choose to give up her citizenship upon marriage, this ought to be a product of her own free will.[70]

The provisions of the 1870 citizenship law that granted citizenship to women upon marriage with a German to some degree undercut state policies of excluding foreign Poles, Jews, and members of various other groups from citizenship. German states were not in a position to control decisions regarding choice of a spouse. Jewish or Polish women generally did not cease to be Jewish or Polish upon marriage with German citizens, especially since it often happened that the Germans they married were also Jewish or Polish, respectively. Rosa Luxemburg was a notorious, if rather unusual, example of the difficulties that might be created for the state. Luxemburg, a leading left-wing Social Democrat in the last decade of the Kaiserreich, was a Jewish immigrant from Eastern Europe who had become a German citizen through marriage. She therefore could not be deported, although the Prussian police would undoubtedly very much have liked to be rid of her.

On the other hand, the rule that women automatically assumed the citizenship of their husbands had certain advantages for state administrators interested in excluding Poles and Jews. Since the majority of immigrants in Germany were male, in most cases marriages between aliens and German citizens involved a woman who was a German citizen and a man who was an alien.[71] When Bismarck expelled some 30,000 Polish and Jewish foreigners from Prussia in 1885 and 1886, Peter Spahn, a Center Party delegate in the Prussian Lower House, protested that the expulsions were being carried out 'against women and children, even in the case, which is the norm, that the women are Prussians [by birth]'.[72] The government response came nine months later, in a second debate on the subject. Wilhelm von Rauchhaupt, the leader of the Conservative party in the Prussian Lower House, told this body in January 1886: 'Gentlemen, one seeks by using this expression "Prussian women" to arouse our national feelings. But it would have been more correct if the gentlemen had simply said: the immigrant Poles married domestic Poles. In this way the expulsion of these married Polish women, who anyway have become foreigners through their marriages, loses its severity.'[73] Prussian Interior Minister Puttkamer refused to consider arguments that marriage to a Prussian woman should protect a man from expulsion. 'To take this [marriage with a former Prussian] into consideration would come close to negating the entire policy.'[74]

Had German women been given the option of retaining their citizenship upon marriage, or becoming dual citizens, the state's power to exclude resident foreigners would have been significantly weakened. This was because German states were generally reluctant to break up families through expulsions. This meant permitting non-German spouses to remain in the country. Blunck, the Progressive Party speaker, touched on this problem in his comments in the Reichstag in 1913. Blunck stated that his party opposed the proposals to permit German women to retain their citizenship even in the event of marriage with someone who was stateless. Such a law would in practice permit the permanent residence of the couple in Germany. 'Our administrative officials would still be in the position to expel the stateless person, but they would then be required to break apart the marriage, and since they quite understandably should not and probably will not do this, the stateless man . . . would in this way acquire the right to reside permanently in Germany.'[75]

Women's groups were not entirely alone in their advocacy of married women's citizenship rights. The liberal *Frankfurter Zeitung* editorialized after the BDF's defeat that 'rarely has the wife been treated so crassly as an unfree, mere appendage of her husband as in this instance'.[76] But the principal allies of women's groups were the Social Democratic Party and the socialist press. The Social Democrats made the issue one of the liberation of women from male domination. Eduard Bernstein, a leading Social Democratic deputy, told the Reichstag that 'a widening [of woman's right to individuality (Persönlichkeit)], not only in legal and political respects, but in all regards, is a necessary consequence of economic changes that have taken place in our society . . .'[77] Bernstein did not mention the importance of traditional family roles.

Despite the efforts of women's groups to convince the conservative side of the Reichstag, in the end only the Social Democrats supported the BDF's petition. The Center and Conservative Parties appealed to the 'indissoluble, holy' character of the marriage bond, in whose 'unity and the unity of the family one of the principal bases of our Christian state' was to be found.[78] The attitude of at least a portion of the Reichstag to the whole issue was perhaps best expressed by the fact that during Bernstein's discussion of married women's citizenship rights it was necessary for the presiding officer to appeal to deputies to continue their private conversations outside the Reichstag chamber, so that Bernstein might be heard.[79] While some National Liberal deputies had promised to support the position of the women's groups, in the end they voted as the government recommended.[80] In an article entitled 'Women without a Fatherland' Helene Lange, the editor of *Die Frau*, bitterly attacked the middle-class parties for sacrificing women's rights on the altar of marital unity. 'The liberal parties again failed completely, and the 'government parties' in a more narrow sense, which so often have felt compelled to defend patriotism against the absence of national feeling and international spirit of the women's movement, have taken the wishes of women to remain true to their Fatherland as an attack on marriage.'[81]

The Great War

Before 1914, German citizenship policies had been crafted, in part, in preparation for war. The war therefore did not alter the basic direction of law and policy. But the war changed the meaning of citizenship. Before the war citizenship determined whether someone might permanently reside in Germany, and, if abroad, enjoy the protection of the state and the right to return. The German citizen had the right to vote, if male, and also, if male, the duty to serve in the army. After July 1914 citizenship meant the difference between being treated like an enemy alien – most foreigners in Germany in July 1914 fell into this category – or as a lawful subject. Aliens were expelled, interned or compelled to remain at their jobs depending on the state administration's calculations of German interests.[82] If living in an enemy country abroad the German citizen also suffered deprivation. Conscription did not merely entail two humiliating years eating dust, but the deadly risks of modern warfare, of machine-guns, artillery and poison gas.

Initially, in the first months of the war, the period when many Germans believed the war would be both successful and short and for a time put aside pre-war enmities, German state administrations permitted hundreds of resident aliens from disadvantaged ethnic and religious groups to enlist, and in this way to gain citizenship for themselves and sometimes for their families. The result, in Prussia, was an increase of some three thousand naturalizations each year over the 1914 figure, at least in 1915 and 1916. This benevolence even extended to foreign Jews. Several hundred of the petitions granted in 1915 were from Jewish men enlisting in the army, a figure for Jewish naturalizations far higher than those recorded before the war.[83] The strictures on the naturalization of Social Democrats were also relaxed. The Social Democrats had voted for the war credits, after all. The Prussian Minister of the Interior informed the head of the district government in Potsdam in January 1915 that, at least with respect to Russian-German immigrants, 'membership in the Social Democratic Party is not at this moment to be given decisive weight, especially when the petitioner has not played a leading role in the party'.[84]

Most foreign aliens in Germany did not benefit from the temporary relaxation of domestic political tensions. Those who were citizens of allied powers, the Austrians and the Italians, were permitted to leave. But in October 1914 the government decided to prohibit the departure of Russian-Polish agricultural workers. Some 300,000 of these migrant laborers were compelled to remain at their jobs in Germany, often against their will. The German Labor Agency recruited an additional quarter million Poles later in the war, often employing duress. Between October 1916 and February 1917 the German army forcibly transported some 60,000 Belgians to work in German factories. This proved so unsuccessful that the German authorities thereafter relied primarily on economic pressure, which they could effectively exert through their control of the Belgian economy. The largest pool of foreign labor was in a very literal sense composed of prisoners, the prisoners of war captured by the German army. There were 1.6 million of these in mid-1916 and 2.5 million by the end of the war.[85]

It is to be doubted whether very many of the foreign recruits for the German economy had much interest in becoming German citizens. This would have meant, among other things, the likelihood of being drafted. At least after the first few months of the war, German states firmly opposed the naturalization of most foreigners. The Prussian government's attitude with regard to the naturalization of most of the foreigners remaining in Germany after the start of the war was summarized in a letter of December 1914 from the Prussian Interior Minister Friedrich von Loebell to Chancellor Bethmann Hollweg. 'With respect to petitions submitted after the start of the war, one can assume that they are intended exclusively or primarily to serve the aim of avoiding surveillance and measures aimed at retaliation. They are therefore in principle to be *rejected*.'[86] The other German states agreed to follow the same principle.[87]

The hardening of attitudes toward foreigners that took place in the course of the war was particularly evident with respect to Jews. Initially the war had brought about a reduction in anti-Semitic agitation. Jews played a leading role in planning the war economy. Concern about the effects of anti-Semitic measures on the attitudes of American Jews may also have played a role, at least at the highest levels of the state. But in 1916 the gloves came off. Pamphlets that characterized Bethmann Hollweg as the 'Chancellor of the German Jews' began to circulate in right-wing circles early in 1916.[88] In October 1916 the Army undertook its infamous tabulation of Jewish soldiers, an undertaking that reflected the widespread suspicion that German Jews were not adequately represented in the most dangerous positions.[89] By the end of 1917, following the failure of the gamble with unrestricted submarine warfare, the entrance of the United States into the war, and, in July 1917, the resignation of Bethmann Hollweg, the general mood had turned so bitter that Jewish leaders seriously feared pogroms. 'They are preparing a scapegoat, which will be sent into the wilderness in the place of those really responsible', wrote the German-Jewish sociologist Franz Oppenheimer in October 1918.[90]

In light of the existence of such attitudes with respect to German Jews, it is not surprising that Jewish foreigners came in for even harsher treatment. In the fall of 1915 the Prussian Minister of the Interior, von

Loebell, prohibited the employment of Russian Jews in industry or agriculture in the eastern provinces.[91] In May 1916 Bethmann Hollweg ordered consulates to grant visas to Russian Jews only in exceptional circumstances, on the grounds that their 'dishonest business methods are damaging to the local population'.[92] In April 1918, on the urging of the Ministry of War, Prussian Interior Minister Wilhelm Drews imposed a total ban on the migration of Russian Jews to Germany, on the grounds that they had proven 'unwilling to work, unclean, [and] morally unreliable'.[93] Shortly thereafter, also on the urging of the Minister of War, the Prussian authorities began deporting foreign Jews found in Berlin.[94] Applications for naturalization from any foreign Jews not enlisting in the Army were throughout the war almost certain to meet with rejection. Near the end of the war even Jews who had enlisted and served in the army found their applications for citizenship rejected.[95]

The war created new reasons for Russian Germans to emigrate to Germany. The position of Russian Germans deteriorated rapidly after the start of the war, in part as a result of the general deprivation, and in part because of Russian suspicions regarding their loyalty. A Russian law adopted in February 1915 prohibited Russian Germans from purchasing land, and required Russian Germans living in a thousand-kilometer-wide zone in the west of Russia to sell their land within ten to sixteen months.[96] The war brought lawlessness and famine. At the same time that conditions in Russia became unbearable for many, the defeat of the Russian army placed over half a million Russian Germans under the direct control of the German army. From February to July 1916 the Fürsorge Verein brought 14,905 Russian Germans to Germany.[97] This pace increased dramatically in 1918. A memorandum written in August or September 1918 estimated that in the previous six months over 100,000 Russian Germans had returned to Germany.[98] Thousands of captured Russian prisoners of war were ethnic Germans, and the German army quickly singled them out for preferential treatment, in the hopes that they would choose to become citizens. The treaty of Brest-Litovsk, by which Bolshevik Russia concluded peace with Germany in March 1918, provided that Germany could freely solicit Russian workers to come to Germany. This included the Russian Germans.[99]

The war also created new missions for the resettled Russian Germans. The deaths suffered during the war had somehow to be made good. German authorities also took into consideration the possibility that Polish migrant laborers might not be as readily available after the war as before. Germany's territorial ambitions provided further grounds for encouraging the Russian German migration. For much of the war the heads of the national and Prussian states and the army planned the annexation of a large strip of Russian Poland, from the territory adjacent to Silesia, Posen and East Prussia. To attach this new property firmly to Germany, the authorities intended to settle it with ethnic Germans from Russia. At least some of the plans envisioned the deportation of the existing population of Poles, Jews and Russians.[100] German estimates of the total population of the territory ranged from two to three million persons, or somewhat more than the total number of Russian Germans.[101]

German annexation plans were a tightly held secret, and the Russian German migrants certainly did not know of the role they were intended to play. The German authorities did their best to prevent the migrants from learning about possible alternatives that did not fit the interests of the state. When German Americans sent Russian German prisoners of war German-language newspapers from America, the German army confiscated them. 'Their content might encourage thoughts of future emigration to overseas lands', noted the War Ministry. 'The fact that the newspapers are missing can easily be explained as a result of English thefts of mail, in the event any questions are posed on this point.'[102] Russian Germans were instruments to be used to further the ends of the state.

While the Russian Germans were the most readily available and desirable source of new 'human material', as the bureaucrats and army officers referred to them, at least some leaders of the state hoped and expected that the end of the war would bring about a vast homecoming of Germans from overseas. Count von Bernstorff, the German Ambassador to the United States, went so far as to predict in March 1917 that 'after the end of the war a large part (ein großer Teil) of the Germans living in North America will have the desire to return to their [German] home'.[103] In March 1918 State Secretary Wallraf of the Reich Office of the Interior expected that at least one million overseas Germans would return after the war. Such an immigration would be 'entirely welcome', he said, from the standpoint of both industry and agriculture.[104]

While the government confidently proceeded with its plans for the massive relocation of ethnic Germans from Russia and around the globe, the reception of the returnees in Germany was not always warm, especially late in the war. In May 1918, for example, the President of the District Government of Hanover wrote to the Prussian Interior Minister urging the rejection of petitions from Russian Germans working in the town of Linden for permission to bring their families from Russia and to settle in the town. The local administration doubted that the men, all prisoners of war, would find employment in the town after the war. It also critized the men's conduct and work ethic.[105] In August 1918 the official in charge of the collection of used clothing in Prussia opposed having a special collection for the Russian Germans – there were already too many collections.[106] And in December 1918 the Ministry of Economy and State Lands and Forests wrote to the Interior Minister urging that the number of ethnic German immigrants be limited, 'keeping in mind the difficulties relating to food, work, and finding housing for the domestic population'.[107] The agency for returning Germans complained to the Prussian Interior Ministry about the problems it was experiencing at the local level. In August 1918 Prussian Interior Minister Drews wrote District Government presidents warning that in many cases ethnic German refugees 'in vain are seeking necessary help . . . and are expelled by police and communal organizations . . . This must change'.[108]

There was one group of Germans whom Prussia and other German states intended to cast off mercilessly: deserters and individuals who failed to report for military service. On 3 August 1914 the Kaiser ordered all German men to return to the Fatherland. This call was repeated several times during the war. The citizenship law of 1913 permitted the state to deprive of their citizenship individuals who did not respond to such a summons. The Army High Command was for the most part prepared to wait until the end of the war to enforce the implied threat of expatriation, but by 1918 the state had deprived 7,000 residents of Alsace-Lorraine of their German citizenship and confiscated their property. The Army firmly intended to pursue all draft-dodgers after the war, but the general amnesty for desertion and failure to report for duty issued by Chancellor Friedrich Ebert on 3 December 1918 prevented this.

Soon after the end of the war it became apparent that many Germans living overseas viewed the loss of German citizenship not as a punishment but as a favor. In England the private property of German nationals had been confiscated during the war, and at the war's end many such individuals sought to regain their possessions by demonstrating that they had in fact lost German citizenship through the passage of ten years from emigration. When the question arose as to whether visits to Germany might have tolled this ten-year period, official German representatives showed some sympathy for the efforts of the individuals who wished to be unburdened of the attachment to Germany.[109] For the most part, however, the German government had an interest in having foreign Germans maintain their German citizenship. In 1919 Germany imposed a series of heavy taxes on all Germans, including Germans living abroad.[110] The prospect of having to pay an inheritance tax to Germany led thousands of German citizens who had emigrated hastily to renounce their German citizenship. 'I must unfortunately confirm', wrote a German embassy official in Chile in 1921, 'that a terribly great movement of German citizens into the Chilean camp has taken place [due to the inheritance tax].'[111] Citizens of other nations, like the English, 'do not give up their citizenship to obtain pecuniary advantages', commented the German General Consul in Norway regarding the receipt of a request from a well-to-do German for release from his German citizenship.[112]

Notes

1. As quoted in the 'Stellungnahme der Vertreter des Reichs-Marineamts in der Sitzung über das Staatsangehörigkeitsgesetz im Reichsamte des Innern' of 30 October 1905. BA, R 1501, Nr. 108030, p. 204RS.
2. Horst Rößler, 'Massenexodus: die Neue Welt des 19. Jahrhunderts', in Klaus Bade (ed.) *Deutsche im Ausland – Fremde in Deutschland: Migration in Geschichte und Gegenwart* (Beck, 1992), pp. 148–9; Peter Marschalk, *Deutsche Überseewanderung im 19. Jahrhundert: Ein Beitrag zur soziologischen Theorie der Bevölkerung* (Ernst Klett, 1973), p. 50.
3. *SBR* (21 February 1912), p. 250D.
4. Of course, the claim that the law created a pan-German state overlooked the existence of Austria-Hungary. The leadership of the German state had no intention of laying claim to the political loyalty of Austrian Germans. Not only was an independent Austria-Hungary, dominated by its German minority, critical to Germany's foreign policy, but union with Austria or large-scale immigration of its ethnic German citizens would have greatly increased the number of Catholics and threatened Protestant control of the State. One of the rare occasions on which this fear was recorded was in 1905, when the breakup of Austria-Hungary as the result of internal conflicts appeared a real possibility. Chancellor Bülow wrote the German Ambassador in Washington that Germany had no interest in absorbing the German territories of the Austrian state. Reprinted in Theodor Schieder, *Das Deutsche Kaiserreich von 1871 als Nationalstaat* (Westdeutscher Verlag, 1961), pp. 91–2. The passage cited was so sensitive that it was omitted from the version published in 1928 in an official document collection. James Joll, *The Origins of the First World War*, 2nd edn (Longman, 1992), pp. 56, 67.

5. *Deutsche Bundesakte* of 8 June 1815, in E. Huber, *Dokumente zur Deutschen Verfassungsgeschichte* (Kohlhammer, 1961), vol. 1, p. 80.

6. Carl von Rotteck, 'Gemeingeist', in C. Rotteck and C. Welcker (eds), *Staats-Lexikon oder Encyklopädie der Staatswissenschaften*, vol. 6 (Verlag Johann Friedrich Hammerich, 1835), p. 450.

7. Letter from General der Infanterie von Gneisenau (no date). GStA PK, HA I, PR 80I, Nr. 2a, p. 17. *SBP,* (17 February 1869), pp. 680–2.

8. The 1848 Frankfurt Parliament had also given voice to dissatisfaction with this clause of the law. *SBF*, vol. 1 (3 July 1848), p. 691.

9. Bismarck to Prussian Interior Minister Friedrich von Eulenburg, 2 March 1869. GStA PK, HA I, Tit. 77, Rep. 227, Nr. 4, Bd. 9, p. 308RS.

10. Memorandum from Bethmann Hollweg, State Secretary of the Reich Office of the Interior, to the Prussian Cabinet, of 22 September 1908, GStA PK, HA I, Rep. 90, 2253, pp. 164–5, 302.

11. *Gesetz über die Erwerbung und den Verlust der Bundes- und Staatsangehörigkeit* of 1 June 1870, Section 21, Paragraph 5. *RGBl* I, p. 355.

12. Memorandum from State Secretary of the Reich Office of the Interior, Bethmann Hollweg, to Chancellor von Bülow, dated 9 September 1908. GStA PK, HA I, Rep 90, Nr. 2253, pp. 154–5.

13. Opinion of the Minister for Foreign Affairs of 12 November 1908. GStA PK, HA I, Rep. 90, Nr. 2253, p. 342.

14. My discussion of the role of the Pan-German League and the German Colonial Society is based in part on the work of Howard Sargent of Georgetown University, who kindly let me see in draft portions of his dissertation on the history of the 1913 law.

15. Letter from Posadowsky to Chancellor Bülow of 6 November 1906. BA R 1501, Nr. 108010, p. 52RS.

16. *SBR* (6 March 1895), p. 1279A.

17. Ibid. (5 December 1896), p. 3755D.

18. Quoted in a letter from State Secretary Posadowsky of the Reich Office of the Interior to Chancellor Bülow of 6 November 1906. BA R 1501, Nr. 108009, p. 41RS.

19. K. Barkin, *The Controversy over German Industrialization, 1890– 1902* (University of Chicago Press, 1970), p. 112.

20. Marschalk, *Deutsche Überseewanderung im 19. Jahrhundert*, pp. 35–7.

21. For a discussion of Tirpitz's role in the Kaiserreich, see Volker Berghahn, *Der Tirpitz-Plan: Genesis und Verfall einer innen-politischen Krisenstrategie unter Wilhelm II* (Droste Verlag, 1971).

22. Letter from Tirpitz to Chancellor Bülow of 10 November 1905, BA R1501, Nr. 108009, p. 247RS.
23. Letter from Tirpitz to the Royal Cabinet of 15 October 1908. GStA PK, HA I, Rep. 90, Nr. 2253, p. 293RS.
24. Letter from Tirpitz to Chancellor Bülow of 10 November 1905, p. 249RS.
25. Letter from Tirpitz to the Royal Cabinet of 15 October 1908, p. 298.
26. Ibid., p. 293.
27. Ibid., p. 298.
28. Ibid., p. 293.
29. Letter from Tirpitz to Chancellor Bülow of 10 November 1905, BA R1501, Nr. 108009, p. 249.
30. Ibid., pp. 248RS–249.
31. Letter from Tirpitz to the Royal Cabinet of 15 October 1908, GStA PK, HA I, Rep. 90, Nr. 2253, p. 298.
32. Tirpitz to Bülow, 13 December 1908, GStA PK, HA I, Rep. 90, Nr. 2253, p. 370. See also the Memorandum entitled 'Stellungnahme der Vertreter des Reich-Marinemats in der Sitzung über das Staatsangehörigkeitsgesetz im Reichsamt des Innern' of 30 October 1905. BA, R 1501, Nr. 108030, pp. 202–5.
33. As noted by Bethmann Hollweg, then State Secretary of the Reich Office of the Interior, in his memorandum to the Prussian Cabinet of 22 September 1908, GStA PK, HA I, Rep. 90, Nr. 2253, p. 165RS.
34. Letter from Tirpitz to Chancellor Bülow of 10 November 1905, p. 249RS–50.
35. Letter from Tirpitz to the Royal Cabinet of 15 October 1908, p. 297RS.
36. Letter from Tirpitz to Chancellor Bülow of 10 November 1905, BA R1501, Nr. 108009, p. 252.
37. Letter from Posadowsky to Bülow of 6 November 1906, p. 48RS.
38. Letter from Posadowsky to Bethmann Hollweg of 18 July 1910, BA R1501, Nr. 108012, p. 234.
39. Opinion of the Minister of Foreign Affairs of 12 November 1908, GStA PK, HA I, Rep. 90, Nr. 2253, pp. 339–40.
40. Memorandum from the Office of the German Consulate in New York, signed Hossenfelder, to Chancellor Bethmann Hollweg, dated 1 April 1910. BA R1501, Nr. 108012, pp. (in order of citation) 328RS, 329, 334RS, 329, 330.
41. Ibid., p. 330. Or, as the Foreign Office put it in a memorandum to Bülow dated 12 November 1908: 'it is not the legal connection [das

staatliche Band], but rather the bond of culture, that ties [emigrants] to Germany . . .' GStA PK, HA I, Rep. 90, Nr. 2253, p. 341.

42. Memorandum from the Office of the German Consulate in New York, signed Hossenfelder, to Chancellor Bethmann Hollweg, dated 1 April 1910, BA R1501, Nr. 108012, p. 325RS.

43. See, as examples of the latter, 'Reichsangehörigkeit', *Hamburger Nachrichten* (21 December 1910), in BA 01.01 (Reichstag), Film 30841, Nr. 670 ('The English principle of the permanence of the quality as a British subject, once acquired, is undoubtedly one strong foundation of Britain's global position. Englishmen know very well that their citizens enjoy the greatest freedom abroad, and yet permit them to continue to be represented by their consulates and diplomatic representatives . . .'); 'Die Wehrpflicht der Auslandsdeutschen und die Erhaltung der Staatsangehörigkeit', *Vossische Zeitung* (18 January 1911), Ibid.; 'Ein nationales Gesetz', *Leipziger Neueste Nachrichten* (6 February 1912), Ibid.; 'Der neue Reichsangehörigkeitsgesetzentwurf', *Schlesische Zeitung* (13 February 1912), Ibid.; 'Das Gesetz über die Staatsangehörigkeit', *Leipziger Volkszeitung* (15 April 1912), Ibid.

44. *SBR* (25 January 1901), p. 903; *SBR* (17 March 1905); *SBR* (26 March 1908), p. 4305.

45. Letter of Chancellor Bülow to State Secretary of the Office of the Interior Bethmann-Hollweg of 7 January 1908, BA R 1501, Nr. 108010, p. 69; Letter of Bethmann Hollweg to Bülow, 9 September 1908, GStA PK, HA I, Rep. 90, Nr. 2253, pp. 152–3.

46. Memorandum of the Prussian Interior Ministry of 11 November 1908, GStA PK, HA I, Rep. 90, Nr. 2253, pp. 353RS–354.

47. Bethmann Hollweg's marginal notations to this effect are found in a memorandum summarizing the results of a survey of embassies and consulates from the Foreign Secretary. Memorandum from Kiderlen-Waechter to Bethmann Hollweg of 10 August 1910. BA R 1501, Nr. 108011, p. 237.

48. Instructions of 31 December 1913 from the Foreign Office to German consulates and embassies. BA R 1501, Nr. 108115, pp. 174–174RS.

49. *Reichs- und Staatsangehörigkeitsgesetz*, *RGBl* I (1913), p. 583 (Section 25). The law provided that the holding of dual citizenship had to be approved by the German state of which the individual was a citizen.

50. Report of Count von Pourtales to Bethmann Hollweg, 16 March 1912. See also the longer report from Pourtales to Bethmann Hollweg dated 14 March 1912. BA R1501, Nr. 108014, pp. 177–9.

Rogers Brubaker has suggested that the 1913 citizenship law amendments 'marked the nationalization, even the ethnicization, of German citizenship'. Brubaker's central claim is that the 1913 debates 'crystallized' a change in the purpose of the citizenship law, not that it dramatically changed its terms. 'In the context of a large and growing immigrant population and demands for easier naturalization . . . the decision to preserve pure *jus sanguinus* invested that legal principle with new meaning, transforming it from a taken-for-granted fact into a self conscious normative tradition.' R. Brubaker, *Citizenship and Nationhood in France and Germany* (Harvard University Press, 1992), pp. 114–15, 119. It is true that debates over the 1913 citizenship law reflected an emphasis on German ethnic solidarity not found in the discussions regarding its Prussian and German predecessors. But Brubaker underestimates the significance of the law's continuing requirement for military service by German emigrants, and hence the ways in which the 1913 law represented a defeat for German nationalists.

51. *Gesetz betreffend die Verfassung des Deutschen Reiches* of 16 April 1871, Section III, in Huber, *Dokumente zur Deutschen Verfassungsgeschichte*, vol. 2, p. 292.
52. Remarks of Social Democratic Deputy Eduard Bernstein, *SBR* (29 May 1913), p. 5302A.
53. Jack Wertheimer, *Unwelcome Strangers* (Oxford University Press, 1987), p. 169. The Prussian government had denied Jewish organizations access to its own statistics. See Memorandum of 6 January 1910 from the Minister of the Interior to all the Oberpräsidenten and District Government Presidents informing them of his refusal to furnish a representative of the Organization of German Jews with this information. GStA PK, HA I, Rep. 77, Tit. 227, Nr. 4, Bd. 21, p. 138.
54. Comments of Reichstag Deputy Dombek, *SBR* (28 May 1913), pp. 5286C–5287C.
55. *SBR* (29 May 1913), p. 5304A.
56. The Prussian government gave the Prussian Progressive Landtag Deputy Fischbeck similar assurances when he pressed it on the question of discrimination against Jews in deciding naturalization petitions. Fischbeck was told that 'the religion of the petitioner is not a matter of decisive importance: every year a large number of members of all religious faiths are taken in the band of citizens'. GStA PK, HA I, Rep. 77, Tit. 227, Nr. 4, Bd. 21, p. 160RS.
57. *SBR* (28 May 1913), p. 5276B.

58. Ibid., p. 5276C–D.
59. Ibid., p. 5279C.
60. Ibid., pp. 5279C–5280A.
61. Ibid., p. 5285D.
62. Ibid., p. 5273A.
63. Ibid., p. 5274C.
64. Ibid., p. 5274–5.
65. The subtitle is taken from an article by Helene Lange lamenting the failure of efforts to grant married women greater citizenship rights. Helene Lange, 'Die Frauen haben kein Vaterland', *Die Frau* 20 (August 1913), p. 641.
66. Barbara Greven-Aschoff, *Die bürgerliche Frauenbewegung in Deutschland, 1894–1933* (Vandenhoeck & Ruprecht, 1981), pp. 107–9.
67. The actions of the Social Democratic Party are described below. The lobbying of Jewish organizations is discussed in Jack Wertheimer, 'Jewish Lobbyists and the German Citizenship Law of 1914: A Documentary Account', *Studies in Contemporary Jewry* 1 (1984), pp. 152–3.
68. Petition of 27 April 1912 from the Federation of German Women's Groups to the members of the Commission for the Revision of the Reich and State Citizenship Law, BA R 01. 01 (Reichstag) Film 30841, File Nr. 670, 88.
69. Lange, 'Die Frauen', p. 642.
70. Ibid., p. 641. Lange's argument was one made generally by women's rights activists with respect to the patriarchal rules of the German Civil Code. Marianne Weber, *Ehefrau und Mutter in der Rechtsentwicklung: Eine Einführung* (J.C.B. Mohr, 1907), pp. 496–7. For a general discussion of the difficulties patriotic German women confronted at the turn of the last century in reconciling expression of the national feelings with their traditional roles, see Roger Chickering, '"Casting Their Gaze More Broadly": Women's Patriotic Activism in Imperial Germany', *Past and Present* 118 (February 1988), pp. 156–85.
71. Table 7, 'Die Ausländer im Deutschen Reich nach den Volkszählungen von 1900, 1905 und 1910', in *Statistisches Jahrbuch für das Deutsche Reich* 33 (1912), p. 6. The table shows that on 1 December 1900, of a total of 757,151 foreigners in the Reich, 303,973 were female. On 1 December 1910 the numbers were 1,236,048 and 531,185, respectively. The imbalance was significantly greater when children below marriageable age were excluded.

See Table 10, 'Staatsangehörigkeit und Alter der ortsanwesenden männlichen Bevölkerung nach Geburtsjahren,' and Table 11, 'Staatsangehörigkeit und Alter der ortsanwesenden weiblichen Bevölkerung nach Geburtsjahren', in *Zeitschrift des Königlich Preussischen Statistischen Bureaus* 28 (1888), pp. 126–7.

72. *SBP* (6 May 1885), p. 1752C.
73. Ibid., (28 January 1886), p. 162.
74. Letter of 26 July 1885 from the Prussian Interior Minister Puttkamer to the Oberpräsidenten of West Prussia and East Prussia. GStA PK, H.A. I, Rep. 77, Tit. 1176, Nr. 2a, Bd. V, p. 407. Puttkamer took a similar stance with respect to the numerous formerly Prussian Jewish women who married foreign Jews. Wertheimer, *Unwelcome Strangers*, p. 45.
75. *SBR*, (28 May 1913), p. 5285B. This argument could have been made just as easily with respect to marriages between German women and foreigners who were not stateless.
76. *Frankfurter Zeitung* (9 June 1913).
77. Remarks of Deputy Bernstein, *SBR* (29 May 1913), p. 5294D.
78. Remarks of Deputy Belzer, Ibid. (28 May 1913), p. 5276A. These comments were fully supported by Giese, a Conservative Party Deputy, Ibid., p. 5282C.
79. Remarks of Deputy Paasche, Ibid. (29 May 1913), p. 5294D.
80. Camilla Jellinek, 'Das Reichs- und Staatsangehörigkeitsgesetz und die Frauen: Ein Epilog', *Die Frauenfrage: Zentralblatt des Bundes Deutscher Fraunvereine* (1 August 1913), p. 1.
81. Helene Lange, 'Die Frauen,' p. 641.
82. See Wertheimer, *Unwelcome Strangers*, p. 56, for an example of a case in which a Jewish man was saved from expulsion in 1914 only by the fact that three of his sons were serving in the German army.
83. But at the end of the war the Prussian War Ministry refused to permit the naturalization of the families of Jews who had enlisted, despite promises to the contrary made at the start of the war. This applied even in cases when the men had died during the war. Egmont Zechlin and Hans Joachim Bieber, *Die deutsche Politik und die Juden im ersten Weltkrieg* (Vandenhoeck & Ruprecht, 1969), p. 277.
84. Letter of the Prussian Minister of the Interior to the District Government President in Potsdam dated 26 January 1915. GStA PK, HA I, Rep. 77, Tit. 226b, Nr. 63, Bd. 1, p. 127.
85. Ulrich Herbert, *A History of Foreign Labor in Germany, 1880–1980*, trans. by William Templer (University of Michigan Press, 1990), pp. (in order of citation) 87, 98, 105, 91.

86. Letter from the Prussian Minister of the Interior to the Reich Chancellor dated 6 December 1914. BAR 1501, Nr. 108020. Emphasis in original.

87. Memorandum entitled 'Aufzeichnung über die Beratungsgegenstände', relating to a meeting in the Reich Ministry of the Interior on 3 September 1920. BAR 1501, Nr. 108021.

88. Zechlin and Bieber, *Die deutsche Politik*, pp. 518–20.

89. Ibid., pp. 527–38. The survey showed that the anti-Semites' claims were false, but then the hatred the survey reflected was not guided primarily by statistics.

90. Ibid., pp. 550–1.

91. GStA PK, HA I, Rep. 77, Tit. 226b, Nr. 66, Bd. 1, p. 1. Trude Maurer estimates that in the course of the war roughly 30,000 Russian–Polish Jews worked as laborers in Germany. A greater number were employed, on a voluntary or compulsory basis, in industries in the conquered territories. Trude Maurer, *Ostjuden in Deutschland 1918–1933* (H. Christians Verlag, 1986), p. 38.

92. GStA PK, HA I, Rep. 77, Tit. 226b, Nr. 66, Bd. 1, p. 2.

93. Order of the Prussian Minister of the Interior to the Presidents of all District Governments dated 23 April 1918. GStA PK, HA I, Rep. 77, Tit. 227b, Nr. 66, Bd. 1, p. 10.

94. Maurer, *Ostjuden in Deutschland*, p. 39.

95. See, for example, the letter from the Police President of Berlin to the Prussian Interior Minister of 16 May 1919. GStA PK, Rep. 77, Tit. 226b, Nr. 65, Bd. 2.

96. Brandes, 'Die Deutschen in Rußland und der Sowjetunion', in K. Bade (ed.), *Deutsche im Ausland – Fremde in Deutschland* (Beck, 1992), p. 123.

97. GStA PK, HA I, Rep. 77, Tit. 226b, Nr. 63a, Bd. 1, p. 225.

98. Memorandum entitled 'Richtlinien für die Regelung der Rückwanderung aus Rußland', undated, in GStA PK, HA I, Rep. 77, Tit. 226b, Nr. 63a, Bd. 3, p. 121. I. Fleischhauer, *Das Dritte Reich und die Deutschen in der Sowjetunion* (Deutsche Verlags-Anstalt, 1983), p. 33, n. 70, gives somewhat lower figures.

99. Zechlin and Bieber, *Die deutsche Politik*, pp. 275–6.

100. Imanuel Geiss, *Die Polnische Grenzstreifen 1914–1918: ein Beitrag zur deutschen Kriegszielpolitik im Ersten Weltkrieg* (Matthiesen, 1960), pp. 84, 88.

101. Ibid., pp. 75, 84.

102. Memorandum of the War Ministry dated 18 July 1916. GStA PK, HA I, Rep. 227, Tit. 63a, Bd. 1, p. 211.

103. Memorandum from Count von Bernstorff dated 25 March 1917. GStA PK, HA I, Rep. 77, Tit. 226b, Nr. 63a, Bd. 2.
104. Minutes of a meeting of 20 March 1918 in the Reich Office of the Interior regarding the return of overseas Germans and ethnic German foreigners. GStA PK, HA I, Rep. 77, Tit. 226b, Nr. 63a, Bd. 2. The *Kriegszeitschrift des Fürsorgevereins für deutsche Rückwanderer* made a similar prediction in its 1 December 1916 issue. Ibid., p. 262.
105. Letter of the President of the District Government of Hanover to the Prussian Interior Minister dated 7 May 1918. GStA PK, HA I, Rep. 77, Tit. 226b, Nr. 63a, Bd. 3, p. 3.
106. Letter from the office of the Staatskommissar für die Regelung der Kriegswohlfahrtspflege in Preußen to the Prussian Interior Minister dated 12 August 1918. GStA PK, HA I, Rep. 77, Tit. 226b, 63a, Bd. 3, p. 201.
107. Ibid., p. 207.
108. Memorandum of the Prussian Minister of the Interior to the Presidents of District Governments dated 23 August 1918. GStA PK, HA I, Rep. 77, Tit. 226b, Nr. 63a, Bd. 3, p. 85RS.
109. See the letters dated 3, 5, and 13 October 1921 to the German Embassy in London, BA, R 1501, Nr. 108022.
110. These taxes are described in a letter from the Reich Minister of Finance to the Reich Minister of the Interior dated 3 August 1920. BA R 1501, Nr 108021.
111. Letter from Dieckhoff, no title given, to the Foreign Office dated 20 May 1921. BA R 1501, Nr. 108022.
112. Letter from the German Counsel in Kristiania to the President of the District Government in Cologne of 2 December 1919. BA R 1501, Nr. 10821.

Part III
Nadir and Transformation, 1918–2000

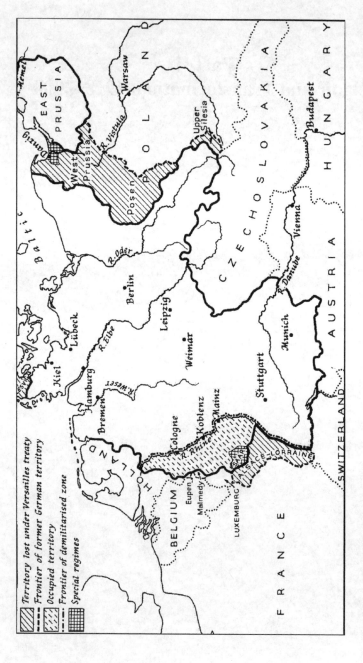

Map 8.1 Weimar Germany in 1919. From William Carr, *A History of Germany 1815–1945*, 2nd edn. (Edward Arnold, 1979). Copyright William Carr 1969, 1979. Reprinted by permission of Hodder Arnold.

-8-

A Cultural or a Racial Nation?

After 1918 a simple and stark division between ethnic Germans and all others replaced most of the highly refined categories of the 1904 Prussian naturalization treatise. The German states, or, as they were called after the war, Länder, of the new Weimar Republic naturalized ethnic Germans almost automatically, barring evidence of serious crimes or treason. States no longer carefully weighed whether potential citizens who were ethnic Germans could be drafted, or would vote for government parties, displace foreign labor, or promote German interests abroad. In part the change reflected the irrelevance of some of the pre-1918 criteria. Germany no longer had a conscript army. State administrations did not steer elections in the fashion that prevailed before 1918, at least in Prussia. Moreover, Prussia and, for shorter periods, the national state, was governed by coalition governments that included the Social Democratic Party: it would have been impossible to exclude sympathizers with that party from citizenship. Weltpolitik belonged to history.

Of even greater importance were the intensified feelings of ethnic solidarity and hatred caused by war and defeat, and the far greater influence of popular opinion on government policy. The war was from the start, in many respects, an ethnic war, of Germans against the other major ethnic groups of Europe. The harsh terms of the Treaty of Versailles, the terrible post-war housing and food shortages, and the inflation that destroyed the German currency between 1919 and 1923 all stoked animosity toward foreigners who had, it seemed, caused and profited from German misery. 'The foreigner is treated in private and in public as an enemy', commented a Spanish reporter in Berlin in May 1923, during the French occupation of the Ruhr and at the height of the catastrophic inflation.[1]

It is remarkable, given this popular mood, and the fact that Europe seemed awash with refugees, from the First World War and the various revolutions and border revisions that accompanied and followed it, that some German Land governments proved far more open to the naturalization of foreigners who were not ethnic Germans, including the most heavily stigmatized group, Jews, than their pre-war predecessors. Prussia, which for almost the entirety of the existence of the republic was ruled primarily by the Social Democratic Party, was the chief instance. This was true especially in the late 1920s, when the German economy seemed to stabilize. Bavaria and other conservative states and political parties bitterly criticized Prussian policies.

A different, less heated subject of debate during the Weimar Republic concerned those provisions of the citizenship law that deprived women of their German citizenship upon marriage with a foreigner. The granting of suffrage to women, and the election of a few women Reichstag deputies, gave women's groups greater political influence than they had had before the war. Nonetheless, the general climate of opinion led them to cast their arguments primarily in terms of the national interest, the fulfillment of traditional female roles, and national ethnic policies, and not to focus primarily on the needs and rights of women. The Reichstag twice expressed support for amending the law, but the Republic came to an end before any action was taken.

Welcoming Ethnic Germans

German states' policy of granting citizenship almost automatically to foreign ethnic Germans was embodied in guidelines regarding naturalization that the Reich Interior Ministry circulated to the different German Länder in June of 1921. According to the guidelines, former German citizens – meaning primarily individuals who had lived in territories taken from Germany by the Treaty of Versailles – were to be rapidly naturalized. Land administrations could assume that they would feel 'solidarity with German political interests – also in conflict with foreign countries'. 'The same holds for ethnic Germans (deutschstämmige Ausländer) who have never been citizens, as long as they preserved the German outlook (deutsche Gesinnung) and German special nature (Eigenart) while abroad.'[2] Particular contrary evidence of disloyalty could call these presumptions into question. For example, while the 1921 guidelines explicitly excluded consideration of political views, foreigners, including ethnic Germans, who had opposed German interests or who constituted a threat to domestic tranquility were to be denied citizenship.

The rules Prussia issued for the benefit of provincial officials suggest how the ethnic standard was applied in practice. The official form – I describe here the version employed in 1929 – instructed officials to ask about the language of instruction in the schools applicants had attended;

whether children in the family were being raised only with a German education, or whether they were also learning a foreign language; whether siblings lived abroad; whether the individual maintained relationships with nationals of his former country; whether the applicant spoke German fluently or with any foreign accent; and, more generally, whether it could be assumed that the person fully shared German nature and ethnicity ('daß er mit deutschen Wesen und Volkstum völlig verwachsen ist').[3] The form also included a series of questions copied from the comparable pre-1918 document, questions designed to elicit information regarding income, work ethic, and also confession. But these questions had become relatively less significant, at least with respect to ethnic German applicants for citizenship.[4] Virtually all ethnic German applicants for citizenship were rapidly naturalized. Prussia granted 114,029 petitions for citizenship from ethnic German foreigners between 1919 and 1931. And since this figure does not include family members, the total number of persons involved was probably three or four times as large as the number of successful petitions.[5]

The willingness of Länder readily to naturalize ethnic German immigrants did not mean that these individuals necessarily found it easy to find a niche within Germany. As noted earlier, local communities sometimes did their best to ward off outsiders, including ethnic Germans, at least in the immediate post-war period. Some Länder sanctioned this practice. In June 1919 Baden gave its communities, for a short period, the power to expel all individuals not belonging to the community, including both Badenese and citizens of other Länder.[6] In October 1923 Bavaria expelled hundreds of Prussians, measures that ceased only when Prussia threatened to take similar actions against Bavarians.[7] This was a return, on a small scale, to pre-1870 legal conditions. The grant of citizenship was only of modest importance if a citizen could not live where he wished.

With the passage of time the treatment of returning Germans by the different Länder seems to have become somewhat less open. In 1924 the head of the Eastern Office of the Foreign Ministry, Ago von Maltzahn, ordered German embassies not to grant entry visas to Nazis and Communists.[8] For a long period the common policy of refusing to naturalize criminals and political extremists prevented the naturalization of Hitler. Hitler's leadership of an attempted coup in 1923 was hard to overlook. It was only a month before the presidential election of March 1932, in which he was the Nazi Party candidate, that Hitler became a German citizen by accepting a minor civil service post in the state of Braunschweig.[9] In the late 1920s the Länder became somewhat less open to ethnic German immigrants from a range of East European countries. In

1927 the Prussian Interior Ministry limited the immediate naturalization of ethnic Germans from Poland to individuals who had emigrated with the approval of the German consulate. All others had to wait at least three years.[10] In September 1929 the three-year residence requirement was extended to all ethnic German returnees, to discourage immigration. The smaller German communities abroad became, the weaker would be Germany's claim to its lost territories.[11] The start of the Great Depression undoubtedly reinforced this tendency.

Anti-Semitism and its Enemies

While the Länder welcomed ethnic Germans as citizens, they imposed a range of barriers to the naturalization of those who were not ethnic Germans. From 1920 all Länder required individuals who were not ethnic Germans to have resided for at least ten years in Germany before they might be considered for naturalization. Some Länder, notably Bavaria, imposed a twenty-year residency requirement, at least with respect to foreigners from Eastern Europe. And even if an applicant met the residency requirement, many Länder were still quite reluctant to grant naturalization.

The hostility to the naturalization of foreigners who were not ethnic Germans was in part a product of the terrible suffering of the war and post-war period. Germans bitterly resented foreigners whose access to foreign currency allowed them to buy German property for a song during the inflation. For example, in 1922 the mayor of a town in the Düsseldorf region demanded the expulsion of a foreigner on the grounds of popular envy. 'In the community there is great discontent regarding the brazen conduct of the foreigner, who is able by paying a high rent to live in an apartment, while many local residents have been waiting for an apartment for over a year.'[12] This story could be multiplied many times over.[13] In a bitter debate on the immigration of East European Jews in the Prussian Parliament in November 1922 the Center Party representative, Loenartz, closed the discussion with a comment with which many, and probably most, Germans would have agreed. 'One thing is certain. The German people will become great again, and Germans living abroad will return to us and our culture only if we . . . firmly protect ourselves against everything that is unhealthy and foreign.'[14] What was foreign seemed to many, by definition, unhealthy.

The animosity toward non-Germans relented to some degree in the mid-1920s, following the stabilization of the mark and a modest economic recovery. But even in this period intense xenophobia remained a significant feature on the middle and right of the political landscape. Carl Schmitt's well-known essay, *The Concept of the Political*, first composed as a lecture in 1927, is a good instance of the widespread influence of this ethnic xenophobia. Schmitt, a law professor at the University of Berlin, wrote that loyalty to an ethnic nation (Volk) provided the fundamental basis for politics, and for permanent conflict among nations. It was the fact that foreigners had a different 'form of life' (Art von Leben) that made foreign nations a threat which 'must be defended against or fought to preserve one's own form of life'.[15] Anti-foreign feeling revived when the Great Depression struck, at the end of 1929. In September 1930 the Nazi Party, the advocate of violently xenophobic and anti-Semitic views, won more than six million votes in a Reichstag election, becoming the second largest party in the state. In 1932 it became the largest party in the Reichstag.

Despite the popular mood, and the extraordinarily difficult conditions, the leadership of the Social Democratic Party never abandoned its pre-war position that long-term residents of Germany should be given the chance to become citizens, if they could demonstrate cultural assimilation. Foreign Jews were the focal point of most of this debate. Before the war some 80,000 foreign Jews lived in Germany, more than 10 percent of the total Jewish population.[16] An additional 40,000 East European Jews had been brought to Germany during the war to work in war industries.[17] And in the aftermath of the war, as a result of pogroms in Poland, the miseries of the Russian civil war and the breakdown of controls over the eastern border, further tens of thousands of Jews entered the country. Popular opinion blamed foreign Jews for taking advantage of the inflation to buy German property at fire-sale prices, for occupying apartments and taking jobs that should have gone to Germans, and for crime and disease.[18] Conservatives feared that East European Jews would infect the German nation with communism.

While Prussia did its best to prevent immigration over Germany's eastern borders with Poland and Czechoslovakia (although the migration of seasonal farm workers from Poland continued on a small scale), it permitted most Jews who had entered Germany after 1914 to remain temporarily, assuming that they were employed.[19] It is true that foreign Jews who were unemployed were, beginning in 1920, placed in internment camps and, if possible, deported.[20] And the state often found ways of making life difficult even for those individuals who had found work.[21] But Prussia did not undertake large-scale deportations. The most important reason, at least in the immediate post-war period, was fear of the Allied response. Wolfgang Heine, the Social Democratic Prussian

Interior Minister in 1919 and early 1920, argued that mass expulsions might 'once again give credence to [war-time] claims of German barbarism'. Some officials hoped that a gentler treatment of Jewish refugees would influence Jewish opinion in America, and that this in turn would lead to a milder treatment of Germany in the ongoing negotiations regarding reparations and territory.[22] Prussian officials also feared that mass expulsions of Jews to Poland or Czechoslovakia might lead these countries to retaliate against their German minorities.[23] Humanitarian considerations were also not entirely irrelevant. In 1919 Jews expelled to Poland faced pogroms. In a debate in 1922 in the Prussian Parliament the Social Democratic Interior Minister, Carl Severing, went so far as to remind the chamber that the immigrants were also human beings, citing Lessing – this provoked laughter from the conservative side of the house.[24]

Prussia not only permitted foreign Jews to continue to live in the state, but to some degree relaxed previous restrictions on their naturalization. Prussian Interior Minister Heine discarded the pre-war naturalization guidelines in mid-1919. In response to an inquiry from the state of Anhalt, Heine wrote that in the future 'even the appearance of discriminatory treatment on the basis of confession would be avoided'. Prussia generally assumed, he stated, that a foreigner who wished to become a German citizen in spite of the military defeat 'has inwardly become firmly attached to the German state (das deutsche Staatswesen)'. In principle all former Germans and also foreigners who seemed desirable additions to the German nation were to be naturalized. Polish and Galician Jews, he wrote, were normally naturalized, 'if their personal conduct is not objectionable, they have resided in Prussia for a long period, and they have found an adequate [economic] position'.[25] Heine sent an order of the same tenor to the Prussian District Governments.[26]

Since Heine's tenure in office was brief, and since the vast majority of Interior Ministry officials had little sympathy with the naturalization policies he proposed, his orders had almost no practical consequences, as indicated by the figures in Table 8.1. Shortly after he left office, in 1920, Prussia imposed a ten-year residence requirement on all applicants for citizenship who were not ethnic Germans. In 1921 this period was raised to fifteen years. In April 1922 the new Social Democratic Prussian Interior Minister, Severing, found it necessary to warn officials against letting anti-Jewish prejudices influence naturalization decisions.[27]

Even the naturalization of a few hundred Jews annually was, however, too much for the conservative Bavarian government. In a long series of dreary memoranda the Bavarian Interior Ministry rejected Prussian

Table 8.1 Naturalization Petitions Granted in Prussia, 1919–1931

Year	Number of naturalization petitions granted	Ethnic Germans ('Deutsch stämmige')	East Europeans of non-German origin	Other non-Germans
1919	3,656	3,437	146	73
1920	5,315	4,997	212	106
1921	6,953	6,536	278	139
1922	10,895	10,243	435	217
1923	17,847	16,778	713	356
1924	11,713	11,117	450	146
1925	8,168	7,749	253	166
1926	10,630	9,445	816	369
1927	10,380	9,371	733	276
1928	11,433	8,999	1,802	632
1929	10,609	8,192	1,816	601
1930	11,667	8,700	2,332	635
1931	10,251	8,465	1,268	518
Total	129,517	114,029	11,254	4,234

Source: 'Nachweisung über die . . . in Preußen erfolgten Einbürgerungen von Ausländern', BA R 43 II/134, p. 20, cited in Maurer, *Ostjuden in Deutschland*, p. 857, n. 162. Since the figures given here are based on the number of petitions granted, the actual number of individuals naturalized, when family members are considered, was probably some three times as great.

claims that Jews could become Germans through cultural assimilation. Bavarian memoranda to the Reich Interior Ministry written in 1928 and 1929 stated the essence of the position, arguing that

> the mastery of the German language, which often is the commercial language of traders in the east, and attendance at German schools, which East Europeans prefer to their own schools simply because they provide superior opportunities for economic advancement, ease the progress of East Europeans in Germany. They offer no assurance, however, that the immigrants inwardly feel and think like Germans.[28]

Bavaria expressed particular concern over the threat posed to German culture by East European Jews who managed to find positions in the academic professions and in professorships at universities.

> The ever increasing entrance of Easterners into the German academic professions (die deutsche Wissenschaft) is a very regrettable fact. It is becoming ever more common for East Europeans, often after only a short residence in Germany, to attain professorships at our German universities and

scientific institutes and to work there as teachers of our German youth, while qualified German nationals are passed over and neglected.[29]

Bavaria advocated a twenty-year residence requirement for Jews and other East Europeans. This would effectively prevent, for the time being, the naturalization of East Europeans who had entered Germany after 1914. And it would permanently keep foreign professionals who had come to Germany as students from achieving the highest positions in their professions. Without German citizenship it was very difficult to find work as a teacher, a doctor, or in many other professional fields, and few could afford to wait twenty years from the start of their studies to start their careers.

Prussia and Bavaria repeatedly came to blows in the Reichsrat – as the Bundesrat, with reduced powers, was called after the war – over Prussian naturalizations of Jewish applicants for citizenship. As in the Kaiserreich, naturalization decisions in the Weimar Republic were made independently by the administration of each state. The 1913 citizenship law had, however, made necessary some consultation between the different Länder. The amended law provided that naturalization could take place only after the Chancellor had established that none of the other states had raised an objection. In the event of a conflict the Bundesrat was empowered to make a decision.[30] As a result of this requirement, each state regularly submitted lists of proposed naturalizations to the Chancellor, who then distributed them to the other states. Bavaria regularly used its powers under this clause to object to all the Jews on Prussia's naturalization lists.

While the Prussian government attempted in the mid-1920s to compromise with Bavaria, it eventually tired of the effort. In April 1927 the Prussian Parliament urged the Prussian Interior Ministry to require only a ten-year residency period for the naturalization of foreigners who were not ethnic Germans.[31] Two months later Prussian Interior Minister Severing informed the other German states of his intention to follow this resolution. 'Solidarity with German culture is to be determined on the basis of habits, speech, upbringing, culture and activities that reflect a German state of mind.'[32] Whereas Prussia naturalized some several hundred East Europeans annually between 1919 and 1927, from 1928 to 1930 this figure jumped to roughly two thousand per year (and these figures do not include family members). Given the number of foreign Jews living in Germany since 1914, however, the figures are still not large. Most of those naturalized had moved to Germany long before 1918. The stiff fees imposed for naturalization, at least with respect to individuals who were not ethnic Germans – after the stabilization of the currency in 1923 500 RM, or roughly three months' salary for a skilled worker – ensured that only the relatively well-to-do would apply.[33] Prussia and its allies had enough votes in the Reichsrat to permit Prussia to ignore the Bavarian objections. The conflict with Bavaria continued with great bitterness until 1931, when the Reichsrat, now dominated by right-wing Land governments, decided to make the twenty-year residence requirement mandatory for all states.[34]

The Citizenship of Married Women

The First World War made clear how critical citizenship was for women as well as men. During the war German women who had married foreigners and still lived in Germany had to report daily to the police, obey an evening curfew, and remain within a confined area. They were not eligible for public financial assistance and often could not send their children to public schools.

The responsibilities middle-class women assumed during the war brought some of them into contact with the discriminatory consequences of the citizenship law. Camilla Jellinek, who became a leader of the efforts to change the citizenship law to better the position of women, led a legal-aid bureau for women. A post-war essay makes clear the influence this experience had on her.

> Before the war the fact that a woman became a foreign citizen [upon marriage with a foreign man] was not given much attention, especially in the lower classes. Many times they did not even realize that they had lost their German citizenship. Nor were they aware of the many difficulties and conflicts that might arise as a result of the involuntary change of citizenship. One did not think about the possibility of war. These women had always lived in Germany, were never abroad, and did not understand that they might become enemy aliens in their own Fatherland. Only the outbreak of the war made the unpleasant consequences of the loss of citizenship quite tangible.[35]

Marie Elisabeth Lüders was another leading advocate of change whose experiences during the war undoubtedly had an important effect in molding her view. During the last two years of the war Lüders headed the central agency for women's labor in the War Ministry. She therefore knew first hand the problems German women who married foreigners encountered in seeking state employment. From 1919 to 1933 Lüders served in the Reichstag as a deputy from the German Democratic Party, a largely middle-class, centrist group. She sponsored half a dozen resolutions on the issue of married women's citizenship. It was in large part as a result of her agitation that the Reichstag twice asked the government, in 1927 and 1930, to propose legislation giving women the right to keep their citizenship upon marriage with a foreigner.[36] The range of grounds on which Lüders campaigned is suggested by a speech she delivered in the Reichstag in June 1930. 'We have the pleasure', she stated,

> of seeing that our demand for the equal treatment of women with respect to nationality has now been accepted by all parties of the Reichstag, excluding only the extreme right . . . We are of the view that on legal, civic (staatsbürgerlichen), humanitarian, and national grounds it is no longer possible to retain the existing treatment of women's nationality. On national grounds, because we believe that we women also have a right to remain attached to the nation from which we come, if we desire, and not simply automatically, by marrying, to be removed from our nation. As a matter of law it seems to us no longer to reflect the fully changed position of the wife, that one treats her simply as an appendage of her husband . . . As a civic question this treatment of the wife no longer corresponds to her civic independence [i.e., a woman's right to vote] . . . We lay the greatest value on being allowed to retain our citizenship, and we also have economic grounds for this aim. It is a well known fact, that through the loss of citizenship most also lose the [economic] bases for their existence. One loses all rights to academic qualifications, positions, and pensions heretofore earned . . .[37]

In contrast to its offhand treatment of the BDF's lobbying in the pre-war years, the Reichstag accorded Lüders's proposal a most respectful hearing.

The opening of universities to women after 1900, and thus access to a range of professions, meant that citizenship became critical for the careers of a small but growing number of women. As Lüders's remarks suggested, a significant number of professions in practice required German citizenship. These included law, medicine, and teaching. By marrying a foreigner a woman might foreclose employment in these fields. This was the case, for example, with respect to B. Petriconi, a German doctor who had married a Peruvian. Petriconi wrote the Reich Interior Minister in 1927 pleading to be permitted to retain her German citizenship.

> As a practical matter the practice of my medical profession will not be possible if I am a foreigner, since, first, I would not be accepted by the Leipzig doctor's

organization, and as a result would not find any support in professional matters, and, secondly, as someone not belonging to the doctor's organization I would not be permitted to work with any regional health-care group. Since most patients belong to these groups, and since every doctor, especially at the beginning of his career, has to depend on seeing such patients . . . the deprivation of German citizenship means preventing me from practicing my profession . . . This is a question of existence for me and my spouse. Your excellency will forgive this repetition and understand that I wish to leave no stone unturned in order to prevent the loss of my nine years of medical education, which after the economic catastrophes is my only possession.[38]

After some six months of appeals the Prussian Interior Minister decided, in January 1928, to permit Petriconi's naturalization, but only because the Reich Justice Ministry had recently agreed in principle to changing the law along the lines Lüders had proposed in the Reichstag.[39]

While protecting and expanding women's civic and political rights undoubtedly played a key role in leading Lüders and Jellinek to advocate a change in the law, the political climate in the 1920s was generally unreceptive to such a focus on individual rights. Lüders often found an appeal to ethnic nationalism more effective. She told the participants in the 1931 German Jurists' Day that

we attempted to change the law [governing the citizenship rights of married women] in 1921 in order to put a stop to the increasing numbers of German-feeling women being made into foreigners by marriage with former Germans who had been forced to give up their citizenships. These [women] would be preserved for Germandom as valuable cultural property by a change in the law governing state citizenship.[40]

Lüders referred here to the millions of ethnic Germans living in territories annexed by Poland, Denmark and France. Economic self-interest often forced them to acquire the citizenship of their new country, but many remained loyal to Germany. When such ethnic German men married women who had remained German citizens, the women lost their German citizenship. Women's-rights activists also spoke more openly of the threat posed to Germany by foreign women who married Germans. In a 1926 article published in a Cologne newspaper, Hedwig Keiler-Neuburger noted that a Frenchwoman who married a German automatically became a German citizen. 'Of what use to us is such a compulsory German (Mußdeutsche)?'[41]

Their appeals to ethnic feeling did not prevent women's groups from also emphasizing the international character of the issue. In 1922 the

United States and Belgium both granted women the right to remain citizens upon marriage with foreigners. If a woman from either country married a German, she became a dual citizen. The American and Belgian laws also ceased to provide for automatic citizenship for foreign women who married male nationals. If a German woman married a citizen of either country she therefore became, at least for a period, stateless. When the BDF appealed to the Reichstag to amend the law in 1925, it did so in part on the basis of the larger international climate. 'With a unity that exists hardly anywhere else the women's movement of the entire world demands the end of a state of affairs under which a woman can be deprived of her citizenship against her will. The danger exists that if Germany does not act rapidly, additional civilized nations will take action before it.'[42] Lüders actively participated in the lobbying efforts of international women's organizations. It was at her suggestion that in 1930 several international women's organizations organized a mass demonstration at the Hague in favor of granting women a choice of nationality.[43]

The pressure exerted by women's groups and their allies was not without effect. An internal memorandum of the Reich Interior Ministry commented in 1927 that 'one has to consider the very strong support for this change . . . Legal-systematic considerations will no longer permit a postponement of the demands of the ladies [die Forderung der Frauenwelt] . . .'[44] The failure of Weimar governments to act despite this pressure may have reflected the press of business and the short lives of cabinets, but probably more important were doubts within the ministries about the wisdom of sanctioning marriages in which the spouses held different citizenships, and also, the token representation of women in positions of power. The Reich Justice Ministry repeatedly warned of difficulties that would arise in determining which state's laws would govern the rights and duties of the wife.[45] While the courts of the husband's country would be inclined to apply its laws to the wife, German courts would tend to apply German laws. The result would be the application of inconsistent rules to similarly situated parties, depending on the forum used.[46] The influence of the view that wives were not entitled to equal rights with their husbands, which the German Civil Code continued to reflect in the Weimar period, doubtless also played a substantial role.

Notes

1. 'Verkehrte Fremdenpolitik', translation of an article from the *Stockholms Dagblad*, 14 May 1923, in BA, R 43 (Reich Chancellory), Film 13441, File 594, p. 171.
2. Memorandum from the Reich Minister of the Interior to the different Länder of 1 June 1921. GStA PK, HA I, Tit. 90, Nr. 2254, p. 379.
3. APW, Polizei Präsidium Breslau, Nr. 863, pp. 10–12.
4. A copy of the version of the form employed in 1923 is found in APW, Polizei Präsidium Breslau, Nr. 862, pp. 119–26.
5. BA R43 II/134, p. 20. Cited in Trude Maurer, *Ostjuden in Deutschland 1918–1933* (H. Christians Verlag, 1986), p. 857.
6. *Verordnung die Beschränkung des Aufenthaltsrechts betreffend* of 12 June 1919, GStA PK, HA I, Tit. 90, Nr. 2254, p. 310.
7. Letter of the Prime Minister of Prussia to the Reich Minister of the Interior of 5 February 1924. BA R 30.01, Film 21507, Nr. 5093, p. 30.
8. Letters of 6 February and 3 April 1924. BA R43, Film 13341, Nr. 594, pp. 202–11.
9. Ian Kershaw, *Hitler 1889–1936: Hubris* (Norton, 2000), p. 362.
10. Letter of 10 September 1927 from the Prussian Minister of the Interior, GStA PK, HA I, Rep. 90, Nr. 2255, p. 136.
11. Memorandum from the Prussian Minister of the Interior of 10 September 1929. NWH RD, Nr. 46976.
12. Letter of 7 February 1922 from the Mayor of Elten to the Landrat of Wesel. NWH RD Nr. 8893.
13. Deputy Bredt of the Economics Party told a comparable story to the Prussian Parliament. *SBP* (29 November 1922), p. 13596.
14. Ibid. (29 November 1922), p. 13622D.
15. Carl Schmitt, *Der Begriff des Politischen* (Duncker & Humblot, 1996; orig. edn 1932), p. 27.
16. J. Wertheimer, *Unwelcome Strangers* (Oxford University Press, 1987), p. 185.
17. Comments of Karl Severing, Prussian Minister of the Interior, during debates in the Prussian Parliament. *SBP* (29 November 1922), p. 13573B.
18. See, for example, petitions submitted to the Prussian constitutional conventions in 1919, which made these claims. *Verfassunggebende Preussische Landesversammlung* (3 October 1919), pp. 4674–5. A similar petition was submitted to the national constitutional convention in the same period. *Nationalversammlung* (30 October

1919), p. 3634. It is a sign of how widespread such assumptions were that even Deputy Fischbeck, a member of the German Democratic Party and a founding member of the Association for Defence against Anti-Semitism, thought that they were for the most part true. *SBP* (29 November 1922) pp. 13588–93.

19. Memorandum of the Prussian Minister of the Interior of 1 November 1919, in BA R 30.01, Film 21507, Nr. 5092, p. 253RS. On the revival of the pre-war importation of Polish farm workers, see the comments of Deputy Cohn, Independent Social Democratic Party, in *SBP* (15 July 1921), pp. 2871B, 2872C.

20. Comments of Deputy Cohn, *SBP* (15 July 1921), pp. 2867B, 2872D. Cohn discussed Prussian expulsions of 450 interned East Europeans.

21. As described by Deputy Cohn in *SBP* (29 November 1922) p. 13603.

22. Comments of Deputy Cohn, Ibid. (29 November 1922), p. 13609A. See also the comments of Prussian Interior Minister Severing, Ibid., p. 13570D.

23. Comments of Prussian Interior Minister Severing, Ibid. (29 November 1922), p. 13571. On the other hand, Prussian officials concluded that Poland was not likely to exert itself energetically on behalf of Polish emigrants who were Jewish. Regine Just, 'Gescheitertes Miteinander: Einbürgerungspolitik und Einbürgerungspraxis in Deutschland von 1871–1933', in AWR-Bulletin. *Vierteljahrschrift für Flüchtlingsfragen* 36 (1998) p. 91.

24. *SBP* (29 November 1922), p. 13573C. A representative of the Prussian government had referred explicitly to the danger of pogroms in explaining, in the fall of 1919, why East European Jews had not been expelled to Poland. *Verfassungsgebende Preussische Landesversammlung* (3 October 1919), p. 4675.

25. Letter from the Prussian Interior Minister to the State Council of Anhalt of 31 May 1919. GStA PK, HA I, Rep. 77, Tit. 226b, Nr. 66, Bd. 1, pp. 20–1.

26. Order of the Prussian Minister of the Interior to the District Governments of 24 June 1919. NWH RD, Nr. 46976.

27. Order of the Prussian Minister of the Interior to the presidents of District Governments of 18 April 1922, NWH RD, Nr. 46976.

28. Memorandum of the Bavarian Interior Ministry to the Reich Ministry of the Interior of 16 March 1928. GStA PK, HA I, Rep. 90, Nr. 2255, p. 148.

29. Memorandum of the Bavarian Foreign Ministry to the Reich Interior Ministry of 23 February 1929. GStA PK, HA I, Rep. 90, Nr. 2255, pp. 301RS–2.

30. *Reichs- und Staatsangehörigkeitsgesetz*, Section 9.
31. Letter of the Prussian Interior Minister to the other German states of 8 December 1927. GstA PK, HA I, Rep. 90, Nr. 2255, p. 142.
32. Letter of the Prussian Minister of the Interior to the Reich Minister of the Interior of 28 June 1927. Ibid., p. 119. Severing here cited the president of the Bundesamt für das Heimatwesen.
33. APW, Polizei Präsidium Breslau, Nr. 863, pp. 10, 46.
34. Maurer, *Ostjuden in Deutschland*, p. 857.
35. Undated essay entitled 'Material von der Auskunft und Hilfestelle über die Wirkung der Bestimmungen des Reichs- und Staatsangehörigkeitsgesetzes vom 22. Juli 1913 auf die mit Ausländern verheirateten Frauen'. From BA Koblenz, Nachlaß Jellinek, Nr. 13. The authorship of the document is not indicated, but its presence in Jellinek's Nachlaß, and the references in the document to the experiences of clinics that aided women, strongly suggest that it came from Jellinek's pen.
36. *SBR* (6 April 1927), p. 3095; Ibid. (24 June 1930), p. 5745. The National Assembly that met in 1919 to draft a new national constitution considered adding a provision to the constitution that would have guaranteed married women the right to keep their citizenship upon marriage. The Assembly rejected such a proposal by what was, apparently, a close voice vote. *Verhandlungen der Verfassungsgebenden Deutschen Nationalversammlung* (15 July 1919), p. 1571B.
37. *SBR* (18 June 1930), pp. 5589A–B.
38. Letter of B. Petriconi to the Reich Minister of the Interior of 7 September 1927. BA R43, Film 13341, Nr. 593, pp. 27–8.
39. Letter of the Prussian Ministry of the Interior to the Reich Chancellory of 4 January 1928. BA R43, Film 13341, Nr. 593, p. 29.
40. Marie Elisabeth Lüders, *Fürchte Dich Nicht: Persönliches und Politisches aus mehr als 80 Jahren, 1878–1962* (Westdeutscher Verlag, 1963), p. 213. For similar summaries of her position see Marie Elisabeth Lüders, 'Staatslose Frauen?', *Die Frau* 30 (November 1922), p. 35; Minutes of a Discussion of Lüders' Proposal by Representatives of the Reich Interior Ministry, the Foreign Office, and the Reich and Prussian Justice Ministries dated 13 March 1922, BA R 1501 (Reich Interior Ministry) Nr. 108059, p. 2.
41. 'Die Staatsangehörigkeit der verheirateten Frau', *Kölnische Zeitung* (13 October 1926), in BA R 1501 Nr. 108061.
42. Letter of the Bund deutscher Frauenvereine to the German Reichstag of 28 May 1925, BA R 1501, Nr. 108060.

43. Lüders's role is mentioned in a pamphlet entitled *Joint Demonstration on the Nationality of Married Women*, at 6. See Bundesarchiv Koblenz, Nachlaß Camilla Jellinek, vol. 13. International efforts to promote the citizenship rights of married women are described in Leila Rupp, *Worlds of Women: The Making of an International Women's Movement* (Princeton University Press, 1997), pp. 146–50.

44. Minutes of 27 October 1927 of a discussion among representatives of the Reich and Prussian Interior and Justice Ministries and the Foreign Office of a Draft Proposal for a law changing the Reich and State Citizenship Law, GStA PK, HA I, Rep. 84a, Nr. 10048, p. 186. The comment was made by Ministerialdirektor Dammann of the Reich Interior Ministry, who chaired the meeting. The meeting followed the adoption by the Reichstag on 6 April 1927 of a resolution urging the Ministry of the Interior to draft a law permitting German women who married foreigners inside Germany to retain their citizenship as long as the couple continued to live in Germany. Ibid., pp. 85, 186.

45. Letter of 28 September 1924 from the Reich Justice Minister to the Reich Minister of the Interior, BA R 1501, Nr. 108059.

46. Minutes of a 13 March 1922 meeting regarding Dr. Lüders's Proposal, GStA PK, HA I, Rep. 84a, Nr. 10048, pp. 58–58RS.

Citizenship as an Instrument of Racial War

The Nazi regime sought to remake German society. It excluded and then killed various political and 'racial'[1] enemies, including communists, Jews, Sinti and Roma, the handicapped, homosexuals, Jehovah's Witnesses, and individuals it considered in various other ways inferior. From ethnic Germans it demanded conformity and enthusiasm.[2]

Since Nazi goals differed fundamentally from those of earlier German states, and since citizenship and naturalization policies directly touched on issues that were central to the Nazi project, to a large extent the legislation which the regime inherited in this area became irrelevant. The powers that existing laws granted to prevent the naturalization of unwanted aliens were relatively insignificant when the fundamental aim was to expel or kill all unwanted individuals, citizens or foreigners, or to employ them as slave laborers.

Nonetheless, as in various other areas of life, the Nazi state found that it could not entirely do without laws. Large groups could not be handled on an entirely individual basis. Bureaucrats required general orders. In parcelling out privileges and burdens the regime found it useful to employ the categories of citizenship. Laws also served as instruments of propaganda. During the war the Nazi state established a range of citizenship categories that corresponded to the racial hierarchy it sought to impose on Europe and to its more immediate wartime needs.

Exclusion: the Pre-war Period

Hitler's brand of anti-Semitism had much in common with the sentiments expressed in the Prussian naturalization treatise of 1904, although his conclusions were far more radical. Both Hitler and many senior Prussian bureaucrats viewed Jews as a 'race', meaning that they considered their various alleged negative character traits ineradicable. As did the drafters of the treatise, Hitler feared Jewish power. Hitler claimed in *Mein Kampf* that in the Vienna of his youth Jews controlled not only the economy, but the trade-union movement and the press. Jews, he argued, were as a result capable of manipulating all levels of the European societies in which they lived into accepting their political goals. Jews' supposed control over the mass media gave them a power far greater than that attributed to them in, for example, *Debit and Credit*. At least those who were being swindled in Freytag's novel understood the nature of the enemy. As his famous discussion of propaganda in *Mein Kampf* showed, Hitler had a very low regard for the ability of most people to think for themselves, including most Germans. He emphasized far more than Freytag the power of Jews to manipulate German society. While Prussian officials drew the conclusion that no further Jewish immigration should be permitted, Hitler went further. Since Jews were disloyal and culturally a menace, he argued, it was necessary not only to prevent further Jewish immigration, but to expel those Jews already in Germany.

The Nazi Party program of 1920, in whose drafting Hitler played a central role, called for the creation of a racial state. All Germans were to be joined in a Greater Germany. 'Only ethnic Germans [Volksgenossen] can be citizens [Staatsbürger]. Volksgenossen are only those who are of German blood, without regard to confession. Therefore no Jew can be a Volksgenosse.' Those who were not Volksgenossen were to be permitted to live in Germany only as guests. If it proved impossible to feed all inhabitants of the state (and Hitler, remembering the famine years of the First World War and the immediate post-war period, clearly believed that on some occasions it would be impossible) then all non-Volksgenossen were to be expelled. 'All immigration of non-Germans is to be prevented. All non-Germans who have immigrated into Germany since the 2nd of August 1914 must be forced to leave.' All owners of, and all writers for, newspapers published in German were to be Volksgenossen.[3]

Given this starting point, it is not surprising that among the Nazi government's first actions, once it had begun to solidify its grip on power, was a ban on the naturalization of East European Jews. On 15 March 1933, six weeks after Hindenburg named Hitler Chancellor and one week after the elections that gave the Nazis and the nationalist right a majority in the Reichstag, the Nazi Reich Interior Minister, Wilhelm Frick, asked the different Land governments to stop naturalizing all so-called 'Ostjuden'. This injunction was reiterated and applied to all 'non-Aryans' in August of the same year.[4] In fact the central government did not have the legal authority to issue orders on this subject to the Länder, but by the middle of March 1933 it had effectively seized control of all the Land governments. Such orders – or 'requests' – did not have to be legal to be effective. In February of 1934 this gap between law and practice was eliminated by the unification of control over citizenship at the national level. Germans ceased to be citizens of each Land and only indirectly of the national state, and became simply Germans.[5] Länder no longer played any role in the granting or denial of naturalization petitions.

Nazi plans required not merely preventing future immigration by unworthy foreigners, but a cleansing of German society. On 14 July 1933 the regime adopted a law permitting the Reich Interior Ministry to deprive of citizenship all individuals naturalized between 9 November 1918 and 30 January 1933.[6] Rules putting the law into effect explicitly provided that 'völkish-national' criteria would determine whether naturalizations had been in the interest of the state.[7] 6,943 Jews were deprived of citizenship, as well as some 3,544 non-Jews.[8] These figures do not include family members, who were also automatically denaturalized at the same time. Most of those who were denaturalized became stateless. Hitler and the right had attacked the Weimar Republic as illegitimate, a regime of traitors. The citizenship law put this claim into effect, for it treated the actions of Weimar governments as in effect void.

At the same time that the Nazi state undertook to undo the naturalizations granted by the previous regime, it threatened to deprive Germans who had fled abroad of citizenship. The law of 14 July 1933 provided for the denaturalization of emigrants whose 'conduct . . . violates the duty of loyalty to the Reich and the [German] Volk and damages German interests'.[9] Individuals who lost their citizenship in this fashion also generally suffered confiscation of their property. Initially the regime proceeded cautiously. Before 1937, 291 emigrants were denaturalized under this provision of the law, albeit often quite prominent ones: among those deprived of citizenship were the writers Heinrich Mann, Ernst Toller, Bertolt Brecht, and Kurt Tucholsky, the Social Democratic leaders Otto Wels and Philip Scheidemann, and Albert Einstein. The Nazi state made more extensive use of the power to deprive emigrants of citizenship from 1937, when it began systematically to denaturalize Jewish emigrants who had not been made citizens during the Weimar Republic. There were 203 such denaturalizations in 1937, 566 in 1938, 1,300 in 1939, and 1,268 in 1940.[10] The main purpose was to legalize the seizure of Jewish property. Since Jews were generally prohibited from taking assets with them when they emigrated, emigrants owned a significant – if diminishing – amount of property inside Germany. If and when they became citizens of other countries it became much more difficult to steal their assets: they could then appeal to their new homelands for protection. The theft of the property of Jewish emigrants was streamlined in November 1941, when a law was adopted that stripped Jews who left Germany of their citizenship upon their departure and provided for the immediate confiscation of their property.[11] Of course, the state hardly needed such formal legitimation, but the bureaucracy functioned much more smoothly if there were laws to sanction its procedures.[12] The deportation of German Jews to the ghettos and death camps in occupied Poland had begun in October 1941, and the November 1941 law became one more instrument in the machinery of genocide.

The Nuremberg Citizenship Law, promulgated in September 1935, divided Germans into first- and second-class citizens through the creation of a new and higher type of citizen, the Reichsbürger. It defined the Reichsbürger to be every German citizen of 'German or related blood who by his conduct shows that he desires and is fit loyally to serve the German Volk and state'.[13] Only Reichsbürger were permitted to vote or to hold public office. Those who were not Reichsbürger retained the subordinate status of German Staatsangehörige. This last category included not only Jews, but also – at least in theory – 'racial' Germans whose conduct had in some way created doubts about their political reliability. The distinctions in the Reichsbürgergesetz provided the legal basis for forcing those Jews who had been permitted to remain in the civil service – because they had served in the First World War, had lost a father or son in the war, or because they had been appointed to the civil service before August 1914 – from their positions.

Between the two classes of citizens there soon developed a third group, individuals with only one or two Jewish grandparents (Mischlinge). Historians have estimated that there were some 150,000–170,000 Mischlinge in Germany in 1933, compared with 500,000 'full Jews'.[14] The status of Mischlinge remained unclear and disputed throughout the Nazi period. While Nazi laws for the most part granted individuals with only one Jewish grandparent the rights of 'Aryan' Germans, those with two Jewish grandparents were in a less secure position. Mischlinge sometimes managed to avoid removal from their government positions after 1935 (although they had been affected by the first purge of the civil service in 1933). Mischlinge were not subjected to the fine imposed on Jews in November 1938, following Kristallnacht, nor to the prohibition on Jewish businesses adopted at the same time. Mischlinge were generally not deported to the death camps, at least if they were not practicing Jews or married to Jews. But Mischlinge with two Jewish grandparents could marry 'Aryans' only with official permission. After 1939 Mischlinge were in general prevented from serving in the army. In the conquered territories of the Soviet Union and Eastern Europe fine distinctions between Jews and partial Jews often were not made by those responsible for the machinery of genocide: all were treated as Jews.

Racial Hierarchies in Conquered Europe

The conquest of foreign territories, beginning with the annexation of Austria and Czechoslovakia, created new conditions and new goals for Nazi citizenship policies. As the war stretched German manpower to the limit, the regime sought to press into military service all those who might possibly be considered German. The category of 'German' expanded. On the other hand, the treatment of non-Germans became harsher, especially in the East. In the annexed part of Poland a special criminal law adopted in December 1941 established draconian punishments for Poles and Jews found guilty of engaging in anti-German behavior. Rations, curfews, housing privileges, the right to travel, where children attended school (for schools and educational privileges generally were firmly divided by 'race'), eligibility for a range of privileged jobs, subjection to slave labor in Germany, deportation to the east and, in 1943 and 1944, evacuation westward: all were imposed, granted or withheld based in part on the identity card an individual held.[15]

Citizenship laws and policies indicate the increasingly radical and coercive character of Nazi racial policies. When Austria was forcibly annexed in March of 1938 all of its 6,759,000 citizens became German citizens, with the distinctions contained in the Nuremberg Citizenship Law.[16] The November 1938 agreement between Germany and Czechoslovakia that regulated the German incorporation of the Sudetenland and its 2,943,000 residents followed roughly the same rule, but provided that the German government had the right to expel non-ethnic German residents of the Sudetenland who had moved there since 1909. All ethnic Germans in Czechoslovakia were given the right to opt for German citizenship, even if they continued to live in Czechoslovakia.[17] When the remainder of Czechoslovakia was conquered in March of 1939 Germany divided it into a Slovakian puppet state and the protectorate of Bohemia and Moravia. In the latter territory, with some 7,485,000 inhabitants, ethnic Germans were made German Staatsangehörige and, under the terms of the Nuremberg Citizenship Law, Reichsbürger: there was no longer an element of choice.[18] The other residents of the protectorate became Staatsangehörige of the protectorate.

Occupied Poland was the site of the Nazi regime's most ambitious racial-engineering measures. Germany divided Poland with the Soviet

Union in September 1939, and in turn split its half of the country into an annexed zone – the so-called Incorporated Eastern Territories (IET) – and the General Government, essentially a colony. The IET held some 9,936,000 persons, of whom fewer than ten percent were at the time of the conquest ethnic Germans.[19] In the IET only ethnic Germans (or those of 'related blood') were permitted to become German citizens, even though the territory had been incorporated into the German state. The citizenship status of individuals who were not ethnic Germans initially remained somewhat murky, in part because the aim of at least some of those making policy was to move them to the General Government.[20] The granting of any German citizenship status to Poles and Jews might have signaled an expectation that Germany intended to permit them to remain in the IET, or that they had the rights of German citizens, for example, to travel freely to other parts of Germany.

While most Jews were deported from the IET eastward to the General Government, initial plans to deport all Poles from the IET proved in the end unworkable. There was simply too little room for them in the General Government. The functioning of the economy in the IET also required their presence. In March of 1941 an official citizenship status was finally created for the inhabitants of the IET who were not ethnic Germans. They became 'Schutzangehörige', or protected subjects, of the German state.[21] This form of citizenship was lost upon emigration from German territory, including deportation to the General Government. By 1942 even the status of Schutzangehöriger was too good for Jews and Sinti and Roma: a decree eliminated the entitlement of formerly Polish Jews and Gypsies to this status.[22] In April 1943 Jews and Gypsies were also deprived of the right to be Staatsangehörige.[23]

Nazi authorities did not consider an immediate clarification of the citizenship status of the Polish and Jewish inhabitants of the newly conquered territories expedient, but they did expend considerable energy creating legal categories for ethnic Germans. The need to distinguish which of the inhabitants of the territories could claim the privileges of being German was in fact a pressing issue. The invading German army, or the SS and police units that followed in its wake, imprisoned or shot tens of thousands of Poles and Jews in the first months of the occupation.[24] By the end of 1940 some 500,000 Jews and 325,000 Poles had been deported to the General Government, in both cases primarily from Wartheland, a district based primarily on the pre-1918 province of Posen.[25] Thousands of Poles rushed to obtain letters from German churches, business associates, and friends that identified them as Germans or friends of Germans, as a means of avoiding these measures.[26] On the other hand, some ethnic Germans may have been treated as Poles. An SS report drafted in September of 1940 found that in Danzig-Westpreußen

> a considerable number of deportations took place out of a fear of competitors and on personal grounds . . . and to acquire the goods of the deportees. One only had to declare that the owners were Poles, find two witnesses who would swear to various general phrases . . . and the fate of the family was decided. The property was shared among the inhabitants of the village . . . It was entirely irrelevant whether the family was of German blood . . .[27]

Since there were rivalries between the SS and the administration of Danzig-Westpreußen this description cannot be taken entirely at face value, but it provides further evidence of the conditions in conquered Poland and of the significance of status as a German or Pole.

The regime's efforts to identify who was an ethnic German were designed to displace ad hoc ascriptions of ethnicity with a centrally directed, objective categorization, to protect ethnic Germans, to prevent Poles from enjoying the privileges accorded Germans, and, above all, to promote the state's project of Germanization. An Interior Ministry memorandum of 25 November 1939 ordered the systematic identification – through questionnaires – of all individuals who might be considered German. The questionnaires asked for information regarding language ability, membership in national organizations, the nationality of the school attended, and persecution as a German by the Polish state.[28] The Interior Ministry's control over access to German citizenship was quickly challenged, however, by Heinrich Himmler, in his capacity as 'Reich Commissioner for the Strengthening of Germandom'. In a decree issued on 7 October 1939, Hitler had ordered Himmler to 'eliminate the damaging influence of foreign national groups that pose a danger for the Reich and the German nation'.[29] It was Himmler who, in September 1940, ordered the police, Nazi Party and state administration in the IET to create a central registry for ethnic Germans, termed the Volksliste.

The September 1940 memorandum, and a March 1941 decree published pursuant to it, divided the Volksliste into four categories or sections, depending on the degree of reliability and 'Germanness' of the individual. The first section of the Volksliste was reserved for ethnic Germans who had been active in the German nationalist cause. Those in the second section were ethnic Germans, but had not been active nationalists. Individuals in the second section were generally not eligible for membership in the Nazi Party. While the instructions issued by Himmler in September 1940 envisioned granting full citizenship, the Reichsbürgerrecht, to all those in the first two categories of the Volksliste, the March 1941 decree only granted them Staatsangehörigkeit. Interior Ministry regulations issued pursuant to the March 1941 decree termed those in the first two sections of the Volksliste merely 'provisional Reichsbürger'. Clearly someone in a position of authority had developed doubts about the political reliability of at least some of the 'Volksdeutsche', or perhaps just wanted to give them an additional incentive for good behavior.[30]

The third and fourth categories of the Volksliste provided a place for individuals who were not deemed worthy of all the privileges granted those included in the first two sections of the Volksliste. The third Volksliste category included individuals of German ancestry who primarily spoke Polish and in other ways behaved like Poles, as well as the Polish spouses of Germans who had been placed in the first or second categories of the Volksliste.[31] The fourth category of the Volksliste was reserved for those ethnic Germans who had been actively pro-Polish, on the theory that they might be reeducated and, furthermore, that it was dangerous to permit people with 'German blood' to remain members of the Polish nation. The March 1941 law provided that individuals in the third Volksliste category might become full German citizens (Staatsangehörige), but only upon petition, in an individualized naturalization proceeding. In January of 1942 the grant of citizenship was made automatic upon admission to the third Volksliste category, but given the form of 'Staatsangehörigkeit auf Widerruf', a status that could be rescinded at any time during the following ten years.[32] Those in the fourth category had to petition for citizenship individually, and if successful were considered 'Staatsangehörige auf Widerruf'.[33] Just as those in the first two Volksliste categories were only provisionally Reichsbürger, so those in the third and fourth categories were only provisionally Staatsangehörige. While it is not clear how much this difference in status mattered, what the distinctions clearly do show is that those who drafted these laws thought it best to encourage a feeling of insecurity even among their fellow ethnic Germans.

Statistics for the city of Posen, the chief city in the province of Wartheland in the IET, show that there was an initial surge of applications for admission to the Volksliste in November 1939. Subsequent high points in applications took place after the German victory over Norway (April 1940), when taxes were reduced for Germans (December 1940), and when Germans, but not Poles, were given ration cards (May 1941).[34] In June 1941, the month of the German invasion of the Soviet Union, the number of applicants dropped sharply. A German victory no longer seemed so certain. From this date it became more common for individuals who had submitted applications to be placed on the Volksliste, or who had been accepted, to attempt to withdraw their applications or reverse their classification. This happened in particular when individuals were drafted to serve in the army. Such persons were subject to imprisonment in concentration camps or, from late 1944, execution.[35] Declaration of nationality was not supposed to be a voluntary matter, but an objective determination of 'racial' identity. Ethnic Germans who refused loyalty to the state were treated as traitors.

The March 1941 decree was strictly construed in Wartheland, but in Danzig-Westpreußen and Upper Silesia, the other districts in the IET, Nazi leaders and their subordinates were far more willing to place individuals who seemed in most respects Polish in the third section of the Volksliste. The administrators of the Wartheland Volksliste were concerned above all to ensure that no Poles snuck their way onto the list. A report drafted between November 1942 and April 1943 by one of the principal administrators of the Volksliste in Wartheland, Herbert Strickner, described the techniques employed to distinguish true Germans from Poles.[36] Knowledge of German meant little, since many Poles had lived in Germany before 1918 and could speak the language with complete fluency. One had to examine the small children in the family, to see which language they were used to speaking. Whether the names of children were Polish or German was also a significant indication of ethnic identity. Religion, the ethnic character of the elementary school chosen for children, and notations regarding ethnicity on Polish military papers were also used to establish eligibility for inclusion on the German Volksliste. In Wartheland 420,000 individuals were placed in the first two categories of the Volksliste and only 65,000 in the third category. In Danzig-Westpreußen the first two categories contained 210,000 persons and the third category 725,000. The results in Upper Silesia were similar to those in Danzig-Westpreußen.[37] While these differences in part were the product of the different relations between Poles and Germans in the districts of the IET, much more significant were the political views of the Nazi officials making decisions.[38]

Inclusion on the Volksliste did not shield individuals from all forms of discrimination. In her study of the status of foreigners in Nazi Germany, Diemut Majer mentions an attempt in 1944 by individuals who had been placed in the third category of the Volksliste to recover plots of land confiscated by ethnic Germans earlier in the war. The police intervened to prevent a reversal of the confiscations, on the grounds that until the individuals whose property had been taken proved their German loyalties they were still to be treated as Poles.[39] Officials in charge of the Volksliste sometimes noted when applications seemed to be based on opportunism. A Wartheland official reported to a superior in August of 1940 that 'when someone recently submitted an application to be [included in the Volksliste] . . . and it was pointed out that the application came rather late [the summer of 1940] there was the innocent response: but earlier one didn't know how the war was going to turn out . . .'[40] It seems likely that such distinctions had consequences.

The Volksliste, or roughly comparable categories, were also employed outside the boundaries of the German state. In the fall of 1941 the General Government created its own form of Volksliste that distinguished between 'deutsche Volkszugehörige' and 'Deutschstämmige', roughly German nationals and those with German origins. In general the administration proceeded with much greater liberality than in Wartheland, for there were far fewer Germans of any kind in the General Government. At least some of the 'deutsche Volkszugehörige' became German citizens.[41] The Reichcommisariat for the Ukraine initially was willing to rely on less formal methods for determining who was to be considered an ethnic German, but Himmler insisted early in the fall of 1942 that the standard Volksliste proceeding be employed.[42] A May 1943 order extended German citizenship to the ethnic Germans in the Ukraine registered in the first and second sections of the Ukrainian Volksliste.[43]

A report filed by an SS team in early 1943 gives a sense of the way in which eligibility for inclusion in the Volksliste was determined in the Ukraine, and perhaps elsewhere as well. The report described an interview conducted by a committee composed of the district commissioner, an observer, an official assigned to the case, an SS officer, one representative each from the Nazi Party and the central administration of the Ukraine, and two representatives of local ethnic Germans.

First the official assigned to the case and one of the representatives of local ethnic Germans spoke. Then the entire family [under consideration] entered the room, which was filled with symbols of the National Socialist Empire. The official assigned to the case . . . reviewed the key facts contained in the questionnaire [that the family had filled out] . . . If certain matters remained unclear . . . the chair of the commission asked questions. [The applicants] were encouraged to behave in a German fashion in selecting a spouse and in their way of life. When youths did not have a regular occupation this was noted, to provide for more appropriate employment. If a non-German spouse was present, he or she was quickly examined to determine mastery of the German language and attitude towards Germandom. Foreign first and last names were changed . . . Then the chairman recommended the inclusion of each individual on the appropriate section of the list, and made it clear to the participants that upon acceptance in the Volksliste they would become German citizens . . .

The ceremony ended with a handshake, further encouragement to behave in a way worthy of Germans, and a Heil Hitler.[44] The assignment of Russian Germans to the appropriate Volksliste category was only partially completed when the German defeats suffered in 1943 and 1944 forced the evacuation of most Russian Germans from the conquered territories of the Soviet Union. Once the refugees reached the temporary safety of camps in the IET or the General Government, the process of racial sorting resumed. Even when labeled as Germans, however, the Russian Germans were often treated only a little better than the Poles both by the state and many of their new fellow citizens.[45]

While the Nazi regime had not initially shown much interest in promoting the rights of German women who married foreigners – the aim was to prevent such marriages from taking place – during the war it generally treated ethnic-German women living in marriages with non-ethnic-German husbands as Germans. This meant, in practice, that they and to some extent also their husbands were protected from the harshest measures taken against various of the groups the regime viewed as racially unfit, and that they retained privileges granted to Germans with respect to rations, housing, curfews and other matters. In Wartheland Nazi authorities took the position that 'it was impossible to include one spouse in the DVL [Deutsche Volksliste] and to leave the other spouse outside it'.[46] The system of privileges and burdens tended to break down if the spouses were placed in different 'racial' categories. The third category of the German Volksliste was created in part to include non-ethnic-German spouses on the Volksliste, and to grant them a species of German citizenship. If a non-German spouse of a German declined to be entered on the German Volksliste, Nazi authorities encouraged the German spouse to seek a divorce. From April 1943 no marriages were permitted, in the IET, between persons who were German Schutzangehörige (i.e. those who were not ethnic Germans) and German citizens.

Continuity and Change

The Nazi regime's answers to the various questions posed by the creation of the German state were both simple and brutal. To the question of how many of the ethnic Germans in Europe were to become citizens of the German national state, the regime had a very simple answer: all. But putting a simple theory into practice when the reality was complex often resulted in policies that were arbitrary, subject to the goals and whims of local officials. The Nazi state relied primarily on racial categories, as it understood the term, to determine whether a person was a German. A cultural definition would have potentially opened the door to the privileges of German citizenship to an indeterminate number of individuals and also would have required the making of difficult judgments about what German cultural characteristics actually were. Of course, the racial definition was also quite murky, but at least in theory it suggested the possibility of drawing bright lines. The major difficulty that remained – in theory – was determining what percentage of German ancestry brought a person within the magic circle of Germandom. This was a question that logic alone could not resolve, and Nazi authorities gave various answers in different places and at different times. In general the weaker the regime felt, the more inclusive was its interpretation of the meaning of German. In Wartheland two ethnic German grandparents were required for inclusion in the first two categories of the Volksliste. In the General Government a single German grandparent, in some cases a single great-grandparent, sufficed.[47]

The answer to the question of whether individuals who were not ethnic Germans might be included in the future German state was also, at least in theory, simple: none. Here there was admittedly a certain amount of slippage. The concept of peoples of 'related blood' was employed to make it at least conceivable that members of certain non-German ethnic groups would be tolerated. These included, according to a 1941 legal commentary by Ernst Huber, the Swedes, Danes, French, Italians and Hungarians.[48] A category that comprised such a diverse range of peoples, and that so closely reflected political expediency and the existing constellation of political alliances in Europe, was clearly subject to change. The regime for the most part simply closed its eyes to the existence of ethnic minority groups inside Germany's 1937 borders – aside from Jews, Sinti and Roma – and members of these groups certainly were not eager to call attention to their distinctive heritage.

The regime's political concepts were as simple as its racism. Domestic political strife was no longer to be tolerated. All political decisions would be made by an objective, all-knowing leadership, and accepted unanimously by everyone. Given these premises, the political content of citizenship ceased to have any significance. The right to vote was meaningless. Of course, there continued to be differences of opinion in society about the various policies of the regime, but the fact that it was impossible to discuss differences openly without risk meant that in fact, over time, far fewer people were willing to conceive of opposition to Hitler's policies. Inside the administration, where it was impossible to avoid a certain initiative, conflicts were increasingly expressed only within a very limited range.

The simplicity of the regime's goals and the brutality of the regime's citizenship policies also reflected Germany's preeminent military position, after 1937. The foreign policy considerations that constrained even Bismarck's treatment of foreigners exercised little restraint on Hitler, again, after 1937. The regime felt constrained to conceal only its most extreme measures, the mass murder of millions of Jews and Soviet POWs, as well as tens of thousands of Poles. It feared both the domestic and foreign policy consequences if these measures became known, for they invited and by the regime's own logic even justified retribution. Hitler was an expert when it came to playing the victim.

To what extent did the Nazi regime's citizenship policies reflect the influence of precedents from Germany history? The regime certainly was skillful at posing as the heir of German traditions, as indicated by the terminology it employed. The creation of multiple classes of citizenship, and the exclusion of Jews, recalled the practices of numerous German communities in the early modern era. Bismarck especially had created a range of useful precedents, including the expulsion of foreign Poles and Jews, the law that deprived certain German Jesuits of citizenship, and his attacks on political parties that failed to support his authoritarian form of rule. To speak most generally, what Nazi citizenship policies shared with those of earlier regimes, and especially those of the Kaiserreich, was an obsessive insecurity. On the other hand, it is also clear that Hitler was not simply continuing Bismarck's policies. The racial utopia, or anti-utopia, Hitler envisioned would have been simply unthinkable to Bismarck. The radical transformation of citizenship policy by the Nazi regime, especially during the war, is one indication – one among many – of the extent to which Hitler broke with nineteenth-century patterns and precedents.

Notes

1. Nazi racial policies have been exhaustively studied. I would like to acknowledge those secondary works that have been particularly helpful in writing this chapter. They are, in the order of their publication, Martin Broszat, *Nationalsozialistische Polenpolitik 1939–1945* (Stuttgart: Deutsche Verlags-Anstalt, 1961); Martin Broszat, 'Volksdeutsche

und Deutschstämmige im GG 1941–1944', in *Gutachten des Instituts für Zeitgeschichte*, vol. 2 (Deutsche Verlags-Anstalt, 1966), pp. 254–61; Diemut Majer, *'Fremdvölkische' im Dritten Reich: Ein Beitrag zur nationalsozialistischen Rechtssetzung und Rechtspraxis in Verwaltung und Justiz unter besonderer Berücksichtigung der eingegliederten Ostgebiete und des Generalgouvernements* (Harald Boldt, 1981); I. Fleischhauer, *Das Dritte Reich und die Deutschen in der Sowjetunion* (Deutsche Verlages-Anstalt, 1983); and D. Gosewinkel, *Einbürgern und Ausschließen* (Vandenhoeck & Ruprecht, 2001). Diemut Majer's classic study has just appeared in English as *'Non-Germans' under the Third Reich: The Nazi Judicial and Administrative System in Germany and Occupied Eastern Europe, with Special Regard to Occupied Poland, 1939–1945*, trans. P. Hill, E. Humphrey, and B. Levin (Johns Hopkins University Press, 2003).

2. For an overview of the various dimensions of the Nazi racial project, see Michael Burleigh and Wolfgang Wippermann, *The Racial State: Germany 1933–1945* (Cambridge University Press, 1991).

3. Program of the National Socialist German Workers' Party of 24 February 1920, articles one, four, five, seven, eight, and twenty-three. *Ursachen und Folgen: Vom deutschen Zusammenbruch 1918 und 1945 bis zur staatlichen Neuordnung Deutschlands in der Gegenwart*, vol. 3, *Der Weg in die Weimarer Republik* (Herbert Wendler, no date), pp. 214–16.

4. Gosewinkel, *Einbürgern und Ausschließen*, pp. 370, 382; Joseph Walk, *Das Sonderrecht für die Juden im NS-Staat: Eine Sammlung der gesetzlichen Maßnahmen und Richtlinien-Inhalt und Bedeutung*, 2nd edn (Müller, 1996), pp. 4, 49.

5. *Verordnung über die deutsche Staatsangehörigkeit* of 5 February 1934, *RGBl* I, p. 85.

6. *Gesetz über den Widerruf von Einbürgerungen und die Aberkennung der deutschen Staatsangehörigkeit* of 14 July 1933, *RGBl* I, p. 480. The law limited the time period within which the denaturalizations could take place to two years: the time limit was later extended to 31 December 1935.

7. *Verordnung zur Durchführung des Gesetzes über den Widerruf von Einbürgerungen und die Aberkennung der deutschen Staatsangehörigkeit* of 26 July 1933. *RGBl* I, p. 538.

8. Hans Lehmann, Introduction, in M. Hepp (ed.), *Die Ausbürgerung deutscher Staatsangehöriger 1933–45 nach den im Reichsanzeiger veröffentlichten Listen*, vol. 1 (Saur, 1985), p. xiii.

9. *Gesetz über den Widerruf von Einbürgerungen und die Aberkennung der deutschen Staatsangehörigkeit* of 14 July 1933, *RGBl* I, p. 480.

10. Martin Dean, 'The Development and Implementation of Nazi Denaturalization and Confiscation Policy up to the Eleventh Decree to the Reich Citizenship Law', *Holocaust and Genocide Studies* 16 (Fall 2002), p. 232.

11. *Elfte Verordnung zum Reichsbürgergesetz* of 25 November 1941, *RGBl* I, pp. 722–4.

12. See Cornelia Essner, *Die 'Nürnberger Gesetze', oder, Die Verwaltung des Rassenwahns 1933–1945* (Ferdinand Schöningh, 2002), pp. 301–2.

13. *Reichsbürgergesetz* of 15 September 1935, *RGBl* I, p. 1146.

14. Avraham Barkai, 'Jewish Life under Persecution', in *German-Jewish History in Modern Times*, vol. 4, *Renewal and Destruction 1918–1945* (Columbia University Press, 1998), pp. 232, 252.

15. See generally Majer, *'Fremdvölkische' im Dritten Reich*, pp. 386–404, 431–59.

16. *Verordnung über die deutsche Staatsangehörigkeit im Lande Österreich* of 3 July 1938, Section 1(2), *RGBl* I, p. 790; *Verordnung über die Einführung der Nürnberger Rassengesetze im Lande Österreich* of 20 May 1938, *RGBl* I, p. 594. The population statistics given here and in the remainder of the paragraph are from *Statistisches Handbuch von Deutschland 1928–1944*, published by the Länderrat des Amerikanischen Besatzungsgebiets (Franz Ehrenwirth, 1949), p. 6.

17. The Czech government had comparable rights with respect to newly arrived ethnic Germans, and non-ethnic Germans in the Sudetenland were given the right to opt for Czech citizenship. *Vertrag zwischen dem Deutschen Reich und der Tschechoslowakischen Republik über die Staatsangehörigkeits- und Optionsfragen* of 20 November 1938, *RGBl* II, p. 897.

18. *Erlaß des Führers und Reichskanzlers über das Protektorat Böhmen und Mähren* of 16 March 1939, Artikel 2(1), *RGBl* I, p. 486.

19. Hans-Christian Harten, *De-Kulturation und Germanisierung: Die nationalsozialistische Rassen- und Erziehungspolitik in Polen 1939–1945* (Frankfurt: Campus, 1996), p. 107.

20. *Gesetz über die Wiedervereinigung der Freien Stadt Danzig mit dem Deutschen Reich* of 1 September 1939, Article 2, *RGBl* I, p. 1547; *Erwerb der deutschen Staatsangehörigkeit in den in das Deutsche Reich eingegliederten Ostgebieten* of 25 November 1939, Section 2, reprinted in *Documenta Occupationis*, vol. 5 (Poznan: Institut

Zachodni, 1952), p. 109. *Erlaß des Führers und Reichskanzlers über Gliederung und Verwaltung der Ostgebiete* of 8 October 1939, Section 6, *RGBl* I, p. 2042. See also Section 2 of the *Erlaß des Führers und Reichskanzlers zur Durchführung der Wiedervereignigung der Gebiete von Eupen, Malmedy und Moresnet mit dem Deutschen Reich* of 23 May 1940, *RGBl* I, p. 803.

21. *Verordnung über die Deutsche Volksliste und die deutsche Staatsangehörigkeit in den eingegliederten Ostgebieten* of 4 March 1941, *RGBl* I, pp. 118–19.

22. Non-ethnic German residents of parts of conquered Yugoslavia were also made 'Schutzangehörige'. Section 3 of *Verordnung über den Erwerb der Staatsangehörigkeit in den befreiten Gebieten der Unterstiermak, Kärtens und Krains* of 14 October 1941, *RGBl* I, p. 649. *Zweite Verordnung über die Deutsche Volksliste und die deutsche Staatsangehörigkeit in den eingegliederten Ostgebieten* of 31 January 1942, Section Four, *RGBl* I, p. 52.

23. *Zwölfte Verordnung zum Reichsbürgergesetz* of 25 April 1943, Section four, *RGBl* I, p. 269. See also the discussion in Gosewinkel, *Einbürgern und Ausschließen*, p. 413.

24. Broszat, *Nationalsozialistische Polenpolitik*, pp. 38–48.

25. Ibid., pp. 65, n. 2, 100. And these estimates may be on the low side, at least with respect to the Polish deportations. Hans-Christian Harten puts the number of Poles deported from the IET before 1944 at 900,000. Harten, *De-Kulturation und Germanisierung*, p. 116, citing Czesław Madajczyk, *Die Okkupationspolitik Nazideutschlands in Polen 1939–1945* (Akademie-Verlag, 1988), pp. 429ff.

26. From the report of SS Obersturmführer and head of the office responsible for composing the Volksliste in Poznan, Herbert Strickner, on the development of the German Volksliste. The report was composed in the fall of 1941 and the spring of 1942. *Documenta Occupationis Teutonicae*, vol. 4, pp. 35–44 (henceforth, *Strickner Report*). Since Strickner was a fanatical National Socialist with his own axes to grind, it is impossible to take the numbers he gives in his report at face value. Nonetheless, it seems plausible that the phenomenon he describes had some basis in reality.

27. Quoted in Broszat, *Nationalsozialistische Polenpolitik 1939–1945*, p. 89.

28. *Erwerb der deutschen Staatsangehörigkeit in den in das Deutsche Reich eingegliederten Ostgebieten* of 25 November 1939, reproduced in *Documenta Occupationis*, vol. 5, p. 108.

29. *Documenta Occupationis*, vol. 5, p. 176.

30. Compare the 12 September 1940 Himmler memorandum entitled *Erlass für die Überprüfung und Aussonderung der Bevölkerung in den eingegliederten Ostgebiete, Documenta Occupationis*, vol. 5, p. 117, with section three of the *Verordnung über die Deutsche Volksliste und die deutsche Staatsangehörigkeit in den eingegliederten Ostgebieten* of 4 March 1941, *RGBl* I, p. 119, and the general instructions regarding enforcement of the 4 March 1941 law in a 13 March 1941 memorandum of the Interior Ministry, *Documenta Occupationis*, vol. 5, p. 130.

31. *Strickner Report, Documenta Occupationis Teutonicae*, vol. 4, pp. 66–7; Himmler's *Erlass für die Überprüfung und Aussonderung der Bevölkerung in den eingegliederten Ostgebiete*, Section A.II. B, *Documenta Occupationis*, vol. 5, p. 115; General instructions regarding of 13 March 1941 of the Interior Ministry, *Documenta Occupationis*, vol. 5, pp. 127–8.

32. *Erlass für die Überprüfung und Aussonderung der Bevolkerung in den eingegliederten Ostgebieten* of 12 September 1940, issued by Heinrich Himmler, Reichsführer SS, in *Documenta Occupationis*, vol. 5, p. 114.

33. *Zweite Verordnung über die Deutsche Volksliste und die deutsche Staatsangehörigkeit in den eingegliederten Ostgebiete* of 31 January 1942, *RGBl* I, p. 51.

34. *Strickner Report, Documenta Occupationis Teutonicae*, vol. 4, pp. 58–9.

35. Broszat, *Nationalsozialistische Polenpolitik*, pp. 135–6.

36. *Strickner Report, Documenta Occupationis Teutonicae*, vol. 4, pp. 35, 323.

37. Broszat, *Nationalsozialistische Polenpolitik*, p. 134. The statistics for Danzig-Westpreußen do not include figures for the city of Danzig.

38. Harten, *De-Kulturation und Germanisierung*, pp. 106–7.

39. Ibid., pp. 427, n. 55, 429.

40. Ibid., p. 429, n. 69. See also Gosewinkel, *Einbürgern und Ausschließen*, p. 412.

41. Broszat, 'Volksdeutsche und Deutschstämmige im GG 1941–1944'.

42. Fleischhauer, *Das Dritte Reich und die Deutschen in der Sowjetunion*, pp. 185–6.

43. *Verordnung über die Verleihung der deutschen Staatsangehörigkeit an die in die Deutsche Volksliste der Ukraine eingetragenen Personen* of 19 May 1943, Section one, *RGBl* I, p. 321.

44. Report of Activities and Experiences with respect to the Delegation to the Reichskommissariat Ukraine, in German Records, Collection of Captured German War Documents, National Archives, Washington, D.C., T 454, R 105, F 1099–1108, as quoted in Fleischhauer, *Das Dritte Reich und die Deutschen in der Sowjetunion*, pp. 188–9.
45. Ibid., pp. 193–236. Comparable to the sorting that took place in the context of the Volksliste was the racial examination of the hundreds of thousands of Germans moved to the IET or the General Government from the Baltic states or conquered territories in the Soviet Union. The Umsiedler were granted (or denied) German citizenship by the agencies in charge of relocating them, but the process had the same uncertainties and arbitrariness that characterized the Volksliste proceedings. Harten, *De-Kulturation und Germanisierung*, pp. 110–15. The exclusion of the Umsiedler from the Volksliste was decreed in January 1942. *Zweite Verordnung über die Deutsche Volksliste und die deutsche Staatsangehörigkeit in den eingegliederten Ostgebiete* of 31 January 1942, *RGBl* I, p. 51.
46. *Strickner Report, Documenta Occupationis Teutonicae*, vol. 4, p. 92.
47. Majer, *'Fremdvölkische' im Dritten Reich*, pp. 425–6.
48. Ibid., p. 416, n. 10.

–10–

A Republican and European
Citizenship Law

The founders of the Federal Republic of Germany had sought as emphatic-
ally as possible to distance the reconstituted state from Nazi crimes and
from the Nazi goal of creating a racially stratified society. The opening
article of the constitution of 23 May 1949 proclaimed that 'the dignity
of man is inviolable'. Article 3 provided that 'all men are equal before
the law' and that 'no one may be disadvantaged or privileged as a result
of his gender, origin, race, language, home or background, beliefs, or
religious or political views'. Article 16 forbade denaturalization except
by the operation of the law and if the affected person would not thereby
be made stateless. This article also made a general offer of asylum to
individuals persecuted on political grounds. The constitution granted
German citizens whom the Nazi regime had deprived of citizenship, and
also their children, the right to again become Germans.[2]

The constitution not only broke with the goals and principles – such as
they were – of the Nazi regime, but also reflected the reality of German
defeat, the division of Germany and the hatred for Germans that Nazi
policies had engendered. It protested the division of the country. The
preamble stated that the constitution had also been created on behalf of
those Germans 'whose participation had been made impossible', those
under Soviet rule. It treated as citizens all those who had been German
citizens in 1937 as well as East European refugees or expellees of German
ethnicity who had come to live within the pre-1938 German borders.[3]
In this way ethnic Germans throughout Eastern Europe were given an
automatic right to refuge. A 1955 law extended German citizenship to
ethnic Germans living outside the 1937 boundaries if Nazi authorities
had enrolled them in the first three Volksliste categories, or if they had on
other grounds been made citizens or 'Staatsangehörige auf Widerruf'.[4]
From 1949 to 1990 over five million ethnic Germans from the German
Democratic Republic and the countries of the Soviet bloc fled to West
Germany and assumed their rights as citizens.[5] This migration slowed

after the building of the Berlin wall in 1961, but then rose again from the 1980s, as the Soviet empire first swayed and then collapsed.

The employment of millions of foreign workers in West Germany, from the 1960s, and an influx of refugees seeking asylum, from the 1980s, posed significant challenges to the goal of creating a society that treated all residents with dignity and as equals. West Germany concluded agreements for the temporary employment of workers with Italy (1955), Greece (1960), Spain (1960), Turkey (1961/1964), Portugal (1964) and Yugoslavia (1968). Of the 3,966,200 aliens in West Germany in September 1973, shortly before the country ended the recruitment of foreign workers, 893,600 were Turkish, 673,300 were Yugoslav and 622,000 Italian. Most were employed in unskilled jobs.[6] This could sometimes be justified initially by their poor command of German and temporary status, but it remained a reality that defined the position of much of the larger group.

Between 1980 and 2000, a total of 2,663,058 persons sought asylum; more than half of this total arrived between 1990 and 1995. The former Soviet Empire, Yugoslavia and Turkey were the chief sources of refugees. Of those who sought asylum fewer than 10 percent obtained it, but the process of adjudication often lasted for years, and many whose applications were rejected remained in Germany even after their rejection.[7] Germany also accepted smaller, more discrete groups of immigrants on a humanitarian basis without requiring individuals to satisfy a court that they had been persecuted or might expect persecution at home. In the early 1980s 33,000 Vietnamese refugees were granted refuge in this way. And since 1991 Germany has permitted the immigration of some 150,000 Jews from the former Soviet Union. These last groups of immigrants were provided many of the social services offered to ethnic German immigrants, such as language courses and assistance with housing.[8] Other asylum seekers were supported at more modest levels while their asylum petitions were being decided. Their ability to work was restricted and they were often required to live in isolated housing projects.[9] By the time refugees began to arrive en masse, popular opinion had become far more hostile to foreigners than it had been in the 1960s, for reasons that will be explored below.[10] In the early 1990s neo-Nazis repeatedly and often violently attacked individual foreigners and the housing provided asylum-seekers. Most, but not all, of the attacks took place in the provinces that before 1990 had been East Germany. This reflected the high level of unemployment and hostility to foreigners found in the new Länder.[11]

A Republican and European Citizenship Law

Table 10.1 Aliens Residing in the Federal Republic of Germany, 1973–2002

Date of Census	Number of foreigners in the Federal Republic of Germany	As a percentage of the total population	Date of Census	Number of foreigners in the Federal Republic of Germany	As a percentage of the total population
30.9.1973	3,966,200	6.4	31.12.1988	4,489,100	7.3
30.9.1974	4,127,400	6.7	31.12.1989	4,845,900	7.7
30.9.1975	4,089,600	6.6	31.12.1990	5,342,500	8.4
30.9.1976	3,948,300	6.4	31.12.1991	5,882,300	7.3
30.9.1977	3,948,300	6.4	31.12.1992	6,495,800	8.0
30.9.1978	3,981,100	6.5	31.12.1993	6,878,100	8.5
30.9.1979	4,142,800	6.7	31.12.1994	6,990,500	8.6
30.9.1980	4,453,300	7.2	31.12.1995	7,173,900	8.8
30.9.1981	4,629,700	7.5	31.12.1996	7,314,000	8.9
30.9.1982	4,666,900	7.6	31.12.1997	7,365,800	9.0
30.9.1983	4,534,900	7.4	31.12.1998	7,319,600	8.9
30.9.1984	4,363,600	7.1	31.12.1999	7,343,600	8.9
31.12.1985	4,378,900	7.2	31.12.2000	7,296,800	8.9
31.12.1986	4,512,700	7.4	31.12.2001	7,318,600	8.9
31.12.1987	4,240,500	6.9	31.12.2002	7,348,000	8.9

Source: Ausländerpolitik und Ausländerrecht in Deutschland, Bundesministerium des Innern (www.bmi.bund.de, accessed on 24 July 2003), 14; Statistisches Bundesamt, *Statistisches Jahrbuch für die Bundesrepublik Deutschland*. The figures exclude foreign military personnel and diplomats.

In the context of the wide-scale employment of migrant workers and the influx of asylum seekers, citizenship law played a function similar to the one it had assumed during the Kaiserreich and in the Weimar Republic. It became a final barrier to the permanent settlement of foreigners who had managed to reside for a long period within the state. The Federal Republic therefore initially found little reason to change those parts of the citizenship law that gave the state administration wide discretionary powers over the granting of naturalization petitions. As in the Weimar period, Land governments used their authority with respect to the naturalization of foreigners to prevent individuals who were not ethnic Germans from becoming citizens. Perhaps surprisingly, the German Democratic Republic also based its citizenship law primarily on the law of 1913, although the GDR was not characterized by much immigration. The GDR's leaders apparently prized the unfettered discretion the law gave them over access to citizenship.[12]

By 1989 some 8 percent of the population of West Germany consisted of aliens. It had become clear that most were not going to leave voluntarily, and, for the reasons discussed below, the state lacked the power, and to some extent was also unwilling, to compel their departure. The center and left of the political spectrum exerted intense pressure on national and Land governments to integrate long-term resident aliens into German society, and under this pressure, and in the absence of viable means of forcing the exit of most of the foreigners in the country, the national government revised the citizenship law. In amendments adopted in 1990, 1993 and 1999 it granted long-term residents a right to naturalization and gave their children German citizenship on birth, although in both cases it imposed conditions designed to prevent dual citizenship. These were revolutionary changes.

Gender and Equality

The treatment of the citizenship status of women also underwent revolutionary change in post-war Germany, although rather more quietly. Article three of the West German constitution provided, in part as a reaction to the subordination of women during the Nazi period, 'that men and women have equal rights'. The adoption of this clause may also have owed something to other legacies of the Nazi period. In the last years of the war and in the first post-war years women had assumed many positions previously limited to men. Moreover, in 1949 significantly more than half of the electorate was female, thanks to Wehrmacht casualties and the continuing internment in the Soviet Union of hundreds of thousands of German POWs.[13] From 1953 most Länder accepted that German women who married foreigners no longer lost their citizenship. Only Bavaria refused to agree that the constitution required a change in the application of the citizenship law to women. National legislation adopted in 1957 confirmed that women no longer automatically assumed the citizenship of their husbands. A report on the question submitted to the Bundestag found the previous rule 'a serious infringement of personal freedom'. The law granted foreign women who married Germans the right to become German citizens at any point during the marriage.[14]

While the 1957 legislation freed women of the necessity of adopting the citizenship of their husbands, it did not create the equal treatment that the constitution had mandated. Foreign men who married German women did not have the right to become German citizens. And as provided by the 1913 law the citizenship of children still followed that of the father, except where children were born out of wedlock. Women had gained the right to determine their own citizenship, but they had little ability to pass their citizenship to their husbands and children.

Changes adopted in 1969 eliminated the right of foreign women to become German citizens on marrying a German, and replaced it with a more limited entitlement that applied to both foreign wives and husbands of Germans. Henceforth foreign spouses were in principle to be naturalized if they showed that they had 'willingly adapted to the German way of life' ('daß sie sich in die deutschen Lebensverhältnisse einordnen'). The spokesman for the government denied in the Bundestag debates that 'this would in the least require the foreign spouse to give up his or her own language or culture'.[15] Spouses who wished to become Germans were, however, required to surrender their previous citizenship. This was new. National guidelines interpreting the law provided that in general naturalization was to be granted to spouses of Germans after five years of residence in Germany, assuming that the marriage had lasted at least two years and the conditions in the law were met.[16]

The change in the law had a range of causes. The number of marriages between German women and foreigners was increasing, thanks in part to the ever-growing number of 'guest workers'. The difficulty foreign husbands of German women experienced in becoming German citizens also created problems for their spouses and for their children. On the other hand, it was becoming apparent that some foreign women were marrying Germans simply for the purposes of obtaining a right to citizenship.[17] The law made obtaining citizenship through sham marriages more difficult. The Bundestag adopted the change unanimously.

In the early 1970s several court cases challenged the rule that children inherited citizenship only from the father as unconstitutional, under the provision of the constitution that guaranteed men and women equal rights. The courts in general agreed with the plaintiffs. It was in part under the influence of these decisions that in 1974 the Bundestag considered and then unanimously adopted legislation establishing that children could inherit German citizenship from either parent. Children were permitted to keep their German citizenship even in cases where they inherited the citizenship of a different state as well.[18] The adoption of the changes owed something to the advocacy of Bundestag deputies from all the major parties who were women, as was noted during the debates on the law.[19] By 1974 the demand for the equal treatment of women's citizenship rights had come to seem self-evident.

'Guest Workers'

The free-trade provisions of the founding treaty of the European Economic Community (EEC), in later incarnations the European Community and European Union, played a critical role in the formation of West German policy with respect to workers both from within and also from outside the EEC. In 1957 the EEC encompassed Belgium, France, West Germany, Italy, Luxembourg and the Netherlands. Article 49 of the Treaty of Rome, signed in March 1957, provided that by the end of 1969 'freedom of movement for workers shall be secured within the Community'. The signatories agreed to abolish discrimination in employment based on nationality and to permit workers to move freely to accept offers of employment and to reside in the state where such an offer of employment had been accepted even after the employment had ended. While Article 49 focused exclusively on workers, the preamble to the Treaty made clear that freedom of movement for persons generally was the ultimate goal. Of the original EEC members it was above all Italy that benefited, as an exporter of labor, from the Treaty of Rome's provisions on freedom of movement. The admission to the European Union of Greece, in 1981, and of Portugal and Spain in 1986, meant that the nationals of these countries, who in the 1980s comprised roughly 12 percent of the foreigners in West Germany, came to be protected by the Treaty of Rome and subsequent European Union rulings, and could be excluded from West Germany only on very limited grounds.[20]

Although the EEC agreement only governed the treatment of citizens of member states, its articles regarding freedom of movement became a model for clauses in treaties entered into between the EEC and Turkey and the EEC and Greece. The September 1963 agreement between the EEC and Turkey provided that 'the Contracting Parties agree to be guided by Articles 48, 49, and 50 [the provisions governing freedom of movement] of the Treaty establishing the [EEC] for the purpose of progressively securing freedom of movement for workers between them'.[21] In 1980, pursuant to a follow-up treaty with Turkey, an EEC commission ruled that a Turkish worker 'duly registered as belonging to the labor force of a member state . . . shall be entitled in that Member State, after one year's legal employment, to the renewal of his permit to work for the same employer, if the job is still available', and after four years of legal employment to have 'free access in the Member State to any paid employment of his choice'.[22] In September of 1990, in a case involving a Turkish worker living in the Netherlands, the European Court of Justice upheld the right of Turkish workers to enforce the 1980 commission rule in court.[23] Thus, EEC treaties, administrative rulings and decisions by European courts sharply limited the power of the West German state to compel the departure of Turkish citizens who came to Germany as 'guest workers'.[24]

The provisions of the Treaty of Rome and EEC treaties with non-EEC states also doubtless affected policies toward states outside the EEC treaty network. West German Labor Minister Walter Arendt and President Karl Carstens orally assured Yugoslav leaders in 1974 and 1983, respectively, that Yugoslav 'guest workers' would not be sent packing when convenient for West Germany.[25] Even when it had not made formal or informal promises, West Germany had to consider that nations that had sent workers might feel unfairly treated if their nationals were singled out for non-renewal of work contracts. It is not surprising that in internal government debates the Foreign Office was often found on the side of those advocating caution in forcing the return of foreign workers to their countries of origin.

It is to Konrad Adenauer, German Chancellor from 1949 to 1963, that the decision to accept the provisions of the Treaty of Rome on freedom of movement, as well as the initial recruitment treaties with foreign states, must be attributed. Adenauer dominated the national government, and it was he who made decisions of this order of magnitude. Adenauer was a firm supporter of the economic and political integration of Germany into Europe, primarily on political rather than economic grounds. He believed European unification on all levels critical to protecting West Germany's political independence against the Soviet threat. He was also convinced that the reestablishment of a unified German state would be achieved only if West Germany became firmly embedded in a larger Europe, for only this would moderate other countries' fears of German power. Adenauer's plan was in fact so successful that it is today easy to forget how intense was the fear of Germany throughout Europe in the 1950s. For all these reasons Adenauer concluded, as he wrote in memoirs published in 1967, that 'every rational German has to welcome the efforts to achieve European unification [europäische Einigung]'.[26]

Pursuant to these deeply held convictions, in instructions dated 19 January 1956 Adenauer ordered his ministers to promote the integration of West Germany into the EEC with 'all relevant means', including the creation of a common European market 'that is similar to the domestic market'.[27] European institutions were to be granted sufficient powers to achieve this end. Freedom of movement within the European Economic Community was an integral part of Adenauer's long-term vision. The EEC agreement with Turkey corresponded with Adenauer's hope that

Turkey would (again) become a close German ally. In the post-war years German officials often considered Turkey a part of Europe.[28] It was convenient for Social Democratic and Free Democratic political leaders in the 1970s to blame Adenauer for having been foolish or short-sighted for having committed West Germany to a policy of freedom of movement, to a limited degree, between West Germany and Turkey, but there was a tendency to forget the larger logic of his policy and the quid pro quos West Germany had obtained.[29]

To what extent did foreign pressures play a role in leading West Germany to recruit migrant workers from other countries? In the late 1950s and 1960s more than a dozen states in southern Europe and also outside Europe pressed the West German government to accept their citizens as migrant laborers.[30] A study of post-war West German migration policies by Johannes-Dieter Steinert finds that it was primarily such external pressure, and not the domestic demand for workers, that led to the signing of the first recruitment treaties. For example, Steinert argues that it was Italian threats to restrict German imports that pushed West Germany into signing a treaty on migrant workers with Italy in 1955.[31] He suggests that the agreement with Turkey was primarily a result of Turkish claims that it would consider a rejection of a treaty 'discriminatory treatment' ('eine Zurücksetzung'), since Germany had established a migrant worker program with Greece. According to Steinert the threat of damage to its international position compelled West Germany to sign the treaty with Turkey ('denn diesem aussenpolitische Argument könnte sich die Bundesregierung nicht entziehen').[32] Steinert also suggests that the recruitment treaties were attractive to West Germany – and often the sending country as well – in part because they provided a means to control and limit the employment of migrant workers by private parties.

While it is true that West Germany was subject to foreign pressures to employ guest workers, the migrant-worker treaties were not foisted on German society against its will. In the 1960s the employment of migrant labor from abroad came to be accepted by most of West German society, even if skeptical opinions were periodically voiced. Following the building of the Berlin Wall in 1961 the flood of refugees from East Germany virtually stopped. Refugees from East Germany had provided a vital source of labor for the West German economic boom of the 1950s, and industry sought to replace them with foreign labor. Pressure from German employers in 1962 and 1963 played a key role in ending the two-year limit on the period for which Turkish workers were permitted to remain in West Germany.[33] In fact certain sectors of the economy had felt a need for foreign labor even before the building of the Wall. Migrant workers contributed far more in taxes and pension-plan payments than the state expected to pay on their behalf. They could be released during a recession, once their work permits expired. For all these reasons, public attacks on the employment of migrant workers were relatively modest in number and extent before the early 1970s. The issue played little role in election campaigns in the 1960s.[34]

West Germans and their political leaders overwhelmingly assumed in the 1960s that almost all of the migrant workers would return to their home countries. The terminology employed with respect to the migrant workers emphasized their temporary status, and also, the voluntary character of their employment. They were not 'Fremdarbeiter', foreign workers, as in the Nazi period, but 'Gastarbeiter', guest workers.[35] This assumption proved most valid with respect to workers from within the European Economic Community, whose home countries became increasingly prosperous in the 1960s and 1970s, and who could, moreover, freely move back and forth between their homes and West Germany. Italy was the principal example. It proved largely invalid with respect to migrant workers from countries that were much poorer than West Germany, and whose relations with West Germany did not offer any assurance that workers who left would be able to return. Turkey and Yugoslavia were the most important countries in this last category.

In November 1973, in the midst of a recession, the national government – from 1969 to 1982 a coalition of the Social Democratic (SPD) and Free Democratic (FDP) Parties – stopped further recruitment of foreign workers. But the national state did not undertake to force most of the migrant workers already in the country to leave. The granting – or denial – of residence and work permits was largely a matter for Land governments or local authorities, although the national government attempted to coordinate local policies. In Bavaria and Baden-Württemberg, Länder governed by the conservative Christian Social Union (CSU) and Christian Democratic Union (CDU) respectively, governments attempted from 1972 onward to limit migrant workers to three- or five-year stays, and in various other ways to promote their temporary residence in Germany. Even in these Länder, however, restrictions on length of residence were only partially put into practice. Policies in Länder governed by the Social Democratic Party, alone or together with the Free Democrats, were more liberal. In North-Rhine Westfalia in 1972; in Hessen in 1973; in Berlin in 1974; and in Hamburg in 1976, Land governments adopted measures designed to permit migrant workers who already lived in West Germany to, as a Hamburg administrative commission put it, 'determine for themselves how long they remain'.[36]

The replacement of the SPD-FDP coalition government with a CDU-FDP coalition in October 1982 led to a far more vigorous effort to repatriate migrant workers. The CDU made the previous government's supposed permissiveness in dealing with foreigners a major issue before the March 1983 national elections. Following the election victory of the Christian Democrats the new Chancellor, Helmut Kohl, publicly announced that 'the number of foreign fellow citizens must be reduced'.[37] At the same time, and in large part thanks to the CDU's electoral tactics, popular opinion had moved sharply against permitting 'guest workers' to remain. In March 1983 pollsters found that 80 percent of West Germans favored requiring foreign workers eventually to leave the country.[38] The recession that began in 1981 doubtless played a role. Unemployment among West Germans jumped from 3.8 percent in 1980 to 9.1 percent in 1983.

To entice migrant workers to leave West Germany, the CDU-FDP coalition government agreed to make lump-sum payments to individuals who left to compensate them for the loss of retirement and unemployment benefits that they would have received had they remained in Germany. Foreigners were given access to low-interest loans to build homes in their countries of origin, provided that they emigrated within a set period to enjoy those homes. Some Länder, notably Berlin (now governed by the CDU) and Baden-Württemberg, independently made modest payments to foreign workers who left. CDU and CSU Land governments, and to a lesser degree other Land governments as well, restricted the right of foreign workers to bring family members to West Germany to join them. In the early 1980s, for example, Bavaria and Baden-Württemberg required the children of 'guest workers' to live in West Germany for eight years before having even a possibility of bringing family members to Germany, and to wait three years after a marriage before – possibly – being granted permission to bring a spouse to Germany. Baden-Württemberg also applied the three-year waiting period to marriages of migrant workers.[39] Those family members who were permitted to come to Germany often found themselves excluded for long periods from the labor market.[40] These measures were not without an effect on the number of aliens in the country, but while some did leave, the vast majority did not.

By the 1980s it had in fact become quite difficult to force many of the 'guest workers' to depart, despite the existence of laws that on their face gave Länder wide discretion to deny residence permits to foreigners.[41] German employers had come to rely on foreign workers. Most were needed even during recessions. European laws and treaties limited the state's power to enforce its laws regarding the residence of foreigners, although the extent of the protection they offered depended in large part on the nationality of the individual and how long he or she had lived and worked in West Germany. Domestic court decisions also limited the discretion of the state. In September 1978 the Federal Constitutional Court ruled that an Indian who had lived in West Germany for twelve years, and whose residence and work permits had repeatedly been renewed, had through the actions of the officials developed a constitutionally protected 'reliance interest' (Vertrauensschutz) in remaining in West Germany.[42] In May of 1987 the same court invalidated the three-year waiting period that Bavaria and Baden-Württemberg imposed with respect to the migration to Germany of foreign spouses of aliens as a violation of Article 6 of the Constitution, which guaranteed marriage and the family 'the special protection of the state order'.[43]

National and Land governments were also sensitive to the charge of racism that might be made if 'guest workers' from non-European ethnic groups were targeted for unfavorable treatment. In part this reflected memories of the Nazi period at home and abroad. A leading academic expert on German citizenship law, Kay Hailbronner, commented in an article written in the mid-1990s that 'everyone who is familiar with the practice of the law that governs foreigners knows of cases in which the regional press has reported on the supposedly inhumane expulsions of foreigners whose children attend German schools and who are seen by employers as reliable workers'.[44] Church and student groups were among the leaders of attacks on efforts to pressure migrant workers and their families to leave Germany.

Naturalization as the Last Barrier

The inability or unwillingness of West German national and Land governments to compel migrant workers and their families to depart made German citizenship law one of the few remaining legal bulwarks against the full integration of resident aliens into German society. No treaties compelled the state to grant citizenship to foreigners. The EEC and successor organizations had left this question entirely within the jurisdiction of its member states. The restrictive emphasis of naturalization policies was reflected in the guidelines Land governments issued regarding the treatment of naturalization petitions, as well as in the national guidelines that replaced these Land directives in 1977.[45]

The national guidelines stated flatly that 'the Federal Republic of Germany is not a land of immigration. It does not desire to increase the number of its citizens through naturalization'.[46] The guidelines required applicants to have lived in Germany for a minimum of ten years prior to naturalization, except if they were ethnic Germans, married to a German citizen, or if there was a 'clear public interest' in a rapid naturalization. Applicants for naturalization had to demonstrate a 'voluntary and lasting inclination [Hinwendung] to Germany', democratic convictions, and 'adaptation to German living conditions' ('Einordnung in die deutschen Lebensverhältnisse'). A criminal record, or repeated disorderly conduct ('Ordnungswidrigkeiten'), as well as 'misdevelopments of the personality' exhibited through, for example, alcohol or drug abuse, were also grounds for the rejection of applications.[47]

Applicants for citizenship from what were termed 'developing countries' were subject to particularly strict rules. Citizens of these countries – which included all of Asia outside of Japan, all of Africa outside of South Africa, all of the Americas outside of the United States and Canada, and all of Turkey – were to be in principle denied citizenship if they had participated in any schooling, training or apprenticeship programs in the Federal Republic.[48] A few limited exceptions were permitted. The guidelines justified the special treatment accorded foreigners from the 'Third World' on the grounds that the purpose of training persons from underdeveloped nations would not be served if the individuals who had benefited did not return to their native countries, and suggested that tensions between West Germany and developing nations might arise if such persons chose to remain in Germany. The Interior Ministry was clearly concerned that this section of the guidelines might be challenged inside and outside of West Germany as being fundamentally a product of racism.

The guidelines stated that 'naturalization should only be granted if it is shown that the applicant will give up his previous citizenship prior to his naturalization [in Germany]'.[49] If surrender of a previous citizenship required the fulfillment of financial or other duties to the state of origin, the applicant was expected to meet these requirements. These provisions of the guidelines in particular affected citizens of Turkey, for Turkish law required Turkish men to perform military service before they were permitted to give up their citizenship.[50] On the other hand, the guidelines provided for certain exceptions. Arbitrary refusals to release citizens or the imposition of burdens that were by international standards onerous as a condition of release from citizenship were not to prevent naturalization. Petitioners who had grown up and been educated in West Germany were not required to fulfill the military service requirements of other countries.[51]

The high fees charged for naturalization may well have deterred a significant number of potential applicants for citizenship. An amendment to the citizenship law adopted in 1970 provided that Land administrators might charge applicants a fee of up to 5,000 marks.[52] The general principle was that the fee imposed should reflect both the administrative cost of processing the petition and the significance of the administrative action for the applicant. Land administrators rated both as significant. In Berlin the usual fee charged in 1987 upon the submission of a naturalization petition was 1,800 DM, and this could be increased if the application raised unusual issues. Spouses of Germans were to be charged only half the usual rate, those who had been granted asylum a quarter.[53]

While the national guidelines posed considerable barriers for foreigners seeking naturalization, in some respects they represented a liberalization of previous Land policies. They did not require a certificate of good health from a doctor, as had North Rhine Westfalia and Rhineland-Pfalz. They did not require that the applicant demonstrate that he would in the future feel 'united with the German people' or that he and his family would henceforth 'belong to the German cultural world' ('Kulturkreis'), as had North Rhine Westfalia. While the pre-1977 Land guidelines generally had not mentioned the issue of dual citizenship, most apparently assumed that retention of a prior citizenship would prevent naturalization, as stated explicitly in the guidelines for North Rhine Westfalia.[54] Here the national guidelines provided for some exceptions to the general rule. Even the fee schedule, as steep as it was, amounted in some respects to a liberalization. In parts of Bavaria fees of up to 12,000 DM had been charged for naturalizations before 1970.[55]

Since the fees imposed on applicants for naturalization were steep and were not returned if a petition was denied, and since the chances for success were at best modest for individuals who were not ethnic Germans or married to a German citizen, it appears that few guest workers applied for citizenship. Furthermore, aside from the expense and effort, applying for citizenship had risks. It was an indication that an individual no longer wished to return to his home country, and this alone might provide Land officials with a reason for refusing to renew residence permits issued on a temporary basis.[56] The difficulty of obtaining naturalization differed significantly from Land to Land. In 1990, for example, one-third of 1 percent of the foreigners living in Bavaria were granted discretionary naturalization by Land authorities. The comparable figure for Berlin was 0.98 percent, or three times the Bavarian rate.[57]

Opening Citizenship to Ethnic Foreigners

By the late 1980s the restrictive naturalization policies of German Länder had created what seemed a permanent and growing alien population. The replacement of an extremely conservative national Interior Minister, Friedrich Zimmermann, by the more moderate Wolfgang Schäuble in April 1989 led directly to a liberalization. Schäuble made the integration of at least a portion of the existing community of foreigners a part of the CDU program. The amendments to the Ausländergesetz adopted in the spring of 1990 provided that petitions for naturalization would usually ('in der Regel') be granted with respect to aliens who had legally lived in the Federal Republic for at least eight years, attended a German school for at least six years, given up other citizenships, and had not been convicted of a crime. To benefit from these rules individuals had to apply for naturalization when they were older than sixteen and before the age of twenty-four. Aliens who had legally lived in West Germany for fifteen years were also usually to be naturalized if they showed that they had given up their previous citizenship, had not been convicted of a crime, and could support themselves and their families. The law incorporated the conditions contained in the federal guidelines regarding exceptions to the prohibition on multiple citizenships. It also reduced the fee for naturalizations that took place under its provisions to 100 marks. This was raised in 1993 to 500 marks, with a provision for reduction in appropriate cases. Both amounts were considerably below the previous norm.[58]

Although the 1990 law encountered a storm of opposition from the Social Democratic and Green Parties, on the grounds that the reforms it contained were inadequate, in fact it was a significant liberalization.[59] In significant ways it realized the goals sketched by the SPD-FDP government some ten years earlier. The number of Turkish citizens naturalized increased dramatically. In 1989 there were 1,612,600 Turkish citizens living in West Germany and 1,713 naturalizations of Turks. In 1999, the last year the 1990 law was in effect, there were 103,900 naturalizations of Turkish citizens. Among the most striking aspects of the application of the new law was the willingness of some Land officials to accept dual nationality. In 1993 45 percent of the individuals who were naturalized who were not Aussiedler, ethnic German immigrants from Eastern Europe and the Former Soviet Union, were permitted to retain another citizenship. This dropped to roughly 20 percent in the course of the 1990s, largely because Turkey eased the re-acquisition of Turkish citizenship, and amended its laws to allow Turks who had given up their citizenship in Turkey to retain most of their previous economic and social rights. More than a few of the Turks who were naturalized after having given up their Turkish citizenship subsequently regained their Turkish passports: the Turkish government has not published the numbers.[60] Exactly how liberally the 1990 law was applied varied considerably from Land to Land, and even within Länder. For example, in 1995 only 10 percent of the successful applicants for naturalization in Bavaria were permitted to keep another citizenship, while in Berlin the rate was 75 percent.[61]

The national coalition government of the Social Democratic and Green Parties elected in 1998 was determined to further promote the legal and social integration of aliens. The law it proposed would have granted citizenship based on birth in Germany, and, furthermore, permitted dual citizenship. The CDU and CSU vociferously opposed the change and undertook a petition drive that targeted the issue of dual citizenship. Some five million Germans signed the petitions. This pressure, and the loss of a regional election in Hessen forced the government to make dual citizenship an exception rather than the norm under the new law.

The new citizenship law adopted in May 1999, with SPD, Green and FDP votes, and also twenty-three abstentions by CDU members of the Bundestag, granted citizenship on birth to all individuals born in the state when at least one parent had legally lived for eight years in Germany and had for three years had an unlimited right to remain. The principal restriction is the requirement that the children of aliens who in this fashion acquire citizenship file, before their twenty-fourth birthday, a declaration that they wish to remain German citizens and, furthermore, demonstrate that they have lost or given up all other citizenships. Dual citizenship is permitted on the same grounds as under the 1990 law, with the addition of a few further exceptions. Citizens of other European Union countries are freed from the requirement that they surrender their previous citizenship, as long as German citizens enjoy a similar right in their country. Some commentators have suggested that the very form of the law will put pressure on administrators to treat dual citizenship liberally. For example, if aliens who acquire German citizenship by birth in Germany have children before they are twenty-three, their children will be German citizens without qualification. In such situations officials may find it difficult to prevent the maintenance of German citizenship by the parent, even if the parent insists on keeping a different citizenship as well. The law also lowered from fifteen to eight years the period of legal residence required of other aliens before they acquired a right to naturalization.[62]

The number of naturalizations of Turkish citizens peaked in the last year before the 1999 law became effective on 1 January 2000. (see Table 10.2) There are several possible explanations, all of which highlight aspects of the new law that restrict access to naturalization. While the residence period required of aliens before a right to naturalization was created was shortened, the 1999 law imposed new conditions on individuals seeking naturalization as a matter of right. For example, it required an adequate knowledge of the German language. It also introduced a requirement that petitioners for citizenship who wished to benefit from this part of the law declare their loyalty to the democratic principles of the Federal Republic. Finally, the law threatened those who acquired, or reacquired, a citizenship in a country other than Germany after becoming German citizens with the loss of their German citizenship. The desire to avoid these provisions was apparently the cause of the spike in naturalizations in 1999.[63]

The liberalization of German citizenship policy was accompanied, and in part made possible, by a tightening of the laws that governed

Table 10.2 Naturalizations of Turkish Citizens in the Federal Republic of Germany, 1982–2002

Year	Turkish citizens naturalized in the Federal Republic of Germany	Turkish citizens in the Federal Republic of Germany	Year	Turkish citizens naturalized in the Federal Republic of Germany	Turkish citizens in the Federal Republic of Germany
1982	580	1,580,700	1993	12,915	1,918,400
1983	853	1,552,300	1994	19,590	1,965,600
1984	1,053	1,425,800	1995	31,578	2,014,300
1985	1,310	1,401,900	1996	46,294	2,049,100
1986	1,492	1,434,300	1997	42,240	2,107,400
1987	1,184	1,481,400	1998	59,664	2,110,200
1988	1,243	1.523,700	1999	103,900	2,053,600
1989	1,713	1,612,600	2000	82,861	1,998,500
1990	2,034	1,675,900	2001	76,573	1,947,900
1991	3,529	1,779,600	2002	64,631	1,912,200
1992	7,377	1,854,900			

Source: Statistisches Bundesamt, *Statistisches Jahrbuch für die Bundesrepublik Deutschland*; correspondence with the Statistisches Bundesamt of 3 September 2003. Since an unknown number of Turkish citizens who gave up their Turkish citizenship to become German citizens may have reacquired their Turkish citizenship without informing the German government, it is possible that, especially since the early 1990s, the number of Turkish citizens has been greater than revealed in this chart.

Figure 10.1 From the photo album of the Musluoglu family, which left Turkey for Germany in 1964. The Turkish caption reads: 'Here begins our history in Germany.' Reproduced with the permission of Klartext Verlag, from Aytac Eryilmaz and Mathilde Jamin (eds), *Fremde Heimat: Eine Geschichte der Auswanderung aus der Turkei* (Essen: Klartext Verlag, 1998).

immigration. The Ausländergesetz adopted in 1990 granted the government expanded powers to exclude newly arriving immigrants. New systems for exchanging information with other European states regarding unwanted foreigners were developed.[64] The rules governing the granting of asylum were tightened. The CDU and SPD agreed in December 1992 to limit the right of asylum to individuals who had not crossed through a member state of the European Union, or other states that respected individual rights, on their way to Germany. This change in the constitution, adopted in June of 1993, drastically restricted who might henceforth apply for asylum. It was easier to liberalize the laws governing citizenship when the government seemed better able to control

Figure 10.2 Medical examination of prospective Turkish migrant workers at the German recruitment office, Istanbul, 1973. Reproduced with the permission of Klartext Verlag, from Aytac Eryilmaz and Mathilde Jamin (eds), *Fremde Heimat: Eine Geschichte der Auswanderung aus der Turkei* (Essen: Klartext Verlag, 1998).

who might come to live in the country. The December 1992 agreement between the SPD and the CDU also placed an upper limit on the number of ethnic-German Aussiedler to be admitted each year. But this number, 225,000, was so high as not to seriously restrict their access to Germany. And this was also true of the new annual limit of 110,000 introduced in 2000.[65]

Rationales

There were a range of reasons for the revisions of German citizenship laws that took place in the 1990s. Since they were often mentioned

Figure 10.3 A Turkish man and his daughter on the way to school, Berlin-Kreuzberg 1978. Reproduced with the permission of Klartext Verlag, from Aytac Eryilmaz and Mathilde Jamin (eds), *Fremde Heimat: Eine Geschichte der Auswanderung aus der Turkei* (Essen: Klartext Verlag, 1998).

together, it is difficult to distinguish which were the most important. The significance of each rationale varied considerably for different political actors, and over time.

Fear of conflict within German society was one ground for the change in the law. This point was stressed both by CDU Interior Minister Schäuble in 1990 and Otto Schily, the SPD Interior Minister, in 1999. Schäuble referred in his remarks to the Bundestag on the proposed Ausländergesetz to the need to preserve 'domestic peace'. He hoped that the law would both prevent the growth of resentment on the part of the aliens in Germany and, by furthering their integration into German society, curb the development of 'radical [right-wing] forces that promote and

The Politics of Citizenship in Germany

Table 10.3 Asylum Seekers in the Federal Republic of Germany, 1975–2002

Year	Number of applications for asylum in the Federal Republic of Germany	Year	Number of applications for asylum in the Federal Republic of Germany
1975	9,627	1989	121,318
1976	11,123	1990	193,063
1977	16,410	1991	256,112
1978	33,136	1992	438,191
1979	51,493	1993	322,599
1980	107,818	1994	127,210
1981	49,391	1995	127,937
1982	37,423	1996	116,367
1983	19,737	1997	104,353
1984	35,278	1998	98,644
1985	73,832	1999	95,113
1986	99,650	2000	78,564
1987	57,379	2001	88,287
1988	103,076	2002	71,127

Source: *Ausländerpolitik und Ausländerrecht in Deutschland*, Bundesministerium des Innern (www.bmi.bund.de, accessed on 24 July 2003), 89; Statistisches Bundesamt, *Statistisches Jahrbuch für die Bundesrepublik Deutschland*.

manipulate enmity to foreigners'.[66] Schily told the Bundestag in May of 1999 that if aliens living in Germany were not given the rights of other Germans, 'the result will be a progressive alienation of the immigrants, the young people who grow up in immigrant families will turn their backs on the society, immigrants will live increasingly in ghettos, [Germans and foreigners will live] in parallel societies'.[67]

Resignation also played an important role. Many Germans who opposed the permanent residence of migrant workers from outside of Europe came to accept that the state no longer had the power to bring about the repatriation of most of the aliens living in the country. Faced with the alternative of permitting a sizable and growing part of the population to remain foreigners while continuing to live in Germany or integrating them more fully into Germany society, this group preferred to permit the foreigners to become citizens. This was one theme of the remarks on the subject of the new citizenship law by Chancellor Gerhard Schröder in his inaugural address to the Bundestag in November of 1998. Both the beginning and ending comments of this part of his speech focused on the need to face what Schröder called 'reality', meaning the reality that recent immigrants were not likely to leave. Schröder began his remarks on the subject of citizenship with this aspect: 'Reality teaches us . . . that in Germany over the past decades an irreversible immigration has taken place.' And he closed this portion of his speech by again referring to the need to face 'realities' ('Wir wollen uns den Realitäten stellen').[68] In less public forums the lack of enthusiasm even in part of the Social Democratic Party – or at least in a part of the audience to which it sought to appeal – becomes clearer. A Social Democratic Bundestag deputy, Dieter Wiefelspütz, one of the SPD specialists on citizenship law, commented during a 1997 debate in Berlin that 'the people who are here now are just not going to leave' ('Wir werden die Menschen hier nicht mehr los').[69]

Another argument employed by those who advocated liberalization of the citizenship law was that the migrant workers had developed over time a legitimate expectation that they would be entitled to remain in Germany. This was the grounds on which the first national commissioner for the Integration of Foreign Workers and their Families, Heinz Kühn, called for an easing of citizenship laws in 1979. 'The migration [of foreign workers], which we once desired and promoted, necessarily created expectations in those who came which cannot, without clear force, be reversed. These expectations must be respected.'[70] In his Bundestag presentation of the 1990 changes in the laws governing foreigners, Interior Minister Schäuble also mentioned, albeit more tersely, 'the hopes and legitimate expectations of the foreigners who are living with us'.[71] Schröder noted in his inaugural address that 'we invited the people who came to us'.[72]

Democratic principles provided a distinct, more positive rationale for granting citizenship. This argument stressed not so much the entitlement that arose from the prior solicitation of migrant workers as a republican conception of the state, one which suggested that a state that failed to represent the population it governed thereby became illegitimate. Schröder repeatedly appealed to the democratic character of the German state, implying that all the permanent residents of Germany were entitled to a range of social and also political rights. Foreigners, he said, 'work here, pay taxes, and obey the law', and on these grounds deserved citizenship. A leading liberal intellectual, Dietrich Thränhardt, has in various publications also stressed the significance of the political rights that would come with citizenship. In describing the effects of the automatic grant of citizenship to ethnic Germans refugees, for example, Thränhardt noted that 'they received a full right to participate [in the political process], so that they were able to set in motion the normal democratic process of articulation of one's views'.[73] Thränhardt's purpose was in part to contrast the effects of the grant of citizenship with respect to Aussiedler with the failure to grant citizenship to aliens who were not ethnically German.

That the question of the political rights of the new citizens may have played a significant, if often hidden, role in debates regarding the new citizenship law – as in the Kaiserreich – is suggested by fears expressed rather late in the process of deliberations by opponents of a more liberal citizenship policy. In February 1999, shortly before the adoption of the revised citizenship law, the Bavarian Interior Minister, Günter Beckstein, a member of the CSU, and a leader of the CDU-CSU Bundestag fraction, Andreas Schmidt, jointly called attention to the political implications of granting immigrants the ballot if they were to retain a non-German citizenship. Both men warned that the new citizens might form minority parties like the Polish Party, and pursue the national interests of foreign countries – Turkey was the main fear – rather than of Germany.[74] While Beckstein and Schmidt focused on the dangers connected with dual citizenship, clearly their fears were not limited to individuals who were dual citizens. Given that as many as a fifth of the voters of Germany might, in something over a generation, be the children or grandchildren of immigrants, it is not surprising that political parties would consider for whom they would vote. The parties that opposed the liberalization of citizenship policies in 1999, the CDU and CSU, probably have some reason to fear that the new citizens will not vote for them.

Finally, a minority have suggested that the new citizenship laws implied, and furthered, a new conception of what the German nation was. In introducing the revised citizenship law to the Bundestag on 7 May 1999, Interior Minister Schily directly addressed the relationship of citizenship policy to national self-understanding. He suggested that the new law both reflected and would promote a fundamental change. Quoting at length from Ernest Renan's famous 1882 essay, 'What is a Nation?', Schily argued that Germany should no longer strive to construct or maintain a homogeneous society. Societies, he argued, including Germany, are held together not by a common ethnicity or language, but by common memories and the desire to live together. Marieluise Beck, a Bundestag member for the Green Party and the Federal Commissioner for Foreigners, made a similar argument. The central question raised by the reform of the citizenship law, she told the Bundestag, was whether Germany could 'as a modern society come to terms with the fact that we live with fellow citizens, men and women, who have the right to be different from the majority of the members of our society? . . . We simply have not yet learned that those who look different and are different have become an integral part of our society'.[75]

The project of European integration stands near the heart of this effort to reshape the meaning of German national feeling. The claim that the citizenship law of 1999 was 'European' was based in part on the perception – and reality – that most other West European countries granted foreigners citizenship far more readily than Germany. This was true in particular of the Netherlands, France and Sweden.[76] The greater tolerance for difference implied in the new citizenship law was also closely linked to the project of a larger Europe. In his May 1999 comments on the citizenship law in the Bundestag, Schily contrasted the 'destructive principle of ethnocracy' with a modern Europe that 'brings together individuals of various biographical and cultural traits'. 'We must understand that in a Europe that is slowly growing together, different nations, cultures, ethnic and language groups will come together in different forms than taken in the homogeneous national-state, which was an error of the previous century.'[77] Beck said, in the same debate, that 'the way toward Europe demands from us, politically and socially, to permit multiplicity, change, and difference, to accept it gladly, as something positive and fruitful . . .'[78] This claim is clearly the most ambitious foundation for the new citizenship law.

Notes

1. The title of the chapter reflects claims often made by the supporters of the German citizenship law adopted in 1999. In his speech opening the Bundestag on 10 November 1998 the new Social Democratic Chancellor, Gerhard Schröder, promised Germans 'a modern citizenship law'. 'We are today democrats and Europeans.' *Verhandlungen des Deutschen Bundestages* (*VDB*), Stenographische Berichte, p. 61. Federal Interior Minister Otto Schily has also emphasized both aspects. 'With the new German citizenship law the previous out-dated laws have been modernized and adapted to a European standard.' *Das neue Staatsangehörigkeirecht*, published by the Ausländerbeauftragte der Bundesregierung and the Bundesministerium des Innern (www.bmi.bund.de: undated, accessed 14 July 2003), p. 7.

2. *Grundgesetz für die Bundesrepublik Deutschland, Bundesgesetzblatt* (*BGBl*) I (1949), Articles 1 (1), 3, 16, and 116 (2). The *Bundesgesetzblatt* is the official journal of laws that succeeded the *Reichsgesetzblatt* in West Germany.

3. Article 116(a) of the Grundgesetz provided that 'Germans in the sense of this constitution are – until otherwise provided by legislation – individuals who hold German citizenship, or who are refugees or

expellees of German ethnicity (Volkszugehörigkeit) or the spouses or offspring of such individuals and have settled within the boundaries of the German state as they existed on 31 December 1937'. *BGBl* I, pp. 15–16.

4. *Gesetz zur Regelung von Fragen der Staatsangehörigkeit* of 22 February 1955, *BGBl* I, 65, Sections 1 and 28. Individuals from Austria, Belgium, Luxembourg and France who were made German citizens by the Nazi regime generally lost this citizenship after the war.

5. This figure is taken from the annual reports of the Statistisches Bundesamt. It is based, for the period from 1949 to 1967, on the number of individuals who applied for assistance from the Bundesnotaufnahme-Dienstellen. For the period after 1968 it is based on the number of ethnic-German returnees, or Aussiedler.

6. U. Herbert, *Geschichte der Ausländerpolitik in Deutschland* (Beck, 2001), pp. 204, 213; Dietrich Thränhardt, 'Die Reform der Einbürgerung in Deutschland', in Forschungsinstitut der Friedrich-Ebert-Stiftung, *Einwanderungskonzeption für die Bundesrepublik Deutschland* (Bonn, 1995), p. 65. Several recent studies have emphasized the diversity of the work experiences of foreign migrant workers, and the fact that not all were unskilled or male or single. But the reality remains that the migrant workers were largely employed in positions that German workers considered undesirable. Anne von Oswald et al., '*Einwanderungsland Deutschland*: A New Look at its Post-War History'; also Esra Erdem and Monika Mattes, 'Gendered Policies – Gendered Patterns: Female Labour Migration from Turkey to Germany from the 1960s to the 1990s', both in R. Ohliger, K. Schönwälder and T. Triadafilopoulos (eds), *European Encounters: Migrants, migration and European Societies since 1945* (Ashgate, 2003), pp. 19–37, 167–85.

7. Bundesministerium des Innern, *Ausländerpolitik und Ausländerrecht in Deutschland* (www.bmi.bund.de: accessed 14 July 2003), pp. 88–9, 96–7; Statistisches Bundesamt, *Statistisches Jahrbuch für die Bundesrepublik Deutschland* (1989), p. 59.

8. *Zuwanderung gestalten*, p. 186; Paul Harris, 'Jewish Immigration to the New Germany: The Policy Making Process Leading to the Adoption of the 1991 Quota Refugee Law', in D. Thränhardt (ed.), *Einwanderung und Einbürgerung in Deutschland*, (Lit Verlag, 1998), pp. 105–47; Paul Harris, 'Russische Juden und Aussiedler', in K. Bade and J. Oltmer (eds), *Aussiedler: deutsche Einwanderer aus Osteuropa* (Universitätsverlag Rasch, 1999), pp. 247–63.

9. The broad range of legal statuses granted to aliens in Germany is described in Lydia Morris, *Managing Migration: Civic Stratification and Migrants' Rights* (Routledge, 2002), pp. 28–52.

10. Mathilde Jamin, 'Migrationserfahrungen: Aus Interviews mit Migrantinnen der Ersten Generation', in A. Eryilmaz and M. Jamin, (eds), *Fremde Heimat: Eine Geschichte der Auswanderung aus der Turkei* (Klartext, 1998), pp. 207–31. Jamin found that Turkish workers initially felt, in general, welcome in Germany, a feeling that changed in the 1970s.

11. Herbert, *Geschichte der Ausländerpolitik*, pp. 296–322. While the level of violence fell after the 1990s, it has remained significant. For an examination of the extent of the integration of foreigners into German society in the 1990s, with a focus on Frankfurt/Main, see Brett Klopp, *German Multiculturalism: Immigrant Integration and the Transformation of Citizenship* (Praeger, 2002).

12. On the citizenship law of the German Democratic Republic see Alexander Makarov, *Deutsches Staatsangehörigkeitsrecht*, (Alfred Metzner, 1971), pp. 595–621. The form taken by the GDR's citizenship policy will not be further pursued in this study.

13. Robert Moeller discusses the genesis of this clause of the constitution in his *Protecting Motherhood: Women and the Family in the Politics of Postwar West Germany* (University of California Press, 1993), pp. 38–75.

14. *VDB* (29 June 1957), pp. 12996–9; Report of 18 May 1957 of the Bundestag Committee for Matters regarding Internal Administration. Ibid., p. 12997C; *Drittes Gesetz zur Regelung von Fragen der Staatsangehörigkeit* of 19 August 1957. *BGBl* I, p. 1251.

15. Elisabeth Enseling (CDU/CSU), *VDB*, Stenographische Berichte, vol. 70 (19 June 1969), p. 13455C. *Gesetz zur Änderung des Reichs- und Staatsangehörigkeitsgesetzes* of 8 September 1969, *BGBl* I, p. 1581.

16. 'Einbürgerungsrichtlinien', Section 6.1. Kay Hailbronner and Günter Renner, *Staatsangehörigkeitsrecht* (Beck, 1991), pp. 635–6.

17. This aspect was mentioned prominently both in the SPD proposal that initiated discussion of the issue, and in the report of the Bundestag Committee of the Interior that recommended a change in the law. See *VDB*, Anlagen, vol. 119 (1968) V/2676; Ibid., vol. 128 (1968) V/3971.

18. *Gesetz zur Änderung des Reichs- und Staatsangehörigkeitsgesetzes* of 20 December 1974, *BGBl* I, p. 3714. The history of the legislation is described in *VDB*, Stenographische Berichte, vol. 90 (5 December 1974), 9053D, and in *VDB*, Anlagen, vol. 191 (1974), 7/2175, p. 6.

19. *VDB*, Stenographische Berichte, vol. 90 (5 December 1974), p. 9058A.
20. Treaty establishing the European Economic Community of 25 March 1957, Articles 3(c) and 48(1), in K. Simmonds and P. Mead (eds), *Encyclopedia of European Community Law, European Community Treaties*, vol. 2 (Sweet & Maxwell), B10046/1; *Statistisches Jahrbuch 1986 für die Bundesrepublik Deutschland*, p. 68.
21. Agreement of September 12, 1963, Establishing an Association between the European Economic Community and Turkey, Article 12. *Encyclopedia of European Community Law, European Community Treaties*, vol. 2, B10046/1.
22. Kay Hailbronner, *Immigration and Asylum Law and Policy of the European Union* (Kluwer Law International, 2000), p. 225. Remarkably enough, this decision was not published.
23. *S.Z Sevince v. Staatssecretaris van Justitie* [1990] ECR I-3461. The court ruled against the plaintiff in the case on other grounds. For a critical discussion of the reasoning in *Sevince*, see Hailbronner, *Immigration and Asylum Law and Policy*, pp. 229–37.
24. For a more detailed discussion of the way in which EEC court rulings limited the powers of the West German government to expel aliens, see C. Joppke, 'The Evolution of Alien Rights in the United States, Germany, and the European Union', in T. Aleinikoff and D. Klusmeyer (eds), *Citizenship Today* (Carnegie, 2001). In 1984 the CDU-FDP coalition government debated prohibiting foreign children over the age of six from entering Germany to join their parents. Foreign Minister Hans-Dietrich Genscher, of the FDP, argued that such a measure would violate undertakings made in the past to the Turkish government and threatened to resign if the change were adopted. The proposal was rejected. Herbert, *Geschichte der Ausländerpolitik*, p. 253.
25. D. Thränhardt, '"Ausländer" als Objekte deutscher Interessen und Ideologien', in Harmut Griese (ed.), *Der gläserne Fremde: Bilanz und Kritik der Gastarbeiterforschung und Ausländerpädagogik* (Leske + Budrich, 1984), p. 118.
26. Konrad Adenauer, *Erinnerungen 1955–1959* (Deutsche Verlags-Anstalt, 1967), p. 252.
27. Ibid., p. 254. The disputes in Adenauer's cabinet that led to the drafting of this memorandum, in particular the reluctance of Economics Minister Ludwig Erhard to accept an economic union with France, are described in Hans Jürgen Küsters, *Die Gründung der Europäischen Wirtschaftsgemeinschaft* (Baden-Baden: Nomos, 1982), pp. 222–6.

28. Schönwälder, *Einwanderung und ethnische Pluralität* (Klartext, 2001), pp. 252–5.
29. Ibid., p. 556, n. 217.
30. Ibid., pp. 247, 251–2, 258, n. 400, 272–3, 343. The countries that solicited the German government to permit their citizens to work in Germany included Bolivia, Brazil, Chile, Hong Kong, India, Iran, Italy, Morocco, Singapore, Thailand, Togo, Tunisia, Turkey, Venezuela and Yugoslavia.
31. Johannes-Dieter Steinert, *Migration und Politik: Westdeutschland-Europa-Übersee 1945-1961* (secolo, 1995), pp. 20, 224, 226.
32. Ibid., p. 307.
33. Schönwälder, *Einwanderung und ethnische Pluralität*, p. 255.
34. Ibid., pp. 345–9, 498.
35. On the changing terminology see Dietrich Thränhardt, 'Die Reform der Einbürgerung in Deutschland', p. 75. 'Guest worker' also had a certain ironic, euphemistic flavor. From the 1980s the more generic term 'foreigner' ('Ausländer') largely displaced 'guest worker'.
36. Karl-Heinz Meier-Braun, *Integration oder Rückkehr? Zur Ausländerpolitik des Bundes und der Länder, insbesondere Baden-Württembergs* (Kaiser, 1988), pp. 77–80, 135–6, 138, 140–2.
37. Ibid., p. 26; Thränhardt, '"Ausländer" als Objekte deutscher Interessen und Ideologien', p. 116.
38. Herbert, *Geschichte der Ausländerpolitik*, p. 241; Meier-Braun, *Integration oder Rückkehr?*, pp. 24, 43; Thränhardt, 'Ausländer als Objekte deutscher Interessen und Ideologien', p. 124.
39. Meier-Braun, *Integration oder Rückkehr?*, pp. 50–2, 56, 86–7, 175, 192. The regulations of Baden-Württemberg, which were issued in 1982 and revised in 1984, are excerpted in the Federal Constitutional Court's decision of 12 May 1987, 2 BvR 1226/83, 101, 313/84, at 76 *Entscheidungen des Bundesverfassungsgerichts*, pp. 1, 4–6.
40. Erdem and Mattes, 'Gendered Policies – Gendered Patterns', pp. 167–85.
41. The relevant statute, the *Ausländergesetz* of 1965, provided that foreign migrant workers could remain in the Federal Republic only if they were in possession of a residence permit (Aufenthaltserlaubnis). This permit could be granted only 'if the presence of the foreigner does not damage the interests of the Federal Republic of Germany'. *Ausländergesetz* of 28 April 1965, Section 2, *BGBl* I, p. 353. Expulsion was permitted, even after the granting of a residence permit, for a large number of reasons, including the commission of a crime, unemployment, or 'if [the] presence [of the foreigner] for

other reasons damages important interests of the Federal Republic of Germany'. Ibid., Section 10.

42. Decision of 26 September 1978, 1 BvR 525/77, 49 *Entscheidungen des Bundesverfassungsgerichts* pp. 168, 181.
43. Decision of 12 May 1987, 2 BvR 1226/83, 101, 313/84, at 76 *Entscheidungen des Bundesverfassungsgerichts*, p. 1. For a discussion that places much more emphasis on the role played by the West German judiciary, see C. Joppke, *Immigration and the Nation-State* (Oxford University Press, 1999), pp. 62–99.
44. Kay Hailbronner, 'Der aufenthaltsrechtliche Status der verschiedenen Gruppen von Einwanderern in der Bundesrepublik Deutschland', in Albrecht Weber, *Einwanderungsland Bundesrepublik Deutschland in der Europäischen Union: Gestaltungsauftrag und Regelungsmöglichkeiten* (Universitätsverlag Rasch, 1997), p. 244.
45. The national guidelines were advisory in nature: one commentator suggests that they had the status of a 'common declaration of intentions'. Thränhardt, 'Die Reform der Einbürgerung in Deutschland', pp. 111–12.
46. 'Einbürgerungsrichtlinien', Section 2.3. Hailbronner and Renner, *Staatsangehörigkeitsrecht*, p. 626. The Hailbronner and Renner commentary reproduces the guidelines with amendments through 1989, and it is this version that will form the basis for the discussion that follows.
47. Ibid., pp. 626–9.
48. Ibid., pp. 631–2, 641.
49. Ibid., p. 633.
50. Thränhardt, 'Integration und Partizipation von Einwanderergruppen im lokalen Kontext,' in K. Bade and J. Oltmer (eds), *Aussiedler: deutsche Einwanderer aus Osteuropa*, (Universitätsverlag, 1999), p. 244; Thränhardt, 'Die Reform der Einbürgerung in Deutschland', p. 72. Turkish citizens were permitted to purchase freedom from military service, but the price was high. Turkey made it easier for emigrants to avoid military service in the 1990s.
51. 'Einbürgerungsrichtlinien', Sections 5.3.3.1, 5.3.3.2, and 5.3.3.6. Hailbronner/Renner, *Staatsangehörigkeitsrecht*, p. 634.
52. *Gesetz zur Änderung von Kostenermächtigungen, sozialversicherungsrechtlichen und anderen Vorschriften* of 23 June 1970, *BGBl* I, p. 805; Hailbronner/Renner, *Staatsangehörigkeitsrecht*, pp. 305–10.
53. Hailbronner and Renner, *Staatsangehörigkeitsrecht*, pp. 198, 505.
54. Makarov, *Deutsches Staatsangehörigkeitsrecht*, pp. 176–7, 192.

55. Hailbronner and Renner, *Staatsangehörigkeitsrecht*, p. 306.
56. This was the situation in the case decided by the Federal Constitutional Court on 26 September 1978, 1 BvR 525/77, 49 *Entscheidungen des Bundesverfassungsgerichts*, p. 168.
57. Thränhardt, 'Die Reform der Einbürgerung in Deutschland', pp. 83, 88.
58. *Gesetz zur Neuregelung des Ausländerrechts* of 9 July 1990, Sections 17–26, 85, 86, 90, *BGBl* I, p. 1354; K. Hailbronner et al., *Staatsangehörigkeitsrecht* 3rd edn (Beck, 2001), pp. 918–25, 845–68. The 1993 law also eliminated the phrase 'in der Regel'. Aliens meeting the terms of the law were thereby given a right to naturalization.
59. Rogers Brubaker's history of French and German citizenship policies, which appeared in 1992, can profitably be read as part of the left-wing critique of the CDU/FDP citizenship-law revisions adopted in 1990. Brubaker disparaged the significance of liberalizing naturalization rules. In his formulation, 'ascription constitutes and perpetually reconstitutes the citizenry; naturalization reshapes it at the margins'. Brubaker, *Citizenship and Nationhood in France and Germany* (Harvard University Press, 1992), p. 81. Brubaker argued that the failure of the Bundestag to adopt a more substantial reform proved that an 'assimilationist citizenship law', one that granted citizenship to all children born in Germany, was 'unimaginable', because Germany lacked a tradition of assimilating all those who were not ethnic Germans. 'There is no chance that the French system of *jus soli* will be adopted; the automatic transformation of immigrants into citizens remains unthinkable in Germany.' Ibid., pp. 177, 185.
60. Heike Hagedorn, 'Administrative Systems and Dual Nationality: The Information Gap', in David Martin and Kay Hailbronner (eds), *Rights and Duties of Dual Nationals: Evolution and Prospects* (Kluwer Law International, 2003), p. 188; Christian Rumpf, 'Citizenship and Multiple Citizenship in Turkish Law', in Ibid., p. 369. Rumpf calls the system developed by Turkey in 1995 'a kind of "hidden dual citizenship"'.
61. Hagedorn, 'Administrative Systems and Dual Nationality', pp. 192–3.
62. *Gesetz zur Reform des Staatsangehörigkeitsrechts* of 15 July 1999, *BGBl* I, pp. 1618–23; Hailbronner et al., *Staatsangehörigkeitsrecht* (2001), pp. 147–65. The Bavarian Minister-President Stoiber stated that the CDU and CSU had collected five million signatures in their petition campaign against the granting of dual citizenship in the

Bundesrat debate held on 21 May 1999. 'Das neue Staatsangehörigkeitsrecht kann in Kraft treten', *Frankfurter Allgemeine Zeitung* (22
May 1999), p. 1.

63. See *Gesetz zur Reform des Staatsangehörigkeitsrechts* of 15 July
1999, *BGBl* I, p. 1618, Article One, sections three, six, and eight,
and Article Two, section one; Hailbronner et al., *Staatsangehörigkeitsrecht* (2001), pp. 336–74, 552–76, 655–718; Christine Kreuzer,
'Double and Multiple Nationality in Germany after the Citizenship
Reform Act of 1999', in Martin and Hailbronner, *Rights and Duties
of Dual Nationals,* pp. 347–59.

64. See generally Hans-Joachim Cremer, 'Internal Controls and Actual
Removals of Deportable Aliens: The Current Legal Situation in
the Federal Republic of Germany', in Kay Hailbronner et al. (eds),
*Immigration Controls: The Search for Workable Policies in Germany
and the United States* (Berghahn 1998), pp. 45–109.

65. *Gesetz zur Änderung des Grundgesetzes (Artikel 16 und 18)* of 28
June 1993. *BGBl* I, p. 1002. Rainer Münz, 'Ethnos or Demos?'
Migration and Citizenship in Germany', in D. Levy and Y. Weiss
(eds), *Challenging Ethnic Citizenship: German and Israeli Perspectives on Immigration* (Berghahn Books, 2002), p. 30.

66. *VDB*, Stenographische Berichte (26 April 1990), p. 16281A,
16284C; 16281B.

67. *VDB*, Stenographische Berichte (7 May 1999), p. 3417D.

68. *VDB*, Stenographische Berichte (10 November 1998), pp. 61–2.

69. *Der Tagesspiegel*, 2 July 1997, p. 2.

70. Karl-Heinz Meier-Braun, *'Gastarbeiter' oder Einwanderer? Anmer-
kungen zur Ausländerpolitik in der Bundesrepublik Deutschland*
(Ullstein, 1980), pp. 24, 36.

71. *VDB*, Stenographische Berichte (26 April 1990), p. 16281B.

72. Ibid. (10 November 1998), p. 61A.

73. Thränhardt, 'Integration und Partizipation von Einwanderungs-
gruppen', p. 245.

74. *Frankfurter Allgemeine Zeitung*, 5 February 1999, p. 2.

75. *VDB*, Stenographische Berichte (7 May 1999), pp. 3449B, C.

76. Meier-Braun, *Deutschland, Einwanderungsland* (Suhrkamp, 2002),
p. 94; Yasemin Nuhoğlu Soysal, *Limits of Citizenship: Migrants and
Postnational Membership in Europe* (University of Chicago Press,
1994), pp. 24–6.

77. *VDB*, Stenographische Berichte (7 May 1999), pp. 3418–19A.

78. Ibid. (7 May 1999), p. 3449D.

Conclusions

The changes in German citizenship and naturalization policies over the past two centuries can be characterized in various ways. The transfer of governmental power from local authorities to central administrations in the nineteenth century, the creation of the modern state, had a range of consequences. The substance of citizenship criteria was to a significant degree a function of the locus of authority over naturalization decisions. In the early nineteenth century, laws and customs regarding admission to citizenship operated to protect local poor chests, and also, to ensure that newcomers would 'fit in' in numerous ways. Communities asked whether the potential citizen – or other potential permanent resident, since there were various kinds of permanent-resident status – would be able to support himself and his family, whether his morals were good, whether he would take too much business away from established trades, who the petitioner's local sponsors were, and what religion he practiced. The needs of the moment, generally economic, played a more important role in making membership decisions than general ideas. Local communities had no need for a fixed and relatively inflexible system of naturalization criteria, and the different levels of membership in fact ensured that a range of standards would be imposed on potential residents.

In the course of the nineteenth century, communities and estate owners in most (but not all) of Germany ceded control over who was entitled to settle in their territories to the central administrations of the different German states. Central administrations usually demanded uniformity and consistency in the formulation and application of rules, and they focused on the needs and goals of the state as a whole, which were often rather different from local needs and goals. Until the 1870s German states – and especially Prussia – generally made economic criteria the most important basis for granting or denying citizenship. Political reliability and moral qualities became more of a focus during or following political crises, which admittedly occurred with some frequency.

The changing political structures of German states also played a decisive role in shaping citizenship policies. The Prussian Untertanengesetz reflected the authoritarian character of the pre-1848 Prussian state in the extraordinary discretion it granted the central administration. The central administration intended to use its control over access to citizenship to establish legal clarity regarding who was a Prussian citizen, to exclude undesirable immigrants, and to force local communities to accept foreigners whose presence would benefit the state economically. It was characteristic of the era that, although most of the conflicts between local authorities and the state administration concerned economic issues, debates were carried on largely in terms of the morality and justice of alternative policies.

The German state founded in 1871 was authoritarian but not Hegelian. Bismarck and his successors used the powers granted in the citizenship law as a weapon – one of many – to manipulate elections. By controlling access to citizenship, states could control access to the ballot. State administrations also crafted citizenship policies to prevent evasion of conscription, to arouse (and respond to) nationalism, and to promote German interests abroad.

That almost all ethnic Germans were welcomed as citizens after 1918 reflected the experience and outcome of the First World War, and also the fact that Germany had become a republic, the greater influence of popular opinion on government policy. Even before 1914 the restrictions on the naturalization of Social Democrats and the tight-fisted treatment of German emigrants had been unpopular with many Germans. The serious consideration that the Weimar Republic gave to granting women the right to retain their citizenship upon marriage with a foreigner was another result of the greater openness of the political system. Women now had the ballot, and women deputies sat in the Reichstag. That the largely Social Democratic government of Prussia naturalized foreign Jews far more readily than pre-war Prussia also reflected the effects of democratization. The Social Democratic Party's leaders believed that all long-term inhabitants of the state were entitled to a certain minimum of political rights, assuming that they became integrated into the society.

The Nazi regime radically remade German society. It excluded and ultimately murdered a range of racial and political enemies and created colonies and vassal states on a vast scale. Citizenship policy was one of many tools it employed to achieve its aims. While existing laws gave the state the power to prevent the naturalization of unwanted new citizens, this was hardly adequate to the ambition of the Nazi project. By the end of the war the regime had created a complicated web of new citizenship categories that corresponded to the racial hierarchy it sought to impose on Europe and to its more immediate wartime needs.

Not all aspects of German citizenship policies can be attributed to political or economic structures. Hitler played a decisive role in formulating the racially exclusionary policies of the Nazi regime. It was Bismarck who ordered the combative methods Prussia employed against Poles and Social Democrats from the 1870s, methods that were to a significant degree followed by the other German states. As we have seen, the Prussian central administration almost certainly would not have been as harsh in its treatment of Poles in Bismarck's absence. Even as conservative a man as Interior Minister Puttkamer clearly and repeatedly opposed Bismarck's expulsion of foreign Poles and even, perhaps, to a degree, foreign Jews. In this way, as in many others, Bismarck left his personal imprint on the form taken by the German national state.

Among the most striking aspects of German citizenship policy through 1945 was the singling out of Jewish applicants for rejection. The Prussian citizenship law of 1842 made the naturalization of Jews alone subject to state control at the highest level. This policy was dropped in the 1860s and 1870s, but was then restored with a vengeance in the 1880s. The elite from which the state administration was recruited was confronted with the reality of Jewish economic success and power, the product of emancipation. The leaders of state administrations often clearly found this deeply threatening. These anxieties were expressed more openly than usual in one of the Bavarian exchanges with Prussia regarding the naturalization of Jews that took place in the 1920s. The memorandum noted the 'ever more frequent entrance of Easterners into the German academic professions . . . while qualified German nationals are passed over and neglected'. These were positions officials wanted for their children, or perhaps had wanted for themselves.

For a very long period, through the 1940s, German citizenship policies treated women primarily as the dependents of men. The citizenship of husbands determined the citizenship of wives. Children inherited their citizenship from fathers. In a very short period of time, between one and two generations, a refusal to even listen to the advocates of equality for women was replaced by a sense that equal treatment of men and women was self-evident. That women had gained the right to vote and serve in parliaments, and that the post-war West German constitution guaranteed equality of rights, clearly played important roles. This study has only touched lightly on the reasons for this transformation. But clearly it was a revolution. And it suggests that other revolutions in drawing the boundaries of citizenship are perhaps also possible.

The German states' relationships with each other and with foreign powers also played a critical role in determining state membership policies. Denial of a petition for citizenship implied the possibility, sooner or later, of expulsion. But expellees have to have a place to go, and expulsions are often viewed as unfriendly acts by the states that are asked to accept the individuals ejected. Prussia's enactment of a citizenship law in 1842 that gave its central administration the right to determine which foreigners could become Prussian subjects reflected its own position of strength among the German states. The increasing emphasis on ethnicity in the naturalization policies of the Kaiserreich was also, in part, a product of German power. The exploitative system of migrant East European labor developed because Germany's eastern neighbors were weaker and less prosperous than Germany, and because the ethnic groups most affected by the discriminatory immigration and naturalization rules, Poles and Jews, were themselves underprivileged minorities in Russia and, to a lesser degree, in Austria-Hungary. The brutality of Nazi policies reflected the regime's military and political power after 1937. West German citizenship policies were also a product of the country's relationships with its neighbors, its initial position of dependence and its desire to be integrated into the larger European community.

How important were citizenship and naturalization policies, and debates over these policies, for German history? In the first two-thirds of the nineteenth century, citizenship was one of the most important focal points of conflict between German states and local authorities. The locus of power over access to citizenship helped define the nature of German states and the societies they governed, whether they were in fact single societies or simply unions of numerous independent societies. By 1848 citizenship had become a key issue for those who wanted to create a German national state. In the period before the First World War citizenship policies kept hundreds of thousands of East Europeans from becoming German citizens, and therefore helped to prevent the creation of an ethnically more diverse society. They promoted, in a modest way, the maintenance of the political status quo, for the new citizens would most likely have voted for opposition parties. From the 1970s citizenship policies have been a focal point of political conflict in the Federal Republic of Germany.

German citizenship and naturalization policies are of interest in part because of the light they cast on the larger processes of change and continuity within German society. The period under study was one of cataclysmic change, in all dimensions: political, economic, social and cultural. The relative stability of the legal regime that governed citizenship is misleading. Laws remained the same only because the latitude they gave state administrations in interpreting them permitted radical changes in the content of policy.

The multiple implications and associations of citizenship and naturalization policies, their centrality to the polity, suggest the significance of the recent changes in German law and policy on this subject. When it granted aliens and their children the right to become German citizens, in a series of laws adopted between 1990 and 1999, the Federal Republic of Germany gave up one of the instruments it and predecessor regimes had employed to mold society, an instrument used for much of this century to promote the ethnic homogeneity of the nation. This change establishes the principle that all long-term residents of the state are entitled to the full range of social, economic and political rights enjoyed by citizens, assuming that they meet a series of conditions that are within the power of most foreigners to satisfy. In part the change in the citizenship law is a response to a reality that many, perhaps most, Germans regret, the presence of a large number of foreigners who have settled more or less permanently in Germany. But the changes also suggest that the Federal Republic takes the position, far more decisively than earlier German states, that it is possible for individuals to be loyal to it without being ethnically German. German identification with republican institutions, and hopes for integration within the European Union, are among the most important bases for the liberalization of the citizenship law, and also provide grounds for hope that foreigners who are not ethnically German may be able to identify with the German state.

While the domestic critics of Germany's new citizenship law, of which there are many, claim that such changes can only legitimately be the result of a national consensus, we have seen that such a consensus rarely, if ever, existed on this subject in the period covered by this study. Just as the boundaries of the German nation and the form of the German state were the subject of intense and irreconcilable differences, so also citizenship and naturalization policies were continuously disputed and repeatedly changed. In these senses recent debates follow a long tradition.

–269–

Select Bibliography

Archival Sources

Archiwum Panstwowe we Wrocławiu, Wrocław (Breslau) (APW)
Police Presidium of Breslau, Nr. 145; 146; 341.
Nowyrudci, Nr. 91.

Badisches General-Landesarchiv, Karlsruhe (BGL)
Abt. 233, Nr. 11143, 3255.
Abt. 236, Nr. 10644.

Bayerisches Hauptstaatsarchiv, Munich (BHM)
Ministry of Foreign Affairs, Nr. 92681.
Ministry of the Interior, Nr. 46204; 71641.
Berlin Embassy, Nr. 1133; 1559.

Bundesarchiv Berlin-Lichterfelde (BA)
BA R 1501 (Reich Office of the Interior), Nr. 108005; 108009; 108010;
    108011; 108012; 108013; 108249; 108250.
BA R 01.01 (Reichstag), Film 30841, File Nr. 670.

Bundesarchiv Koblenz
Nachlaß Camilla Jellinek

Geheimes Staatsarchiv Preußischer Kulturbesitz, Berlin-Dahlem
    (GStA PK).
HA I, Rep. 76IV, Sekt. 1, Abt. XVI, Generalia Nr. 10, Vol. 1.
HA I, Rep. 77, Tit. 226b, Nr. 63, Bd. 1.
HA I, Rep. 77, Tit. 227, Nr. 4, Bd. 1–22.
HA I, Rep. 77, Tit. 227, Nr. 4, Beiheft 1–24.
HA I, Rep. 77, Tit. 227, Nr. 44, Bd. 1, 1–3.
HA I, Rep. 77, Tit. 227, Nr. 53, Beiheft 2.
HA I, Rep. 77, Tit. 311, Nr. 34, Bd. 1–7.
HA I, Rep. 77, Tit. 1176, Nr. 2a, Bd. 4; Bd. 5; adh 1.

Bibliography

HA I, Rep. 77, Tit. 1176, Nr. 68, Beiakt 3.

HA I, Rep. 80 Staatsrat (printed documents), Nr. 124; 221; 266; 286, 286a–d.

HA I, Rep. 80 I, gen, Nr. 4a, Bd. 26, Debates of the Staatsrat.

HA I, Rep. 89, Nr. 15694; 15695; 15713; 16786; 16788.

HA I, Rep. 90, Nr. 2253; 2254.

HA I, Rep. 90a, Abt. B, Tit. III/26, Nr. 6, Bd. 93; Bd. 97.

HA I, Rep. 120, A.V.1, Bd. 1.

HA XIV, Rep. 205, Nr. 2; 16.

HA XVI, Rep. 30, Abt. I, Nr. 1120; 1048; 1060.

Nordrhein-Westfälisches Hauptstaatsarchiv, Düsseldorf (NWH), Regierung Düsseldorf (RD), Nr. 558; 582; 9157; 11979.

Stadtarchiv Munich, RA 48062–48111.

Official Publications and Journals

Allgemeine Deutsche Biographie (Berlin: Duncker & Humblot).

Allgemeines Landrecht für die Preussischen Staaten von 1794, ed. Hans Hattenhauer (Neuwied: Luchterhand Verlag, 1996).

Bundesgesetzblatt.

Corpus Constitutionum Marchicarum, oder Königl. Preußis. und Churfürstl. Brandenburgsche in der Chur- und Marck Brandenburg, auch incorporirten Landen publicirte und ergangene Ordnungen, Edicta, Mandata, Rescripta, u. von Zeiten Friedrichs I Churfürstens zu Brandenburg, u. bis ietzo (Berlin, 1736).

Gesetzsammlung für die Königlichen Preußischen Staaten.

Handbuch über den Königlich-Preussischen Hof und Staat (Berlin: Decker).

Ministerial-Blatt für die gesammte innere Verwaltung in den Königlich Preußischen Staaten.

Mittheilungen des statistischen Bureaus in Berlin.

Preussische Jahrbücher.

Protokolle der deutschen Bundesversammlung.

Reichsgesetzblatt.

Statistik des Deutschen Reichs.

Statistisches Handbuch von Deutschland 1928–1944, published by the Länderrat des Amerikanischen Besatzungsgebiets (Munich: Franz Ehrenwirth, 1949).

Statistisches Jahrbuch für das Deutsche Reich.

Bibliography

Statistisches Jahrbuch für das Königreich Bayern.

Statistisches Jahrbuch für die Bundesrepublik Deutschland.

Stenographischer Bericht über die Verhandlungen der deutschen constituirenden Nationalversammlung zu Frankfurt am Main, ed. Franz Wigard (9 Vols; Frankfurt/Main, 1848–1849).

Stenographische Berichte über die Verhandlungen des Preussischen Hauses der Abgeordneten.

Stenographische Berichte über die Verhandlungen des Preussischen Herrenhauses.

Stenographische Berichte über die Verhandlungen des Reichstags des Norddeutschen Bundes.

Stenographische Berichte über die Verhandlungen des Reichstags.

Verhandlungen des Deutschen Bundestages.

Vierteljahrshefte zur Statistik des Deutschen Reichs.

Vollständige Sammlung der Großherzoglich Badischen Regierungsblätter von deren Entstehung 1803 bis Ende 1841 (Mannheim: Verlag von J. Bensheimer, 1844).

Zeitschrift des Königlich Preussischen Statistischen Bureaus.

Zeitschrift des Königlich Preussischen Statistischen Landesamts.

Secondary Literature

Abrams, L., 'Concubinage, Cohabitation and the Law: Class and Gender Relations in Nineteenth Century Germany', *Gender & History* 5 (1993), pp. 81–100.

Adenauer, K., *Erinnerungen 1955–1959*, Stuttgart: Deutsche Verlags-Anstalt, 1967.

Anderson, M., *Practicing Democracy: Elections and Political Culture in Imperial Germany*, Princeton: Princeton University Press, 2000.

Bade, K., 'Arbeiterstatistik zur Ausländerkontrolle: die "Nachweisungen" der preußischen Landräte über den Zugang, Abgang und Bestand der ausländischen Arbeiter im preußischen Staat 1906–1914', *Archiv für Sozialgeschichte* 24 (1984), pp. 163–284.

——, (ed.) *Deutsche im Ausland – Fremde in Deutschland: Migration in Geschichte und Gegenwart*, Munich: Beck, 1992.

——, *Europa in Bewegung: Migration vom späten 18. Jahrhundert bis zur Gegenwart*, Munich: Beck, 2000.

——, '"Preußengänger" und "Abwehrpolitik": Ausländerbeschäftigung, Ausländerpolitik und Ausländerkontrolle auf dem Arbeitsmarkt in Preußen vor dem Ersten Weltkrieg', *Archiv für Sozialgeschichte* 24 (1984), pp. 91–162.

Barclay, D., *Frederick William IV and the Prussian Monarchy, 1840–1861*, Oxford: Oxford University Press, 1995.

Barfuß, K., *'Gastarbeiter' in Nordwestdeutschland 1884–1918*, Bremen: Selbstverlag des Staatsarchivs der freien Hansestadt Bremen, 1986.

Barkai, A., 'Jewish Life under Persecution', in *German-Jewish History in Modern Times*, vol. 4, *Renewal and Destruction 1918–1945*, New York: Columbia University Press, 1998.

Barkin, K., *The Controversy Over German Industrialization, 1890–1902*, Chicago: University of Chicago Press, 1970.

Beck, H., *The Origins of the Authoritarian Welfare State in Prussia: Conservatives, Bureaucracy, and the Social Question, 1815–1870*, Ann Arbor: University of Michigan Press, 1995.

Belzyt, L., 'Die Zahl der Sorben in der amtlichen Sprachenstatistik vor dem Ersten Weltkrieg', in H. Hahn and P. Kunze (eds), *Nationale Minderheiten und staatliche Minderheitenpolitik in Deutschland im 19. Jahrhundert*, Berlin: Akademie, 1999.

Berdahl, R., *The Politics of the Prussian Nobility: The Development of a Conservative Ideology 1770–1848*, Princeton: Princeton University Press, 1988.

Bering, D., *The Stigma of Names: Antisemitism in German Daily Life, 1812–1933*, trans. N. Plaice, Ann Arbor: University of Michigan Press, 1992.

Best, H. and Weege, W., *Biographisches Handbuch der Abgeordneten der Frankfurter Nationalversammlung 1848/49*, Düsseldorf, Droste Verlag, 1996.

Blanke, R., 'Bismarck and the Prussian Polish Policies of 1886', *Journal of Modern History* 45 (1973), pp. 211–39.

——, *Prussian Poland in the German Empire (1871–1900)*, New York: Columbia University Press, 1981.

——, *Polish-speaking Germans? Language and National Identity among the Masurians since 1871*, Cologne: Böhlau, 2001.

Blasius, D., *Ehescheidung in Deutschland, 1794–1945*, Göttingen: Vandenhoeck & Ruprecht, 1987.

Bödiker, T., 'Die Auswanderung und die Einwanderung des preussischen Staates', *Zeitschrift des Königlich Preussischen Statistischen Bureaus* 13 (1873).

Brandes, D., 'Die Deutschen in Rußland und der Sowjetunion', in K. Bade (ed.), *Deutsche im Ausland – Fremde in Deutschland: Migration in Geschichte und Gegenwart*, Munich: Beck, 1992.

Broszat, M., *Nationalsozialistische Polenpolitik 1939–1945* Stuttgart: Deutsche Verlags-Anstalt, 1961.

——, *Zweihundert Jahre deutsche Polenpolitik*, Munich: Ehrenwirth, 1963.

——, 'Volksdeutsche und Deutschstämmige im GG 1941–1944', in *Gutachten des Instituts für Zeitgeschichte*, vol. 2, Stuttgart: Deutsche Verlags-Anstalt, 1966, pp. 254–261.

Brubaker, R., *Citizenship and Nationhood in France and Germany*, Cambridge MA: Harvard University Press, 1992.

——, 'Homeland nationalism in Weimar Germany and "Weimar Russia"', in R. Brubaker, *Nationalism Reframed: Nationhood and the National Question in the New Europe*, Cambridge: Cambridge University Press, 1996, pp. 107–47.

Burger, H., 'Paßwesen und Staatsbürgerschaft', in W. Heindl and E. Saurer (eds), *Grenze und Staat Paßwesen, Staatsbürgerschaft, Heimatrecht und Fremdengesetzgebung in der österreichischen Monarchie 1750–1867*, Vienna: Böhlau Verlag, 2000, pp. 3–172.

Busch, O., *Military System and Social Life in Old Regime Prussia, 1713–1807: The Beginnings of the Social Militarization of Prusso-German Society*, trans. John Gagliardo, Atlantic Highlands NJ: Humanities Press, 1997.

Carsten, F., *The Origins of Prussia*, Oxford: Clarendon, 1959.

Chickering, R., '"Casting Their Gaze More Broadly": Women's Patriotic Activism in Imperial Germany', *Past and Present* 118 (February 1988), pp. 156–85.

Cremer, H., 'Internal Controls and Actual Removals of Deportable Aliens: The Current Legal Situation in the Federal Republic of Germany', in K. Hailbronner, D. Martin, and H. Motomura (eds), *Immigration Controls: The Search for Workable Policies in Germany and the United States*, Providence: Berghahn, 1998, pp. 45–109.

Dean, M., 'The Development and Implementation of Nazi Denaturalization and Confiscation Policy up to the Eleventh Decree to the Reich Citizenship Law', *Holocaust and Genocide Studies* 16 (Fall 2002).

Documenta Occupationis Teutonicae, vols 4, 5, Poznan: Institut Zachodni.

Doege, M., *Armut in Preußen und Bayern (1770–1840)*, Munich: Kommissionsverlag UNI-Druck, 1991.

Dronke, E., *Polizei-Geschichten*, 1846; reprint, Göttingen: Vandenhoeck & Ruprecht, 1968.

Erdem, E. and Mattes, M., 'Gendered Policies – Gendered Patterns: Female Labour Migration from Turkey to Germany from the 1960s to the 1990s', in R. Ohliger, K. Schönwälder and T. Triadafilopoulos (eds), *European Encounters: Migrants, migration and European societies since 1945*, Aldershot: Ashgate, 2003, pp. 167–85.

Bibliography

Eryilmaz, A. and Jamin, M. (eds), *Fremde Heimat: Eine Geschichte der Auswanderung aus der Turkei*, Essen: Klartext, 1998.

Essner, C., *Die 'Nürnberger Gesetze', oder, Die Verwaltung des Rassenwahns 1933–1945*, Paderborn: Ferdinand Schöningh, 2002.

Eyck, F., *The Frankfurt Parliament*, London: St Martin's Press, 1968.

Fahrmeir, A., *Citizens and Aliens: Foreigners and the Law in Britain and the German States 1789–1870*, New York: Berghahn, 2000.

Feldman, D., *Englishmen and Jews: Social Relations and Political Culture 1840–1914*, New Haven: Yale University Press, 1994.

——, 'Was the Nineteenth Century a Golden Age for Immigrants? The Changing Articulation of National, Local and Voluntary Controls', in A. Fahrmeir, O. Faron, P. Weil (eds), *Migration Control in the North Atlantic World: The Evolution of State Practices in Europe and the United States from the French Revolution to the Inter-War Period*, New York: Berghahn, 2003.

Fichte, J., 'Beitrag zur Berichtigung der Urtheile des Publicums über die französische Revolution', in *Sämmtliche Werke*, vol. 6, Berlin, 1845.

——, 'Reden an die deutsche Nation', in *Sämmtliche Werke*, J.H. Fichte (pub.), vol. 7, Berlin, 1846.

Fleischhauer, I., *Das Dritte Reich und die Deutschen in der Sowjetunion*, Stuttgart: Deutsche Verlags-Anstalt, 1983.

Freytag, G., *Soll und Haben*, Eschborn: Verlag Dietmar Klotz, 1992.

Friedrich, K., 'The development of the Prussian town, 1720–1815', in P. Dwyer (ed.), *The Rise of Prussia 1700–1830*, Harlow: Longman, 2000, pp. 129–50.

Geiss, I., *Die Polnische Grenzstreifen 1914–1918: ein Beitrag zur deutschen Kriegszielpolitik im Ersten Weltkrieg*, Lübeck: Matthiesen, 1960.

Gillis, J., *The Prussian Bureaucracy in Crisis, 1840–1860: Origins of an Administrative Elite*, Stanford: Stanford University Press, 1971.

Gilman, S., *The Jew's Body*, New York: Routledge, 1991.

Gollwitzer, H., *Die Standesherren: Die politische und gesellschaftliche Stellung der Mediatisierten 1815–1918*, Stuttgart: Friedrich Vorwerk Verlag, 1957.

Gosewinkel, D., 'Die Staatsangehörigkeit als Institution des Nationalstaats: zur Entstehung des Reichs- und Staatsangehörigkeitsgesetzes von 1913', in R. Grawert, B. Schlink, R. Wahl, J. Wieland (eds), *Offene Staatlichkeit: Festschrift für Ernst-Wolfgang Böckenförde zum 65. Geburtstag*, Berlin: Duncker & Humblot, 1995, pp. 359–78.

——, 'Staatsbürgerschaft und Staatsangehörigkeit', *Geschichte und Gesellschaft* 21 (1995), pp. 533–56.

———, '"Unerwünschte Elemente" – Einwanderung und Einbürgerung der Juden in Deutschland 1848–1933', *Tel Aviver Jahrbuch für deutsche Geschichte* 27 (1998), pp. 71–106.

———, *Einbürgern und Ausschließen: Die Nationalisierung der Staatsangehörigkeit vom Deutschen Bund bis zur Bundesrepublik Deutschland*, Göttingen: Vandenhoeck & Ruprecht, 2001.

Grawert, R., *Staat und Staatsangehörigkeit: Verfassungsgeschichtliche Untersuchung zur Entstehung der Staatsangehörigkeit*, Berlin: Duncker & Humblot, 1973.

Groeben, H., *Aufbaujahre der Europäischen Gemeinschaft: Das Ringen um den Gemeinsamen Markt und die Politische Union (1958–1966)*, Baden-Baden: Nomos, 1982.

de Groot, G., *Staatsangehörigkeitsrecht im Wandel: Eine rechtsvergleichende Studie über Erwerbs- und Verlustgründe der Staatsangehörigkeit*, Cologne: Carl Heymanns Verlag, 1989.

Grosse, P., *Kolonialismus, Eugenik und bürgerliche Gesellschaft in Deutschland 1850–1918*, Frankfurt/Main: Campus Verlag, 2000.

Gröwer, K., '"Wilde Ehen" in den hansestädtischen Unterschichten 1814–1871', *Archiv für Sozialgeschichte* 38 (1998), pp. 1–22.

Haake, P., *Johann Peter Friedrich Ancillon und Kronprinz Friedrich Wilhelm IV von Preußen*, Munich: Oldenbourg Verlag, 1920.

Hagedorn, H., 'Administrative Systems and Dual Nationality: The Information Gap', in David Martin and Kay Hailbronner (eds), *Rights and Duties of Dual Nationals: Evolution and Prospects,* The Hague: Kluwer Law International, 2003, pp. 183–200.

Hagen, W., *Germans, Poles, and Jews: The Nationality Conflict in the Prussian East, 1772–1914*, Chicago: University of Chicago Press, 1980.

Hailbronner, K., 'Der aufenthaltsrechtliche Status der verschiedenen Gruppen von Einwanderern in der Bundesrepublik Deutschland', in Albrecht Weber, *Einwanderungsland Bundesrepublik Deutschland in der Europäischen Union: Gestaltungsauftrag und Regelungsmöglichkeiten*, Osnäbruck: Universitätsverlag Rasch, 1997.

———, *Immigration and Asylum Law and Policy of the European Union*, The Hague: Kluwer Law International, 2000.

Hailbronner, K. and Renner, G., *Staatsangehörigkeitsrecht*, Munich: Beck, 1991.

Hailbronner, K., Renner, G., and Kreuzer, C., *Staatsangehörigkeitsrecht*, 3rd edn, Munich: Beck, 2001.

Hamerow, T., *The Social Foundations of German Unification, 1858–1871*, Princeton: Princeton University Press, 1969.

Bibliography

Harris, J., *The People Speak! Anti-Semitism and Emancipation in 19th Century Bavaria*, Ann Arbor: University of Michigan Press, 1994.

Harris, P., 'Jewish Immmigration to the New Germany: The Policy Making Process Leading to the Adoption of the 1991 Quota Refugee Law', in D. Thränhardt (ed.), *Einwanderung und Einbürgerung in Deutschland*, Münster: Lit Verlag, 1998, pp. 105–47.

——, 'Russische Juden und Aussiedler: Integrationspolitik und lokale Verantwortung', in K. Bade and J. Oltmer (eds), *Aussiedler: deutsche Einwanderer aus Osteuropa*, Osnäbrück: Universitätsverlag Rasch, 1999.

Harten, H., *De-Kulturation und Germanisierung: Die nationalsozialistische Rassen- und Erziehungspolitik in Polen 1939–1945*, Frankfurt: Campus, 1996.

Hauser, O., 'Polen und Dänen im Deutschen Reich', in T. Schieder and E. Deuerlein (eds), *Reichsgründung 1870/71: Tatsachen, Kontroversen, Interpretationen*, Stuttgart: Seewald, 1970.

Heffter, H., *Die Deutsche Selbstverwaltung im 19. Jahrhundert: Geschichte der Ideen und Institutionen*, 2nd edn, Stuttgart: K.F. Koehler, 1969.

Hegel, G.W.F., *Grundlinien der Philosophie des Rechts oder Naturrecht und Staatswissenschaft im Grundrisse*, in *Sämtliche Werke*, vol. 7, Stuttgart: Frommanns, 1952.

Hehemann, R., *Die 'Bekämpfung des Zigeunerwesens' im Wilhelminischen Deutschland und in der Weimarer Republik, 1871–1933*, Frankfurt/Main: Haag und Herchen, 1987.

Heindl, W., and Saurer, E. (eds), *Grenze und Staat Paßwesen, Staatsbürgerschaft, Heimatrecht und Fremdengesetzgebung in der österreichischen Monarchie 1750–1867*, Vienna: Böhlau Verlag, 2000.

Herbert, U., *A History of Foreign Labor in Germany, 1880–1980*, trans. by William Templer, Ann Arbor: University of Michigan Press, 1990.

——, *Geschichte der Ausländerpolitik in Deutschland: Saisonarbeiter, Zwangsarbeiter, Gastarbeiter, Flüchtlinge*, Munich: Beck, 2001.

Higham, J., *Send These to Me: Immigrants in Urban America*, Baltimore: Johns Hopkins University Press, 1993.

von Hippel, W., 'Bevölkerungsentwicklung und Wirtschaftsstruktur im Königreich Württemberg 1815/65: Überlegungen zum Pauperismusproblem in Südwestdeutschland', in U. Engelhardt, V. Sellin, and H. Stuke (eds), *Soziale Bewegung und politische Verfassung: Beiträge zur Geschichte der modernen Welt*, Stuttgart: Ernst Klett, 1976, pp. 270–371.

Hochstadt, S., 'Migration in Preindustrial Germany', *Central European History* 16 (1983), pp. 195–224.

——, *Mobility and Modernity: Migration in Germany, 1820–1989*, Ann Arbor: University of Michigan Press, 1999.

Hoffmann, J., *Uebersicht der Bodenfläche und Bevölkerung des Preussischen Staats*, Berlin, 1817.

——, *Die Bevölkerung des Preussischen Staats nach dem Ergebnisse der zu Ende des Jahres 1837 amtlich aufgenommenen Nachrichten*, Berlin, 1839.

——, 'Über die Besorgnisse, welche die Zunahme der Bevölkerung erregt', in J. Hoffmann, *Sammlung kleiner Schriften staatswirtschaftlichen Inhalts*, Berlin, 1843.

Huber, E., *Deutsche Verfassungsgeschichte seit 1789*, vol. 4, *Struktur und Krisen des Kaiserreichs*, Stuttgart: Kohlhammer, 1969.

—— (ed.), *Dokumente zur Deutschen Verfassungsgeschichte*, 2 vols, Stuttgart: W. Kohlhammer Verlag, 1961.

Hull, I., *Sexuality, State, and Civil Society in Germany, 1700–1815*, Ithaca: Cornell University Press, 1996.

Jackson, J., *Migration and Urbanization in the Ruhr Valley, 1821–1914*, Atlantic Highlands NJ: Humanities Press, 1997.

Joppke, C., *Immigration and the Nation-State: The United States, Germany, and Great Britain*, Oxford: Oxford University Press, 1999.

——, 'The Evolution of Alien Rights in the United States, Germany, and the European Union', in T. Aleinikoff and D. Klusmeyer (eds), *Citizenship Today: Global Perspectives and Practices*, Washington: Carnegie Endowment for International Peace, 2001.

Just, R., 'Gescheitertes Miteinander: Einbürgerungspolitik und Einbürgerungspraxis in Deutschland von 1871–1933', in AWR-Bulletin, *Vierteljahresschrift für Flüchtlingsfragen* 36 (1998).

Kaltwasser, I., *Häusliches Gesinde in der Freien Stadt Frankfurt am Main: Rechtsstellung, soziale Lage und Aspekte des sozialen Wandels 1815–1866*, Frankfurt am Main: Waldemer Kramer, 1989.

Kaplan, M., *The Making of the Jewish Middle Class: Women, Family, and Identity in Imperial Germany*, New York: Oxford, 1991.

Katz, J., *Out of the Ghetto: The Social Background of Jewish Emancipation, 1770–1870*, Cambridge MA: Harvard University Press, 1973.

Koselleck, R., *Preußen zwischen Reform und Revolution: Allgemeines Landrecht, Verwaltung und soziale Bewegung von 1791 bis 1848*, 3rd edn, Stuttgart: Klett-Cotta, 1981.

Kraus, A., *Die Unterschichten Hamburgs in der ersten Hälfte des 19. Jahrhunderts: Entstehung, Struktur und Lebensverhältnisse. Eine*

Bibliography

Nipperdey, T., *Deutsche Geschichte 1800–1866, Bürgerwelt und starker Staat*, 6th edn, Munich: Beck, 1993.

——, *Deutsche Geschichte 1866–1918*, vol. 2, *Machtstaat vor der Demokratie*, 2nd edn, Munich: Beck, 1993.

Noiriel, G., *The French Melting Pot: Immigration, Citizenship, and National Identity*, trans. G. de Laforcade, Minneapolis: University of Minnesota Press, 1996.

Oswald, A., Schönwälder, K., and Sonnenberger, B., '*Einwanderungsland Deutschland*: A New Look at its Post-War History', in R. Ohliger, K. Schönwälder and T. Triadafilopoulos (eds), *European Encounters: Migrants, Migration and European Societies since 1945*, Aldershot: Ashgate, 2003, pp. 19–37.

Panayi, P., *Ethnic Minorities in Nineteenth and Twentieth Century Germany: Jews, Gypsies, Poles, Turks and Others*, Harlow: Longman, 2000.

Pech, S., *The Czech Revolution of 1848*, Chapel Hill: University of North Carolina Press, 1969.

Pulzer, P., *The Rise of Political Anti-Semitism in Germany and Austria*, rev. edn, Cambridge MA: Harvard University Press, 1988.

——, *Jews and the German State: The Political History of a Minority, 1848–1933*, Oxford: Basil Blackwell, 1992.

van Rahden, T., 'Die Grenze vor Ort – Einbürgerung und Ausweisung ausländischer Juden in Breslau 1860–1918', in *Tel Aviver Jahrbuch für deutsche Geschichte* 27 (1998), pp. 47–69.

——, *Juden und andere Breslauer: Die Beziehungen zwischen Juden, Protestanten und Katholiken in einer deutschen Großstadt von 1860 bis 1925*, Göttingen: Vandenhoeck & Ruprecht, 2000.

Rauchberg, H., 'Zur Kritik des Österreichischen Heimatrechtes', *Zeitschrift für Volkswirtschaft, Socialpolitik und Verwaltung* 2 (1893), pp. 59–99.

Rehm, H., 'Der Erwerb von Staats- und Gemeinde-Angehörigkeit in geschichtlicher Entwicklung nach römischem und deutschem Staatsrecht', *Annalen des Deutschen Reichs für Gesetzgebung, Verwaltung und Statistik* XXV (1892), pp. 137–282.

Rumpf, C., 'Citizenship and Multiple Citizenship in Turkish Law', in D. Martin and K. Hailbronner (eds), *Rights and Duties of Dual Nationals: Evolution and Prospects*, The Hague: Kluwer Law International, 2003, pp. 361–73.

Rürup, R., 'Die Emanzipation der Juden in Baden', in A. Schäfer (ed.), *Oberrheinische Studien*, vol. 2, Bretten: Druckerei Esser, 1973.

Sahlins, P., *Unnaturally French: Foreign Citizens in the Old Regime and After*, Ithaca NY: Cornell University Press, 2004.

Schinkel, H., 'Armenpflege und Freizügigkeit in der preussischen Gesetzgebung vom Jahre 1842', *Vierteljahrschrift für Sozial- und Wirtschaftsgeschichte* 50 (1964), pp. 459–79.

Schmitt, C., *Der Begriff des Politischen*, Berlin: Duncker & Humblot, 1996; orig. edn 1932.

Schneider, H., *Der Preussische Staatsrat: Ein Beitrag zur Verfassungs- und Rechtsgeschichte Preussens*, Munich: Beck Verlag, 1952.

Schönwälder, K., *Einwanderung und ethnische Pluralität: Politische Entscheidungen und öffentliche Debatten in Grossbritannien und der Bundesrepublik von den 1950er bis zu den 1970er Jahren*, Essen: Klartext, 2001.

Schubert, E., *Arme Leute: Bettler und Gauner im Franken des 18. Jahrhunderts*, Neustadt a.d. Aisch: Commissionsverlag Degener & Co., 1983.

Schwartz, M., *MdR Biographisches Handbuch der Reichstage*, Hanover, Verlag für Literatur und Zeitgeschehen, 1965.

Schwarz, S., *Die Juden in Bayern im Wandel der Zeiten*, Munich: Günter Olzog, 1963.

Shorter, E., *Social Change and Social Policy in Bavaria, 1800–1860*, Dissertation: Harvard University, 1967.

Soysal, Y., *Limits of Citizenship: Migrants and Postnational Membership in Europe*, Chicago: University of Chicago Press, 1994.

Spencer, E., *Police and the Social Order in German Cities: The Düsseldorf District, 1848–1914*, De Kalb: Northern Illinois University Press, 1992.

Spenkuch, H. (ed.), *Die Protokolle des Preussischen Staatsministeriums 1817–1934/38*, vol. 7, *8. Januar 1879 bis 19. Marz 1890*, Hildesheim: Olms-Weidmann, 1999.

Steinert, J., *Migration und Politik: Westdeutschland-Europa-Übersee 1945–1961*, Osnabrück: secolo, 1995.

Steinmetz, G. *Regulating the Social: The Welfare State and Local Politics in Imperial Germany*, Princeton: Princeton University Press, 1993.

Stern, F., *The Politics of Cultural Despair: A Study in the Rise of the Germanic Ideology*, Berkeley: University of California Press, 1974.

——, *Gold and Iron: Bismarck, Bleichröder, and the Building of the German Empire*, New York: Alfred A. Knopf, 1977.

Stolleis, M., 'Untertan-Bürger-Staatsbürger: Bemerkungen zur juristischen Terminologie im späten 18. Jahrhundert', in R. Vierhaus (ed.), *Bürger und Bürgerlichkeit im Zeitalter der Aufklärung*, Heidelberg: Schneider, 1981, pp. 65–99.

Stübig, H., 'Die Wehrverfassung Preußens in der Reformzeit: Wehrpflicht im Spannungsfeld von Restauration und Revolution 1815–1860', in

Bibliography

R. Foerster (ed.), *Die Wehrpflicht: Entstehung, Erscheinungsformen und politisch-militärische Wirkung*, Munich: Oldenbourg, 1994.

Thränhardt, D., '"Ausländer" als Objekte deutscher Interessen und Ideologien', in H. Griese (ed.), *Der gläserne Fremde: Bilanz und Kritik der Gastarbeiterforschung und Ausländerpädagogik*, Leverkusen: Leske + Budrich, 1984, pp. 115–32.

——, 'Die Reform der Einbürgerung in Deutschland', in Forschungsinstitut der Friedrich-Ebert-Stiftung, *Einwanderungskonzeption für die Bundesrepublik Deutschland*, Bonn (1995), pp. 63–116.

——, (ed.), *Einwanderung und Einbürgerung in Deutschland*, Münster: Lit Verlag, 1998.

——, 'Integration und Partizipation von Einwanderergruppen im lokalen Kontext', in K. Bade and J. Oltmer (eds), *Aussiedler: deutsche Einwanderer aus Osteuropa*, Osnabrück: Universitätsverlag Rasch, 1999, pp. 229–46.

Toury, J., *Die politischen Orientierungen der Juden in Deutschland: Von Jena bis Weimar*, Tübingen: Mohr, 1966.

Treue, W., 'Adam Smith in Deutschland. Zum Problem des "Politischen Professors" zwischen 1776 und 1810', in W. Conze (ed.), *Deutschland und Europa, Historische Studie zur Völker- und Staatenordnung des Abendlandes, Festschrift für Hans Rothfels*, Düsseldorf: Droste-Verlag, 1951, pp. 101–33.

Trevisiol, O., *Scheidung vom Vaterland: Die Einbürgerung von italienischen Migranten im Deutschen Kaiserreich am Beispiel von Konstanz*, magi-e-forum historicum, Bd. 3: www.magi-e.historicum.net/reihe/magi-e_band_03.pdf, 01.04.2003 (accessed on 4 August 2003).

Urbanitsch, P., 'Die Deutschen', in *Das Habsburgermonarchie*, vol. 3/1, Vienna: Verlag der österreichischen Akademie der Wissenschaften, 1980.

Ursachen und Folgen: Vom deutschen Zusammenbruch 1918 und 1945 bis zur staatlichen Neuordnung Deutschlands in der Gegenwart, vol. 3, *Der Weg in die Weimarer Republik*, Berlin: Herbert Wendler, no date.

Vagts, A., *Deutschland und die Vereinigten Staaten in der Weltpolitik*, vol. 1, New York: Macmillan, 1935.

Vick, B., *Defining Germany: The 1848 Frankfurt Parliamentarians and National Identity*, Cambridge MA: Harvard University Press, 2002.

Volkov, S., *Die Juden in Deutschland 1780–1918*, Munich: Oldenbourg Verlag, 1994.

Walk, J., *Das Sonderrecht für die Juden im NS-Staat: Eine Sammlung der gesetzlichen Maßnahmen und Richtlinien-Inhalt und Bedeutung*, 2nd edn, Heidelberg: Müller, 1996.

Walker, M., *Germany and the Emigration 1816–1885*, Cambridge MA: Harvard University Press, 1964.

——, *German Home Towns: Community, State, and General Estate 1648–1871*, Ithaca: Cornell University Press, 1971.

Walzer, M., *Spheres of Justice: A Defense of Pluralism and Equality*, New York: Basic Books, 1984.

Weber, Marianne, *Ehefrau und Mutter in der Rechtsentwicklung: Eine Einführung*, Tübingen: J.C.B. Mohr, 1907.

Weber, Max, *Wirtschaft und Gesellschaft: Grundriss der verstehenden Soziologie*, vol. 1, Tübingen: J.C.B. Mohr, 1956.

Wehler, H., 'Von den "Reichsfeinden" zur "Reichskristallnacht": Polenpolitik im Deutschen Kaiserreich 1871–1918', in H. Wehler, *Krisenherde des Kaiserreichs 1871–1918*, Göttingen: Vandenhoeck & Ruprecht, 1970.

——, *Das deutsche Kaiserreich: 1871–1918*, Göttingen: Vandenhoeck & Ruprecht, 1973.

——, *Deutsche Gesellschaftsgeschichte*, 3 vols, Munich: Beck, 1987–95.

Weil, P., *Qu'est-ce qu'un Français? Histoire de la Nationalité Française depuis la Révolution*, Paris: Bernard Grasset, 2002.

Weinacht, P., '"Staatsbürger" Zur Geschichte und Kritik eines Politischen Begriffs', in *Der Staat: Zeitschrift für Staatslehre, Öffentliches Recht und Verfassungsgeschichte* 8 (1969), pp. 41–63.

Wendelin, H., 'Schub und Heimatrecht', in W. Heindl and E. Saurer (eds), *Grenze und Staat Paßwesen, Staatsbürgerschaft, Heimatrecht und Fremdengesetzgebung in der österreichischen Monarchie 1750–1867*, Vienna: Böhlau Verlag, 2000, pp. 173–344.

Wertheimer, J., 'Jewish Lobbyists and the German Citizenship Law of 1914: A Documentary Account', *Studies in Contemporary Jewry* 1 (1984), pp. 140–62.

——, *Unwelcome Strangers: East European Jews in Imperial Germany*, New York: Oxford University Press, 1987.

Wildenthal, L., 'Race, Gender, and Citizenship in the German Colonial Empire', in F. Cooper and A. Stoler (eds), *Tensions of Empire: Colonial Cultures in a Bourgeois World*, Berkeley: University of California Press, 1997.

——, *German Women for Empire, 1884–1945*, Durham NC: Duke University Press, 2001.

Wollstein, G., *Das 'Großdeutschland' der Paulskirche: Nationale Ziele in der bürgerlichen Revolution 1848/49*, Düsseldorf: Droste, 1977.

Zechlin, E. and Bieber, H., *Die deutsche Politik und die Juden im ersten Weltkrieg*, Göttingen: Vandenhoeck & Ruprecht, 1969.

Bibliography

Ziekursch, J., *Das Ergebnis der friderizianischen Städteverwaltung und die Städteordnung Steins*, Jena: Hermann Castenoble, 1908.

——, *Hundert Jahre schlesischer Agrargeschichte: Vom Hubertusburger Frieden bis zum Abschluß der Bauernbefreiung*, 2nd edn, Breslau: Preuss & Jünger, 1927.

Ziemske, B., *Die deutsche Staatsangehörigkeit nach dem Grundgesetz*, Berlin: Duncker & Humblot, 1995.

Zuwanderung gestalten Integration fördern, Bericht der Unabhängigen Kommission 'Zuwanderung', www.bmi.bund.de: 4 July 2001, accessed on 14 July 2003.

Index

Adenauer, Konrad, 241–2
Agrarian League (Bund der Landwirte),
    118
Alexander II (tsar of Russia), 111, 118
Alsace-Lorraine
    citizenship, 77, 125, 189
    demographic statistics, 2
    official fears, 8, 125
    political loyalties, 2, 78, 92
Anabaptists, 28
anti-Semitism, 35n48
    attacks on, 82, 181, 206
    concealment or denial, 141, 180,
        194n56
    euphemisms, 118–19
    fear of Jewish power, 117–21, 147, 186,
        205–8, 217–18
    naturalization policies and, 9, 68–9, 98,
        131n26, 140, 143–4, 146–57, 179–81,
        186–7, 205–9
    Nazism and, 217–22
    rationalizations, 98, 116–17, 127,
        146–9, 186–7, 205
anxiety, regarding
    Catholics, 100, 114–15, 143, 190n4
    crime and foreigners, 25, 41, 43, 46–7,
        100, 146, 205, 246
    disloyalty of foreigners, 3, 8, 114–15,
        122–3, 146–52, 256
    economic competition, 17, 65–9, 206–8,
        236–7, 244
    international vulnerability, 4, 112,
        174–6, 184–7, 241–3
    journeymen and the working class, 58,
        84–90, 143–4
    political power of ethnic minorities,
        115, 119–23, 133n43, 147, 151–2,
        256
    poverty, 17–18, 41, 88
    revolution, 58, 83–90

Social Democratic Party, 114, 141–3,
    155–7, 185
    see also anti-Semitism
Arendt, Walter, 241
assimilation, 77–8, 149–52
Association for Defense against Anti-
    Semitism (Verein zur Abwehr des
    Antisemitismus), 120
asylum, 235–6, 251–2
Aussiedler, 6, 235–6, 252
Austria, 20–22, 33n27, 37, 40, 77, 221
Austria-Hungary, 90, 113–4, 141, 178,
    185, 190n4

Baden, 91, 203
    foreign Jews, 68, 153–4
    freedom of movement, 37–38
    naturalizations, 65–67
Baden-Württemberg, 243–5
Bamburger, Ludwig, 116
Bavaria
    expulsions, 19–22, 100, 107nn72–3,
        163n52, 203
    foreign Jews, 68, 202, 204, 206–9
    freedom of movement, 37–8
    'guest workers', 243–5
    naturalizations, 68, 153, 204, 206–9,
        243–5, 247, 249
Bebel, August, 173
Beck, Anton, 180–1
Beck, Marieluise, 256–7
Becker, Bernhard, 83
Beckstein, Günter, 256
Behrens, Franz, 159
Belgium, 176, 185, 211, 240
Belzer, Emil, 180
Berlin
    expulsions, 44–5, 84
    'guest workers', 243, 247, 249
Belgium, Belgians, 90, 185–6, 240

Index

Bernstein, Eduard, 179, 184
Bernstorff, Johann Heinrich von, 188
Bethmann Hollweg, Theobold von, 177–9, 186–7
Bismarck, Otto von
    authoritarian methods, 91–2, 111–14, 118–23, 171, 267
    expulsion of foreign Jews and Poles, 111–14, 116–23
    Kulturkampf, 100, 114–5
    liberal phase in domestic policies, 77–8, 92–4, 98–9
    Poles, 99–100, 111–12, 115, 120–4
    useful precedents for Nazis, 229
Blasius, Dirk, 84
Bleichröder, Gerson, 116
Blunck, Andreas, 181, 183
Braun, Karl, 22
Brecht, Bertolt, 219
Broszat, Martin, 127–8
Brubaker, Rogers, 6–7, 194n50, 263n59
Bülow, Bernhard von, 172, 176–8
Burschenschaften (student fraternities), 118

cameralism, 27, 29
Caprivi, Leo von, 124–5
Carstens, Karl, 241
Catholics, 30, 100, 114–5, 190n4
Center Party, 114, 122, 143, 180, 183–4, 204
charity
    foreigners, 41, 47
    local poor, 17, 19, 41, 45, 47
Christian Democratic Union, 243–4, 248–53, 256
Christian Social Union, 243–4, 256
citizenship
    based on descent, 7, 55, 59, 62–3
    based on place of birth, 7, 62–3, 82, 125, 181, 249
    dual, 59–61, 175, 179, 183–4, 238–9, 246, 248–50, 256
    duties, 5, 60–61, 184–90, 225, 250
    local forms, 17–19, 24–6
    rights
        employment opportunities, 5, 65–7, 85–6, 156, 210–11
        freedom to move and work, in some instances, 30, 65–9, 159, 240–2

protection against private denunciation, 156
protection from expulsion by home state, 5, 21–7, 64–5, 152, 157
right to marry, in some instances, 5, 85–90, 154–6, 244–5
suffrage, in some instances, 5, 156–7, 255
world wars and, 184–90, 221–7
see also gender and citizenship
Citizenship Law of 1842 (of Prussia), 4
    gender, 63–65
    implementation, 65–69
    influence of foreign laws, 62–3
    origins, 55–62
Citizenship Law of 1870 (of the North German Confederation and German Empire)
    citizenship of emigrants, 169–72
Citizenship Law of 1913 (of the German Empire)
    influence on Nazi legislation, 9, 217, 227–9
    military service, 176–9
    naturalizations, 179–81
    popular pressure, 169, 172–5, 177
Citizenship Law of 1999 (of the Federal Republic of Germany) citizenship on birth, 5–6, 249
    dual citizenship, 248–50, 256, 263n62
    grounds for, 252–7
    long-term residents, 249–50
class, economic
    citizenship of German emigrants and, 175, 178–9
    expulsions as tool to discipline and punish the poor, 84–90, 94, 100, 142–3, 155–7
    moral judgments based on, 41, 44, 47, 57, 84–7, 157–8
Colonial Society (Deutsche Kolonialgesellschaft), 172–3
colonies
    racism in, 112–13
common good (Gemeinwohl)
    naturalization decisions and, 61, 65–9
    preemption of local rights and, 28–9, 37, 46

Index

class domination and, 44, 100,
102nn72–3
foreigners living in 'concubinage', 85–9
foreign Poles and Jews 1885–6, 118–24,
126–9
Germans after the Second World War,
235
Jews to death camps, 220
treaties governing, 6, 22, 26, 33n26,
34n30, 62
within German states, 22, 41–5, 100,
203

Fahrmeir, Andreas, 6
farm workers, *see* laborers
Federation of German Women's Groups
(Bund Deutscher Frauenvereine),
182–4, 210, 212
Fichte, Johann Gottlieb, 29–30, 35n48
First World War, 184–90
foreign policy
ethnic Germans abroad, 4, 158–9,
172–5, 179, 187–8, 221–7 relations
with Austria-Hungary, 112, 124
relations with Russia, 58, 111–12, 124,
158–9, 179
relations with the United States, 144,
175, 205–6
treatment of foreigners and, 2–3, 112,
124–6, 129, 141, 205–6, 219, 229,
236, 240–6, 268
France, 78, 90, 112–13, 123, 211, 228, 240
influence on Germany, 6–7, 43, 62–3,
125, 257
Frankfurt Parliament of 1848, 79–83
freedom of movement, 79–81
individuals who were not ethnic
Germans, 81–3, 101n1
Free Democratic Party, 242–4, 248–9
freedom of movement, 4, 28, 42–8
foundation of national unity, 79
right of all Germans, 79–80
solution to the problem of pauperism,
27–8, 45–7, 79–80
French Civil Code of 1803, 7, 62–4
Freytag, Gustav, 116–17, 147, 218
Frick, Wilhelm, 218
Friedrich Wilhelm III (king of Prussia),
57–8

Friedrich Wilhelm IV (king of Prussia),
48, 60, 85–6

gender and citizenship
see married women and citizenship
Genscher, Hans-Dietrich, 260n24
German Civil Code, 195n70, 212
German Confederation (Bund), 22–7, 77,
170
German Democratic Party, 209
German Democratic Republic, 237–8
German-Americans, 144–6, 176–7, 188
Gneisenau, August Neidhardt von, 170
Gosewinkel, Dieter, 7–9, 128
Goßler, Gustav von, 120–1
Great Britain, 90
immigration and citizenship policies, 6,
63, 113
influence on Germany, 62–3, 190,
193n43
see also England
Greece, 236, 240
Green Party, 248–9, 256–7
'Guest Workers' (Gastarbeiter), 236–7,
240–5
guilds
egoism of, in view of central
administrations, 28, 46, 67
restricting access to citizenship of
outsiders, 24, 28, 37, 65–7, 84
Gulden, Gustav, 79

Haegy, Franz, 143
Hailbronner, Kay, 245
Haller, Carl Ludwig von, 60
Hamburg, 24–6, 243
Hanemann, Johann Heinrich Ludwig, 23–6
Hanover, 24–6
Hardenberg, Karl August von, 43–5
Hasse, Ernst, 172
Hauser, Oswald, 127–8
Hegel, Georg Friedrich, 28–30, 37–8
Heine, Wolfgang, 205–6
Herbert, Ulrich, 8
Hermann, Friedrich, 80
Hildebrand, Bruno, 80
Himmler, Heinrich, 223, 226
Hinckeldey, Carl Ludwig von, 84
Hindenburg, Paul von, 218

Index

Index

economic and political self-interest and, 43–4, 46–7, 57, 116–19, 126–7
  ideology of the reaction of the 1850s, 83–87
  rationale for anti-Semitism, 116–19, 126–7, 148, 185–6
  traditional rights and, 28, 41, 44–8, 67

Napoleon I (emperor of France), 21, 29, 63
national feeling, 78
  of Czechs, 83
  of Germans, 1, 29–30, 79–83, 169, 172–9, 201–4, 223–9, 256–7, 269
  of Poles, 114–5
National Liberal Party, 114, 126, 171–2, 180, 184
National Union of Commercial Employees (Deutschnationaler Handlungshilfenverband), 118
naturalization
  fees, 208–9, 247–8
  German ethnicity, 202–4, 221–7, 235, 246
  incentive for good behavior, 94, 98, 143, 154–7, 159
  National Guidelines for Naturalization of 1977, 245–7
  Prussian Administrative Treatise on Naturalization of 1904
  anti-Semitism of, 140, 146–9
  conscription and, 143–6, 148–51
  Czechs and Danes and, 151–2
  discarded, 206
  German-Americans and, 144–6
  Poles and, 149–51
  secrecy of, 141
  Social Democratic Party and, 142–3
  standards for in pre-1848 Baden, 65–7
  standards for in pre-1848 Prussia, 67–9
Nazi regime
  denaturalizations, 219
  'racial' citizenship categories, 220–7
Netherlands, Dutch, 92–3, 126, 176, 240, 257
Neubach, Helmut, 126–7
Nicholas I (tsar of Russia), 58
Nipperdey, Thomas, 128, 129n2
nobility
  see East Elbian landowners, estates
North Rhine Westphalia, 243, 247

Palacký, František, 83
Pan-German League (Alldeutscher Verband), 172, 175
Poland, Poles, 205–6, 211, 221–6
  conscription, 143–4
  demographic statistics, 2, 115
  farm laborers, 92–4, 98, 120–6
  national aspirations, 114–5
  naturalizations, 92–100
  Nazi policies, 221–7
  official fears, 8, 92–3, 99–100, 112, 120–3
  rebellions, 92–3, 114, 117
police, 21, 84–89, 143, 152
Polish Party, 114, 122
Portugal, 236, 240
Posadowsky-Wehner, Arthur von, 172, 176
Pourtalès, Friedrich von, 179
poverty
  grounds for excluding foreigners, 17–24, 27, 41–5, 47, 57, 80, 143
Progressive Party (and successor parties), 122, 180–1
  Jewish voters and, 119–21, 133n43, 147
Prussia
  liberal constitution of, in German context, 27–9, 40, 57, 63–9
  local barriers to movement in, 37–48
  migration to, from, and within, 19–22, 56–9, 84–100
  reaction in 1850s, 83–91
  see also Bismarck, Citizenship Law of 1842, East Elbian landowners, expulsions, naturalization
Puttkamer, Robert von,
  expulsions of Jews and Poles, 115, 118–23, 127, 183
  tension with Bismarck over expulsions, 118–21, 127

Quakers, 28

racism, 112–3, 148, 217–21, 227–8, 266
Rayski, Ferdinand von, 23
Reichensperger, August, 80
Reichhaupt, Wilhelm von, 183
Remscheid, 88–90
Renan, Ernest, 256